PASSION
AND
PARADISE

Related titles from Herder & Herder

PASSION
AND
PARADISE

HUMAN AND DIVINE EMOTION
IN THE THOUGHT
OF GREGORY OF NYSSA

J. WARREN SMITH

A Herder & Herder Book
The Crossroad Publishing Company
New York

The Crossroad Publishing Company
16 Penn Plaza, 481 Eighth Avenue
New York, NY 10001

Printed in the United States of America

Library of Congress Cataloging-in-Publication Data
Smith, J. Warren, 1964–
    Passion and paradise : human and divine emotion in the thought of Gregory of Nyssa / J. Warren Smith.
        p.   cm.
    "A Herder and Herder book."
    Includes bibliographical references and index.
    ISBN 0-8245-1944-2 (alk. paper)
    1. Gregory, of Nyssa, Saint, ca. 335–ca. 394. 2. God–Worship and love–History of doctrines–Early church, ca. 30–600. 3. Love–Religious aspects–Christianity–History of doctrines–Early church, ca. 30–600. I. Title.
BV4817.S52 2004
233′.5–dc22
                                                                            2004006965

1 2 3 4 5 6 7 8 9 10   10 09 08 07 06 05 04

In Memoriam

My Father,
Dr. W. Thomas Smith
(October 20, 1923–June 3, 1986)
Professor of Church History,
Interdenominational Theological Center (1974–86),
whose vivid lectures made church history come alive,
inspiring my theological curiosity

and

My Mother,
Barbara Sullards Smith
(July 25, 1925–March 31, 2000),
whose indefatigable devotion encouraging, reading, and typing papers
enabled a dyslexic son to overcome and find fulfillment in the academy.

Contents

Acknowledgements

In 1989 during my seminary days at Yale Divinity School, I was fortunate enough to do an internship teaching Religious Education at the Nyadire Secondary School in Zimbabwe. Prior to these travels, I had already become keenly interested in patristic thought. During that year abroad, however, my study of the early church and the Hellenistic world became more serious. By the light of a kerosene lantern, I read the apologists of the second century, Plato's *Timaeus,* and Marcus Aurelius's *Meditations.* The greatest impression by far was made by Gregory of Nyssa. I was particularly struck by Rowan Greer's description in *Broken Lights and Mended Lives* of Nyssen's realized eschatology. My captivation with his vision of the Christian life as a proleptic participation in the eschaton was the seed of my 1999 Yale dissertation which lies before you. Since I began writing this dissertation eight years ago, scholarly examination of Nyssen's corpus has experienced a revival among students of theology and Christian antiquity. This recent growth industry in Nyssen scholarship has not left us with a definitive account of his theology. On the contrary, so theologically rich are his texts that no single generation of scholars can offer an exhaustive analysis of Nyssen's thought. My modest hope is that this volume will be an aid to students of all levels as they read Nyssen's probative and provocative works for themselves.

This book has been nurtured by the love and labor of many colleagues and friends. I am grateful to the Theology and Ancient Christianity faculties of Yale's Department of Religious Studies, especially Harry Attridge who graciously consented to be a reader at the last moment, Cyril O'Regan who before and after his departure for Notre Dame offered valuable insights that helped me conceptualize certain problematic sections of this book, and Marilyn McCord Adams in whose office and company I enjoyed many hours working through the philosophical issues behind Nyssen's theology. Most of all I am indebted to Rowan A. Greer who first taught me how to read the fathers, introduced me to Gregory of Nyssa, and guided my reflections upon his corpus with comments and suggestions as voluminous and helpful as they were gracious. His friendship and council continue to be a rich blessing. No one can successfully pass through a Ph.D. program without the support of dear colleagues: Jaime Clark-Soles, Stephen Chapman, Stephen Davis, Amy Laura Hall, Jeff Hensley, Allen Hunt, Rebecca Krawiec, Dan Lee, Julia Rusling, Kevin Mongrain, Guy Nave, George Parsenios, Regina Plunkett-Dowling, Brian Stiltner, and my roommate, Bill Alexander. Nor could New Haven have been a home to me had it not been for the Christian community I enjoyed at Hamden Plains United Methodist Church. I am thankful as well for the support and evangelical fellowship of A Foundation for Theological Education under the leadership of Edmund W. Robb, Jr., Edmund W. Robb, III, Steve Harper, and the John Wesley Fellows. I want to thank the editors and staff of Crossroad Publishing Company, especially John Eagleson, who prepared and set the manuscript, and most of all John Jones, whose encouragement, suggestions, and constructive criticism were invaluable in converting a dissertation to a book. I am grateful for his friendship and support of this project from the beginning. I deeply appreciate the painstaking work of David Moffitt, who checked the Greek references and my transliterations. Roger Owens graciously offered to proofread endnotes, and for that thankless job I am grateful. Most of all I am indebted to my wife, Kimberly Doughty, for her inexhaustible patience, her meticulous proofreading, and our life together.

May 11, 2004
Lake Junaluska, North Carolina

Introduction

The study of theologians of the distant past, like eschatological speculation itself, can resemble the experience of gazing through a smoky, semitransparent window. At the same moment that we see what lies on the other side, we are inevitably confronted with our own reflection. Indeed, the way students of the early church have rediscovered Nyssen's writings in the last century and a half reflects their own theological and cultural concerns. Accordingly, let us begin this study with an outline of Nyssen's historical circumstances, a summary of questions central to his theological anthropology, and various approaches to Nyssen's thought that commentators have followed, indicating the place of this study within that larger conversation. While the details of this third part may be of primary interest to specialists, the general trajectories traced here are of some importance for our study.

The Ancient and Modern Background

This book is a study in Christian theological anthropology. The writings of Gregory of Nyssa, the great Cappadocian theologian, have wielded tremendous influence on our thinking about this topic. At the core of Nyssen's anthropology is his interest in the paradoxical character of human nature. On the one hand, man is an exalted being created in the image of the God who is impassible, not subject to emotions or passions. Endowed with rationality that in some ways mirrors God, human beings have the capacity of partaking in the divine nature and enjoying fellowship with their Creator. On the other hand, human beings are fleshly beings, with the same sensual appetites possessed by nonrational animals, such as those connected to eating and mating. These impulses are not evil in themselves: they promote the survival of the individual and the species, and help bring Adam's race to the destiny God wills for it — as Nyssen calls it, the *plērōma*. Nonetheless, because humans dwell simultaneously in the two worlds of sense and intellect, there is always a possibility of conflict between the desires and longings of the rational

1

and corporeal natures. When passions gain the upper hand, and we use our rational nature only in the calculating pursuit of mundane goods, our conformity with the likeness to God is compromised, and we create misery for ourselves and those around us.

How, Nyssen asks, can human beings made in the likeness of the supremely wise and benevolent God live in such misery of their own creation? And what if anything can man do to escape this misery? How can we strip away the layer of grime, both to restore our happiness and to restore the image that enables us to enjoy communion with God? Granted that we can never overcome the absolute divide between the eternal God and temporal creatures, in what sense can the finite be united with the Infinite? Surrounding these questions are others: What does it mean to be made in the image of God? Does the body bear the marks of the divine image, or are these reserved for the soul? How has sin compromised the *imago Dei*? What is the nature of the passions? If they are not inherently the source of sin, did God make them for some holy purpose? Does the purification of the soul require the elimination of the passions or merely some transformation? If the passions can be sublimated, how might they serve the soul's ascent to God?

Why choose Gregory of Nyssa as a theological conversation partner for reflection on theological anthropology? What aspect of a fourth-century bishop from the rugged backwater province of Cappadocia could be valuable for contemporary reflection on what we might call the human condition or the nature and destiny of man?

Nyssen seeks to unpack the riddles of anthropology from two starting points — theology and eschatology. Although for a man of his era Nyssen was quite knowledgeable in the sciences of biology and human physiology, and reflective about our experience of life, he reasons not from the human experience to the divine, but from the divine to the human. Starting with the claim of faith that God made man in his image, Nyssen reasons that we cannot know who we are except by knowing the triune God who has revealed himself in the works of his economy. Therefore the nature of the God in whose image we are made, and with whom we shall have communion, must be the starting point for questions of human nature.

Nyssen's other approach to anthropology is eschatology. In line with the old adage that "you can't understand the acorn until you've seen the oak tree," Nyssen assumes that resurrected humanity — the new creation — shall be the consummation of God's creative purpose for humankind. God's creative intention for humanity, articulated in the words of Genesis 1:26, "Let us make man in our image, after our likeness," is finally fulfilled in Christ's eschatological kingdom. Since the end shall be like the beginning, Nyssen reads the creation narrative of Genesis through the lens of Jesus' apocalyptic sayings from the canonical Gospels. In the revelations of what humanity shall be, we see what God intended for us in the beginning.

Nyssen's eschatology, however, is always tied to his understanding of man's present condition. There is a difference between our present and future conditions: In the eschaton will be eliminated any aspects of our present humanity that are alien to the *imago Dei,* anything that causes our present misery and is incompatible with the blessedness God wills for us in the fullness of time. Nevertheless, Nyssen does not overdetermine this difference as a rupture or strong dualism: God has called the material creation good in the beginning; it can never become merely an epiphenomenal good that will pass away altogether. Indeed, the present age and the age to come are continuous in significant ways. The new heaven, the new earth, and the new humanity are a *renewed* and perfected heaven, earth, and humanity, not different ones. Moreover, the eschatological vision is not simply an abstract or speculative object of human longing in some postponed future, but the basis for hope in the present. For Nyssen, the humanity of the resurrection — what we shall be — is the standard for the Christian living in the present. The Christian life is a proleptic participation in the life to come. In other words, we embrace in the present the life that shall be ours in the future. What we shall become determines what we strive to be in the here and now. Eschatology, reflection on the destiny of humankind, sets the goal for our present journey. We look ahead to the eventual transformation of our passions in the eschaton, and we strive to begin bringing about this transformation through ascetic discipline in the present.

This book, therefore, is an exploration of Nyssen's theory of the restoration of the divine image through the transformation of the passions both in this life and in the eschaton. Nyssen speaks of this transformed passion using a paradoxical phrase, "impassible desire." This phrase has usually been understood in this way: the desire ceases to be a passion in the pejorative sense when it shifts its focus from the fleshly and mundane to the goodness of God himself. This interpretation, while correct, needs to be enriched. What happens to the dynamics of human love, as we usually understand it, when we love an infinite, eternal, and perfect God? How is our eschatological desire for the God who is "all in all" different from the desire for God we experience every day, a desire

amid the temptations and struggles of the present age? I will seek to unpack various possible meanings that the expression "impassible desire"
might have for Nyssen.

Such a paradox can be understood only within the context of Nyssen's
theory of the soul's dynamics. As we shall see, Nyssen maintains that
the life of the soul and that of the body are inextricably bound. Both
body and soul shall be redeemed, and their redemption is interrelated.
Nevertheless, his account of our eschatological destiny is not univocal.
At times he focuses on the restoration of the body in the resurrection, at
other times, on the soul's purification. He never integrates these varied
accounts into a unified vision of the eschaton, and what such a vision
might look like, particularly as it bears upon the question of the body,
lies outside the scope of this book. Rather I want to focus on Nyssen's
intricate accounts of the soul's spiritual journey to its eschatological destiny in God and the process of transformation that occurs en route and
in the end.

By way of introduction to this project in historical theology, we
may situate Nyssen's anthropology and eschatology within the broader
contexts of Nyssen's own thought and theological career, and of our
contemporary discussion of Nyssen's thought.

The Historical Backdrop of the Fourth Century

Gregory of Nyssa (331/340–395), with his elder brother Basil of
Caesarea (329/330–379) and Basil's friend, Gregory of Nazianzus (329–
390), were the most influential theologians in the Eastern church during
the second half of the fourth century. Known collectively as the Cappadocians, these three men secured at the Council of Constantinople (381)
a victory for the Nicene theological formula, affirming the co-eternality
and consubstantiality of the Son and the Father.[1] Though not silencing
the Arian views that had dominated fourth-century theological discussion, Constantinople forever identified such views as heretical. While
bringing one chapter of church history to a close, they helped open a
new chapter, and by affirming the full humanity of Jesus, in opposition
to Apollinaris, they played a central role in the early phase of the Christological controversy that was to occupy the theological attention of the
church, East and West, throughout the first half of the fifth century.

Basil and Nyssen were born to the purple-bordered toga. Their family belonged to the *decuriones,* the class of landed elites whose wealth
and *dignitas* made them suitable assistants to the imperially appointed
governor in the provincial assemblies. In recognition of this service to

the empire, the men of the family received the honor of wearing the distinctive purple stripe lining the border of their toga. Their family estate was located in the coastal region of Pontus, which from the reign of Trajan had been incorporated into the Cappadocian province until Diocletian's reorganization of the empire.[2] Their paternal grandmother, Macrina the Elder, had been converted to Christianity by the preaching of Gregory Thaumaturgos, who, together with his brother, Athenodore, studied under Origen in Caesarea of Palestine before coming to Neocaesarea in Pontus. Origen's basic sensibilities about the value of the classical philosophical tradition for understanding the Christian faith were, to some degree, passed down from Macrina to her son, Basil the Elder, to whom she taught the faith using a creed written by Gregory Thaumaturgos for the church at Neocaesarea.[3] Basil and Nyssen could also claim to have relatives among the Forty Martyrs of Sebaste for whom their mother, Emmelia, erected a tomb to house their relics.

Their parents, Basil the Elder and Emmelia, had ten children. The eldest, Macrina the Younger, helped her mother raise and educate the children after their father's untimely death. Nyssen credits her with turning her younger brother Basil away from the vainglorious pursuit of rhetoric to the philosophical life of a Christian — that is, to the ascetic service of the church. Macrina herself, following the tradition of the virgin St. Thecla, adopted a life of celibacy and contemplation, and ultimately persuaded Emmelia to convert the family estate into a monastic community for women seeking to escape the destitute life on the streets and devote themselves to a life of prayer and asceticism. Of the other four daughters, nothing is known.

Basil pursued his formal studies in Antioch and then Athens, where he met Gregory of Nazianzus. Although his primary area of study was rhetoric, Basil seems to have read widely in the sciences. Around the time of his baptism, Basil abandoned his career as a teacher of rhetoric in Cappadocia and left home. Perhaps inspired by stories of St. Antony, he set off on a tour of the monasteries of Egypt. Upon his return to Cappadocia, Basil established a monastic community of his own in the mountains near the family estate. Basil's community integrated the life of study and contemplation with service and hospitality for the poor and sick.[4] In 365, the year after he published his refutation of the *Apology* written by the Neo-Arian Eunomius of Cyzicus, Basil was appointed as assistant to Eusebius, bishop of Caesarea, whose health had been deteriorating. When Eusebius died five years later, Basil succeeded him as bishop of the principal episcopal see in Cappadocia. In addition to Basil, Gregory tells us of two other brothers — Naucratius, who for a while followed in his father's footsteps as a rhetorician before entering into a kind of hermitic retreat and dying in a hunting accident, and Peter, who became bishop of Sebaste.

Unlike his older brother, Basil, Gregory of Nyssa received no formal education. Yet his knowledge of biology and philosophy, which he tells us he learned from his siblings Basil and Macrina the Younger, was formidable. By Nyssen's own account, as a young man he had little zeal for the church and was at best indifferent to his heritage as a descendent of martyrs. He was content to marry, move far away from the strong hand of Emmelia, and teach rhetoric as his father had done.

It is hard to locate a single, decisive turning point in Nyssen's life. He tells us that after a dream in which he was attacked by the Forty Martyrs of Sebaste for his spiritual apathy, he repented of his indifference. Even so, this was no radical conversion, and his maturation in the faith was gradual. This changed in 372, when Basil appointed Nyssen to the relatively insignificant see of Nyssa.

By temperament, Nyssen was retiring. He appears to have been more at home in the solitude of his study than in the competitive and often vicious arena of ecclesial politics, in which he proved hopelessly naïve. From the beginning, his life as bishop was dominated by the fierce contest between the Arians and the pro-Nicenes for control of Cappadocia. The emperor Valens, unlike his predecessor, the orthodox emperor Jovian, was a strong supporter of the Arians. In an attempt to weaken Basil's authority, Valens divided the civil diocese of Cappadocia, thereby reducing the number of sees within Basil's sphere of influence. Basil responded by appointing his brother to Nyssa and his friend, Gregory of Nazianzus, to the see of Sasima to shore up the pro-Nicene control over Cappadocia against the Arians. The Arians challenged the legitimacy of Nyssen's ordination; Valens supported the challenge and dispatched his representative, Demosthanes, to prosecute Nyssen on the spurious charge of embezzlement. The Arians finally succeeded in exiling Nyssen from his see for three years. However, in 378 after Valens's inglorious death on the field of Adrianople, the new emperor, Gratian, a devoted adherent to Nicaea, reinstated Nyssen to his see. If Valens's death had been a serendipitous turn for the pro-Nicene party, the next year the winds of fortune blew against them: Basil died.

Arguably, Basil had become the leader of the pro-Nicenes. It was he who had reconciled the supporters of Nicaea with the Homoiousian party of Basil of Ancyra; their concern was that Nicaea's description of the Son as consubstantial (*homoousios*) with the Father might be another form of modalism that did not adequately express Scripture's distinction between the members of the Godhead. Basil's development of the description of the Persons of the Trinity as *hypostases* added the nuance of "difference" to the Nicene language of *homoousios* necessary to eliminate the hint of Sabellianism dividing the Homoiousians from the pro-Nicenes.[5] Now they could present a united front against the Homoians and the Neo-Arians.

With Basil's passing, Nyssen, together with Nazianzen, emerged from out of his brother's long shadow. In his early writings, such as *On Virginity,* Nyssen had sought to explain the theological rationale behind the ascetic life of self-denial practiced in Basil's monastery and codified in Basil's monastic rules. Following Basil's death, Nyssen took up the task of completing his brother's unfinished theological projects. His *On the Making of Man* is intended to complete Basil's *Hexaemeron;* similarly Nyssen's *Against Eunomius,* composed about the same time as *On the Making of Man,* was his attempt to carry on Basil's refutation of the Neo-Arian, Eunomius of Cyzicus. That Nyssen had come into his own right was apparent when Theodosius I summoned the Council of Constantinople in 381. Not only were the two Gregorys among the 150 bishops invited, but when Meletius of Antioch, who was the presiding bishop, died during the Council, Nazianzen succeeded him as the Council's president, and Nyssen was asked to deliver his funeral oration. Indeed Constantinople's alteration of the Nicene Creed followed the Cappadocian formula, "one *ousia* in three *hypostases.*" Thus Nyssen's Trinitarian writings as well as his presence, though to a lesser degree than Nazianzen's, proved instrumental in fashioning the Orthodox interpretation of the Triune God depicted in Scripture.[6]

After Constantinople, Nyssen was content to return to his pastoral duties among his flock at Nyssa. Yet he by no means faded into obscurity. He continued to be held in high regard by Theodosius, who called upon him to deliver the funeral orations for his wife, the empress Aelia Flacilla, in 383, and then for his daughter Pulcheria in 385. In that same year, Nyssen weighed in on a new controversy stirred up by the writings of Apollinaris.[7] His greatest speculative works, *Commentary on the Song of Songs* and *Life of Moses,* were probably not written until a few years before his death around 395.

It was amid these theological and ecclesiastical disputes that Nyssen's theological anthropology, especially that articulated in *On the Making of Man* and *On the Soul and Resurrection,* was developed. In fact, his thoughts on the nature and destiny of humankind emerged in conjunction with two projects not primarily concerned with issues of anthropology: the rehabilitation and appropriation of Origen's thought, and the refutation of Eunomius and the Anomoeans. Due at least in part to Gregory Thaumaturgos's influence in Pontus and specifically on Nyssen's grandmother, the Cappadocians were attracted to Origen's theology. At Basil's hermitage in Pontus, Basil and Nazianzen around 358 compiled an anthology of Origen's thought, entitled the *Philocalia*. The passages anthologized, especially those from Origen's *On First Principles* and *Against Celsus,* were intended to illustrate the usefulness of the classical philosophical tradition for Christian interpretation of Scripture and for speculation on the nature of God and human beings. Origen's allegorical method, used for retrieval of the spiritual meaning of troubling passages of Scripture, served as a model for the Cappadocians' approach to the spiritual interpretation of Scripture. Nyssen's homilies on the Song of Songs show Origen's exegetical influence. Yet equally clear is that Nyssen did not follow in lockstep with Origen's interpretation. Rather, in the spirit of Origen, he was free to pursue a completely different line of interpretation.[8] The Cappadocians also were drawn to Origen's use of the erotic and mystical tradition of Plato's *Symposium* to explain asceticism as a means of purifying the soul's love for God — an erotic love that raises the soul toward mystical union with God.

At the same time that the Cappadocians valued Origen's creative intellectual imagination, they recognized the problematic character of his thought. Origen's integration of Platonic and Christian elements appeared at points dangerously syncretistic. In *On First Principles,* Origen speculates that the material world was created by God as a result of the fall of preexisting rational beings. Insisting that all rational creatures are created in the just and benevolent wisdom of God, he concludes that the inequality among rational creatures must be the result of our merit or demerit rather than an injustice on God's part. The rational creatures, who fell away from God because they were satiated with God's goodness, were given bodies that, in contrast to the blessed life of communion with God, were the source of discomfort and suffering. The painful life in the body was not a basely punitive contrivance. On the contrary, the misery of their embodiment rekindles that desire — a desire that had grown cool and no longer bound them to God — for the soul's return to God. Paradoxically, the coarseness of the flesh that was the source of heaviness for the soul, preventing it from enjoying blessed communion with God, actually arouses in the soul the very warmth of affection and longing necessary to shed the coarse and heavy garment that is the body and return to God fully appreciative of the goodness of its life in God.

In contrast with the account of the body in the Gnostic myths of creation, Origen views embodiment as salutary and redemptive. The body, along with the whole of the material creation, is part of God's plan for the restoration of rational creatures. Despite the misery caused by the body, its role in God's salvific plan makes it a good for fallen souls, just as a hospital, for all its unpleasantness, is beneficial for the sick. Eventually, all rational beings shall, though perhaps after the passage of many lives in the world, acquire love suitable for their reunion with the divine Word. For Origen, the soul uses its convalescence in the body as a preparation for its ascent back to God. Rather than indulging its desire for comfort and ease, the soul practices a life of self-denial and the mortification of the flesh in order that its desire for God may be intensified and so hasten its return to the Divine.

While the Cappadocians followed Origen, rather than Athanasius, in centering their soteriology on the purification of the soul's desire for God, there was much in Origen's account of the creation to give them pause. Is the material world, as Origen claims, good only in its temporary function as a means of the soul's convalescence? This seemed inconsistent with the vision of Genesis 1 that God saw the goodness of his creation, which suggested that the material universe possessed an intrinsic goodness that is a lasting component of God's economy. To take another example, Nyssen shared Origen's view that every soul would eventually experience salvation, but he rejected the idea of the transmigration of souls, which Origen incorporated from Plato; if one maintained that the soul's location in the cosmic hierarchy was determined by the merit of its free will, this seemed to suggest that the soul of a human being could fall into the body of an irrational animal.

Even more fundamentally troubling for Nyssen is Origen's explanation of the fall. Those rational beings who have been given the ultimate gift of beholding the supremely beautiful One and participating in his supreme blessedness—could they ever reach the point of satiation with God? Nyssen clearly believed not: the purified soul united with God in contemplative participation is supremely blessed, and so cannot be satiated with God's goodness, cannot as it were be too full of God. Nyssen nevertheless was left with the challenge of explaining how the soul can desire to contemplate God for all eternity. As we will see, the genius of Nyssen's solution to the problem of satiation lay in his account of the way the soul dynamically participes in the Divine. This account, which explains both the soul's redemption in this life and its beatific union with God in the eschaton, grew out of the doctrine of God he developed in his polemics against the Neo-Arians.

As mentioned previously, a second crucial set of circumstances shaping his anthropology was the ongoing battle with the Anomoean party or Neo-Arians, who opposed the Council of Nicaea's declaration that the Son is coeternal and consubstantial (*homoousios*) with the Father. Eunomius of Cyzicus (325–395), who succeeded Aetius (300–370) as leader of the Neo-Arians in 370, rejected the consubstantiality of the Son with the Father by arguing that the generation of the Son within the Godhead contradicted the very essence (*ousia*) of God.[9] Based on his semantic theory derived from Plato's *Cratylus* that names are an imitation or reflection of the essence of the entities they name, Eunomius maintained that the essence of God was knowable. The Father was one God who was *ingenerate*. The Son, however, was begotten of the Father or generate. Were the Son to have been generated by the Father at the level of his essence, the Godhead would have had to undergo some internal change, but God is immutable. Moreover, since the begetting of offspring entails passion, the Father's begetting of the Son from his *ousia* would mean that the Godhead was not impassible. Therefore, the Son did not share the same *ousia* as the Father; rather he was the product of the Father's activity rather than essence, and the essence remained unaffected.

At the risk of oversimplification, let me summarize Nyssen's argument here. His reply to Eunomius began by challenging Eunomius's epistemological presupposition. God at the level of his essence is unknowable, Nyssen asserted. The Godhead is known through his self-revelation in his creative and redemptive activities (*energeia*). The divine essence, however, cannot be known, because God is infinite and eternal Being. In contrast, we, as creatures created in time, are inherently temporal and finite. Since the finite cannot enclose the infinite, our minds can never comprehend God. How, therefore, can we who cannot comprehend the divine claim to know the very essence of God? Since the divine essence is unknowable, Eunomius cannot say that God is essentially *ingenerate*. Therefore, the Son, as generated by the Father, is not by definition *essentially* different from the ingenerate Father. Moreover, the Father's generation of the Son does not entail a change in the essence of the Godhead or introduce passion into the impassible deity.

The dispute with Eunomius over the divine essence and the divinity of the Son had serious implications for Nyssen's anthropology. First, Nyssen's distinction between the infinite and eternal God and finite and time-bound creatures raises questions about the nature of human participation in and fellowship with God. How can a finite creature be united in contemplative participation with an infinite God who is beyond human comprehension? If fellowship with God entails an imitation of the divine nature, how does the finite take on the likeness of the Infinite? To put it simply, how does the absolute ontological gap between the Creator and the finite creature affect the way the creature knows and loves the infinite God? One of Nyssen's greatest contributions to theological anthropology, his theory of epectasy — the soul's eternal movement into God's infinite being — offers an account of the *koinōnia* of the finite with the Infinite. We see, therefore, how significant his theory of God as infinite was for the rest of his theology.

Second, as a result of his insistence on the impassibility of the Godhead, Nyssen was committed to preserving *apatheia*, impassibility, as one of the virtues inherent in human nature made in the image and likeness of God. Eunomius had charged that the generation of the Son at the level of the divine essence introduces passion into the Godhead. In this context, Nyssen argues that the Father remains impassible because the Father's generation of the Son is not at all like the manner by which human fathers beget their offspring. Since God is impassible, by extension those creatures made in the image of God must also share in his *apatheia*. This theological claim, however, raises the anthropological problem of how creatures made in the image of a passionless God can be afflicted by passions. The mere presence of the passions in human beings seems to belie the claim of Scripture that we are made in the image of God. While Nyssen would have had to address this issue regardless of his dispute with Eunomius, the Trinitarian controversy, which was concurrent with his writing of *On the Making of Man* and *On the Soul and Resurrection*, forced the issue of the passions and the *imago Dei* to the foreground of his anthropological reflections.

Gregory of Nyssa in the Modern Mind

The renewal of interest in Gregory of Nyssa in the West has its origin in the Neo-Patristic movement in Roman Catholicism during the first half of the twentieth century. Hans Urs von Balthasar, Jean Daniélou, and Henri de Lubac sought to enrich Catholic theology by retrieving and incorporating the voices of the Eastern Fathers — voices ignored because of what was perceived as a near-hegemony of the Thomistic tradition.[10] Among the voices they helped recover for Protestants and Catholics alike was that of Gregory of Nyssa.

Over the course of the last century, the scholarly engagement with Nyssen's thought has followed three trajectories. The first two lines of inquiry concern his thought as a philosophical system with a strong mystical component, and later the sources of his thought in classical and Hellenistic philosophy. Von Balthasar's *Présence et Pensée* cele-brated Nyssen's thought as the harmonization of idea and drama, or a philosophical system with "religious realization."[11] On this reading, Plotinus creates an irreconcilable division between the One who is be-yond being and Mind or ideas, which belong to the realm of beings. By contrast, Nyssen's negative theology, which does not place God be-yond being, holds that in the mystical experience of God's simplicity we know God with certainty by feeling his presence. Daniélou's 1944 dis-sertation, *Platonisme et théologie mystique,* though appreciative of the Platonic influences upon his thought, focused on the mystical movements of his theology that he described as "epectasy."[12] Nyssen's significance as the mediator of the classical mystical tradition to Christianity, espe-cially with his influence upon Pseudo-Dionysius, was explored in Walther Völker's *Gregor Von Nyssa als Mystiker*[13] and more recently in Andrew Louth's *Origins of the Christian Mystical Tradition.*[14] Nyssen and his Cappadocian contemporaries were viewed, as Werner Jaeger declared, as the height of a synthesis between the philosophical tradition of classical Greece and orthodox Christianity. For Jaroslav Pelikan, the Cappado-cian project is an engagement with Hellenism, the form taken by classical culture by the end of the fourth century A.D.[15]

Was Nyssen's thought a benign synthesis of the classical and the Christian preserving the distinctly Christian voice, or was his brainchild a hyper-Hellenized Christianity, in which essential components of the Gospel were sacrificed for philosophical concerns? This is the under-lying concern of the second trajectory of Nyssen studies, the search for Nyssen's sources. Herald Cherniss's *The Platonism of Gregory of Nyssa* was one of the early works to address this issue.[16] In his response to Karl Gronau's 1908 dissertation, which argued for Nyssen's reliance upon Posidonius for his anthropology,[17] Cherniss argues that Nyssen, despite his initial interest in studying the literature of classical antiquity, was pushed by his domineering sister Macrina, and his older brother, Basil, into the episcopacy.[18] As Nyssen's intellectual tendencies and sympathy for Platonism demonstrate, his theology is an example of how devout faith "drawn by the spell of reason" attempts to unite the contradic-tory and incompatible theses into a harmonious synthesis.[19] Ultimately, however, Cherniss concludes, "it seems that, but for some few ortho-dox dogmas which he could not circumvent, Nyssen has merely applied Christian names to Plato's doctrines and called it Christian theology. These few dogmas, however, make of his writings a sorry spectacle."[20] Nyssen's allegiance to Plato led him to attempt to integrate the streams of his Platonic thought with his religious sentiments in a manner that failed to serve either.[21]

Cherniss's work bred interest in Nyssen among classicists and historians of philosophy who sought to locate the classical and Hellenistic sources of his thought. Much of this work has been helpful in illustrating the breadth of Nyssen's knowledge of moral philosophy, medicine, natural science, and cosmology. Some important works in this vein include A. H. Armstrong's "Platonic Elements in St. Nyssen of Nyssa's Doctrine of Man,"[22] and John F. Callahan's "Greek Philosophy and the Cappadocian Cosmology."[23] Charalambos Apostolopoulos's dissertation, *Phaedo Christianus Studien zur Verindung und Abwägung des Verhältnisses zwischen dem platonischen "Phaidon" und dem Dialog Gregors von Nyssa "Über die Seele und die Auferstehung,"*[24] has provided a form-critical study of Nyssen's reliance upon Plato's account of Socrates' deathbed dialogue, the *Phaedo,* as the model for his own deathbed discussion with Macrina in *De Anima et Resurrectione.*

Anders Nygren includes Nyssen among the culprits of antiquity responsible for confusing the uniquely Christian concept of *agape* with the pagan notion of *erōs.*[25] While he is right that Nyssen uses a motif of *erōs* to describe the soul's ascent to God and at time equates *agape* with *epithymia,*[26] Nygren's sweeping account of *agape* in the history of Christian doctrine pays, as we shall see, insufficient attention to Nyssen's account of the eschatological transformation of *epithymia* into *agape.*[27]

Even Werner Jaeger joined other Protestant critics of Nyssen's synergism. Having devoted much of his later years to the study of Nyssen and the production of critical editions of his writings, Jaeger's criticism of Nyssen is meticulously supported by his reading of the corpus. Although more appreciative of Nyssen's conscious attempt to balance Greek *paideia* and Christian dogma than Nygren was,[28] Jaeger concludes that Nyssen's incorporation of the Platonic notions of the soul's ascent to God is highly problematic for Christian soteriology, which rests upon a strong doctrine of grace. While he admits that the Christian ascetic movement of the fourth century did not find its impetus in Neoplatonism, Jaeger contends that the theological grounding Basil and Nyssen sought to provide the monastic movement reflected the mutual permeation of Christian piety and Greek philosophy typical of Alexandrian theology. The result was that philosophy not merely functioned as the explanatory handmaiden of theology, but was integrated into Christianity forming a true synthesis — the creation of a "new philosophical and rationalized form of Christianity."[29]

While Jaeger acknowledges that the charge of Semi-Pelagianism is somewhat anachronistic, he nonetheless assumes that the same concern for moral perfection in reaction to spiritual laxity, which was of chief concern for Pelagius, was also a driving force in the ascetic piety of Eastern monasticism. He demonstrates that Nyssen does not have a highly developed doctrine of grace or, at least, that it is a notion quite distinct from that assumed in the Protestant formula "justified by grace through faith."

While theologians must ever be watchful for syncretistic moves that might compromise the authentic voice of the Faith, much of the criticism from Cherniss, Nygren, and Jaeger reflects the haunting influence of Harnack. As I will show in chapter 2, Nyssen's primary commitment is not to philosophical consistency but to the church's teachings that "give fullness to understanding." The unsystematic character of his anthropology reflects his sense of the limited and fragmentary vision of the Divine that is the highest level attainable by theological speculation. While paying close attention to Nyssen's use of philosophy, my greater concern is to elucidate the way his doctrinal commitments gave shape to his speculations and became the source of his (unsystematic) anthropology. As to the question of grace and free will, Jaeger, by focusing so closely on *De Instituto Christiana*, does not have a narrative framework in which to show concretely the synergy of divine assistance and human initiative. By considering the issue in the context of Nyssen's threefold cycle of ascent, i.e., purification, illumination, and unification, as presented in *De Vita Moysis*, I show that Nyssen does indeed give priority to God's initiative.

The third movement in Nyssen scholarship might be termed The Erotic Nyssen. In the wake of Peter Brown's *The Body and Society: Men, Women, and Sexual Renunciation in Early Christianity* (1988),[30] students of the Cappadocians have turned their attention to Nyssen's ascetic theology, with special focus on his views of the body and gender, virginity, and the passions. Caroline Walker Bynum has demonstrated not only the complexity and confusion of Nyssen's account of the body of the resurrection, but more importantly the significance of eschatology as the lens through which to examine his anthropology.[31] Nyssen's account of the resurrection, seen as a "restoration" of human nature as God intended it, provided the rationale for ascetic mortification of the flesh; at the same time, as Teresa Shaw has shown, his knowledge of human physiology greatly influenced his conception of how the flesh might be controlled to provide great purity for the soul.[32] Verna Harrison's work pointed out Nyssen's paradoxical treatment of gender: On the one hand, virginity is a way of transcending gender and embracing the divine image in which there is no gender; on the other hand, Nyssen freely uses distinctly male and female qualities in his figurative depiction of the assorted forms of our communion with God.[33]

Among the most provocative recent studies of Nyssen have been those that discuss the positive role of the passions and the erotic in Nyssen's asceticism. Mark Hart has sought to soften what to modern ears appears to be harsh — Nyssen's critique of the institution of marriage as the source of all vices, in favor of the superior life of celibacy.[34] The loathsome picture of marriage and the almost idealized view of the celibate life Nyssen presents in *On Virginity* should not, Hart suggests, be taken at face value. Rather the extreme nature of the rhetoric signals that Nyssen intends the reader to read his account of marriage ironically. Celibacy is not so much a strength as an accommodation of human weakness for those who cannot resist the temptation of becoming entangled in the worldly desires and ambitions one faces in family life. The stinging critique of marriage is not intended to praise celibacy, which is not a mode of life superior to married life. Instead it is a call to the higher life, free from hedonism and worldly ambitions — the very life to which all Christians, married or single, are called.[35] On this provocative reading, Nyssen is the good rhetorician whose description of marriage plays on the prejudices and passions of ordinary Christians with pedestrian values to inspire them to pursue a higher way of living.[36] Ultimately, by showing that the married life and the contemplative life are not mutually exclusive, Hart claims, Nyssen "provides a nondualistic understanding...of asceticism."[37]

Recently John Behr, seeking to bolster Hart's reading of *On Virginity,* argues through a close reading of *On the Making of Man* that God intended the union of the rational and irrational natures in humanity to bring material creation to perfection — raising the corporeal above base necessity — when ordered by reason.[38] He concludes, therefore, that for Nyssen gender and sexuality are an essential part of human nature both in the beginning and eschatologically.[39] Together Hart and Behr have offered a rereading of Nyssen that finds a positive function of sexuality in his ascetic theology.

Similarly, Rowan Williams's rereading of *On the Soul and Resurrection* advanced an argument for the vital role of passions, such as grief, in the soul's spiritual ascent. He explains that the opening scene of the dialogue, in which Macrina allows her brother to shed copious tears mourning the passing of Basil and grieving Macrina's suffering and nearness to death, dramatically illustrates the soul's integral union with the body as reflected in the role of emotions in the soul's quest for understanding. Macrina uses Nyssen's grief for spiritual pedagogy: "We should not know how little we understand the soul if we did not give way to the full instinctive weight of grief," which is aroused by "our fundamental uncertainties or confusions about the nature of the soul, its independence and immortality."[40] The discontinuity between Macrina's pastoral approach at the outset of the dialogue and her harsh critique of the passions, including grief, later in the dialogue should, Williams concludes, suggest to us that her view of the passions is not as rigid and negative as her initial argument suggests. Her toleration of Nyssen's outburst foreshadows her final movement from an ethic characterized by *apatheia* to one of Aristotelian moderation.

This recent reevaluation of Nyssen's view of human passion and the soul's heavenly ascent, of the erotic and the ascetic, has naturally led to a renewed fascination with the vivid and erotically charged account of the soul's mystical union with God in Nyssen's *Commentary on the Song of Songs*. Building on the work of Hart, Behr, and Williams, Martin Laird has persuasively argued that Nyssen in his homilies on the Song of Songs uses sensually potent images of the Canticle to train our desire for God.[41] Its paradoxical language leads readers through the "noetic-erotic" dynamic of desiring what is known only partly and what is beyond their grasp. Yet in the apophatic experience, the inability to grasp the infinite God who is beyond language and the noetic realm is not the cause of anxiety or frustration, but of greater desire for God.

This book properly belongs to the discussion in Nyssen scholarship I have called the "Erotic Phase." While it shares many of the essential assumptions about Nyssen's anthropology, it does not follow these assumptions to the same conclusion. It is, I hope, a voice of caution against the temptation felt by all students of historical theology, to hear their own theological voice and concerns in the voice of a thinker with whom they feel a great sympathy.

On the one hand, I agree that Nyssen is not an extreme ascetic who sought to purge the soul of all its emotions; he is not Evagrius Ponticus. I also agree that in Nyssen's later works, such as his *Commentary on the Song of Songs,* he is more comfortable retaining the language of desire (*epithymia*) than he was in some of his earlier texts, such as *On the Soul and Resurrection.*

On the other hand, in the recent movement to recover an ascetic theology that allows a positive role for the emotions, especially desire, in the soul's movement into God, Nyssen's thought has been sanitized, rendered more coherent and consistent than it actually is and, accordingly, more palatable to modern sensibilities. Hart's reading of *On Virginity,* for example, which softens a seemingly antiquated indictment against marriage, gains much of its plausibility by its "nonsynthetic" approach, with an absence of discussion of Nyssen's ascetic writings such as Nyssen's treatment of Macrina, the paragon of celibate self-discipline and purity,[42] and his account of the origin of gender in *On the Making of Man*.

Similarly, Behr overstates the place of sexuality in Nyssen's thought. He is right that Nyssen portrays human beings as the union of the non-rational nature of the animals with the rational nature of God and the angels, brought together in order that the nonrational corporeal creation may be brought to perfection. Indeed the logic of this strand of Nyssen's argument *should* lead him to the precise conclusion Behr suggests — if, that is, Nyssen were fully consistent. He is not. For other strands of his argument in *On the Making of Man* suggest that gender was not part of God's original purpose for humanity (embodiment without gender, to mention one) and, in fact, that the passions seem to grow out of the addition of gender.

Rowan Williams's reading of Nyssen's account of the passions in *On the Soul and Resurrection* is essentially correct: the rational soul needs a desire — an impulse arising from the appetitive faculties and directed toward God — in order for contemplative communion with God. Yet Williams interprets Nyssen's view of grief in his deathbed conversation with Macrina in a way that reflects a more modern, pastoral approach to bereavement than Nyssen in fact has. While the logic of Nyssen's treatment of grief *could* lead to the pastoral sensitivity Williams imagines, this is not a conclusion Nyssen himself adopts or would even need to adopt according to the logic of his system. His grief is not a healthy emotion that ultimately inspires his quest for knowledge about the nature and destiny of the soul; instead it is a disturbance of the soul, one that hinders his ascent to God and must be healed as his sister awakens him to the hope of the resurrection.[43]

While Nyssen does not advocate the elimination of passions, understood in their neutral sense as *emotions,* nevertheless, some emotions with which contemporary Christians are comfortable, Nyssen is not. It is important to distinguish where Nyssen's argument *might* have proceeded, or where as a matter of constructive theology and psychology we would have liked it to go, from where it does in fact proceed. Nyssen, though a careful thinker, is not always neat. Certain recurring concerns or views, particularly those relating to asceticism, are essentially consistent throughout his corpus. To take one example, in his earlier and later writings he maintains that desire is inherently morally neutral, and that when desire is controlled by reason, it is necessary for our participation in God. Nyssen has many religious commitments, however, and not all of them are easily integrated. For example, he affirms that the *imago Dei* is without gender and that we shall be restored to it eschatologically; at the same time he must acknowledge the goodness of God's creation and the place of marriage in that creation. Similarly, he maintains that man's relation with God will always be erotic; yet he also holds that desire is transformed by our eschatological experience of God. There are ways of trying to harmonize these ideas and ways of suggesting that they are irreconcilably at odds. Nyssen does neither. So when discerning some trajectories in his thinking, we honor his voice, as with all voices of the tradition, both by taking him seriously as a living source of illumination — not a mere artifact of a distant age — and by acknowledging his *difference* from us, as another voice that challenges our theological assumptions.

Summary of the Argument

This book attempts to recover Nyssen's understanding of the erotic relation of humanity with God in all its historical messiness, and then, amid the various avenues of his thought, to ask whether his varied and apparently contradictory treatments of the erotic might be linked together to give us a fuller account of the transformed nature of human *erōs* in the eschaton. This account tries to be faithful to the texts of Nyssen's corpus and in so doing reveal an implicit coherence to the foundational vision of Nyssen's ascetic theology, if not a coherence of all the details.

The first two chapters lay out Nyssen's conception of God's creative intention for humanity as made in the *imago Dei;* this discussion will draw primarily from *On the Soul and Resurrection* and *On the Making of Man.* From this account of Nyssen's psychology — how the divine image is reflected in the soul, the significance of gender, and the soul's relation to the body — we are prepared to examine his treatment of the emotions and passions in chapter 3. Based on his account of the divine image and his interpretation of the creation account of Genesis 1, we will see why the passions pose an anthropological problem for Nyssen. Yet as his account of the passions illustrates, the problem lies not with human embodiment per se but with the judgments and orientation of the soul. Consequently, his soteriology focuses upon purifying the soul's desires.

Chapters 4 through 6 introduce Nyssen's account of how our desire is trained, according to his theory of epectasy — the soul's eternal movement into God. A concept emerging from his attempt to refute Origen's theory of satiation, epectasy explains how the soul's desires are transformed, and how the transformed desires enable the soul to encounter the wonder of God's infinite being. Chapter 6 offers an account of the ascent to God from *Life of Moses* that rests on the psychological dynamics developed in *On the Making of Man* and *On the Soul and Resurrection*. In the last chapter, we come to the final test for our understanding of the role of the erotic in Nyssen's eschatology. For here we see the messiness of Nyssen's view of desire. On the one hand, in *On the Soul and Resurrection* Nyssen insists that, eschatologically, the soul's experience of God as the "all in all" transforms desire (*epithymia*) into the pure love of *agape*, which is characterized by an eternal enjoyment of God in which time consciousness is lost. On the other hand, in *Commentary on the Song of Songs* his account of epectasy asserts that the soul never ceases to desire God. To be sure, Nyssen's account of our love of God in his theory of epectasy rests upon the unchanging relation of Creator and creature; therefore, in a very real sense, the *fundamental* character of our love does not change with the passing of the present age and the advent of the age to come. It shall always be erotic. Yet the question remains: How does the coming of the eschaton change the character of our love? How does the new experience of God as "all in all" transform the nature of human *erōs?*

CHAPTER ONE

The *Imago Dei:* The Foundation of Nyssen's Psychology

"And God said, 'Let us make man in our image [*kat'eikona*] and according to our likeness [*kath' homoiōsin*]'" (Gen. 1:26). The *imago Dei* (image of God) is the appropriate place to embark on our study of Gregory of Nyssa's theory of human nature because it is the essence of that nature. For Nyssen, these words establish God's creative purpose for making man and lay the foundation for Nyssen's understanding of man's place in the divine economy. They explain the distinctiveness of this bipedal creature who walks with erect posture and whose facial structure allows him to produce not grunts but an array of sounds and combinations of sounds to express thought and intention. They enable Nyssen to account for the great paradox that is man: a creature who despite his physical weakness dominates all other animals, including those whose brute strength and speed far surpass his own. The *imago Dei* is the principal biblical rubric around which Nyssen constructs his theory of the soul. Although he will describe the body as "a mirror of the mirror" reflecting the divine beauty, it is the soul that properly speaking was made like the divine, thus mirroring the divine virtues.[1] These lines from Genesis explains man's relationship to the Creator, and consequently man's ability to participate in the mind and being of God. In this respect, the *imago Dei* is for Nyssen the starting point for man's unceasing journey into the Infinite. It encapsulates the origin of human nature and its eschatological destiny. At the same time that Genesis 1:26–27 articulates the exalted nature of man, it also raises a profoundly troubling question: How can a creature of such vaunted origins and nature live a life of misery more resembling that of the beasts than the blessedness of the deity in whose image he is made? How can a creature whose nature has been invested with the marks of royal dignity live such an ignoble existence? The issue of this discontinuity between the vision of human

21

nature in Genesis 1 and its present condition dominates Nyssen's early anthropological writings.

Although Nyssen's discussion of the *imago Dei* has been explored by patristic scholars,[2] an overview of his account is necessary here for understanding his conception of the distinctive features of human nature — the passions. Nyssen's view of the passions is intelligible to modern readers only when we first understand his vision of the excellence and beauty of the divine archetype with which they are in tension. Thus we must begin by examining how the *imago Dei* functions theologically for Nyssen in delimiting the boundaries between the Creator and the creature.

Common Ground: Man's Structural Likeness to God

In Nyssen's thought, the *imago Dei* establishes man's *similarity* and *dissimilarity* to the Divine. Therefore it serves two equally important functions in his thought. First, the image refers to that common ground created by God on which he and his creatures might meet and by which people might share in the goodness of the divine nature. Therefore, the *imago Dei* establishes the basis for that communion between the Creator and his creatures which is our ultimate *telos*. Second, because an image is not identical with the archetype, it is inherently dissimilar to the one whose likeness it bears. Therefore, the biblical concept of the *imago Dei* becomes Nyssen's way of speaking of our inherent difference from God.[3] Thus it provides an anthropological foundation for preserving the ontological distinction between the Creator and the creature.

The human soul bears the likeness of God in two senses: structurally and morally. The image of God in the first sense as the soul's structural or formal similarity to the divine nature refers to the construction of human nature with those faculties discernible in the divine. Even as the form of a tool is crafted to serve the craftsman's purposes, so too, Nyssen says, the artificer (*aristotechnēs*) of our form fashioned it for the work of royalty.[4] The royal activity for which our nature was made is exercising dominion over the creatures of the earth (Gen. 1:26) as God's benevolent viceroy of creation. If man is to rule all lower life forms, he must possess the powers of the one who is ruler over the whole cosmos. Chief among these is the capacity as a rational being for self-governance (*autexousia*). Man's rational nature is the most basic sense in which we possess a likeness to the divine nature. "You see in yourself," Nyssen writes, "word [*logos*] and understanding [*dianoia*], an imitation of the very Mind and Word [of God]."[5] The rational faculties of the soul confer upon humankind the capacity for self-governance, commonly called "free will."[6] Here we must exercise some restraint, and avoid importing notions of the will influenced by later debates in Western Christianity about the freedom of the will. Unlike the way Augustine eventually characterizes *voluntas*,[7] Nyssen does not describe the will *as* a faculty separate from the intellect.[8] It is simply a by-product of the soul's rational nature and therefore a capacity of the soul's rational faculty. In other words, the soul's intellectual capacities for reasoning (*logos*), discriminating (*diakrisis*), and contemplation (*theoria* or *dianoia*) enable the soul to have knowledge of both the sensible goods of the material world and the intelligible goods of the divine and heavenly realm.[9] From this knowledge the soul is able to judge the relative merits of these goods and thus determine which goods should be sought above all else and which are of secondary importance. Nonrational animals have neither the knowledge of intelligible goods nor the capacity to be critically reflective about the drives of instinct. Consequently, they do not have the freedom to seek any goods except those pleasing to the body's senses. Moreover, lacking the power of critical reflection, their actions are directed almost entirely by instinct. In other words, Nyssen would say, they are wholly subject to forces of material necessity. Human beings, by contrast, because they can know and compare a variety of goods, have the capacity to be self-critical of their desires and impulses. Therefore, the rational soul is free in the sense that it is not subject to any external necessity. Freedom from necessity is the mark of man's royal nature. For even as God could not be truly sovereign over his creation if his will were in any sense determined by external forces, so too human beings must possess a similar autarchy in order to fulfill their royal commission.[10]

This capacity for freedom to choose is a prerequisite for virtue. Nyssen explains the correlation: "preeminent among all [virtues of our nature] is the fact that we are free from necessity, and not in bondage to any natural power, but have decision in our own power as we please; for virtue is a voluntary thing, subject to no dominion: that which is the result of compulsion and force cannot be virtue."[11] His meaning is twofold. On the one hand, freedom is a precondition for virtue since that which is done mechanically under coercion is neither blameworthy nor laudatory. On the other hand, the true excellence of a life devoted to the good cannot be achieved if the soul is weighted down by the serious limitations imposed by the constraints of one's material existence. This latter meaning is Nyssen's primary concern.

Macrina lists four other structural features of the soul that it shares with its divine archetype: intellect, incorporeal nature, weightlessness, and transcendence of spatial dimension.[12] In both *On the Making of*

Man and *On the Soul and the Resurrection,* Nyssen compares the soul's capacity to permeate and govern the whole of the body without being localized in a single member to God's omnipresent workings in creation. The mind's capacity for reason and language in human nature is an imitation of the divine Logos.[13] This implanted mind (*enkeimenos nous*) that penetrates and works in all parts of the body also has the godlike power of apprehending the world through the senses.[14] Indeed, *nous* and the body (*sōma*) are not welded together; rather the intellectual and immaterial mind is mingled with the senses through which the external world is apprehended.[15] Evidence of this is found in the judgments that arise simultaneously with sense perception even though they are separate faculties.[16] These judgments coordinate diverse sense data into a coherent and unified picture of one's experience.[17] It is interesting that although Nyssen in *On the Making of Man* explicitly indicates that the mind is not confined to a single organ of the body, it is not until *On the Soul and the Resurrection* that he recognizes nondimensionality as a feature of incorporeal nature.[18]

This model of the soul stands in striking contrast with Stoic and Epicurean materialist models of the soul. The nondimensionality of Nyssen's incorporeal soul is clearly grounded in common orthodox beliefs about God. Since the divine nature is incorporeal, it is not located in space and time. Consequently it both transcends creation and at the same time penetrates the entirety of the cosmos. Thus the soul's nondimensionality is analogous to God's omnipresence. At the same time, Nyssen insists upon the psychosomatic unity of the person — a unity analogous to God's immanence in creation. Although the soul is incorporeal and, therefore, not confined to any portion of the body, the soul is, for Nyssen, inextricably united to the body. As we shall see, this does not mean for Nyssen that the soul is confined to the grave when the body dies. Rather the nondimensionality of the soul enables it to be united to the body in the grave and at the same time enter into Abraham's bosom.

The body too — as the servant of the soul — bears the trappings of the soul's royal image. Our rational nature is outwardly observable in the form of the body, which both enables the cultivation of the rational faculties and allows the intellectual powers of the mind to be manifest. God equipped man with hands that allowed the form of the face to be shaped such that articulate speech is possible.[19] Had man not been given hands that were capable of holding, carrying, and manipulating tools food supplies, and so on, then his mouth would have been shaped like that of a dog's, which is capable of carrying and dragging food. Such a mouth does not have the form that allows for an articulation of sounds more nuanced than grunts and howls. Moreover, Nyssen says that our upright posture is a sign of the royal dignity of our nature. For unlike beasts that walk stooped with the submissive posture of a slave, human beings walk erect with their heads lifted up toward the heavens.[20] Thus man bears the structural image of God in the form of the body as well as in the powers of the mind. Extending the idea of the image of God to the body, however, represents a tension or even a contradiction with Nyssen's insistence upon the soul's distinction from the body.

Common Ground: The Moral Likeness

Endowed with a structural likeness to the divine nature through its rational faculties, the human soul is capable of bearing the *moral likeness* to the beauty of God's perfection. Since God is incorporeal, the divine beauty cannot refer to any physical quality. Rather the beauty of God's nature is, Nyssen says, contemplated in terms of God's *aretē*. In Homeric culture *aretē* referred to the preeminence of the Homeric heroes. By the fourth century B.C. as Greek city-states such as Athens had replaced monarchy with a democratic polity, Plato and Aristotle used *aretē* to describe a moral and intellectual excellence or virtue that includes prudence, temperance, forbearance, and justice — qualities necessary for citizens in a democracy — in addition to qualities of strength, speed, cunning, and ferocity that characterize the excellence of warrior princes, such as Achilles and Odysseus. Nyssen construes God's *aretē* in the language of Scripture as righteousness (*dikaiosunē*), purity (*katharotēs*), blessedness (*makariotēs*), and goodness unalloyed with evil. To these he adds the Stoic term *apatheia,* which carries for Nyssen the dual sense of impassibility and sinlessness.[21] *Apatheia*, when used by Nyssen as an attribute of God, refers to the divine transcendence or aseity and immutability. Unlike material creatures that are subject to change and often suffer change at the hands of some external force of nature, God, because he transcends the physical realm of change, is eternal and immutable. His transcendence means that the Divine is not subject to any external force that might cause God to suffer change. It is in this sense that God is impassible. Therefore, divine *apatheia* is synonymous with God's freedom from necessity.

Nyssen's ascription of *apatheia* to God in both *On the Making of Man* and *On the Soul and Resurrection* reflects certain critical theological issues that arose during the ongoing Trinitarian controversies. In 380/381 at the same time he was writing these anthropological treatises,

Nyssen was responding to the Neo-Arians' denial of the consubstantiality of the Son and the Father. Eunomius charged that if the Son were
begotten within the being of the Father, such generation necessarily entailed passion or change in the Father's *ousia,* thus compromising the
Father's rationality and freedom.[22] Nyssen's inclusion of *apatheia* among
the virtues proper to the *imago Dei* was intended to reaffirm Nicene orthodoxy's belief in God's freedom and immutability and to show the
coherence of his Trinitarian theology and his anthropology.

The second meaning of *apatheia* as sinlessness carries the idea that,
since God is incorporeal and perfect, he does not experience evil emotions or impulses (*pathē*), such as anger or lust, that are triggered by
threatening or pleasurable stimuli.[23] Unlike mortals for whom these emotions obscure their intellects' apprehension of the Good, God is never
moved from the Good that resides within his very being. This sense of
divine *apatheia* is Nyssen's way of articulating the biblical concept of
God's absolute purity and holiness.[24] Even as the beauty of God's nature
is contemplated in terms of his virtues, so too our royal lineage is denoted
by the presence of the same virtues as those of our archetype. Nyssen
enumerates these same divine virtues as those intended for human nature. The supreme virtue that is the height of all God's perfections is
love (*agapē*). Without love, the divine stamp upon our nature is corrupted and distorted.[25] Love is the sine qua non of the moral image of
God. God adorns human nature, Nyssen says, with these qualities in
the same way that an artist making a portrait of a king would incorporate symbols of his royal power, for example, scepter, diadem, and
purple robe, in the painting.[26] Neither the virtues that constitute man's
moral likeness to God, nor even those that constitute the structural likeness are unalterably fixed in the individual. Rather our likeness to God
depends upon our participation in God's goodness: "He made human
nature participant in all good; for if the deity is the fullness of good, and
this [i.e., human nature] is His image, then the image finds resemblance
to the Archetype in being filled with all good."[27] The implication is that
unless we share in the divine virtues we fail to reflect the nature of the
divine archetype and so cease to be in the image of God.[28] This does
not, however, mean that unless the soul perfectly and fully embodies
the divine goodness, then the *imago Dei* is lost. For it is impossible for
the finite and created soul to possess the sum of God's infinite goodness
and virtues. Yet Nyssen maintains that the human soul, like a mirror,
can possess a likeness to God only as long as it reflects his image to the
extent of its capacity. He writes, "The mind, as being in the image of
the most beautiful, itself also remains in beauty and goodness so long as

it partakes *as far as is possible* in its likeness to the archetype."[29] This
is the logic of the metaphor: as a mirror that is turned from the subject
does not bear the subject's reflection, so too the human soul, if it is not
fully centered upon God who is the source of virtue, no longer reflects
the image of the subject.[30] Nyssen carries the metaphor further: If the
mirror's reflective surface is obscured by some foreign substance such as
dirt or corrosion, the image it reflects is distorted.[31] Similarly, the soul
cannot embody the divine virtues unless any impurity that impedes its
participation in God is removed.[32] Thus, man's structural likeness to the
divine enables him to possess the moral likeness through a sustained and
dynamic connection between the soul and its Creator.

The Unlikeness of God and Man

Although being made according to the image of God (*kat' eikona theou*)
establishes the common ground of rationality necessary for commerce
between God and humanity, Nyssen recognizes that the language of
image and archetype implies *dissimilarity* as well as likeness. While the
metaphor of an image in a mirror suggests that the reflection bears
certain similarities to the appearance of the subject, it also implicitly
assumes that the two are not identical but different. These differences
between human nature and its archetype are of three types: (1) inherent
ontological differences, (2) created differences that were fashioned by
God in anticipation of the sin, and (3) differences due to corruption after
the sin. First, the inherent ontological differences reflect the ontological
divide between the created being of man and the eternal and absolute
being of the Creator. God who is without beginning or end is a perfectly
self-sufficient and self-subsisting being and as such is the sum and source
of all goodness. Nothing can be added to his nature nor can anything be
taken from him. In contrast, people, who occupy the realm of becoming,
are in a state of perpetual movement either toward greater and greater
likeness to God or in decay embodying less and less of God's goodness.
The goodness of the creatures' being is not their own, but is completely
derived from their participation in God's being. The creature, therefore,
comes into being from nothing and so is a part of the world of change.
By virtue of our created nature, we differ from God fundamentally in
that we are mutable while God is immutable.[33]

This point of dissimilarity can never be overcome. We will always be
incomplete, ever in a state of becoming; while God is always fully actualized Being. Although one of Nyssen's chief presuppositions is that man
must be like God in order to know God, this point of dissimilarity does

not inherently create an obstacle to our communion with God. Rather, as we shall see, our state of perpetual becoming is the basis for Nyssen's conception of our dynamic participation in God. By contrast the other two types of dissimilarity between God and human beings do pose a problem for the soul's communion with God — these are dissimilarities that must be overcome. The second and third classes of unlikeness are not inherent in our nature as is mutability. The second class are those differences incorporated by God into the form of our nature: gender distinctions and the nonrational faculties. The third class, the passions, were not a part of God's design and are, for Nyssen, a level of difference that separates man from God. The origin of these dissimilarities can be found in Nyssen's exegesis of the first creation story in the first chapter of Genesis.

Creation in the Image:
Nyssen's Exegesis of Genesis 1:26–27

From his close reading of Genesis 1, Nyssen notices a theologically problematic detail. In verse 26, God deliberates about what form is most suitable as the archetype for human nature and settles upon his own rational nature as the image according to which humanity shall be made. Then in verse 27, the Septuagint says, "And God made the man, according to God's image [*kat'eikona theou*] he made him, male and female he made them." Reading Genesis through the light of the New Testament, Nyssen views the division of humanity into male and female (in the third clause) as at odds with the creation of humanity in the divine image (in the first and second clauses). For in the baptismal formula of Galatians 3:28 Paul declares that in Christ there is neither male nor female.[34] How could God make humanity male and female and at the same time make man according to his own likeness in which there is no gender difference? If Christ, as the archetype of human nature, lacks gender, how is one to account for the incorporation of this alien feature into human nature? When Nyssen links Galatians 3:28 to Genesis 1:27 by identifying Christ as the archetype, he is not reverting to an archaic "image Christology" that speaks of Christ as the image of God in whose likeness humanity is made. He avoids any reference to Colossians 1:15, in which Paul calls Christ "the image of the invisible God." Such an allusion would have played into the hands of the anti-Nicene factions. For to call Christ the image of God implies that Christ, though like God, is different from God and so not *homoousios* with the Father. Rather Nyssen's point is that Christ's divine nature, which is the paradigm of human nature, has no

gender division.[35] So how can man be made in the image of a genderless
God and also be stamped with gender? Nyssen reconciles the apparent
contradiction through a careful analysis of the change of pronouns in
the Septuagint's version of Genesis 1:27. He observes:

> There is an end of the creation of that which was made "in the
> image": then it [i.e., Scripture] makes a resumption of the ac-
> count of creation, and says, "male and female created He them."
> I presume that everyone knows that this is a departure from the
> Prototype [*tou prōtotypou:*] for "in Christ Jesus," as the apostle
> says, "there is neither male nor female." Yet the phrase declares
> that man is thus divided [*diērēsthai*]. Thus the creation [*kataskeuē*]
> of our nature is in a sense twofold [*diplē*]: one made like to God,
> one divided according to this distinction: for something like this
> the passage darkly conveys by this arrangement, where it first says,
> "God created man, in the image of God created He *him*," and
> then, adding to what has been said, "male and female created He
> *them*," — a thing which is alien from our conceptions of God.[36]

Since Paul expressly concludes that the divine is devoid of gender, Nyssen
concludes that man cannot be made male and female and *at the same
time* be made in the image of that supreme nature that is not divided
into gender. This reason leads Nyssen to another conclusion: Genesis
1:27 is describing the twofold aspect of humanity's creation. Genesis
1:27b— "according to God's image he made him"—refers to the "creation" of a single humanity[37] whose nature reflects God's own rational
nature without any of the physical characteristics by which the sexes are
divided. Genesis 1:27c — "male and female he created them" — refers
to a later act of creation when God fashioned the first human beings
as embodied creatures marked phenotypically as male or female. The
term "image of God" denotes all the goodness of God's nature that he
graciously shares with us out of the munificence proper to his nature.[38]
Thus the "image of God" according to which the soul was fashioned is
distinguished from the nonrational nature added by the divine artificer
as a prudent afterthought.

The reason God introduces the adulterant of gender to the divine
image Nyssen locates in God's anticipation of the fall. Knowing that
man's nature is inescapably subject to change and flux,[39] God foresaw
that man's immature and mutable nature would fall away from him in
disobedience and so come under the penalty of death.[40] Because the fall
would result in the corruption of human nature such that we would
no longer be able to procreate in the manner of angels,[41] God decided

to divide humanity into male and female. The division of the race into genders allows for procreation after the manner of beasts[42] — a manner of procreation that accommodates the sensual orientation after the fall. Nyssen argues that God "... formed for our nature that contrivance for increase which befits those who had fallen into sin, implanting in humankind, instead of the angelic majesty of nature that animal and nonrational mode."[43]

When Nyssen speaks of the bestial mode of procreation as God's "contrivance ... which *befits* those who had fallen into sin," he implies that Adam and Eve's disobedience was a turn from angelic life of contemplation befitting rational creatures to an indulgence in sensual pleasures characteristic of nonrational animals whose souls can grasp only sensual goods. Having tasted the pleasures of the senses, Adam and Eve thenceforth share an orientation to the pleasures of the body. Therefore, God uses this orientation as the mechanism that will draw them together for the purpose of procreating. This "contrivance" that comes to human nature by its kinship with irrational animals is the impulse to breed out of a desire for sensual pleasure.[44]

The corruption of our nature and "declension from the angelic life" is explained by Nyssen's idea that the body is the "mirror of the mirror" that is the mind's reflection of the divine nature.[45] In other words, as the souls of our first parents turned from contemplating the beauty of God's intelligible goodness to the inferior beauties of sensible goods, the mirror of their souls ceases to reflect the beauty of the passionless archetype and increasingly takes on the image of beasts and their passions. As a result of being given this nature common with beasts for the purpose of reproduction, human beings were also created with the nonrational nature of beasts, which gives them a capacity for passion not present in the impassible divine archetype.[46] Although the capacity for the passionate means of procreation is contingent upon the irrational faculties with its appetitive drives, Nyssen explains that the presence of these passions was not a part of God's intention for our nature but the necessary corollary to the means of procreation God willed: "These attributes [e.g., *thymos* and *epithymia*], then, human nature took to itself from the side of the brutes; for those qualities with which brute life was armed for self-preservation, then transferred to human life, became passions. ... All these and the like affections entered man's composition by reason of the animal mode of generation."[47] This capacity for passion as the precondition for bestial procreation Nyssen speaks of as a weakness inherent in our nature.[48]

For Nyssen, the paradox of human nature is articulated in the words of Psalm 48:13 (LXX): "And man being in honor did not know it, he is compared to uncomprehending beasts and he was made like them." Man's honor is that God made him in His own image, rational like the angels, but He also made him with instinctual responses to pain and pleasure, like animals. Nyssen concludes: "For [man] truly was made like the beasts, who received in his nature the present mode of transient generation, on account of his inclination to material things."[49] A troubling question, however, emerges from Nyssen's explanation of Genesis 1:27c: Was man's inclination toward material goods, which he says prompted God to give man a common nature with the animals including gender and the passions, in fact caused by the presence of the nonrational impulses of our bestial nature? In other words, was man's susceptibility to sensual temptation that caused the fall the result of God's giving us a share in the nature of nonrational animals? Was the cure for death in fact the cause of the fall? These questions we will leave for our discussion of the passions.

The two aspects that Nyssen finds in God's fashioning of humanity in Genesis 1:27 raise another question. If the first aspect, the image, was a single, non-gendered humanity, what was it? Was it the "Platonic form" of humanity? Was it an androgynous prototype? And in what sense was it "created"? Gerhardt Ladner argues persuasively that for Nyssen, the first clause of creation in Genesis 1:27b does not refer to the development of the ideal human being or the essence of humanity. In a sense, Nyssen maintains, God already determined the highest quality of human nature in his choice of himself as the archetype in Genesis 1:26. He makes the point that the hortatory subjunctive "Let us make man in our image" is an act of deliberation whereby God settles upon the pattern after which man is to be made. Nyssen writes,

> While the worlds . . . are laid as a foundation of the universe, the creation is, so to say offhand by the divine power, existing at once by his command, while council precedes the making of man; and that and that which is to be is foreshown by the Maker in verbal description, and of what kind it is fitting that it should be, and to what archetype it is fitting that it should bear a likeness . . . so that he has a rank assigned to him before his Genesis, and possesses rule over the things that are before his coming into being.[50]

In other words, God decides before the actual creation of man what faculties man will need in order to exert dominion over the earth. They are the rational faculties and derivative virtues discussed earlier. Here these faculties and virtues function not merely to distinguish the image

from the body and the material creation but also to show that the freedom of the image is a means towards exercising dominion over creation.
I shall return to this problem later in the argument. For the moment,
however, my concern is to interpret God's first fashioning of humanity
as Nyssen understands Genesis 1:27. What he says is that God fashioned
the *plērōma,* or plenitude, of the human race, that is, all human beings
who ever will be born.[51] Nyssen writes: "In saying that 'God created
man' the text indicates, by the indefinite character of the term, all humankind; for was not Adam named here together with the creation.... Yet
the name given to the man created is not the particular, but the general name."[52] Then the features of our nature that are not constituent of
the divine image, for example, gender and nonrational impulses, were
added. For Ladner, the first creation is important because it contains
that original spiritual condition to which man will be "restored" at the
resurrection.[53]

The only limitation of Ladner's reading of Nyssen is that he takes
Nyssen too literally in his description of a double creation. He is certainly
right that Nyssen does not view the first creation as the construction of
the form of human nature; nevertheless, one cannot view the *plērōma*
simply as consisting of all human beings endowed with individuated
subsistence.[54] First, if one takes the *plērōma* to refer to the totality
of individuals existing as pure rational beings prior to their *incorporation* with irrational appetites and gender, then Nyssen's concept of
the *plērōma* is barely distinguishable from Origen's theory of the host
of rational beings abiding individually prior to their fall into material,
embodied existence. Nyssen devotes too much time to rejecting Origen's
theory of the preexistence of souls apart from bodies to be read as claiming that the soul exists in some prior disembodied state until its birth.[55]
Second, Nyssen says that the *plērōma* exists only at the level of God's
foreknowledge. He explains the nature of the creation of the *plērōma:*
"The entire plenitude of humanity was included by the God of all, by
his power of foreknowledge, as it were into one body, and that this is
what the text teaches us.... For the image is not in any one part of our
nature ... but this power extends equally to all the race: and a sign of
this is the implanted mind alike in all: for all have the power of understanding and deliberating."[56] From a human perspective, the "all" of
whom Nyssen speaks are distinct individuals, presumably all the individuals who will ever exist and who will complete the finite number
of individuals who make up the *plērōma.* But in God's foreknowledge,
they have no substance of their own. In this way, Nyssen's account of
the *plērōma* does not correspond to Origen's preexisting rational beings

that had independent subsistence. Nyssen is conscious of the difference
between God's creative intention and God's actual creation of people as
discrete beings. As Rowan Greer has observed, when Nyssen speaks of
God's creative planning in Genesis 1:26, he uses the word, *ktisis*, which
can be translated "creation." But when speaking of God's act of actually fashioning humanity in Genesis 1:27, he uses the word *kataskeuē*,
which describes the work of a craftsman fashioning his creation.[57] Genesis 1:27, therefore, does not refer to two different creations fashioned at
two distinct moments. It seems that the human *plērōma* is something actually fashioned and yet somehow incomplete until the requisite number
of individuals has been made.

The *Plērōma* and Human Nature

I have suggested that we find several oppositions in Nyssen's thought:
God's intention for creation in Genesis 1:26 as opposed to his actual
fashioning of humanity in Genesis 1:27; the image of God as opposed
to the addition of the male-female distinction; and the first fashioning
of the *plērōma* of humanity as opposed to its eschatological actualization. It is understandable that critics might interpret these oppositions
as a reflection of Philo of Alexandria's treatment of creation and suggest
that Nyssen has the idea of a double creation. In treating the opening chapters of Genesis Philo notices that there are two accounts of the
creation of humanity. Although the narrative suggests that the creation
occurs in various stages, in fact God made the cosmos simultaneously
in one moment.[58] This is the case with the making of man as well. In
De Opificio Mundi, Philo explains that Genesis 1:26 describes the formation of generic humanity devoid of the particularities, such as gender,
which distinguish the individual from the whole.[59] The molding of Adam
from the dust in Genesis 2:7 is an amplification of Genesis 1:27 with
the introduction of gender in Genesis 2:18–22. The rational faculties
of these individuals are a reflection of the ideal man created in Genesis 1:26.[60] These two different accounts do not, however, represent two
separate moments of time since God makes the world in a single act
of creation; rather their narrative expresses the logical priority in God's
creative activity.

For Philo, this creative activity, which is instantaneous and occurs
outside of time is the creation of the *paradeigmata* or ideas upon which
God the demiurge fashions the material creation.[61] The *paradeigmata*
are the universals that are ontologically prior to and independent of the
particular creatures to which they give their form. Although he does not

speak of two times, in a logical sense Philo does have the idea of a double creation that attributes priority to the intelligible world, now understood as the sum of the Platonic forms and as placed in God's mind.

As much as Nyssen has been influenced by Philo, however, we cannot read any of this into Nyssen's thought. In a passage in his *Apologia in Hexaemeron*, Nyssen discusses the opening words of Genesis. He points out that the Hebrew has been translated as either *en archēi* or *en kephalaioi*. This does not matter, since both words imply that there is a sense in which God created the world collectively or all at once. "Beginning" can refer to the point that begins a line. In this sense the beginning *arche* in Genesis 1:1 is the moment that initiates the sequence of time. The moment is without interval, but implies the intervals that follow. Nyssen requires that this "moment" represents the "extremity" of creation. Perhaps it is to be equated with "the principles, the causes, and the powers of all existing things." "God laid the foundation of the world in a moment and in the first impulse of his will. The essence of each of the things that exist ran out together from here — heaven, the ether, stars, fire, air, sea, earth, living things, plants." All that follows from this first moment of creation "is seen by the divine eye and manifest to the word of his power, that Word which, as the prophecy says, 'knows everything before it comes to be.' (Daniel 13:42 LXX)"[62]

It will be obvious that Nyssen does not understand the simultaneity of creation the way Philo does. Nyssen's God does not create an intelligible world that is instantiated in the universe as we know it. Instead, the "moment" for Nyssen is the actual creation of what we can construe as the potentialities of the creation, understood as a process unfolding from this beginning towards its goal.[63]

A more fruitful approach to understanding what Nyssen means by the first fashioning of the *plērōma* of humanity is to be found in his eclectic integration of Platonic and Aristotelian theories of universals. Like Plato, Nyssen holds to the belief in a universal human nature. In his work *On the Premature Deaths of Infants,* Nyssen says that there is a "single, uncreated, eternal nature [*physis*] . . . [that is] the same forever" of which all other natures, including human nature, are produced. He proceeds to describe this human nature as "a mixture from divine sources, the godlike intellectual substance being in him united with earthly elements . . . fashioned . . . to be the incarnate likeness of the divine transcendent power."[64]

If the anthropology in *On the Premature Deaths of Infants* is consistent with the account of man's creation in *On the Making of Man,* then it seems that the above conception of "human nature" corresponds to the *plērōma* of humanity that Nyssen locates in Genesis 1:27. What is interesting about his comment in *On the Premature Deaths of Infants* is that the generic human nature includes both the image and the body. "In saying that 'God created man' the text indicates, by the indefinite character of the term, all mankind...yet the name given to the man created is not particular, but the general name."[65] This generic name and nature includes the divine image, "For the image is not in part of our nature, nor is the grace in any one of the things found in that nature, but this power extends equally to all the race...for all have the power of understanding and deliberating, and all else whereby the divine nature finds its image in that which was made according to it."[66]

The first creation of humanity refers to God's deliberative act of creating all human beings, i.e., the *plērōma*, according to the divine archetype endowed with the rational faculties of apprehension, understanding, and free choice. Being made "according to God's image," this single man representing the *plērōma* embodies both the virtues of God's moral image as well as the rational faculties that comprise the structural image of God. As such the *plērōma* reflects God's universal *intention* for humanity; it is the ideal: who God wills us to be and who we shall become at the end of the age. The man of the first creation is not therefore the prototype of the species. Moreover, this understanding of universal human "nature" differs markedly from Plato's theory of universals. The theory of the forms presented in *Phaedo*, *Republic* III and V, and *Parmenides* attempts to solve the problem of "the one and the many" by identifying the universal essence that unites all things of a particular type. The *eidos* consists of *only* the essential qualities that unite a group of diverse things under a single name, such as chair or virtue. The form, therefore, transcends the particular material instantiations of it. In other words, it contains none of the particular features distinctive of a Duncan Fife chair that are wholly absent from a Frank Lloyd Wright chair. But for Nyssen, the *plērōma* includes both universal characteristics of human beings and the particular individuals who will share in that nature. Thus the universal is inseparable from the particular. Johannes Zachhuber puts it well; all natures, including human nature, are, for Nyssen, "incorporeal being, albeit of a particular kind."[67]

Nyssen's integration of the form with the particular is similar to Aristotle's approach to the problem of universals. Unlike his teacher, Aristotle held to what Guthrie calls "the primacy of the particular." That is, what really exists are individual objects (chairs, dogs, human beings) or instances of behavior (prudence, benevolence, fortitude). All individual chairs are called chairs because they share a common formal and final cause. The form (*eidos*) is "the essence and primary substance of each thing."[68] The *eidos* that makes the particular chair a chair is real, but it has no existence independent of the particular chairs in which the form inheres. Contra Plato, the form does not subsist in some eternal and immutable realm. Thus, for Aristotle, there is no *eidos* separable from the particulars.

Nyssen's theory of the creation of the *plērōma* presents the universal human nature as having no subsistence apart from the particular people with whom God will invest this nature.[69] Yet Nyssen, unlike Aristotle, views human nature existing at the level of God's foreknowledge and creative intention prior to the existence of any particular human being. Thus human nature itself is logically prior to any particular instance of it because it was created outside of space and time. Nyssen's integration of a Platonic understanding of human nature as an intelligible and eternal reality with an Aristotelian concern for the particular is similar to Proclus's attempt to reconcile Plato and Aristotle. In his *Commentary on Timaeus*, Proclus contends that *phusis* mediates the particular with the intelligible. It is the matter-inhering form (*enylon eidos*) that is logically prior to the particular and gives the particular its essence by virtue of its immanence in the particular.[70]

The *imago Dei* is central to our understanding of Nyssen's anthropology since he equates the divine image with the powers and virtues of the soul, to the exclusion of the body. Yet because he so strongly links the image of God to the soul, one wonders whether the body is included in the *plērōma*. Nyssen writes,

> I think that by these words Holy Scripture conveys to us a great and lofty doctrine; and the doctrine is this. While two natures — the divine and incorporeal nature, and the irrational life of brutes — are separated from each other as extremes, human nature is the mean between them: for in the compound nature of man we may behold a part of each of the natures... of the Divine, the rational and intelligent element, which does not admit the distinction of male and female; of the irrational, our bodily form and structure, divided into male and female.[71]

Nyssen's own interpretation of the double character of God's actual creation of humanity identifies the first aspect "in the image of God" with man's intellectual faculties proper to the rational soul; the second aspect of creation is associated with the nonrational elements of our nature, among which he includes gender. He acknowledges that human nature is a hybrid of the divine and rational element with the bestial and nonrational nature. In this regard, his statement is consistent with his description of human *physis* in *On the Premature Deaths of Infants.*

To argue that the first fashioning of humanity does not include the body created two problems. First, if the first fashioning is only of the image of God, only of the intellectual and spiritual faculties, then how are we to account for the nonrational elements of the soul that are related to the needs of the whole body and not simply to the bestial mode of procreation? Moreover, when Nyssen speaks of humanity as harmonizing the entire creation, the body is described as an instrument enabling humanity to have a relationship to beasts and the lower orders of creation.[72] Second, Nyssen goes on to say that the eschatological humanity will be restored to the pure image of God as found in the first man. He writes, "the man that was manifest at the first creation of the world, and he that shall be after the consummation of all are alike: they equally bear in themselves the Divine image."[73] If eschatological humanity will be "alike" to the *plērōma* of humanity of the first fashioning, and if we affirm the general resurrection of the body, then it is hard to see how the body would be excluded from the first fashioning.

On the other hand, there are certainly passages in Nyssen's writings that emphasize a humanity made in the divine image, uncompromised by the nonrational nature of animals. On this reading the human nature in the eschaton is freed, not only from gender, but also from the nonrational nature that necessarily co-exists with the sentient soul of any animal. The relationship of the nonrational nature to the sentient soul will become clear in the next chapter. For the time being, however, it is enough to say simply that Nyssen has unnecessarily created this problem by equating the nonrational nature of beasts as a whole with the bestial mode of procreation between the male and female of the species.

At this point our study comes to a critical juncture. So far we have seen the positive relation of the rational or spiritual to the nonrational or bodily natures of human beings. Yet when we turn to the subject of gender and the *imago Dei*, we encounter Nyssen's more negative treatment of the irrational and the bodily natures. These contradictory views of human nature ultimately lead Nyssen to two soteriological trajectories; one route emphasizes the redemption of the body in the resurrection, the other, the purification of the soul. The latter, his theory of *epektasis*, is the branch of his soteriology with which this investigation is primarily concerned.

The problem of the twofold character of the first fashioning of humanity can be addressed if we first recognize that Nyssen uses the theory to express three concerns. First, and most basic, is the exegetical problem

inherent in Genesis 1:27. The interpretation lets him explain away what
he views as the contradiction between man's being made in the image of
God and the division of humanity into the sexes. Second, it allows him,
as *On the Making of Man* (16.9) suggests, to describe the composite
character of human nature. Humanity possesses both the godlike intellectual faculties and virtues as well as the nonrational, precritical faculties
proper to animals. But third, as *On the Making of Man* (16.17) suggests,
Nyssen employs the theory to link God's creative purpose "in the beginning" to the eschatological consummation of the divine economy, which
is the basis of his reworking of Origen's idea of *apokatastasis* — the end
shall be like the beginning.

There is an ambiguity here. Are we to link this third concern to the
first and argue that the addition of male and female, and, presumably, of
the body represents a corruption of the beginning that will be eliminated
in the end? Or are we to link the third concern to the second one and
say that "male and female" can refer to the body, concluding that the
body is somehow integral to both the beginning and the end? For the
moment the most important point to make is that this third concern is
the overarching agenda of *On the Making of Man*. In his introduction to
the treatise, Nyssen explains the goal of the project: "For it is necessary
to know those things concerning man which came to be — of that which
we believe to *have come to be,* of that which we expect to appear *later,*
and of that which is *now* seen."[74]

Nyssen's order is confusing to modern readers who think of time in
linear terms: the past precedes the present from which we look to the
future that shall come to us. But Nyssen proposes to discuss the past and
the future and then present state of humanity. This curious order is not
the order of topics to be discussed; rather it reflects his presupposition
that humanity in the creation at the beginning and at the end of time
possess a similar nature that stands in stark contrast to human nature
in the present. He introduces his investigation of Gen. 1:27 with this set
purpose: "Let us turn our inquiry to the question before us, — how it is
that while the deity is in bliss, and humanity is in misery, the latter is yet
in Scripture called 'like' the former?"[75]

The conclusion to which his view of the twofold aspect of creation
leads is that God willed that human beings share in his divine nature in
order that we might partake of divine bliss. This bliss is our eschatological destiny once the image is fully actualized, and was compromised by
the passions of our nonrational nature that are the source of our misery. The problem is that corrupting passions are linked with gender. In
his reading of Genesis 1:27, Nyssen notices that when God actualized

his intention to create humanity in his image and likeness, he does so by adding "male and female" to the image. The implication of Nyssen's interpretation is that the image is compromised by the passions of our nonrational nature. This makes it seem as though the body is itself an obstacle to the full actualization of the image. Moreover, in the discussion that follows, his emphasis is upon the gender distinction as God's addition to the image as a remedy for the fall of the image. We have already noted the confusion caused by this idea. The bestial form of procreation, meant as a remedy for sin and death, begins to look like the occasion for the fall. In this pejorative view of gender, the male-female "addition" to the image is no more than a temporary device since the eschatological humanity in Christ will exclude the male-female distinction.

This conclusion, however, contradicts Nyssen's view of the body as central to God's purpose in the creation of man. Through the bodily senses, the soul is able to experience the goods of material creation and so know the goodness of the Creator.[76] The embodiment of the rational soul allows man to act as the steward of the material and nonrational world. Nyssen even goes so far as to suggest that God intends to use the union of the rational and the nonrational in man to sanctify and unite all of creation.[77] And lastly, Nyssen does not view the body as epiphenomenal, as does Origen. Rather he contends that the resurrection body is the very material body of this life, only glorified.[78] (It should be noted, however, that his doctrine of the resurrection is hardly systematic, much less coherent.)[79] If eschatological humanity has put on an incorruptible material body, and if this humanity is like the humanity of God's first fashioning, then the human nature that was the product of God's creative intention was also embodied (even if lacking gender). Thus, although the body is not itself the image of God, Nyssen cannot be read as viewing it as an impediment to communion with God.

The Second Aspect of the Making of Man: Gender

As we have seen, Nyssen understands Genesis 1:27 to refer to the actual fashioning of humanity, but he can also treat the last clause of the verse as an "addition" of the male and female distinction to the image. It is difficult not to be reminded of Philo's view that in Genesis 1:27, God's division of the genus *anthrōpos* that is made in the divine image into the species male and female occurs outside of time: "This though its individual members had not yet taken shape."[80] Later, commenting on Genesis 2:7–8, Philo says, "By this also he shows very clearly that there

is a vast difference between the man thus formed and the man that came
into existence earlier after the image of God: for the man so formed is
an object of sense-perception . . . consisting of body and soul, man and
woman, by nature mortal; while he that was after the (divine) image
was an idea or type or seal, an object of thought, incorporeal, neither
male nor female, by nature incorruptible."[81] Here Philo clearly equates
the divine image with the universal human nature that contains none
of the individuating characteristics, such as gender, that are present in
the body of a particular person. Though at odds with his own earlier
interpretation of Genesis 1:27, this passage of Philo views gender as
coming into being in the second or actual, temporal creation.

As we have seen, however, Nyssen does not strictly follow Philo. For
the first creation, in Nyssen's theory, is not of the *paradeigma* of humanity (as in Philo's reworking of Plato's *Timaeus*), but of the universal
humanity expressed together with the plenitude of particular human beings. Nyssen is not committed to a strictly Platonic model, as is Philo.
Nevertheless, his understanding of the second aspect of creation, the
male-female distinction, reflects the influence of both Philo and Origen.

Nyssen's use of *kataskeuē*, that is, the actual fashioning of material
by the craftsman into the intended object, suggests that this fashioning
includes both the image and the male-female distinction. In 16.6, he
excludes Adam from the first part of the verse because the term used
is the general one, *anthrōpos*. But it seems possible to argue that the
addition of the male-female entails the fashioning of the first human
beings. The distinction between *ktisis* and *kataskeuē* — being created as
opposed to being fashioned — would follow the distinction in Rufinus's
Latin translation of Origen's *Homilies on Genesis* between God's *making*
of the immortal soul in his image (Gen. 1:26–27) and God's *forming* the
bodies of Adam from the dust of the ground and of Eve from Adam's
rib (Gen. 2:7).[82]

Nevertheless, since Nyssen also uses *kataskeuē* to refer to the double aspect of human nature as a whole, the question cannot be resolved
solely by examining his vocabulary. Later, in his account of the delayed
resurrection Nyssen implies that we can make a distinction between the
making of an image and the addition of male and female, and that
he associates Adam and Eve with the addition. Having quoted Genesis 1:27a/b, he comments: "Accordingly, the image of God, which we
behold in universal humanity, had its consummation then; but Adam as
yet was not; for the thing formed from the earth is called Adam, by ety-
mological nomenclature."[83] While the divine image exists in the mind of
God and was actually created, gendered humanity does not exist until

Adam is formed from the earth. If this is the case, then the second aspect of creation refers to God's bringing into actual existence the first members of the human race. The anthropological significance of the creation of gender in time, and not as part of God's intention in Genesis 1:26, is that it removes gender from the essence of human nature and stresses its ad hoc nature. In other words, if Nyssen had placed the creation of gender in God's eternal mind, then gender would be included in the universal human nature. Thus he reinforces the point that gender is not an essential or ultimately meaningful component of human nature.

Of course, the logic of the various passages we have examined implies that the creation of the *plērōma* refers to the *potential* existence of each individual human being — a potential that begins being *actualized* with the making of Adam and Eve. This process of actualization continues through time until the final person foreknown by God is born.[84] With that birth the plenitude of the human race has been consummated and the resurrection can begin.[85] Perhaps Nyssen is not explicit on the point because he recognizes that from the perspective of the eternal God who stands outside of time the creation of the plenitude of humanity at the beginning of time and its consummation at the end of time are simultaneous.[86]

Ultimately, the importance of the second aspect of creation is the way this theory leads Nyssen to view both universal human nature and human beings in their present constitution. To begin with, Nyssen's interpretation establishes a fundamental equality between men and women at the level of their shared intellectual nature. Although he maintains that human nature as a whole is comprised of both the incorporeal-intellectual nature and the material-sensual nature of animals, primacy is given to the rational faculties of the soul over the nonrational faculties. As we shall see, Macrina even identifies the rational faculties that bear the image of God as the *essence* of human nature since it is these faculties that are distinctive of human beings.[87] This reading establishes this equality between the sexes by giving priority to man's intellectual nature and relegating the difference between male and female to an ad hoc contrivance for the purpose of reproduction. The intellectual nature is that which, as we have seen, enables us to participate in the life and being of God that is our highest good. When the soul's contemplative participation in and enjoyment of God's goodness is understood in the context of Nyssen's doctrine of epectasy — the immortal soul's eternal movement into the infinite divine — then the soul's intellectual faculties are integral to humanity's primary eschatological activity.

By contrast, the division of the human race into male and female serves our transient need for perpetuating the species. This understanding of the soul might appear to compromise the doctrine of the resurrection. The fact that Nyssen speaks of the resurrection as spiritual may indicate his awareness of the problem. But even if we can distinguish gender from the body as such, Nyssen can follow Jesus' pronouncement that in the resurrection people will no longer marry or be given in marriage since there will be no death and hence no need for procreation. Nyssen concludes that the resurrected humanity will embrace that virginity which Adam and Eve enjoyed before the fall into sin and before their experience of sexual pleasure. If the resurrection bodies are the same material bodies we have now, then presumably they will retain the marks of gender. Even as the mouth, though still a part of the resurrected body, will not be needed to eat food for physical nourishment, so too the sex organs will play no purpose in the Kingdom where the absence of death eliminates the need for procreation.[88] The genitalia will have no greater significance for life in the resurrection than the appendix has for modern human beings. Not only will there be no procreative need for sex; more to the point, the soul having recovered its pre-Fall purity will not be concerned with sensual pleasures, but only with the joy of those intelligible goods that are the proper objects of a rational creature's intellectual love. This reorientation of the soul from the sensual to the intelligible means that the marks of gender that divide the race into the sexes will lose their social significance; gender consciousness will slip from human experience. Men and women will no longer view each other or themselves as male or female. To whatever extent people will be conscious of one another, they will view each other only as creatures in and through whom they experience the goodness of God, who eschatologically shall be "all and in all."[89]

Nyssen's appraisal of gender through the lens of creation as well as eschatology leads him to view gender as an accidental rather than an essential quality of human nature. It is accidental in that it is the result of the accident of sin and the fall into passionate sensuality; it need not have been necessary for the fulfillment of God's purpose. Nyssen argues that, even if there had been no Fall and hence the need for the bestial mode of procreation requiring the division of the sexes, the *plērōma* would have been achieved through an angelic, asexual mode of procreation.[90] Gender adds nothing to man necessary for the attainment of his *telos,* contemplative communion with God. Such contemplation is within the capacity of the intellectual faculties. Even the extent to which the nonrational faculties of the soul can be harnessed to serve the intellectual faculties' ascent to God, gender and sexuality in themselves do not contribute to the soul's pilgrimage. Although the physical form of resurrected humanity retains gender, the difference between male and female, as I suggested above, does not contribute at all to our eschatological existence. At most the marks of gender, like the form of the eyes or nose, merely establish the continuity of an individual person's identity between the two ages. Even so, the qualities of the soul — its degree of purity or corruption — more than the markings of the body, denote the identity of the individual.[91]

By treating gender as an accidental rather than an essential component of human nature, Nyssen treats the female differently from how she is treated in the anthropologies of classical and late antiquity. On the one hand, Nyssen's theory stands apart from the androgyne tradition of Plato's *Symposium*. In Aristophanes' ironic encomium on *Eros*, he explains why human beings are drawn to sexual union with each other. He tells the comic myth that originally human beings were round, two-faced, quadrapedal hermaphrodites (*amphoterōn*) whose locomotion resembled the tumbling of acrobats.[92] Zeus and the other gods punished these creatures for conspiring against them by splitting each into two. Once split in two, each person now possesses a single gender.

But Aristophanes' myth is not merely providing an etiology of gender and sexual orientation. For at this point, the comic mask of Aristophanes' story is removed revealing its true, tragic character. Once divided each loses the strength and vigor of her previous condition.[93] And what strength she retains is consumed by the frenetic search for her other half, in the hope that through sexual union the original unity of the individual might be regained.[94] Yet sexual liaisons are short lived and the sense of wholeness for which human beings seek is never achieved. The speech is not concerned with one gender more than the other. Both share the need to find their other half. The point is that Aristophanes' primordial hermaphrodites are quite different from Nyssen's man of the first creation. Whereas the hermaphrodite is already sexed, equipped with some combination of genitalia (male-male, female-female, or male-female), Nyssen's prototype perfectly bearing the image of the sexless God is wholly without gender.

Nyssen's understanding of the baptismal formula from Galatians 3:28 is different not only from Aristophanes' myth but also from the androgyne anthropologies that were present in Hellenistic Judaism and Christianity.[95] Nyssen's difference with the hermaphroditic and androgyne models can best be seen in the way these models treat gender in the present. The hermaphroditic model views individuals as fundamentally incomplete and therefore needing to find in another person that other half whereby they are made whole. For Nyssen, however, "the Other" in whom the individual finds perfection and happiness is not another mortal, but God. There is nothing that an individual as a man or as a woman lacks that is essential for happiness. Happiness, for Nyssen, is not found in the binary relations between men and women, but between creature and Creator. This is the presupposition behind Nyssen's view of the life of virginity. For, as we shall see, virginity for Nyssen embraces that prototypical humanity that is without gender. Moreover, Nyssen's view differs from that tradition that interprets the *imago Dei* as a composite of the masculine and the feminine.[96] For such a model assumes that there are virtues inherent in either the male or the female that the other lacks.[97] For Nyssen, no individual is dependent upon another person (save Christ) to be reformed in the image of God and gain salvation. For gender is simply an ad hoc physical attribute, completely unrelated to the divine image that defines the highest faculties of human nature.

Nyssen's conception of the *imago Dei* results in a different view of women from the one found in many Christian and non-Christian discussions of the sexes in classical and late antiquity.[98] For example, Philo rejects the hermaphroditic model from the *Symposium,* interpreting Genesis 1:27 as God's creation of human nature that includes the addition of the species male and female (which are alien to the divine image) to the genus, *anthrōpos.* Yet Philo in his interpretation of the making of Eve from Adam's rib (Gen. 2:21–22) identifies the masculine with the rational faculties of mind or *nous* while the feminine that is formed from flesh he associates with the lower faculties of sense perception or *aisthēsis.* Moreover, the female is associated with sexuality, which arouses among men desires for bodily pleasures that are the cause of evil.[99] The result of his analysis of Genesis 2 is that the masculine is equated with the rational character proper to the image of God. Women, therefore, acquire the image of God by forsaking that which is feminine and becoming masculine, that is, rational.[100]

Similarly, Origen associates *spiritus,* the higher divine quality in human beings, with the male and *anima,* that which animates the body, with the female. If the *anima* does not submit to the masculine, *spiritus,* then sin results.[101] One finds a parallel to this tradition in the conversation between Simon Peter and Jesus in the Gospel according to Thomas 114. When Peter asks if Mary should leave the disciples since she, as a woman is not "worthy of life," Jesus responds, "I am going to attract her to make her male so that she too might become a living spirit that resembles you males. For every female (element) that makes itself male will enter the kingdom of heavens."[102] Precedent for such a view among orthodox Christians is common. Jerome viewed the renunciation of sex among female virgins as tantamount to the abandonment of the feminine. The virgin had metaphorically become male.[103]

Nyssen's treatment of gender stands in striking relief against this background. Because all human beings were created in the *plērōma* and bear the image of God, all members of the human race possess a higher nature that is fundamentally rational. Moreover, since the division of human-kind into male and female is not included in God's creative intention but comes only as an accommodation for sin, Nyssen does not associate the masculine with the rational while identifying the feminine with the nonrational. Nyssen associates both maleness and femaleness with sensuality; consequently, the female cannot be exclusively linked to sexuality and sensuality, thereby being the cause of sin. Cline Horowitz's reading of *On the Making of Man* 16 misses the mark when she claims, "Gregory of Nyssa thought the mention of woman was a forecast of sin and a need for an animal mode of procreation."[104] For the reference to "man" in Genesis 1:27c was just as much an adulterant of the *imago Dei* as was "woman." Rather men and women share an equal capacity for rationality and an autocratic will. Thus each is capable of participating in God's goodness and embodying the virtues that constitute God's moral likeness. Within the logic of his reading, Nyssen's assertion that the virgin transcends her nature as a woman does not mean, as Jerome claims, that she has become male. Rather she has transcended gender altogether, bearing the intellectual nature that is superior to the masculine.

Although Nyssen does assume that women have a weaker constitution than men,[105] he nevertheless does not here view the reclamation of the *imago Dei* as the masculinization of women. In *The Life of Moses*, however, he lapses into an association of the female with the material and the male with virtue.[106] This is inconsistent with his theoretical discussion of gender in *On the Making of Man*. He may well be following the rhetoric of Philo[107] and Origen;[108] yet unlike either of them, he never gives any theoretical or exegetic reason for identifying the female with the passionate and the masculine with the rational. After all, as Verna Harrison observes, "Gregory envisages the distinction between male and female specifically in terms of the biological reproduction, not as a functional cosmic, ontological, or spiritual reality."[109] In fact, the passage from *The Life of Moses* is as inconsistent with *On the Making of Man* (16) as is his *Commentary on the Song of Songs*, in which eschatological humanity is portrayed as feminine.[110] Perhaps the best explanation for

this contradiction internal to Nyssen's corpus is Elizabeth Clark's suggestion that this language recognizes the full humanity of women and
yet is itself constrained by its androcentric culture.[111] Thus Nyssen's theory, in contrast with Philo's, does not privilege one sex over the other,
but instead establishes the *theoretical* basis of equality among men and
women for the hope of godlike virtue.

One of the guiding principles in Nyssen's anthropology is that the end
is like the beginning. The creation of man in the image of God and the
eschatological destiny of man are inseparable. The language of Genesis
1:26–27 does not, for Nyssen, describe present humanity, but points
forward describing the incorruptible glory that human nature shall put
on at the resurrection. Likewise, the eschatological exaltation of humanity can be conceived only as the fulfillment of God's creative intention
declared in Genesis 1. He speaks of it alternatively as the consummation of the *plērōma* and the restoration of creation. Jesus is the nexus of
Nyssen's salvation history. He as the image of the invisible God is the
archetype. He is also the "man from heaven" who is "first born from the
dead" — the one whose bodily resurrection is the hope and the paradigm
of resurrected humanity.[112]

Through baptism, the Christian is united with Christ in his death and
resurrection, thereby becoming a participant in the eschatological humanity that Christ's death and resurrection inaugurate. Thus for Nyssen
the baptismal formula from Galatians 3:27–28 is crucial: "For as many
of you as were baptized into Christ have put on Christ. There is neither Jew nor Greek, slave nor free, male nor female." This proclaims
the vision of resurrected humanity that bears the image of God uncompromised by alien features such as gender. But Nyssen also maintains
that through the leavening of humanity in the Incarnation,[113] the Christian's life in the church is a life of proleptic participation in the humanity
of the resurrection described in the baptismal formula. In other words,
Nyssen holds that the Christian is able to order her life in the present in
such a way as to transcend her gender and embody a soul possessing the
purity of the *imago Dei*. As we shall see in chapter 7, Macrina through
her ascetic discipline and her devotion to a life of virginity so suppresses
the passions of her nonrational nature — that nature associated with the
second creation — that he speaks of her as transcending her gender, in a
real sense no longer being a woman.

Before we can explore Nyssen's soteriology, which explains how the
soul is able to control, sublimate, and even transcend the impulses and
emotions of man's lower bestial nature, it will be necessary to examine
his psychology. Specifically, a partial cause for the ambiguity about the

place of the body in his theory lies in Nyssen's failure to explain in *On the Making of Man* 16 exactly what human faculties and impulses are subsumed under the term "nonrational nature." Having defined the passions as the product of man's nonrational nature, Nyssen, if he is to insulate God from the charge of creating the cause of sin, must locate his theory of the passions within the context of a dynamic theory of the soul that opens the possibility for the soul's virtuous life within the body. In other words, in order to understand how Nyssen is able to speak of the Christian's transcending her nature in this life, we first must understand his conception of the relationship between the rational faculties that bear God's image and the nonrational faculties that bear the image of the beasts. The problem of the body will not disappear, but the concern in what follows will be with Nyssen's understanding of the image of God and of the spiritual destiny of humanity.

CHAPTER TWO

Nyssen's Eclectic Psychology

The soul, as we have seen, is the locus of the divine image in man. For it is the soul that possesses the rational faculties that constitute man's structural likeness to God. Consequently, the qualities of purity, *apatheia,* and love that constitute God's moral virtues — those virtues wherein the beauty of God's nature is contemplated — are qualities of the soul. Yes, Nyssen does speak of the body as the mirror of the mirror; that is, the body possesses qualities of the soul, such as immortality and impassibility, which the soul communicates to the body through its hegemonic dominion over the body. But all the virtues that comprise the moral image of God are properly characteristics of the soul. Although Nyssen shared Athanasius's concern for the divinization of the flesh, of greater importance by far for his soteriology was the purification of the soul so that it might properly participate in and enjoy the goodness of God. Yet at the same time that the soul's rational faculties fit man for communion with God the soul was also the animating principle of the material body. As a hybrid between the intellectual creature, like the angelic host, and the corporeal creation, the human soul is fashioned, not only to ascend to its lofty heavenly goal, but also to coordinate those basic functions necessary to sustain the life and health of the body.

Moreover, as we shall see in the next chapter, those activities of the soul that serve the needs of a sentient, embodied creature are not, for Nyssen, antithetical to the soul's higher rational activities. Rather they are necessary for the intellectual soul's ascent to God. Thus the life of the soul divided in its jurisdiction between the heavenly and the mundane can be understood only in terms of a dynamic coordination of the faculties appropriate to each realm. In order to understand this coordination of its faculties, we need to understand how Nyssen conceives of the soul's governance of the body. In fact, I will argue, Nyssen's apparent ambivalence toward the emotions in *On the Soul and the Resurrection* both originates and is ultimately resolved through his understanding of the trichotomous structure of the soul. His account of the nature and structure of the human soul, in some ways, is as confusing as his theory of the passions. For although Nyssen, through the voice of Macrina, repudiates certain doctrines of the soul espoused by Plato and Aristotle, his own theory turns out to be highly influenced by both models. He employs an Aristotelian structure and yet preserves the metaphorical language associated with Plato's tripartite soul to explain the tensions between the soul's various impulses and operations.

At first glance his disavowal of Plato and Aristotle appears disingenuous, given his reliance upon no minor elements of their respective psychologies. Indeed it has led some scholars to think that Nyssen's theory of the soul is baptized pagan philosophy without any substantial transformation of the classical models. Nyssen's eclectic borrowing from these traditions, I will argue, suggests that he has no dogmatic commitment to either tradition. The real transformation of the classical model, as we shall see in subsequent chapters, is visible once one considers the character of the soul's participation in God. For the time being, however, it is necessary to examine Nyssen's indebtedness to the traditions of classical philosophy. Specifically, we need to examine two models of the soul, each of which commanded the attention of students of human psychology in late antiquity: Platonist and Peripatetic. Nyssen articulates a conception of the soul governed by certain biblical categories, such as the *imago Dei,* which place his psychology in opposition to these traditions. At the same time, it is the idiosyncratic permutations of these models that reveal how he borrows from these schools in order to describe a soul that best accommodates his overriding religious concerns. Thus we can see how his theological concerns shape his appropriation of late antique insights into human psychology. Before turning to our examination of the various theories of the soul that influenced Nyssen's psychology, it may be helpful to explain what I mean by calling Nyssen's psychology eclectic.

The intellectual culture of the Hellenistic age has commonly been described as "eclectic" in the pejorative sense of the word. Eduard Zeller dismissed the successors of Plato and Aristotle and Zeno as "lacking the vigorous constructive speculation," being without "the capacity for original work, seeking for a solution in some kind of compromise."[1] Even in its neutral meaning, the joining of streams of thought from different philosophical systems, the term "eclectic" is not an adequate term to distinguish Hellenistic philosophy from philosophy in any other age.[2] After all, no one would suggest that they were the only group of philosophers to be influenced by the thought of more than one philosophical tradition.

This engagement with diverse schools of thought, contrary to Zeller's assertion, need not be a sign of deficient intellectual imagination. On the contrary, though their work is not of the same caliber as the giants of Hellenic culture, their efforts to incorporate congenial features and to reconcile seemingly conflicting opinions of various classical schools indicates that the succeeding generations of intellectuals recognized the wealth of insight bequeathed to them by their classical predecessors. For example, Plato's thought, according to Aristotle, largely followed the Pythagoreans but also included Cratylus and Heraclitus's view of the sensible world as the realm of flux as well as Socrates' concern for universals as the basis of ethics.[3] Similarly, the Middle Platonism of Antiochus of Ascalon (ca. 130–68 B.C.) sought to prove the compatibility of Platonism, Aristotelianism, and Stoicism.

Arguably the integration of various philosophical traditions is not the mere ad hoc union of fundamentally incompatible philosophical notions — patchwork philosophy. Rather the eclectic incorporation of ideas from rival schools reflected the conviction that there was a common ground upon which the different traditions relied that could enable Stoicism, for example, to inform the thought of the Academy. When Antiochus succeeded Philo of Larissa as head of the Academy, Platonism shifted away from the skeptical philosophy that had characterized the temperament of the "New Academy" under Arcesilaus (ca. 316–241 B.C.) to a *dogmatic* form of Platonism. As a student in the Academy under Polemo, Arcesilaus read Plato's early dialogues, leading him to conclude that neither the senses nor the mind can arrive at knowledge in any definitive sense. His method of dialectic revived the Socratic approach to questioning that challenged all opinions without offering any positive conclusions.[4] Indeed, Cicero viewed Arcesilaus's skepticism as the revival of the spirit, not merely of Socrates, but of Plato's dialogues in which "all things are inquired into and no certain statement is made."[5] Arcesilaus was not, for all his attacks upon Stoicism, a throwback to the Old Academy, but eclectically incorporated Pyrrho's skepticism with the epistemology of Plato.[6]

Eclecticism was not confined to the New Academy. Zeno attended the lectures of Polemo and incorporated the tradition of the Old Academy into his own brand of Stoicism. Thus Hankinson has observed that the dispute between Arcesilaus and Zeno was less the conflict between two radically opposed systems of thought and more a contest between two claimants to the philosophical legacy of Socrates.[7] In contrast with Arcesilaus's skeptical attitude toward the possibility of knowledge, Antiochus's dogmatic philosophy appealed to the Stoic epistemology and ethics to advance Platonism's objections to moral relativism.[8] However, the materialist component of Antiochus's system borrowed from Stoic psychology led him to abandon Platonism's traditional identification of the highest good with an ideal belonging to a transcendent and intelligible realm. In this respect his appropriation of Stoicism was, from the perspective of other Middle Platonists such as Philo, Plutarch, and Cicero, not comparable to the eclectic Platonism of the New Academy. It was so syncretistic as to cease being true Platonism.

Philo and Plutarch follow Antiochus's dogmatic approach to philosophy, yet their systematization of Platonism took a decidedly different form. Both were eclectic, Philo influenced by Stoic ethics and the Neo-Pythagoreans and Plutarch by Peripatetic ethics. Yet both spoke of the *summum bonum* in the language of Plato's *Theaetetus* as conformity to the image of the Divine, rather than as "living in accordance with nature."[9]

To summarize, generally speaking almost all the philosophical schools have been eclectic in some sense in that they have drawn upon the insights of other philosophers who were not members of their particular school. Yet, more technically speaking, the eclectic quality of Hellenistic thought before Antiochus is distinct from the dogmatic tendencies of Middle Platonism. The former refers to the incorporation of features from other philosophical traditions that possessed a family resemblance to another school of thought. This eclectic appropriation of diverse philosophical positions was intended to supplement the deficiencies in one's own tradition. The latter refers to the systematization of philosophy with the intent of reconciling the differences between the major schools.

Gregory of Nyssa is philosophically eclectic, but theologically kaleidoscopic. His eclecticism reflects his attitude toward philosophy vis-à-vis Scripture. That is, he is not committed to any one philosophical system, but will borrow from each what is useful for explaining his theological position. Thus he is eclectic in that his borrowing is not at all systematic, nor is he principally concerned with being philosophically coherent. Theologically, Nyssen cannot be viewed as systematic. His use of theological vocabulary is inconsistent and his varied discussions of key doctrines, such as the resurrection, cannot easily be drawn together into a coherent system. The alternative to a dogmatic theology is a kaleidoscopic theology, a theology that by twists and turns describes different facets of the God whose infinite virtues are seen through the prism of his self-revelation in the Incarnation.

The Development of Plato's Soul

Plato's early discussion of the nature of the soul is tied to two central themes in his thought: knowledge is recollection and the soul is immortal. In Plato's account of Socrates' deathbed discourse, Socrates claims that the unitary nature of the soul is necessary for the soul's transcendence of the body in death. Were the soul composite, it could be broken down into its constituent parts, even as the body is dissolved into dust (*Phaedo* 78B–C). The soul's essential simplicity (*axysuntheton*) he bases on its invisibility. In this respect the soul is like the invisible, intelligible entities that can be grasped only by the intellect. Since the soul and the intelligible share the quality of invisibility, Socrates concludes that the soul also shares the property of imperishability (79A–B). Socrates' demonstrates the soul's capacity to subsist independent of the body based on his theory of *anemēsis*. Plato in *Meno* offered proof for the theory of recollection that served as the epistemological basis for Socrates' pedagogy in his account of Socrates' questioning the uneducated slave boy about geometry. From the boy's ability to recognize the truth of Socrates' statements about geometrical shapes, Plato concludes that the boy could agree with Socrates' statements because in some sense he already had knowledge of geometry (82C–E). Similarly, in *Phaedo,* Socrates argues that equal things and the idea of the Equal are not identical. Moreover, the idea of the Equal is necessary to make judgments about the similarity or dissimilarity of objects. Since we make such judgments from the time of our birth, the idea of the Equal must exist in the soul prior to our birth (75C). Thus the soul itself must exist prior to its life in the body (76E). Since the soul was imperishable, and therefore immortal, its nature was divine, like the intelligible entities.

Consequently, the philosopher's life is devoted to purifying the soul of the errant opinions and desires derived from its sojourn in the body by living a life separated from the sensual orientation of the body and centered upon the truth that is accessible to the intellect alone. The life of the philosopher is an anticipation of the soul's ultimate separation from the body at death.[10] If the soul has sufficiently purified itself of the errors of the body, it may be released from its migratory cycles of reincarnation[11] and enter into the heavenly realm of truth with the gods (63C). For this reason, Socrates does not fear drinking the hemlock (58E). This unitary paradigm failed, however, to explain the intersection of the soul and body necessary for the soul to function as the animating principle of the body.[12] Equally problematic for Plato's model of the unitary soul is the question of the location of the passions. Do the emotions and sensual impulses reside in the body or are they found in the soul?

In *Phaedo*, Plato speaks of the passions (*pathē*) and desires (*epithymia*)
as residing in the body (66C). If the passions reside in the soul itself,
then the soul seems to have some nonrational component. Thus the soul
would not be simple or purely rational. In order to preserve the soul's
simple nature and with it the hope of immortality,[13] Plato is forced to
locate the passions and desire in the body. The problem is that the separation of the soul and body in death does not in itself constitute a
purification of the soul. Rather the souls that have not been purified by
the study of philosophy are weighted down with the heavy and pon-
derous "bodily element" (81C–D) in the soul. As a consequence of the
soul's sustained contact with the body, the experience of pleasure and
pain acts as "another nail to rivet the soul to the body and weld them
together" (83D). By contrast the soul of the philosopher "drags nothing
bodily with it" at death (80E). Self-restraint or moderation aids the philosopher's turn from the body and senses (83B–C); for instead of being
excited by desires (*epithymia*) and passions (*pathē*) such that one acts to
satisfy them the philosopher is either dismissive or disdainful (*oligōros*)
of the impulse or handles it in an orderly fashion (*kosmiōs*) (68C). Thus
he says that the soul does not give in to emotions, such as thirst or
hunger as feelings of the body (*tois kata to sōma pathesin*) (94B). Similarly, Odysseus's soul is master over the impulses of his heart (94D).
The philosopher, therefore, turns from the body to the invisible realm of
the intelligible and thereby "keeps away from pleasures [*hēdonē*], and
desires [*epithymia*] and grief [*lupē*] and pain" (83b).

This language raises a number of problems. If the passions are located
in the body and not the soul, then presumably death itself would free
the soul from the passions by separating it from their source, the body.
Yet he asserts that the unpurified soul even after its separation from the
body is weighted down with heavy bodily elements, which continually
draw it to the sensible goods of the flesh. If the passions and desire are
located in the body and not the soul, then what are the "nails" that
rivet the soul to the body? What is the "heavy bodily element" that
weighs down the unpurified soul? Since the soul is incorporeal, it cannot
literally contain the material stuff of the body. It can only be that the
soul develops a habitual orientation to the things of the body. Such an
orientation or inclination must be some form of attraction or desire to the
sensible goods of the body. Moreover, although he locates the passions
in the body, Plato also comments that the soul is responsible for its
embodiment; "this imprisonment . . . is due to desires, so that the prisoner
[i.e., the soul] himself is contributing to his own incarceration most of

all" (82E). How can the soul be culpable for its own incarceration if the cause of the imprisonment, i.e., the desires, lies within the body?

Plato recognizes that the model of the simple, divine soul is not adequate to explain the soul's corruption and its attachment to the things of the body that hinder its ascent to the intelligible realm. At the same time, he does not want to give up the soul's immortality. In *Republic, Timaeus,* and *Phaedrus,* Plato introduces his new psychological model, the tripartite soul that enables him to address both issues. In his discussion of the nature of justice in *Republic,* Plato argues that there is a correlation between the justice of the city and the just ordering of the souls of its citizens. More to the point, the rightly ordered social hierarchy of the city governed by wisdom mirrors the justly ordered soul (434E-435E).

If *Republic* is viewed with a concern to psychology rather than politics, Socrates' account of the three-tiered social strata of the *polis* is an allegory of the soul that enables Plato to dissect the invisible soul and illustrate the workings of its primary powers. Plato splits the soul into three parts. First, the rational part (*logistikon*) of the soul corresponds to the philosopher king since it alone is able to grasp the good of the whole organism and thus rightly order all other parts of the soul to do what is within their power to serve the collective attainment of that good. The lowest part of the soul is the nonrational or appetitive part (*epithymētikon*), which consists of the soul's desires and attraction to those sensually pleasing objects that provide nourishment and security for the body. This part corresponds to the commercial sector of the city's society, which seeks to acquire the goods and services (by production or expansion) that sustain the material health of the body politic. The third part of the soul links the higher and lower parts; it is the spirited part (*thymētikon*).

The function of the spirited part of the soul is most easily apprehended by understanding the work of its social counterpart, the guardians. In Plato's polity the guardians are philosophical dogs who preserve the just ordering of the polis by keeping the commercial segment of the city in check. The guardians are educated in philosophy and so are allies of the philosopher king (440A–B). The king grasps the collective good that the city's commercial interests cannot, because they know only the goods of their particular *niche.* The guardians preserve the harmony of the city by imposing moderation (*sōphrosynē*) upon diverse interests and desire of the commercial sector. They insure that the commercial interests do not try to usurp the place of the philosopher king by making their particular interest or desire the supreme good of the whole city (432A). Therefore, the guardians insure that the city moves collectively toward the common good by seeing to it that each citizen performs her particular task, each of which contributes to the attainment of the good (433A–B). By keeping the lower part of the city subordinate to the wiser and better part of the city, the right order of the social hierarchy that is the essence of political justice is preserved.

Similarly, the spirited part of the soul keeps the soul's appetite for sensual goods in check. It does not wholly suppress the desires, but prevents these powerful impulses from distracting the soul's pursuit of the higher good determined by the intellectual part of the soul (430A–B). Therefore the spirited part of the soul is associated with the fighting spirit of self-discipline that "screws up [one's] courage to the sticking point" to resist the impulse to follow the pleasurable route of least resistance (429C–D). This tripartite division enables Plato to locate the "earthly element" that weighs the soul down in the soul's appetitive faculties. The divine quality is located in its higher, rational part of the soul.

Yet even in *Republic* Plato is concerned that this division compromises the soul's immortality. Consequently in book 10, he explains that the soul in its pure state did not possess these desires until it was united with the body.[14] In *Timaeus,* Plato explains the soul's composite constitution of the rational and nonrational parts through his myth of the soul's creation — a double creation, as it turns out. The immortal soul is fashioned by the Demiurge and bears the image of its Creator. This rational soul is handed over to the lesser gods who make for it a mortal body. To the immortal soul the gods attach another soul that is mortal and is responsible for animating the body. This lesser, mortal soul is the locus of the nonrational impulses and emotions that lead the rational soul into evil (42D–E).[15] This solution is not wholly satisfactory. For if the nonrational components of the soul were mortal even as the body is mortal, then at death the immortal soul would be separated not only from the mortal body, but also from the mortal parts of the soul. Thus while Plato's tripartite soul explains how the "earthly element" resulting from its embodiment adheres to the rational soul, the "double creation" narrative from *Timaeus* does not explain how that "earthly element" can continue to corrupt the rational, immortal soul after death.

Since Nyssen explicitly comments and builds upon the tripartite soul described in *Phaedrus,* a close examination of the "chariot myth" from this dialogue is in order. Socrates' allegory of the chariot in *Phaedrus* illustrates for Plato the dynamic relationship between the passions or emotions and the soul's rational faculties. In the context of the dramatic developments of the dialogue, one sees the importance for Plato of clarifying this relationship. The myth follows Socrates' dual suggestion that the beloved cannot be viewed merely as a means to satisfy the lover (241C) and that the erotic movements of the soul can be self-destructive madness (242C). Plato needs to reconcile the immortal and divine nature of the soul, which gives every individual worth, with the nonrational character of erotic impulses. How can the soul genuinely be immortal if it possesses a volatile principle of motion that may lead to self-annihilation?[16]

The form of the soul, which is indeed beyond the descriptive powers of mortals, can, Socrates says, be likened in its composite nature to a chariot drawn by two winged horses steered by the charioteer. The soul of the gods possesses a pair of steeds of equally good breeding. The pair of horses representing the human soul, in contrast, are of mixed dispositions; one is noble (*kalos* and *agathos*) in constitution and breeding, but the other is of the opposite temperament (246B).[17] Although Plato never provides his reader with a clear interpretation of the symbolic significance of the elements of the chariot, Socrates' narrative of the chariot's journey to the outer regions of heaven offers some basis for informed speculation. At its most basic level, the figure of the chariot depicts the interaction between the horses, which provide the power to move the chariot, and the charioteer, who determines the chariot's destination and steers the horses along the best route to its objective. The horses, therefore, represent the principles of movement in the soul, and the charioteer is a figure for that faculty which determines its ends and the best means for the attainment of its goals. From the narrative, Socrates is clear that the charioteer is a type for the intellect, that "pilot of the soul." For it is the charioteer who tries to gain a glimpse over the firmament into the realm of true knowledge containing those formless, colorless, and intangible essences of justice and temperance, visible only to the mind (247C–D). Thus even as the horses are the source of movement for the charioteer, the other two faculties are the soul's source of movement that enables the intellect to fulfill its search for the True and the Good.

The meaning of the horses in the allegory is something of a puzzle for interpreters. They cannot refer to the body itself since they are both equipped with wings that enable them to ascend to the realm beyond the heavens — something the body could never do. The wings denote that godlike nature that enables them to venture close to the formless (*aschēmatistos*) and incorporeal (*anaphēs*) realm of true knowledge.[18] The wings represent the divine virtues of the soul, e.g., beauty (*kalon*), wisdom (*sophon*), and goodness (*agathon*), necessary for its contemplative participation in the transcendent realm of eternal ideas.[19] Yet how can he suggest that a horse, which has an evil disposition, possess such wings of virtue? Of the second horse of ignoble birth and breeding Socrates says that the chariot's ascent to the heavenly realm is nearly impossible "for the horse of the evil nature weighs the chariot down, making it heavy and pulling toward the earth the charioteer whose horse is not well trained" (247B). The horse's tendency to pull the chariot down may simply be Socrates' way of illustrating how evil in the soul prevents the intellect from ascending to the intelligible realm with ease. This horse's heaviness may well signify that impulse within the soul that is attracted, not to the ethereal and the intelligible, but to the earthy and the sensual.

Since Socrates speaks of this horse as having the wings of virtue by which it can ascend to the banquet of the gods, the horse cannot itself be intrinsically evil. Rather it makes better sense to view this horse as denoting the nonrational appetitive faculty, which though naturally oriented toward the sensual, can be directed to loftier goods. This view is supported by Socrates' description of the horse as one not well trained by the charioteer. Were this horse's problem simply its inherent body mass, training would not enable the horse to climb into heavens. Thus it is legitimate to view the ignoble horse as symbolizing an impulse or appetite of the soul, which without the training and guidance of the intellect would be drawn down to corporeal things pleasing to the senses. Based on this interpretation of the ignoble horse, the good and beautiful horse symbolizes those impulses of the soul which, through their training in the virtues, possess a sufficient measure of beauty and goodness and wisdom to be drawn toward the Beautiful and the Good residing in the intelligible realm above the heavens (*hyperouranion*). Thus the difference between the horses is that the horse of noble constitution represents the impulses well trained and guided by reason, while its less docile counterpart symbolizes the impulses of the soul not trained in virtue.

The fact that it has wings, malnourished though they are, indicates that the other horse has the capacity for such training — a potential for divine ascent into the heavens. Thus, I would argue, the two horses represent the two possible and competing orientations of the soul's appetitive faculty. The allegory describes the human condition as suffering from an abiding conflict within the soul between two antithetical orientations of the soul's appetitive faculty. The philosopher is distinguished from the masses of humankind in three possible ways. Either she so thoroughly

trains the soul in the way of reason that its spirited faculty, represented
by the well-bred horse, is strong enough to compensate for the heaviness of the carnal impulses of the appetitive faculty. Alternatively, the
philosopher by ascetic discipline so weakens the soul's appetite for the
sensual good that it offers less resistance to the pull of her soul's desire
for the intelligible goods.

There is a third way in which the metaphor of the two horses may be
construed. Through training, the horse of less noble breeding may develop strong enough to raise the soul toward heaven. Such fortified wings
might represent the sublimated form of desire or *erōs* for beauties beyond those of earth. This is a very different view of the soul's nonrational
or appetitive impulses. In the first two interpretations, the philosopher
tries to negate or minimize the effect of the sensual desires either by
compensation or deprivation. In the third interpretation, however, the
philosopher harnesses the energy of the desiring faculty to aid the soul's
heavenly ascent by sublimating or reorienting its desire from the sensual
and mundane to the intelligible and eternal. By training the soul's desires
the philosopher's soul comes to resemble the soul of the gods that Plato
depicts as a chariot drawn by equally well trained steeds. As we will see,
it is this latter view that Nyssen will employ to describe the dynamic
relationship between the soul's faculties that enables the soul's ascent
to God.

Aristotle's Psychology

Aristotle's mature doctrine of the soul developed in three distinct
stages.[20] Initially in *Eudemus* his view was indistinguishable from that
of his teacher, Plato. As presented in *Phaedo*, the soul, though immortal
and capable of subsisting independently of the body, is in this life shack-
led with the heavy confines of the flesh. Death, far from being an object
of fear, offers occasion for joy, for it alone brings the soul's ultimate
emancipation. Later, however, Aristotle comes to see the soul, not as a
uniquely human endowment, but as common to all plants and animals.
This "instrumentalist" view maintains that the soul and body are two
distinct substances united in the body. The soul, while having the body as
its locus, uses the body's structure for its own ends. At this middle stage,
Aristotle is not yet ready to claim that the soul's unity with the body is
indissoluble. To the contrary, in spite of its attachment to its corporeal
abode it is not limited to the body, but has the capacity to partake of an
independent, disembodied existence.

By the time he writes *De Anima*,[21] however, Aristotle's reflection on the psychosomatic union leads him to offer a definition of the soul that precludes the possibility of the soul's subsisting in a disembodied state. At the beginning of Book II he introduces the hylemorphic theory of the soul. As all entities are composite beings — the product of form (*eidos*) or actuality imposed on the pure potentiality of matter (*hylē*) — so, too, all living creatures are composed of the body and the soul that give form and activity to the matter. Thus the soul is the form of the body (412a20). Following the logical and grammatical maxim that a thing (subject) is what it does (predicate), Aristotle can say that in the activity that the soul provides to the body the soul gives actuality to the body's material potentiality. The act of the soul now gives the body its predicates, its history, its life.[22] If we say that the soul is known by the activities of the body, then we could say that the activity of seeing is derived from the powers of the soul conferred upon the eye.[23] That activity of seeing, however, is inseparable from the physical structure of the eye. So too, both a body and a soul are necessary to form a human being.[24] Although Aristotle does not explicitly state the implications of the hylemorphic theory of the person that the soul cannot transcend the body in death, the implication is clear: if the soul is simply the power to engage the body's activities — activities that are dependent upon the structure and fitness of the body to be accomplished — then there is no way of thinking that the activities of the body can continue once the body ceases to live and its structure is reduced to dust.

Even having articulated the hylemorphic theory, Aristotle does not completely abandon the hope of some transcendence in death. The key question is: Is there a part of the human person — an activity — that is not totally reliant upon the instrumentality of the body? Earlier in Book I, he says that mind (*nous*) is a divine substance (*ousia*) that is indestructible (*ou phtheiresthai*).[25] Moreover, having just said that the soul and body exist in an indissoluble unity even in death, Aristotle refuses to close the door on the question of the immortality of the soul. "It is also uncertain," he writes, "whether the soul as an activity bears the same relation to the body as the sailor to a ship" (413a7–9). Even as a sailor carries out activities in a ship but is not dependent upon the ship in order to perform them, so, he muses, are there contemplative activities proper to the intellectual activity of the soul that do not require the mediation of the body's structures? "But in the case of the mind [*nous*] and the thinking faculty [*theōrētikos*] nothing is yet clear; it seems to be a distinct kind of soul, and it alone admits of being separated, as is the immortal from the perishable" (413b25–28).

The matter hinges on whether the theoretical reflections of the mind are inexorably tied to the senses. If the speculative work of *nous* (as in the case of the perfect unmoved mover who has himself as the sole object of thought) has itself as the object of its thoughts, then the intellect might be independent of the body's senses. Moreover, influenced by Anaxagoras, Aristotle insists that for the mind to know it must be unmixed (*amige*). Yet does this mean unmixed with respect to the body or to the object of its thought? No clear answer follows. Ultimately the conundrum is reducible to two options. Either the soul is not simple, and *nous* is separable from the rest of the soul's powers with the body because the powers cannot exist separately from the body, or *nous* is not a separable feature of the soul, but a part of the indivisible *psyche*, which is the form of the body. If Aristotle is read to hold the former view, then one can speak of the soul as being immortal. If, however, the latter opinion is true, then even though the theoretical activity does not require the sense organs, the intellect can have no disembodied subsistence.[26]

Parameters for the Use of Philosophy

Before turning to Nyssen's judgment on the usefulness of these doctrines from classical psychology, we need to be aware of the place Nyssen gave to philosophy in Christian theology. It must be said at the outset that for all his reliance upon these philosophical schools, Nyssen is conscious that the Christian philosopher cannot appropriate the pagan models whole cloth. The teachings of Scripture limit what philosophical material the Christian may incorporate into her own thought. The Christian, Macrina asserts, is not absolutely free in her speculations to base her opinions on the present, outward appearances. Rather she is limited both in her premises and her conclusions by the claims revealed in Scripture, which acts as "a rule of dogma and law."[27] Suspicious even of adopting the philosophical arguments to justify faith claims, Macrina employs a trope common in early Christian writings that contrasts the virtue of the church's simple and unadorned style (in which the truth of the faith is transparent) with the ornate and complicated syllogisms of the philosophers (which make untruths appear believable).[28] Macrina's initial repudiation of Plato and Aristotle serves as a way of setting boundaries determining the extent to which the Christian can employ the idiom of the Academy or the Lyceum. Ultimately, it is the idiom of Scripture that sets the terms of the inquiry; for it is Scripture that provides the final answer which the Christian philosopher seeks to understand. Yet, I will argue, once the Rule of Faith establishes the boundaries of the discourse, Nyssen feels free to borrow in a highly eclectic fashion the metaphors and tropes of pagan thought to serve his theological agenda.[29]

Nyssen's theory of the soul's structure in *On the Soul and the Resurrection* is not presented at the outset of the dialogue and then used systematically as the basis from which his subsequent account of the passions is deduced. Rather his account of the soul's structure is refined at various stages in the dialogue to accommodate Macrina's progressively more nuanced account of the passions. Since the final account of the soul explains Macrina's theory of the sublimation of the passions, for the sake of clarity I will begin by sketching out his psychology in order to elucidate the logic guiding their subsequent discussion about the passions.

Macrina's account of the soul begins as her attempt to allay her brother's grief-induced doubts that the invisible soul exists. Her argument for the soul's existence starts with an examination of the soul's various activities.[30] Even as the invisible deity is known by his activities in the world, so too the unseen soul is known by the body's outward and visible movements. Nyssen then presses his sister to explain the nature of the one soul that is responsible for seemingly contradictory movements. In other words, how can she explain the presence of nonrational impulses, such as lust or anger, in a soul that is essentially rational and intellectual?[31] Are the desiring and spirited faculties, out of which these impulses arise, proper to the essential nature of the soul or are they something distinct and separate? Have they been part of the rational soul "from the beginning" or were they "something additional"? These questions force Macrina first to define the general parameters for their discussion of the nature of the soul and then to describe the soul's origin and structure. Macrina begins setting the boundaries for their investigation by ruling out those features of Greek pagan psychology that prima facie are incompatible with Christian anthropology.

Macrina's Judgment on Plato and Aristotle

Initially, Macrina rejects Stoic and Epicurean theories of the soul as problematic because their materialist tendencies cause them to reject a central claim of Christian anthropology, that the soul is immortal.[32] Having already dismissed Epicurean and Stoic psychology, she directs her comments first to Aristotle and then to Plato. She does not refer to Aristotle by name directly; instead she simply alludes to "the philosopher after [Plato]" who claimed to have proved "the soul to be mortal."[33] Although Aristotle's conclusion regarding the soul's immortality is subject to some

interpretation, Macrina certainly saw Aristotle's view that *nous* is inseparable from *psychē* (that is, the form of the body) as a proof for the
mortality of the soul. Moreover, while Aristotle was merely tempted to
call the human soul, or at least *nous,* a divine thing, Macrina felt no hesitation at affirming such an exalted view of man. Moses quoted the divine
meditation prior to creation, "Let us make man in our image, according to our likeness." The filial resemblance of Adam's soul to God was
for Macrina more than a poetic sentiment; it was the primary assumption of her anthropology. Since, therefore, the essence of the human soul
must conform with the divine nature, which is immortal, the rational
soul in its essence cannot be mortal.[34] It is interesting that Macrina mentions Aristotle in regard to the question of the soul's mortality and yet
does not group him together with the Stoics and Epicureans. One explanation may be that, because Nyssen does rely heavily on Aristotle's
trichotomous theory of the soul, he needs to establish from the outset
how he is different from Aristotle. In other words, the Christian philosopher may employ the hylemorphic theory so long as one does not accept
the conclusion about the mortality of the soul to which Aristotle's theory
led him.

Macrina also rejects Plato's allegory of the chariot in the *Phaedrus.*[35]
The metaphor is problematic for her because it attributes nonrational
appetites to the soul. Thus the Platonic soul is not simple and intellectual but is composite, possessing both rational and nonrational faculties.
Given her criticism of Aristotle for asserting that the soul is mortal, one
might expect her concern about the chariot allegory in *Phaedrus* to be
a fear that this tripartite model implies that the soul is composite and
therefore mortal.[36] Yet there is nothing in her description and subsequent
critique of the chariot myth from which one can conclude that she sees
this tripartite model as compromising the unity of the soul and therefore implying that the soul is mortal.[37] This model for the soul proves
unsatisfactory for Macrina because of the theological implications for
one who holds that the soul is the image of the impassible God. The
Phaedrus model assumes that the human soul is a composite of both
rational and nonrational faculties. Such a claim is untenable for Macrina, since it imputes a principle of nonrationality to the divine nature,
which is the archetype of the human soul.[38] One might answer Macrina's objection by distinguishing those properties of the soul that bear
the structural image of God and those features alien to the divine image
which were added to accommodate human nature after the fall into sin.
That there are elements alien to the *imago Dei* in the soul is not the
issue for Macrina. Rather the problem is that Plato's chariot allegory

from *Phaedrus* suggests that the soul is *essentially* a compound of the rational and the nonrational. In order to understand Macrina's concern, we must understand her theory of predication upon which her objection to the *Phaedrus* rests.

In *On the Soul and Resurrection*, Nyssen articulates, through Macrina's voice, a theory of predication that creates for him the same difficulty in that work that his theory of the "double creations" does in *On the Making of Man*. Namely, it excludes from his definition of human nature anything that is alien to the divine nature. Aristotle's theory of predication holds that a thing is defined in terms of its *genera* and *differentiae*.[39] In other words, the taxonomy of an animal or plant is determined by the similarities of its nature to other creatures and at the same time by those characteristics that are unique to that species. Macrina, however, contends that the essence of a thing is not located in those general features shared with other beings (*koinoi*). Rather it is in the *idia*, i.e., those special characteristics that set it apart from all other beings, that one finds the essence of a thing.[40] Thus a proper definition of the human soul must identify those attributes that distinguish human beings from all other creatures. The uniqueness of humanity Macrina naturally locates in the *imago Dei*. No feature of the human constitution can comprise the essence of man's nature that is not proper to the nature of the divine archetype of the soul.[41] In a similar way, Nyssen in *On the Making of Man* says that the name of a thing refers to what it is in its perfect state. Even though the human soul possesses characteristics, such as the nutritive and perceptive faculties, common to plants and nonrational animals, man should neither be thought to possess three different souls nor to belong to same class of creatures as turnips or turtles. Rather, the soul is named for that state of perfection toward which it is moving. He concludes, "Thus as the soul finds its perfection in that which is intellectual and rational, everything that is not so may indeed share the name of 'soul,' but is not really soul, but a certain vital energy associated with the appellation 'soul.' "[42]

The key to determining the chief end in which a thing finds its perfection lies in its "powers." Unlike a stone carving which has the size, shape, and painted color of a loaf of bread, real bread has "the power of being food." Therefore, because the human soul has the highest powers of a soul, i.e., those of rationality, it is properly called a soul only with respect to its intellectual nature. For this reason, Nyssen refuses to describe man as a "microcosm" of the universe. Such reduces the dignity of human nature to that of a mouse or a gnat. For, even though man

shares with the mouse and gnat the same universal elements, human beings are not defined principally by their material causes. Rather man is
defined with reference to that in which his greatness lies, his likeness to
the nature of the Creator.[43]

This theory of predication is the cause of an internal contradiction in
Nyssen's thought. For, as we shall see, the soul undergoes development
within the body taking a form that corresponds to the form of the body
at each stage of its development. Therefore, the soul at its earliest stage
resembles the soul that moves plants and then later the soul of sentient
animals before becoming the rational human soul. This theory of the
soul's development reflects Nyssen's notion that God intentionally made
man a hybrid of the rational and the embodied so that man might rule
creation and so that God might use the union of the rational and the
material as the means by which Christ might unite all things in himself.

When Macrina rejects Plato's incorporation of the appetitive faculties
into the human soul, she is not denying that human beings have desire
(*epithymia*) and irascibility (*thymos*) any more than she would deny the
presence of the faculties of perception, nutrition, and growth. Rather
she denies that these faculties are constitutive of the soul.[44] *Thymos* and
epithymia, like all emotions, should be regarded as warts on the outer
surface of the soul, considered part of it because they are joined to it,
though not essential to the soul's complexion.[45]

From her theory of predication, Macrina not only delimits the boundaries between the human soul in its essence and its appetitive baggage
common to all sentient creatures; she also deduces from this premise the
moral imperative that people should purge themselves of their nonrational passions in order to conform to their impassible and supremely
rational archetype. With her call for the extirpation of the passions,
Macrina adopts a posture not unlike certain radical stoics.[46] Since reason is in constant conflict with these emotions, the virtuous man is one
who is free from anger or desire. The preeminent example of such a
sage in Scripture is Moses, who proved himself superior to both desire
and anger. Appealing to Numbers 12:3, Macrina explains that Moses'
meekness illustrates his "incapacity for anger [which] is shown through
mildness and an aversion to wrath — and that he desired none of the
things the desiring element in many people is directed towards."[47]

Macrina can make the bold assertion that Moses was *incapable* (*to
aorgeton*) of *thymos* because she defines *thymos,* not in terms of the
emotional or physiological reaction to some irritating sense stimulus,
but narrowly in terms of its objective, namely, harming someone who
is bothersome or unpleasant.[48] Because Moses has managed to suppress

or purge himself of these emotions he is more fully human and bears a greater resemblance to the divine nature than those whose rational souls are dominated by the emotions. Thus the eradication (*keitai*) of these alien qualities (*allotriosis*) of the soul is necessary in order for human beings to conform to their proper nature.[49] As will be seen in the next chapter, Nyssen forces Macrina to modify her view of the emotions. Yet in order to understand her reconception of the passions, one must understand Nyssen's theory of the soul's structure and the relationship between the various faculties.

The Trichotomous Structure of the Soul

Although Nyssen explicitly refuses to employ the language of microcosm and macrocosm to describe human nature, his psychology as well as his understanding of the place of man in God's redemptive economy presuppose that the order of human faculties mirrors the natural order of created beings. God created human beings, he says, as the convergence of the rational and nonrational natures in order to unite and so redeem both the corporeal and the spiritual or intelligible realms of creation. Nyssen observes that the order of the creation narrative in Genesis 1 parallels the physical and metaphysical order of the universe. This hierarchy consists of a spectrum from the completely intellectual (*noeron pantōs*) beings at the apex of creation to the corporeal beings (*sōmatika*) that comprise the vast number of lower and simpler forms for creation. The corporeal creation is divided between the inanimate (*apsycha*) creatures that, lacking a soul, are lifeless (e.g., purely inert substances) and the animate beings (*empsycha*) that, being endowed with a soul, participate in life (*to metechon zōēs*). Of the living creatures, there are three classes: first, at the bottom are nonsentient beings (*anaisthēta*), then sentient beings (*aisthētika*) that lack rational faculties (*aloga*), and last the highest of corporeal creatures, sentient beings endowed with the blessing of rationality (*noeron* and *logikon*). According to Nyssen, the narrative of Genesis 1 describes how the "life-giving power" (*hē zōtikē dynamis*) of God united itself with matter, giving life to the corporeal creatures, beginning at the bottom with the nonsentient creatures proceeding to the sentient beings, and finally to the intellectual and rational creature, man.[50]

Similarly, in *On the Making of Man*, Nyssen claims that concealed within the cosmological narrative of Genesis, Moses handed down a "hidden doctrine" that reveals that "the power of life and soul may be considered in three divisions." These three types of the soul constitute three modes of participating in life. They are the vegetative soul, the sentient soul with its "power of management according to the senses," and finally the rational soul.[51] Thus because in human nature the nutritive and sentient powers of the soul are conjoined to the rational faculties that allow them to be ordered by the mind, human nature is nothing short of "perfect bodily existence."[52] This union of the vegetative, the sentient, and the rational in Adam provides the mechanism by which God will perfect, not simply human nature, but all of creation with the advent of the last Adam. For when the divine Logos, the seat of all rationality, is united with human nature, which (by virtue of its rational faculty) is most suitable to act as the temple of the divine reason, he is united also with the nonrational and lower natures of creation. Because human nature is the nexus of all levels of created nature, Christ as leaven begins to permeate and perfect the entirety of the cosmic hierarchy in which human nature participates.

The soul, which distinguishes the living corporeal beings from the lifeless, is the animating principle of the body, responsible for all activity and movement. The simplest form of the soul found in the nonsentient corporeal beings, i.e., plant life, is limited to vegetative activity. This most basic movement of the soul is the plant's organic ability as a living creature to undergo growth, development, and reproduction. The fundamental movements that the soul produces in a plant are largely directed by its appetitive faculty (*orexis*), which enable plants to draw to themselves those things necessary for their nourishment and growth.[53] The movement apparent in a maple tree, for instance, consists very basically in the root's drawing in water and nutrients from the soil, in the process of photosynthesis, and in its respiration. Though Nyssen does not give any elaboration of the soul's operation in nonsentient creatures, presumably the appetitive soul is also responsible for movements involved in pollination and reproduction. In these simple life forms the activities of the soul are elementary. Because plants, at least from Nyssen's antique biological understanding, lack sensory experience of their environment, their appetitive faculty is automatic, influenced, not by an "awareness" of their surroundings but by their own internal need or lack of need for water, nutrients, or sunlight.[54]

Turning to consider the sentient creatures, Nyssen assumes that as one ascends the hierarchy of corporeal beings, the soul at each stage adds a new set of faculties to those of the stage immediate below it. The higher form appropriates and transforms the features of the lower form. Thus Nyssen speaks of the nonrational soul of sentient creatures as the animating principle of the body that "puts a vital power into the organic body by the activity of the senses."[55] By this he means that, because sentient beings possess the same needs as plants to acquire means of sustenance and to procreate, they are likewise endowed with this appetitive faculty; yet these appetitive impulses, unlike those in plants, are informed by their sensual experience of their surroundings.

Thus unlike plants whose appetitive faculty enables them merely to ingest the nutrients, water, and sunlight immediately present to the plant's roots or leaves, sentient creatures possess an instinct to *seek* nourishment and to reproduce informed solely by its experience of sense data as either pleasant or unpleasant. For example, a male cape buffalo's search for a water hole and the grassy savannah is a reaction in the appetitive faculty prompted by the memory of the pleasing taste of cool water and lush grass. Similarly, the buffalo's appetitive impulse may cause him to react to the odor of a nearby lioness either by fleeing out of fear or by lowering his great horns and charging the predator. In creatures endowed with the ability to perceive both those things that provide for and things that threaten their survival, the appetitive drive (*orexis*) basic to all living beings takes the form of desire (*epithymia*) and irascibility (*thymos*). Consequently for Nyssen, *epithymia* and *thymos* are the primary sources of motion in sentient beings.[56]

As the last of God's creation, human beings, Nyssen claims, are that nexus of the created order in which all three vital forms of life are united.[57] In the soul of man, therefore, "the faculties peculiar to the nonrational nature are mingled with the intelligible nature."[58] There are three important consequences of this *mingling* of the rational and the nonrational. First, man's rational nature works through and requires the aid of the nonrational faculties. As Macrina puts it,

> It is not possible for the power of reason to be present in the corporeal life except through the senses and since perception comes under the heading of the nonrational, existence of our soul comes about through its one essential feature [i.e., rationality] and its relation to the qualities joined to it.[59]

Presumably she means that the rational faculties rely upon the faculties of sense perception to provide raw data from which inferences may be drawn. To say that the rational soul requires the aid of nonrational faculties of the senses is not to imply that the rational soul is absolutely dependent upon the body. Since the rational soul, which bears the image of God, shares with its Creator and divine Archetype intellect and an incorporeal nature, it is neither confined to a single locus in the body[60] nor lacks the capacity for existence independent of the body.[61] Macrina's point is that the rational soul in its embodied existence is dependent upon the body for apprehension of the sensible reality and for the expression of its rationality. Nyssen maintains that the form of the body, which is constructed to serve the purposes of the rational soul, possesses a structural likeness to God. He compares the faculties of perception proper to the nonrational soul with the divine power of apprehension; thus the body and the sentient soul bear the reflection of their maker.[62] The rational soul's reliance upon the body and the nonrational soul indicates how thoroughgoing is Nyssen's idea of the psychosomatic unity of the person. Consequently it implies that the *imago Dei* is reflected in the totality of the person — even in this instance in the nonrational faculties of the soul. To be sure, Nyssen can restrict the image to the soul; but even where he does, his tendency is to make the body integral to the image from the perspective of the way the image functions.

Second, as sentient beings whose movements are predicated on the reactions of the appetitive faculty to their perception, human beings' reaction are forms of *epithymia* and/or *thymos*. In other words, the appetitive faculty, from which one seeks out both the means of sustenance for one's personal survival and a mate for the perpetuation of the species, is informed primarily by sense data. The immediate reactions either of fear and anger (*thymos*) to painful or unappealing sensations or of desire and longing (*epithymia*) to pleasing sense data are the principal emotions (*pathē*) by which all other actions are derived.[63] Consequently, Nyssen contends that all other emotions are mere extensions of desire and/or spiritedness. Commenting on the emotion of grief (*lupē*), Macrina illustrates how this one emotion is a form of both *epithymia* and *thymos*. We suffer, she says,

> ... the languishing of the spirit, because of our inability to take vengeance on those who have offended us, [which] produces grief, and the despair of not having what we desire and the deprivation of what is agreeable to us creates this gloomy disposition in our consciousness.[64]

In other words, grief over the loss of a loved one is both the sadness resulting from unsatisfied desire to be with one's beloved and the emptiness of spirit resulting from a recognition of one's impotence to gain redress for one's loss. It is because Nyssen reduces all emotions to some direct manifestation or consequence of desire that he locates man's capacity for *agapē* in the desiring faculty, *epithymētikon*.

There is yet a third important implication of the mingling of the rational and nonrational natures: man's appetitive faculty is informed

by those goods that can be apprehended only by his intellectual faculty. Even as the appetitive faculty of the vegetative soul takes on the
new characteristics of *epithymia* and *thymos* in animals that possess the
power of sense perception, so too the appetitive impulses of man's nonrational nature take on a new, distinctly human character. Human beings
endowed with rational faculties possess, not simply a sensual awareness of their immediate surroundings and situation, but an intellectual
awareness of that intelligible realm and its goods that transcend one's
immediate sense experience. Consequently, in the rational soul the appetitive impulse responds with desire for those transcendent, intelligible
goods apprehended by the intellect. The introduction of this transcendent awareness of the intelligible goods, however, does not completely
override the soul's attraction to the sensual goods. As a creature of both
realms — the senses and the mind — man dwells in a state of constant
tension within his appetitive faculty, a conflict between his desire for the
goods perceived by the eyes and ears and touch and his longing for those
goods beheld solely by the eye of the intellect.

To summarize, Nyssen views the embodied rational soul as such a
thorough blending (*dia pasēs ideas tōn psychōn*) of the rational and nonrational faculties that it produces a metamorphosis within the appetitive
faculties of the soul's lower elements. The human soul is a "commixture
[*anakrasis*] of the intellectual essence with the subtle [*lepton*] and enlightened [*phōtoeides*] element of the sensitive nature."[65] He is able to speak
of certain faculties of the nonrational nature as (*lepton*) and (*phōtoeides*)
because there is a sense in which the assimilation of the sentient soul into
the rational soul has altered the character of the sensible soul. In other
words, although the nonrational faculties man shares with the beasts
have an innate tendency toward sensual goods, man's appetitive faculties also have acquired an orientation that is unprecedented among the
lower animals. The soul of man longs to understand the meaning of life
as well as to enjoy its mundane moments. One's irascible nature can as
easily be stirred to indignation by foolish or hubristic opinions as it can
be inflamed with rage by a threat to one's child.

Thus Nyssen can speak of man's sensitive nature as being "midway"
(*mesōs*) between the vegetative (*hylōdesteras*) and the rational soul. He
says the sentient nature is "coarser than the [intellect] and as it is more
refined than the [vegetative soul]." It is coarser than the intellect since
by itself, the senses cannot apprehend the more ethereal goods. Moreover man's sensual nature bears a primordial crudeness because it is still
disposed to desire the lesser goods of the body. At the same time, it is
more refined than the vegetative faculty. For it is not wholly turned in

upon itself satisfying merely the physical needs of the body. The result of this blending of the different forms of the soul is that in man the rational and nonrational need not stand as opposing impulses. Rather they can form an "alliance" (*oikeiōsis*), which not only transforms man's sensual nature, but also aids the rational nature in achieving its natural end.

Tripartite or Trichotomous Soul?

What sort of soul has Nyssen described? What is its pedigree in classical psychology? According to Cherniss, he has adopted Plato's tripartite model as chiefly described in *Republic* and in the chariot metaphor in *Phaedrus*. The allegory of the chariot was Plato's depiction of the soul as having both a rational element, which is immortal and divine, and an nonrational part, which is associated with the mortal body. In this way Plato was able to acknowledge the passionate element in human nature without giving it a purely material cause and at the same time preserve a sense of the soul's immortal nature. According to Cherniss, Nyssen recognized that this allegory introduces a partition of the soul yet at the same time retains its immortal aspect.[66] The division of the soul into the intellect represented by the charioteer and the desiring and irascible parts represented by the two horses corresponds to the tripartite character of the soul depicted in the much longer allegory of the soul, *Republic*. Comparing Plato's psychological allegory of Glaucus the sea-god (611D), whose divine nature is crusted over with barnacles, to Macrina's description of the *epithymia* and *thymos* as warts growing on the outside of the soul but not proper to its essential rational and godlike nature,[67] Cherniss argues that Nyssen follows Plato in adopting a tripartite model of the soul that is nonetheless unified, divine, and immortal.[68]

The most succinct statement of Nyssen's view of the soul Cherniss finds in the *Canonical Epistle:* "There are three around [*peri*] our soul which have been contemplated according to the first division: the intellect (*to logikon*), the desirous part (*to epithymētikon*), and the irascible part (*to thymoeides*)."[69] Similarly commenting on the significance of the two doorposts and the lintel upon which the blood of the Passover lamb was smeared in the Exodus narrative, Nyssen identifies these three pieces of wood as types for the three parts of the soul: the intellect (*logistikon*), the passion of desire (*epithymētikon*), and the spirited passion or gumption (*thymoeides*).[70] Even when Nyssen speaks of the passions of the soul as impulses (*hormai*) and movements (*kinēmata*),[71] Cherniss concludes that here *hormai* and *kinēmata* are tantamount to parts (*meroi*) of the soul.[72] Thus each part, when suitably controlled by reason, fulfills its particular duty promoting harmony and justice within the soul and in relation to God and one's fellow creatures.

When one examines *On the Making of Man*[73] and *On the Soul and the Resurrection*,[74] however, one encounters a different account of the threefold structure of the soul. In both works Nyssen explains, as has already been discussed in this chapter, that there are three forms of the soul corresponding to the three general types of animate creatures. The simplest is the vegetative soul of plants. Then slightly more complex are animals whose souls possess both the powers of the vegetative soul of plants, but also the powers of sense perception. This is the sentient soul. Finally in humankind God creates us with the rational soul, which, in addition to the powers of the vegetative and sentient, possesses the powers of the intellect. Nyssen is explicit that this division of the human soul, which is a blending of all three types of soul, is a division of powers (*dynameis*), "[Moses'] discourse then hereby teaches us that the power of life and soul [*tēn zōtikēn kai psychikēn dynamin*] may be considered in three divisions (*en trisi diaphorais*). For one is only a power of growth and nutrition."[75]

The division of the powers of the soul between the vegetative, sentient, and rational conforms, not to the threefold division in Plato, but to that in Aristotle. To begin with, he defines living creatures as those beings that have mind (*nous*), sense perception (*aisthēsis*), and movement (*kinēsis*) either internal or with respect to location in space.[76] Like Nyssen, Aristotle divides these faculties along a hierarchy of creatures from plants with only the powers of internal movement necessary for growth and reproduction to animals that have the powers of sensation to human beings who have the vegetative, sentient, and rational. Concomitant with the powers of perception come the appetites (*orektikon*), which principally include desire (*epithymia*), drive (*thymos*), and choice (*boulēsis*).[77] Thus both Nyssen and Aristotle divide the human soul according to a taxonomy that reflects its relationship to the souls of other living creatures. Michel Barnes rightly points out that Nyssen's psychology follows Aristotle's in another important way. By speaking of the soul as one divided into three distinct powers, Nyssen has achieved a way of speaking of the soul as having essential unity in contrast with the awkward Platonic language of different parts of the soul. Hence Nyssen and Aristotle view the soul as trichotomous rather than tripartite.[78]

How then does one reconcile Nyssen's tendency in some texts to write of the soul's threefold nature as consisting of intellect, desire, and gumption and in other texts speaking of the threefold division as vegetative, sentient or appetitive, and rational, with desire and gumption being twin features of the appetite part of the soul? Can these be reconciled or is this simply an example of Nyssen's penchant for selecting whatever philosophical language best suited his theological purposes at the time?[79] While I will argue that the latter view is an expression of his more mature and more carefully developed anthropology, I nevertheless see no need to see these two views as utterly incompatible. Rather, even as Aristotle's, and even more so Posidonius's, view of the soul as trichotomous rather than tripartite reflects an evolution in Plato's model and the eclectic nature of later Greek anthropology, so too one can read Nyssen's trichotomous view of the soul in *On the Making of Man* and *On the Soul and the Resurrection* as reflecting a more nuanced consideration of the diversity of activities of the soul.

Unlike *De Virginitate* or *De Vita Moysis* or the *Canonical Epistle* in which the nature of the soul is touched upon only indirectly, *On the Making of Man* and *On the Soul and the Resurrection* are texts devoted principally to questions surrounding the origin, character, and end of man. In these latter works the nature of the soul is one of the chief subjects of his inquiry. Not surprisingly, therefore, in them one expects to find a more focused and considered examination of the soul. Yet in these works, Nyssen nowhere speaks of the soul using the term *meros*, or part. Instead he marshals the terms *orexis, hormai, dynamis,* and *kinēmata*. This is no random choice of terms or uncritical borrowing from other philosophical schools. Rather the language that Nyssen employs to describe the soul reflects the extent to which the soul falls within the grasp of human understanding. Macrina, responding to Nyssen's materialist objections to the existence of the soul as something distinct from the body, suggests that even as God's invisible presence is *seen* giving *being* and order to creation so too *the soul's* life-giving activities *are observed* in the body.[80] *Because of its visible movements in the body, we can believe in the invisible soul's existence.*[81] Thought and imagination are the movements (*kinēsis*) and activities (*energeia*) of the mind.[82]

Against the backdrop of the Neo-Arian controversy, Nyssen's theological analogue as the basis of his description of the soul is understandable. Even as God, though his essence is beyond the comprehension of creatures, is known by his activities, his *energeiai,* in the world, so too the soul, though its essence is a mystery to the intellect,[83] is knowable solely by means of our observation of its activities. Consequently the language Nyssen uses to speak of the soul's nature is derived from the epistemological basis of any discourse about the soul's nature, i.e., its visible effects upon the body. Cherniss asks the rhetorical questions, "What is a power or activity but a part of the soul?" Perhaps the question should be reversed; "In what sense can a unitary and immaterial substance, such as the soul, have *parts?* In such a context what can we mean by 'parts'?" Indeed, the only way that which is immaterial and simple can be thought of as having "parts" is if the term "parts" is a very general way of speaking of its activities. Thus the language of "parts" is replaced by the more accurate designation of "powers" and "activities."

It also might be argued that Nyssen even in his earlier works does not speak of actual parts within the soul. In the *Canonical Epistle,* the three aspects pertaining to the soul, Nyssen says, are "contemplated [*theōroumena*] according to the principal division [*diairesin*]." Nyssen does not say that the soul *has* three parts; rather he simply says that the three most important things about the soul are divided or classified in our contemplative inquiry. Thus the division is not proper to the nature of the soul, but the product of our speculations (*theōria*) about the soul. Similarly in the *theōria* of *The Life of Moses* the lintel and doorposts are figures (*ainigmatōn*), which break the soul down into its general activities (*physiologountos*) to illustrate how God's grace affects the whole of the soul. So the image divides (*diairousa*) the soul into the intellect, desire, and gumption. Since the soul is not three but one, as Nyssen is insistent, *to logistikon, to epithymētikon,* and *to thymoeides* represent conceptual divisions among the various general powers or activities of the soul.

Nyssen's psychology of the single soul that is possessed of both the godlike faculties of the intellect and the brute-like faculties of sense perception and carnal appetites is fundamental for understanding his soteriology. For it illustrates Nyssen's conception of man's identity based on his place in creation and his role in the divine economy. The intellect defines humanity both with respect to our origins and with respect to our destiny. For the intellect, as man's created likeness to God, establishes the potential for man's fulfillment of his supreme end, beatific union with God. At the same time because man is the nexus of material creation, he finds both his ability to mediate God's goodness to the lower creatures through his dominion but also his ability to be corrupted, becoming barley distinguishable from the beasts. It is for this reason that we can appreciate why Nyssen retains the language associated with Plato's tripartite division of the soul in the chariot myth from *Phaedrus.* Aristotle's trichotomous soul satisfies Nyssen's scientific bent to describe the soul organically so as to explain its development in union with the body. But the imagery from *Phaedrus* — language Macrina herself will use — gives him the poetic model to describe the tension between the rational and nonrational faculties of the soul. From this sketch of the ordering of the soul, we are able to turn to the problem of the passions and examine how this trichotomous psychology explains the internal conflict within the soul and yet holds out the hope that the intellect will establish right order over man's lower nature in order that the soul might be fully redeemed and perfected.

CHAPTER THREE

The Nature of the Passions

The human soul, in Nyssen's early anthropology, reflects man's amphibious nature possessing both the rational faculties that enable man to participate in God's goodness and the faculties of the vegetative and sentient soul that allow him to acquire and utilize the material goods necessary for bodily existence. Consequently, the soul's rational powers are capable of apprehending the intelligible goods of God and so bear the moral image of God. At the same time, the soul's sentient powers can apprehend phenomena in the environment that may be sensually pleasing or threatening to life and limb. Even as the soul is affected by its apprehension of the Divine, so too it is affected by its experience of both attractive and unpleasant sense data. Nyssen uses Aristotle's trichotomous model of the soul to describe the organic nature of the soul and the way the higher powers of the soul change the character of its appetitive impulses. Yet he retains the language of Plato's tripartite soul to illustrate the tension inherent in man's amphibious nature. The metaphor of the chariot is descriptive, not only of the conflict between the goods of the body and those of the soul, but also the dynamic tension between the desires rooted in the sensual world and the higher faculty of the soul whereby desire serves the intellect in attainment of its goods proper to man's higher nature.

Ultimately, however, Nyssen bends both models of the soul to serve theological interests. In other words, Gregory of Nyssa's eclectic treatment of the emotions is ultimately determined, not by philosophical concerns, but by his sense of obligation to be faithful to the teachings of Scripture — particularly its presentation of human nature as well as its proscriptions on virtue and vice. Nevertheless, his theory of the soul as a trichotomous unity mixed with the metaphorical depictions of the soul adapted from Plato enables him to describe the principal source of evil in human existence as well as the means by which the evil associated with the passions may be overcome. I want to suggests that because

Nyssen draws heavily upon Aristotelian psychology as well as Platonic he is able to present the passions, not simply in the dualistic terms of a conflict between the impulses of the body and those of the mind, but in terms of mistaken or corrupt judgments of the mind — failures of the intellect. I will begin by tracing Nyssen's presentation of the dialectical unfolding of his view of the passions through his deathbed conversation with Macrina in *De Anima et Resurrectione*.

Nyssen's Dialectical Presentation of the Passions in *De Anima et Resurrectione*

Thesis: Macrina's Initial Pejorative Account of the Passions

The tension between the higher and lower elements of human nature is worked out dramatically in Nyssen and Macrina's discussion of the nature of the passions and the dangers associated with them. From the beginning, Macrina offers a flatly negative assessment of the passions, regarding them as antithetical to man's true, rational nature. All emotions, she contends, are ultimately derived from or are expressions of desire (*epithymia*) and our spirited faculty (*thymos*).[1] Yet *epithymia* and *thymos* are not proper to our rational nature, but are the appetitive impulses inherent in our brutish or nonrational nature.[2] Consequently, Macrina assumes that the emotions are innately oriented to evil. *Thymos*, for example, is not of a neutral disposition; rather it is the impulse or desire to do injury to anyone who annoys us.[3] Even Nyssen's tears of grief (*lupē*) over the loss of Basil and his emotional distress upon seeing his sister on her deathbed elicit a gentle reproach from the dying Macrina. Sorrow over the death of a loved one is not befitting one who holds to the hope of the resurrection.[4] Since these emotions in particular, as well as the *epithymia* from which all emotions proceed, are proper to a nonrational, corporeal nature and so utterly incompatible with the supremely rational divine nature, they ought not be deemed proper to the nature of one created in the image of God.[5] Thus she concludes that the passions *epithymia* and *thymos* ought only be viewed as warts,[6] external blemishes upon the rational soul, which should be purged[7] by means of ascetic mortification of the flesh.[8]

Antithesis: Virtuous Emotions in Scripture

Nyssen shows reluctance to abandon these emotions, however, and his reluctance is not merely conventional but scriptural. Without disagreeing with his teacher's assessment of the rational character of man's higher nature, or her identification of emotions with man's brutish nature, Nyssen challenges her conclusion that *epithymia* and *thymos* are *incompatible* with humanity's godlikeness and so must be *purged*. Such conclusions about incompatiblity, he notes, are themselves incompatible with the witness of Scripture. Far from viewing emotions as intrinsically unholy and unbefitting saints, both the Old and New Testaments portray a variety of emotions, including *epithymia* and *thymos,* as virtues God not only tolerates but favors.[9] For example, in Daniel's vision along the banks of the Tigris, he is addressed by a heavenly figure as *anēr epithymion* and told not to fear because he set his heart to understand the words of the Lord.[10] In the book of Numbers, Nyssen says, Phineas made propitiation with God by means by his *thymos.*[11] Fear, which Macrina equates with a weakening of *thymos,*[12] is extolled in Proverbs as the source of wisdom. And Paul contrasts "godly grief" (*hē kata theon lupē*), which leads to repentance and salvation with "worldly grief," which yields only death.[13] From these and other examples, Nyssen asserts, "Scripture shows that it is not necessary for us to think of these qualities as base passions, for they would not, then, be under the heading of the attainment of virtue."[14] More importantly, Nyssen reminds Macrina[15] of her own admission that *epithymia* and *thymos* are essential for the soul's ascent to and union with God in the present life.[16]

These radically different assessments of the passions pose a real problem for Nyssen. Macrina's view raises troubling questions — questions that cannot simply be dismissed as an Eastern tendency toward Manichaeism. How can human beings possess the princely autarchy proper to creatures fashioned in the image of a passionless God when they are constantly beset with fleshly drives and impulses? How can man's fiery instinct to lash out against his rivals be reconciled with the merciful benevolence of God that we are called to imitate? How can the sensual and self-serving drive of *epithymia* be compatible with the self-sacrificing love of Christ? How can *epithymia* and *thymos* be viewed as anything but a hideous growth to be seared from the surface of the soul, or as tares destined to be separated from the wheat at the end of the age and destroyed? Yet this paradox of human nature is called into question by the perspective of Scripture. Macrina presents the *problem* from experience: More often than not the conflict between rational and nonrational natures produces a destructive rather than a constructive tension. Yet the witness of Scripture provides the *answer* that Nyssen must ultimately accept, namely, the emotions can themselves be redeemed and even play an essential role in our salvation. The real project for Nyssen is to explain

how the same nonrational nature that seems to be at cross-purposes with
our lofty rational nature can, as Scripture claims, serve the spiritual ends
of the soul. Nyssen establishes the groundwork for his final solution to
this conundrum by explaining how *epithymia* and *thymos* operate in
man, as in any sentient creature, as the twin principles of motion, a
function propelling the soul toward its divinely ordained ends.

Synthesis: Emotions as Either Vice or Virtue

The turning point in Macrina's account of the passions comes with
Nyssen's enumeration of instances in the Septuagint and New Testament
where *epithymia, thymos*, and *lupē* are depicted as virtues (56C). Challenged by this compelling litany of virtuous emotions, Macrina retracts
her earlier claim that the passions must be extirpated. She reconsiders
the moral character of the emotions, beginning with a more nuanced
account of the place of the appetitive powers of the soul in relation to
its essential, rational faculties proper to the divine archetype. Here she
introduces her theory of the emotions as residing on "the borderland"
(*en methorioi*) of the soul. Given the dialectical character of the rational
soul's union with the faculties of the sentient soul, Nyssen's psychosomatic anthropology provides a clear answer to the ancient question, "Do
the passions lie in the soul or in the body?" Because the primary passions
of *epithymia* and *thymos* are the form of the appetitive impulses proper
to nonrational creatures, they lie within the realm of the sentient soul.
When however the emotions are united with the rational soul and so are
enabled to be directed to either the spiritual and intellectual goods or
the sensual goods, they become elevated to a "middle ground" between
the coarsely material vegetative and sentient souls and the incorporeal,
rational soul.

   The passions for Nyssen lie in what he calls the borderland between
the sensual, bodily activities of the soul and its transcendent, intellectual
activities. Yielding to Nyssen's argument that *thymos, phobos,* and *epithymia* are treated by Scripture as virtues, Macrina explains that she did
not mean by calling the emotions "warts" on the soul to imply that they
are inherently inclined to vice. Nor did she intend to say that they are an
alien infirmity impeding the rational soul's journey to its natural end. She
acknowledges the need for a distinction between those activities of the
soul *proper (kata physin autēn)* to its rational nature and those "on the
margin" (*en methorioi*) of the soul. The activities proper to the intellectual nature of the human soul are those by which "the image of the divine
grace" is preserved, e.g., contemplation (*theōrētikēn*), distinguishing between types of phenomena (*diakritēn*), and speculation (*epoptikēn*). In

contrast, the activities that are not proper to the rational soul but are the product of its union with the body and the sentient powers of the soul are those required to act toward either the good or its opposite.[17]

Here Nyssen is using the structure of the soul and its relation to the body to explain the distinction between the contemplative life on the one hand and the moral life on the other. The former faculties are proper to our nature because they are also proper to the divine nature and so will always be needed for the fulfillment of man's supreme end, communion with God. The latter faculties Macrina speaks of as being on the "border" of the soul because, in light of her theory of predication, they do not distinguish human beings from other sentient beings. More importantly, *epithymia* and *thymos* are placed on the outer fringe of the rational soul because they serve an ancillary role, enabling the individual to act morally in the face of mundane dilemmas and temptations in his present existence. I have described them as "ancillary" because, as will be seen more fully in subsequent chapters, the eschatological redemption and perfection of creation will eliminate tensions in our existence from which temptations arise. Then we will have no need for the virtues of "godly grief" or "courage." In our present situation, however, the moral activities of the soul are necessary for ordering our life so that the intellect may pursue the higher, contemplative ends proper to our nature. Thus Nyssen presents the moral life as subordinate to, yet an essential precondition for, the life of contemplation.

Nyssen's hierarchical arrangement of the moral and intellectual virtues reflected in Macrina's view of the "borderland" is found in Nyssen's discussion of Paul's distinction between the carnal man, the natural man, and the spiritual man in 1 Corinthians 2:14–15 and 3:3. These three types of people, he says, reflect Paul's understanding of the threefold powers of the soul.[18] The carnal man's preoccupation with satisfying the stomach reflects the working of the appetitive faculty of the soul common to all sentient creatures. In contrast the spiritual man "perceives the perfection of the godly life." The natural man, however, holds "a middle position with regard to virtue and vice, rising above the one, but without pure participation in the other."[19] Unlike in his description of 1 Thessalonians 5:23, which he interprets as an allusion to the threefold powers of the human soul, the distinction between the carnal man and the natural man is determined, not on the particular power of the soul at work, but the end toward which the power is directed. The carnal man is centered on the sensually pleasing objects to which his appetites are inclined. In contrast, the natural man "rises above" the carnal man. For the natural man is the virtuous pagan whose attention is not wholly fixed upon the desire of the flesh, but is also reflective and philosophical. Yet, in contrast with the spiritual man, his contemplations are informed only by his reasoned consideration of the world as it now is constituted.[20]

In the distinction between the natural man and the spiritual man, Nyssen is formulating what in the Western church would be called a "nature-grace" distinction.[21] The spiritual man possesses a knowledge of the perfect, contemplative life that is to come — a life characterized as being graced. Although Nyssen does not say that the spiritual man possesses the gift of perfect reflection of the divine beauty conferred by grace, he would say that the mere knowledge of such perfection is not man's natural knowledge of God or human nature, but is revealed knowledge imparted by grace through the Holy Scriptures. The natural man lacks a knowledge of his eschatological destiny. Nor does he have knowledge of Christ, the archetype and paragon of human excellence. The natural man represents the sentient nature in man because he is not necessarily oriented toward either the flesh (as the beasts) or the intellect (as the angels). He lives in a realm of tension between these desires and consequently feels an attraction to both. Thus the natural man possesses the freedom to choose between these competing goods. Macrina says that the moral activity on the margin of the soul is not distinctive of man's principal activity of contemplation, which reflects the divine image. Yet since the activities of the moral life rely upon the nonrational faculties of *epithymia* and *thymos*, which have no corresponding feature in the passionless divine nature, Macrina will insist that the moral life reflects, not the *imago Dei*, but the virtues needed in the tension-filled situation of our present existence.

Nyssen, however, insists elsewhere that man's moral freedom is a principal locus of man's reflection of the divine image. In *De Hominis Opificio* (16.9), Nyssen says that man's dignity lies in bearing the image of the king of creation. He, like a prince who acts as his father's representative, has been given the capacity to rule over creation. The soul of man has the capacity to rule over his own corporeal nature. Even as God's rationality frees him from all necessity and so endows him with absolute liberty, human beings endowed with reason are freed from a life of uncritical submission to desires for immediate and short-term goods. As a rational, sentient being, therefore, man possesses the faculties in the "borderland" of the soul — faculties that enable him to be a responsible moral agent.

Locating the emotions on the "borderland" of the soul, Macrina has established the psychological foundation for her new account of the morally neutral character of the emotions. Retreating from her definition

of the passions, such as *thymos,* as having some inherently malign intention (such as doing harm to one's enemies), Macrina concedes that the
emotions *(pathē)* are not inherently evil;[22] rather they should be viewed
as having the potential to be directed either toward a good end or an
evil one. This modification of Macrina's original position is significant
because it establishes that an emotion in itself is morally indifferent, and
therefore, it should be judged solely in terms of the end toward which
it is directed. In the larger design of the dialogue, this is the first step
toward Macrina's acknowledgment of the spiritual importance of *epithymia* and *thymos* as the sources and incipient forms of all emotions.
The immediate consequence of her concession, however, is that she begins to move from her earlier opinion, which viewed the rational and
nonrational faculties as being in irreconcilable opposition to each other,
to her final recognition that the mingling of the rational and nonrational
in the human soul enables reason to control and define the character of
human desires.

Macrina first explicitly acknowledges the morally neutral character of
the emotions when she concedes to her brother that:

> If reason, which is the special ingredient of our nature, is in con-
> trol of these faculties imposed upon us externally, then, as Scripture
> has made clear through the symbol of man being ordered to rule
> over all nonrational things, none of these faculties within us is acti-
> vated towards the service of evil — fear engenders obedience, anger
> courage, cowardice caution; the desiring faculty fosters in us the
> divine and pure pleasures.[23]

Here Nyssen begins to articulate the distinction between the emotions
as neutral impulses *(hormai)* and the passions *(pathē)* as impulses allowed to follow their natural attraction to mundane, sensual goods.[24]
By speaking of reason's controlling the nonrational impulses and thereby
cultivating a desire in the soul for the Divine, Macrina is appropriating
the Platonic model of that dynamic relation between the rational and the
nonrational faculties of the soul that enables the soul to ascend to God.
To illustrate the disastrous consequences when reason does not control
the appetitive impulses, Macrina explicitly employs Plato's metaphor of
the chariot. "If reason lets go the reins [it is] like a charioteer who has
become entangled in his chariot and is dragged along by it, being pulled
wherever the nonrational team carries him."[25] If reason controls the nonrational impulses, then *thymos,* for instance, is not harmful or destructive
but manifests itself as a virtue, courage. If on the other hand, reason does
not maintain a firm rein on nonrational impulses, then the emotions or

passions take control. leading the soul toward evil. As in the *Phaedrus*
the "nonrational team" of horses represents the appetitive impulses that
act as the principles of movement in the soul.

Unlike Plato, however, Macrina does not distinguish one of the horses
as signifying an impulse innately directed to the good, as represented by
the horse of noble breeding. Rather she holds that man's nonrational
appetitive faculty is naturally oriented toward the sensual. Yet it is this
nonrational emotion of *agapē*[26] or *epithymia* — this longing for some
desirable object — that rouses the soul from lethargy and inactivity and
propels it toward its end. Were desire wholly absent from man's nature,
Macrina asks rhetorically, "what would draw us to a union with celestial
things? If love [*agapē*] is taken away, how shall we be joined to God?
If our anger [*thymos*] is quenched, what weapon shall we have against
the Adversary?"[27] To illustrate the point Macrina employs a political
image. The impulses of desire are analogous to the throng of common
soldiers and lieutenants who are pledged to the service of a king. When
properly controlled and directed, these vassals enable the sovereign to
attain the objectives of state.[28] It is only by the presence of this deep
desire and yearning for God that the soul can be turned from the sensual
and be drawn into communion with the Divine. This ascent of the soul,
Macrina cautions, is possible only if reason maintain firm and constant
control of these nonrational appetites. Through this argument that the
moral character of our emotions is determined by whether or not they
are controlled by reason and directed to the good, Nyssen has begun to
offer the first solution to the problem of the passions.

Nyssen's First Solution: The Passions Rightly Ordered

The intellect's capacity to control the emotions provides an alternative to
Marcina's earlier insistence that the soul must be purged of the impulses
and feelings of the lower faculties of the soul. Man's rational faculty
exerts control over the appetitive faculty in two ways. First, by being
able to discern the proper end for which the material goods were created,
reason trains the soul to seek those material goods that its body genuinely
needs rather than those that merely *appear* desirable. Without reason,
Macrina says, the human soul loses its likeness to God and acts more
in the manner of beasts.[29] Lacking reason, nonrational beasts respond
solely to sense stimuli. The pleasing sensations they pursue and seek out;
the unappealing they shun.

In many cases there may be a natural correlation between what is
pleasing to the senses and what is good for the individual or the species.

To put it simply, animals are not conscious of the goods (such as the right amount of protein and iron for producing muscle tissue or a diverse gene pool) necessary for their individual or collective survival. Yet these ends are fulfilled by the animal's instinctive attraction to the sensually alluring quality in those foods that satisfy the creature's bodily needs. Thus the lion's appetitive impulse is instinctively predisposed toward the smell and taste of meat or by the alluring odor of the lioness in heat. Through the desire or revulsion stimulated by the appropriate sense stimuli, the *teloi* of the natural order are achieved. Yet Macrina observes that the nonrational impulses of animals uncontrolled by reason often create an excessive rage or desire that is self-destructive. "Through their passions," Macrina contends, "they destroy each other being dominated by rage, and the powerful carnal impulses do not operate for their own good."[30] This self-destructive behavior occurs because, lacking reason, animals have no way of distinguishing their needs from their desires; they seek what is pleasing rather than what is beneficial. They are unable to weigh and calculate the relative good of their object. Thus two male lions may inflict great harm on each other fighting for control of a pride of lionesses; the desire for territory and mating partners drives them to excessive violence. Without the restraining judgment of reason, the intensity of desire exceeds the worth of the goods sought.

In human beings, reason maintains control by enabling man to distinguish between the apparent good of an object and its genuine good. The apparent good is that good apprehended by nonrational creatures through the senses. Reason, however, enables man to transcend the pleasantness of an object's sight or taste or smell and determine the good of the object based on what is needed by the individual and whether or not the object in question satisfies these needs. Her point is that reason, by giving man the ability to think about causal relations — about ends and means — enables man to assess his own needs then evaluate the good of an object in terms of its ability to meet those needs.

The second, and more important, way in which reason controls man's appetitive faculties is by directing them to what Macrina calls "lofty goods." The scope of man's desires (*epithymia*) is broader than that of nonrational creatures because of the greater variety of goods that his rational faculties apprehend. In other words, man's intellect enables him to grasp intelligible goods that cannot be discerned by the senses. Unlike animals that apprehend only those goods that are sensually pleasing, human beings, endowed with an intellect, can apprehend goods that transcend those particular goods immediately accessible through the senses.

The soul, therefore, Nyssen can say, is drawn to God through desire even as a lover of music might be drawn off the street into a church by the melodious voices of a choir.[31] It is the intellect that apprehends the beauty of the heavenly spheres, and the soul, excited by the mind's glimpse of the Beautiful, is filled with desire for God.[32] Thus the *epithymia* characteristic of the appetitive faculty in sentient creatures now has undergone a conversion of sorts. Originally, it was directed through the senses to those things necessary for the survival of the individual and the species. Now pointed by the wise charioteer to that which is truly desirable, the horses of the soul raise their heads from their downward course to the sensual goods and set their focus on the intelligible realm of the Divine.

The soul, with its newly felt longing for God, has just begun its heavenward ascent. This marks only a change of focus in the appetitive faculty from the sensual to the intelligible. Although this reorientation of desire is a crucial development in the soul's disposition, it is not sufficient for the soul to attain the final blessedness of divine communion. For the soul must overcome the inertia of its own ever-present desire for material goods. Thus the soul's initial movement toward God and its perseverance in its quest is effected by an arousal of the spirited faculty, *thymos,* concomitant with the new spark of desire within the appetitive faculty. As has already been established, Nyssen views all emotions as expressions or manifestations of either *epithymia* or *thymos.* And although he speaks of them as independent, he does seem to allow, as in the case of grief, that the impulse of *thymos* to seek retribution may be aroused when an object of one's desire has been stolen or destroyed. The impulses of the spirited faculty is largely derivative or a consequence of the impulse of *epithymia.* In a positive context, *thymos* is the source of gumption or drive, which rallies and coordinates the emotions and faculties of the soul to pursue the object of desire.

Thus with its first impulse of desire for God, the soul does not passively admire its beloved from afar, but immediately rises from its lethargy and musters all its energy to overcome any and all obstacles that separate it from its beloved. In other words, awakened by *epithymia* the spirited faculty has the capacity to override other emotional impulses and reactions to sense stimuli that might impede the soul's pursuit of its object. Thus a lioness's desire for meat may be so strong as to inspire the emotion of courage (*thymos*), which suppress its fear of the vastly larger and dangerous cape buffalo, which is her target. In a spiritual context, therefore, when reason controls the appetitive faculty, setting union with God as the chief object of desire, reason also gains control over the lesser emotions by the sublimation of the irascible faculty. *Thymos* now takes the form, not of anger, which seeks to harm, but of courage or discipline, which overcomes the emotions of fear or instincts (such as man's predilection for the easy over the difficult and for the pleasurable over the unpleasant) that might cause the soul to turn aside from its quest. Thus even as the lioness's desire for food produces the emotion of *thymos,* which suppresses the instinctual fear of the cape buffalo, so too the soul filled with *epithymia* for God sublimates the bestial *thymos* and so gains the courage and strength to beat down those sensuous impulses that might tempt the soul and divert it from the pursuit of God to a lesser good.

This is precisely what Macrina has in mind when she says, "The seed of anger [*thymos*] is not [usually] directed toward courage, but arms itself for battle on the side of its own kind, namely, the nonrational." Still she asks, "if our anger is quenched, what weapon shall we have against the Adversary?"[33] The sublimated form of *thymos,* courage, steels the soul against the sensuous temptations by which Satan draws the soul from God. If the supreme emotion that is determinative of all other emotions can be set unwaveringly toward the highest good, then the power of all secondary emotions can be controlled and used to facilitate, rather than hinder, the soul's participation in God. In this way, Nyssen provides an alternative to Macrina's earlier radical theory of eradicating the passions. Now emotions, when rightly ordered by the intellect, which inspires in the *epithymētikon* desire for the goods appropriate to our nature, not only cease to be an impediment to the soul's ascent to God, but actually enable it to attain this end. Because the intellect can rightly order the impulses of our nonrational nature, it illustrates at the microcosmic level God's redemptive and perfecting economy in which reason shall come to rightly order the rest of the material creation or bring it into a harmonious union.

Nyssen's presentation of the relation between *epithymia* and *thymos* is interesting philosophically because it marks a radical reworking of Plato's account of this dynamic in *Republic* and *Phaedrus.* In *Republic,* the guiding principle is that the just *polis* is akin to the just soul; both are just because they achieve an internal harmony through the right ordering of their members. In the just city state, each of the three strata of society (e.g., the philosopher king, the guardians, and the commercial interests and laborers) carries out only its particular function and does not presume to do the work of another class.[34] For Plato, this order is preserved by the guardians whose principal function is to keep the commercial interests of the *demos* from supplanting the philosopher king's wise coordination of the city's resources for the collective good.[35] The city's threefold class structure (as do the charioteer and the two winged horses from *Phaedrus*) corresponds to the tripartite structure of the soul, i.e., the intellectual part (*logistikon*), the spirited part (*thymētikon*), and the appetitive part (*epithymētikon*).[36] Even as the guardians of the city follow the philosopher king and hold at bay the commercial interests that are constantly attempting to pursue their own private and immediate interests rather than the good of the whole, so too the spirited part of the soul forms an alliance with the intellectual part to restrain the impulse of the appetitive part from pursuing the sensual and mundane goods that it wants — goods that may not be in the overall interest of the person. Plato's expressed assumption is that the alliance of the intellect and the spirited part is possible because they are alike; both are noble in nature.[37] Similarly, in *Phaedrus* the spirited part of the soul is represented by the horse of noble breeding that uses its strength to counterbalance the opposing downward movement of the horse of low breeding, i.e., the appetitive faculty. In both works, however, the point is not that the appetites should be eliminated but that they are kept in check and their energy harnessed to enable the soul to achieve the goods grasped by reason.

Nyssen retains the Platonic metaphor to preserve the latter dynamic. But because he clearly places *thymos*, along with *epithymia*, in the sentient soul, Nyssen views *thymos,* not as an intrinsically noble feature of the soul akin to the intellect, but as a nonrational impulse that often becomes the ally of desire. As a faculty proper to the sentient soul, therefore, the spirited faculty is naturally and habitually oriented toward stimuli from the sensible realm. Moreover, because it is not derivative of the intellectual soul, the spirited faculty has no self-critical component. In other words, *thymos* may be inflamed by the perception of threat or insult but is incapable of adjudicating whether that perception is accurate or whether the degree of anger is proportional to the threat or insult. Therefore, *thymos* uncontrolled by reason is as likely as *epithymia* to spiral out of control, resulting in unwarranted injury to oneself or others.

Nyssen also deviates from Plato in that within his Christian anthropology the spirited faculty is subordinate to the ends of love or Christian desire. In other words, the spirited faculty coordinates the powers of the lower soul to attain the object of desire. This dynamic he can explain easily using his organic Aristotelian model of the soul. Because the spirited faculty and the appetitive faculty are powers of the soul derived from the soul's powers of sense perception, the action of the spirited faculty is often a *reaction* to the arousal of the desire for some sensually pleas-ing good. In cases, therefore, where there is some obstacle preventing the soul from attaining the object of its desire, *thymos* plays an auxil-iary role to *epithymia*. In the case of a hungry lion that sees a recent kill being eaten by a pack of hyena, its *thymos* is the burst of violent roaring and snapping that drives the hyenas away so that the lion can eat his fill. Similarly in human beings, *thymos* may take the form, to use an example from Shakespeare, of Macbeth's screwing his courage to the sticking point to do that difficult but necessary deed to secure the crown of Scotland. In both cases, the spirited faculty serves the appetitive faculty.

Likewise in the case of the ascent to God, the soul's movement to God arises out of a desire for the divine beauty glimpsed by the intel-lect. This movement is aided by the spirited faculty that spurs the soul on even in the face of obstacles. Thus, as Macrina says, *thymos* is the soul's courage that overcomes Satan's temptations. The rational soul's love of God rules the lower impulses of the soul through the power of the spirited faculty. Christian love, rightly understood as sublimated *epi-thymia*, is the principal cause for the soul's movement to God. *Thymos* is a secondary, but necessary, impulse that facilitates the soul's move-ment toward the Divine. That is, *thymos* is the emotion associated with the ascetic discipline necessary for the ascent. Nyssen does not explore the phenomenon of competing desires, i.e., the desire to be obedient to God in conflict with the desire for comfort or in the case of martyrs to continue living. The logic of Nyssen's thought, however, suggests that *thymos* in a very Platonic fashion takes the form of righteous anger that suppresses this lower desire so that the desire informed by the intellect may be fulfilled.

Nyssen's theory of the sublimation of the passions — arising out of Macrina's representation of the ethical capacities as lying on the margin of the soul — ultimately does not solve the problematic tension between the divine similitude and the bestial drives and affections that have trou-bled Nyssen from the outset of the dialogue. However carefully Macrina has qualified and modified her earlier views, Nyssen never fully rejects certain fundamental assumptions in his sister's anthropology — assump-tions that necessarily exclude *epithymia* and *thymos* from the character of the human soul in its final and perfect form. Macrina's harsh doc-trine of the passions early in the dialogue is seriously tempered; it is not, however, completely dismissed. Many of her early core assumptions are retained and serve to shape opinions developed later in their conver-sation. Thus Macrina's final account of the passions marks a genuine synthesis of her first account, which centers on the distinctive, godlike nature of the human soul and of Nyssen's argument from Scripture about virtue. It is appropriate, therefore, to ask which elements of Macrina's earlier account of the soul have not been aborted.

First, Nyssen calls into question neither his sister's theory of predication nor her equating the essence of human nature with the intellect that alone bears the image of God. Indeed, the latter claim is the fundamental assumption underlying her distinction between the proper function of the soul and those marginal, ethical activities.[38] As has already been discussed, the idea of blending the rational and nonrational during the soul's maturation in the body leads Nyssen to distinguish the moral faculties that occupy the borderland of the soul from the speculative faculties that are proper to the soul. In light of Macrina's assertion that only the rational element of the soul is identical with the image of God, it appears that Nyssen is making a correlation between the rational and the contemplative. Certainly Nyssen would not deny that a morally virtuous soul, especially one whose chief disposition is love, reflects the Beauty of the divine nature.[39] Yet by equating the rational with the image of God and identifying contemplation as the proper activity of the rational soul, he assumes that humankind most fully bears the image of the Creator when engaged in theoretical and scientific reflection. As will be shown below, however, man's rational faculty must serve two ends. First, the intellect, to borrow Plato's charioteer analogy, must bridle and steer man's bestial yearnings and impulses so that, second, the intellect may gaze upon the intelligible beauty of the heavenly realm. Thus man's intellect establishes harmony between the body and the soul by properly ordering the appetites of the soul; consequently the soul abides in that peace requisite for the contemplative life.

Second, Macrina's earlier poetic, though unflattering, comparison of the passions to warts attached to the surface of the soul is not wholly abandoned. To be sure, her tone changes; she does not speak of them with so pejorative a metaphor. Nevertheless her description of the passions (56C) as existing "around the soul" (*peri tēn psychēn*) or "on the outer surface" (*dia to prospephykenai*) of the soul is not wholly incompatible with her later view of the passions (57C) as being at the margin or border (*en methoriōi*). The latter image portrays the relation of the appetitive faculties and the intellect as being interrelated rather than having the relation of a parasite to its host. Although the appetitive faculty is vital for the moral activities that free the intellect for its principal, contemplative occupation, by speaking of the passions as *en methoriōi* Nyssen has quite literally marginalized the emotional element of the soul.

It is but an ancillary faculty serving the contingent needs of the embodied soul.

Even as the moral virtues (which are dependent upon the appetitive and spirited faculties) are not ends in themselves but preconditions for the blessed life of contemplation, so too, the rationally controlled appetites are not constitutive of human nature in its purest and ultimate form. While Macrina's notion of the passions as existing in a borderland enables her to speak of a dynamic relation between the appetitive and the rational faculties — a model that recognizes the importance of the appetitive faculty in the spiritual life of believers, nevertheless, this distinction will allow Nyssen later to speak of a radical, eschatological purgation of the passions that will restore the human soul to its unalloyed intellectual nature. Nyssen expresses this synthesis by employing the metaphors and psychological models taken from classical and Hellenistic philosophy. It would be a mistake, however, to assume that Nyssen's use of these models causes him to appropriate a Platonic or Aristotelian or Stoic theory of the emotions whole cloth. Rather, when one compares Macrina's final account of the passions with classical and Hellenistic theories, one sees the points of difference between Nyssen's moral theology and the theories of various schools of philosophy. These elements from secular philosophical anthropology and ethics Nyssen appropriates in his typically eclectic manner to serve his soteriological concerns. Moreover one sees how his adaptation of these pagan models to aid his principal theological understanding of the nature and destiny of humanity radically reshapes the meaning conveyed by these models.

Nyssen and Classical Views of the Passions

On the nature of the emotions there was one view commonly held among philosophers of classical antiquity. According to Martha Nussbaum, human emotions were considered forms of *orexis,* which is commonly translated "desire." Nussbaum, however, argues that *orexis* was not understood in antiquity as a purely mechanical response to sense stimuli. Rather, she says it was assumed to be an "intentional awareness" (i.e., a judgment based on an individual's needs, memories, fears, and loves),[40] which is based on an individual's beliefs or opinions. These emotions were not viewed as inherently irrational; rather, all emotions were rational in the sense that they were derived from the intellect's judgments about one's beliefs or perceptions. Hence they were rational inasmuch as there was a reason for the emotion.

Ultimately they would be judged as rational or irrational in the normative sense depending on the character of the beliefs (i.e., the reasonableness of the belief or perception) that elicit the reaction.[41] For instance, according to Aristotle a feeling of anger stems from the belief or perception that one has been unjustly wronged or injured in a serious way. Although the mere belief of injury is sufficient to provoke anger, whether the reaction is justified depends upon the truth of the perception (i.e., that the person at whom I am angry is in fact the one responsible for the injury or that I did sustain some real injury). Aristotle, therefore, viewed virtue, not as the elimination of emotions, but as their moderation under the control of reason, thereby maintaining psychological balance (*symphōnein*).[42] In fact, he views emotions, such as anger, as being necessary for virtue. The virtue of "mildness" (*praotēs*) is Aristotle's term for appropriate anger, i.e., sufficient anger to defend one's loved ones and property in situations entailing real threat.[43] Whether one's anger is appropriate depends solely on the accuracy of one's judgment of how imminent and grave the threat is.

This Aristotelian model of the cognitive character of emotions was reflected particularly in the Platonic and Stoic distinction between *hormai* and *pathē*. *Hormai* traditionally denoted the instinctual animal impulses aroused by sense stimuli. Heirocles and Seneca viewed *hormai* as an inherent desire to live according to nature and escape any unnatural condition. For example, a tortoise's attempt to right itself after falling on its back or an infant's attempt to stand though she keeps falling down are both examples of creatures driven by natural impulses to do what nature intended them to do.[44] These efforts reflect the teleological impulses of nature "hardwired" into all animate creatures.

While *hormai* as natural impulses were viewed as morally neutral, *pathē* were morally problematic. A passage from Seneca illustrates this Greek distinction. In *On Anger,* he argues that feelings like fear are merely physiological or psychological reactions, as when the sight of food makes a dog salivate or the sight of a crouching cheetah sends a surge of adrenaline through the impala's body; these cannot be called passion (*adfectus*) in the pejorative sense. In human beings, the "butterflies" in the stomach of a soldier arming for battle or of an orator seconds before ascending the rostrum are but involuntary movements of the mind caused "by chance" (*fortuito*), i.e., some occurrence beyond the intention or control of the individual. The Greek term *hormai* corresponds to these mental movements caused by chance; therefore, they are not in themselves blameworthy, but morally neutral in character. *Hormai* correspond with Zeno's description of *propatheia,* which is the state where one experiences the onset of spontaneous, instinctive feelings, preliminary to passion, evoked by some perception.[45]

In contrast to *hormai, pathē*, or in Latin *adfecti*, are passions in the pejorative sense. Seneca says that passion consists not of the instinctual reactions themselves (i.e., the *hormai*), but in "surrendering to" the impulses rather than acting according to reason. It is *consent* to the impulses that is sufficient for an emotion to bear the pejorative label "passion." Whenever any man thinks that he has been injured, Seneca says, he naturally feels the impulse to exact retribution; but the wise man who governs himself according to reason will promptly be "dissuaded by some consideration [and] immediately calms down." In such a situation, he concludes, "This I do not call anger, this prompting of the mind which is submissive to reason; anger is that which overleaps reason and sweeps it away."[46] By this reasoning Seneca disagreed with Aristotle's view that anger was necessary for virtue. On the contrary, it militated against virtue. To act either out of emotion rather than reason or even to act with accompanying emotions to "spur you one" was dangerous, he held, because once the emotions have any influence over one's actions they quickly build up a momentum of their own that overpowers reason and inevitably leads to excess.

Chrysippus centuries before Seneca had spoken of *pathē* as forms of errant belief or judgment (*doxa/krisis*) that are accompanied by an excessive inclination or violent movement (*plēronazousa hormē*) in the mind. These judgments entailed the perception of sense data accompanied by a critical rejection or acceptance of the data.[47] Plutarch in *On Moral Virtue* (C) characterized Chrysippus's view of the passions as when the *hegēmonikon* experiences some disturbance of emotion by which it "is hurried on to something outrageous which contravenes the convictions of reason. Passion, in fact, according to [Chrysippus] is a vicious and intemperate reason, formed by an evil and perverse judgment which has acquired additional violence and strength."[48] Galen reports that although Chrysippus had in his younger days located the passions in a nonrational faculty (*alogos dynamis*) of the soul, he eventually abandoned the Platonic tripartite model in favor of a unitary view of the soul.[49] If the soul is not divided between rational and irrational components, then *pathos* can be explained only as an error in judgment or in perception or both.[50]

Chrysippus's monistic psychology left no room for internal conflicts as the Platonic model allowed. Moreover, he was concerned that if passion is outside of the realm of the intellect then reason could not control it. If passion is simply mistaken judgment, then education that trains one to make correct judgments should enable one to achieve freedom from passion (*apatheia*).[51] By defining emotions as judgments, he aligns them with cognitive rather than physiological activity. Thus Chrysippus shares with Aristotle a clear dissociation of the passions from the mere animal reactions to sense stimuli.[52] The disturbances of the mind characteristic of *pathē* are simply poor judgment. Although Chrysippus and Seneca are both optimistic that the properly trained intellect can avoid erroneous or perverse judgment, Seneca is more inclined to locate the impetus for the passions in the immediate and uncritical reactions of instinct to which the intellect gives its assent.[53]

The classical distinction between *hormē* and *pathē* is not wholly absent from Nyssen's moral theology. Yet he was not thoroughly consistent in preserving the distinction.[54] As suggested above, Nyssen uses *hormē* in two senses. On one hand, he associates the faculty *epithymētikos* with *hormē*, meaning that *hormē* is an inclination of the appetitive faculty triggered by sense stimuli and manifest as either desire or revulsion.[55] On the other hand, he will speak of *hormē* as the particular impulse or reaction of some stimuli. In Macrina's chariot metaphor, she interprets the charioteer's being hurled from his chariot and dragged headlong to destruction as illustrating how "the impulses [*hai hormai*] are transformed into a state of passion [*eis pathos*]" commonly observed among nonrational beasts.[56]

Here *hormai* could be taken to mean either the drives of the soul, such as *epithymia*, or the drives aroused by some sensation. The impulses (plural) are turned over into passion (singular). The apparent meaning is that the impulses or reactions enter into a state called passion, which here is not a neutral state but one that is morally suspect. The soul is said to enter into the chaos of *pathos* when the *sensation* of the emotions (*hormai*) — be it the elixir of rage as in the "rebel yell" before an attack or the sudden and paralyzing wave of nausea sweeping over a soldier at the mere sight of an advancing enemy's battle line — dictates one's action. Thus the *hormē* is not evil in itself. In Macrina's interpretation of Jesus' parable of the wheat and the weeds, the "good seeds" represent *hormai*,[57] which are the raw material of either moral excellence or vice.

The real source of confusion comes in Nyssen's use of the term *pathos*. As illustrated in Macrina's chariot metaphor, it denotes the uncritical and unrestrained and ultimately self-destructive pursuit of some lesser good. This is by far the predominant context in which he uses *pathos*. Yet at the outset of Macrina's reconsideration of the passions, she explicitly offers a definition for the term *pathos*. Commenting on the faculties of the nonrational nature, Macrina observes that "these qualities that come to be in us are called *pathē*,"[58] which, when mingled with rational nature, give people the capacity for moral decision making, and which, when controlled by reason, do not lead people to evil conduct.[59] By the end of this same passage, however, she seems to revert to her earlier view of *pathē* as specifically referring to instances where evil results when reason has failed to exert due control. In the examples of Daniel and Phineas, in whom *epithymia* and *thymos* were virtues because they were channeled by reason for the service of God, Macrina contends that *epithymia* and *thymos* should not be termed "passions." For a passion refers to any desire for or excitement about ends unbefitting children of the heavenly king; "When the activity inclines towards the worse we call it passion."[60] Thus it seems that *pathē* is used by Nyssen to mean both the morally neutral emotion traditionally identified with *hormai* and at the same time what Seneca calls "passion" properly speaking, i.e., when reason abdicates its rule giving the emotions sovereign sway over the soul. The passions, therefore, are animal instincts not rationally motivated for the ends proper to man's intellectual nature.[61]

While one great strength of the Platonic paradigm is that it recognizes and takes seriously humanity's innate, uncritical drive for immediate gratification, which reflects kinship with lower animals, its inadequacy, however, lies in its basic simplicity. The explanation of nonrational behavior as the result of a predisposition for sensual goods is easily applied to the behavior of animals and young children. The problem of the passions is not explained in terms of war between the body and the soul. It is a struggle between competing impulses *within* the soul. Despite his failure to be consistent in his use of *hormai* and *pathē*, Nyssen is explicit that in their morally laden sense passions, though rising out of our animal impulses, are distinctively human.[62] For Nyssen's purposes, the simplicity of the model is its virtue; for it serves one of the principal aims of his ascetic moral theology: calling Christians to be conscious of and to exert control over our bestial impulses, which frequently are at cross-purposes with the impulses of our proper nature as creatures bearing the image of the supremely rational God. Thus Nyssen's model establishes a rationale for an ascetic mortification of the flesh.

Yet it is a model that often proves too mechanistic to account for the intricate drives of man the political animal. Aristotle and Chrysippus rightly object that because human beings are rational creatures our emotions (*pathē*) are not simply reactions of the appetitive faculty to goods or evils either immediately present or remembered. Rather emotions reflect the *orexis* that is informed by certain natural orientations of the soul[63] and by judgments about present circumstances or past experiences. In other words, our reactions to the immediate unfolding of events will be based on judgments that are a synthesis of our knowledge of the present situation and our predispositions or prejudices based on past experiences. We draw instant analogies between the present and past related occurrences that we experienced personally or about which we have been told. In the case of Aristotle's distinction between fright and fear,[64] the *hormē* of fright or alarm at the sight of an approaching enemy is not simply a reaction to sense data. Rather, as Nussbaum would argue, even the emotion of fright is informed by *orexis* or one's "intentional awareness" of the situation in which the sense data is received. Thus the approaching enemy are viewed, not simply as people, but as hostile people. Moreover it may well be informed by judgments of the enemy's past actions, e.g., whether they are merciful to their captives or slaughter their prisoners.

The Platonic metaphor of the chariot is not, however, fully sufficient to describe this character of the passions. For, although all emotions are expressions of *epithymia* or *thymos,* not all emotions can be explained simply as the response to some sense stimuli that is either pleasing or threatening. Since emotions arise out of the individual's "intentional awareness," these reactions rest upon certain judgments about the world. For a lioness they may be informed by concerns for protecting her cubs from hyenas or finding food for the pride. In the case of human beings whose intellect's capacity for self-transcendence, memory, and imagination exceeds that of a lioness, the scope of our "intentional awareness" far exceeds that of animals. Thus the neutral impulses, when used for the service of corrupt human ends, assume a more odious form than found in nonrational animals. "Thus the rising anger in human beings is indeed akin to the impulse of the brutes but it grows by the alliance of thought: for thence come malignity, envy, deceit, conspiracy, hypocrisy; all these are the result of the evil husbandry of the mind."[65] The very alliance of the intellect and the appetites whereby the soul ascends to God can also be perverted. The appetites can so dominate the soul that the intellect is used to serve the appetites by devising ever more sophisticated ways of attaining base goods. The significance of judgments as the basis for emotions began to emerge in Plato's later works but was more fully developed by Aristotle and the Stoics. In the fourth century A.D., Nyssen too had begun to incorporate the connection of emotions and judgments into his treatment of the passions.

Passion as Errant Judgment

Once Nyssen has accepted that emotions are in themselves morally neutral, the criterion for adjudicating whether a given emotion is a virtue or a vice hinges upon the judgment that arouses the emotion. For example, the emotion of desire rests upon the soul's judgment of what is desirable. Whether an individual's desire is appropriate or not, i.e., whether it is a virtue like the love for God or a vice like lust, depends on the accuracy of his judgment of the object's value in relation to the cosmic hierarchy of goods. Nyssen views the sin that results from uncontrolled *pathos* as closely associated with errant judgment. Commenting on Jesus' parable of the wheat and the weeds, Macrina says,

> We think that by "the good seed" the Word indicates such impulses [*hormas*] of the soul each of which, if it works solely for the good, bears all together the fruit of virtue in us. However, when sin is sown among these [impulses] concerning the *judgment of the good* [*peri ten tou kalou krisin di'hamartian*], that which is good according to its own nature is obscured [*epeskotisthe*] when mixed with the blades of deception [*blastou tes apates*].[66]

In his tortured Greek, Nyssen seems to suggest that the nonrational impulses of the soul, including *epithymia* and *thymos,* which are given to the soul for the pursuit of virtue, become vices when they are led astray by a mistaken judgment or misapprehension of the good. Similarly, in his *Commentary on the Song of Songs* XI, Nyssen, describing the former life of the bride in the Song of Songs before she has attained perfection, i.e., freedom from the passions, writes, "There was a time when the bride was dark, cast into darkness by the unenlightened beliefs... being weakened by the forces waging their war within her... ignorant of herself."[67] Here he is making a correlation between the moral character of the bride's soul and her mistaken opinions about the good and the real. In this respect, Nyssen's account of the passions possesses an affinity with Chrysippus's and Zeno's view of the passion as errant belief or judgment (*doxa/krisis*), which produces violent movement (*pleonazousia horme*) in the mind. Since Nyssen, unlike Chrysippus, preserves a trichotomous model of the soul,[68] which includes the nonrational appetitive faculties, his account is closer to Zeno's view of the passions as the *result* of errant judgment than to Chrysippus's view that the passions are *identical* with mistaken opinions.

One example of *pathos* manifest principally as the result of errant judgment is grief, *lupē.* Nyssen's dialogue *On the Soul and Resurrection* provides an excellent case study of *pathos*. Unlike some instances such as moments of lust or gluttony or cowardice where the emotional excess is closely tied to the immediate presence of a particular sense datum, grief is an emotion whose causes lie deeper in the individual's psyche. To be sure, grief may well be triggered by seeing or hearing or smelling something that either reminds a person of a departed loved one or causes one to anticipate one's own imminent or possible demise. At the outset of the dialogue when Nyssen goes to Pontus to seek comfort from Macrina, he tells us, "As we met each other, the sight of my teacher reawakened the grief within me for she was already ill and close to death."[69]

As the dialogue unfolds, Nyssen makes it clear that the grief that was aroused within him in the instant he saw his sister cannot be explained simply or even principally as a reaction to the her sickly appearance. Rather early in the course of Nyssen's conversation with his sister, Macrina identifies the cause of her brother's grief as an errant judgment or a failure of belief, specifically his fear about the soul's fate at death. In the dialogue, Nyssen's grief is not primarily sadness over the temporary separation from the brother whose company he will miss. Rather it is his suspicion that the soul is mortal. As the physical distress of Nyssen's grief begins to ease, Macrina begins to rein in her brother's soul, reminding him of Paul's words from 1 Thessalonians 4:13: "It is not right to grieve for those who are asleep, since we are told that sorrow belongs to those who have no hope."[70] With these words of reproof — the first Macrina utters in the dialogue — we see Macrina's recognition of the cause behind Nyssen's *pathos,* i.e., his failure to believe or to be suitably confident in the hope of eternal life.

As their conversation proceeds, her suspicion proves well founded. For Nyssen offers a litany of reasons why the fear of death is one of our most natural impulses. Capital punishment is the most feared sentence a criminal can receive because it brings the ultimate punishment, being stripped of all life's goods. For the same reason, medicine is among the most revered professions; indeed all human activities, he claims, are devoted to sustaining life and forestalling death. When Macrina asks why death is to be feared, Nyssen compares looking at a corpse to seeing the thin, black wick of a newly extinguished candle. Just as the candle's flame is gone, so too the life-giving principle of the body has disappeared to who knows where and will not return.[71] Thus grief is primarily the mistaken belief that death entails not a temporary but a permanent loss of life and an eternal separation from those we love. For at the heart of Nyssen's sadness is the conflict between his longing (*epithymia*) for his departed brother and his despair of ever seeing Basil again — a despair arising out of his judgment concerning the finality of death.[72]

This point Nyssen makes explicit in Macrina's rhetorical question to her brother, "Isn't this what disturbs and distracts you, the fear that the soul does not last forever, but leaves with the dissolution of the body?" With Macrina's opening words from 1 Thessalonians, Nyssen states the central theme of the dialogue: the passion of grief that disorders the soul is overcome and the soul is rightly ordered only when the intellect is grounded in the theological virtue of hope, specifically the hope of the resurrection of the body. The remainder of the dialogue, therefore, recounts Macrina's attempt to explain the reasonableness of Christian hope. Here we see Macrina as the physician who heals Nyssen's distraught soul by her apologetic for the doctrine of the resurrection and the immortality of the soul. The physical distress accompanying Nyssen's grief she initially eases by allowing him to vent his *pathos,* and the sadness of his soul she dispels by showing the error of his suspicions about the soul and by restoring the eschatological hope of eternal life.

I agree with Rowan Williams that grief is a product of the appetitive faculty and of the spirited faculty that together constitute the soul's principle of movement. Indeed, *lupē,* as an expression of *epithymia,* has that chief characteristic of *erōs,* a deep desire for that which is absent[73] or lacking.[74] In my view, however, Williams is mistaken in his assumption that because grief is a form of desire it is necessarily the mechanism that moves the soul's search for the object of its love. While grief certainly is an expression of desire for one who is absent, Nyssen is explicit that grief is *frustrated* desire, which results in the languishing of *thymos.*[75] The key point is that in order for *epithymia* to energize the soul and set it in motion toward its object, there must be the *hope* of attaining the goal.[76] Macrina, therefore, argues that hope is the supreme precondition necessary for the soul's forward movement. *Epithymia* is sustained by the interplay of dialectic between hope and memory. "Hope," says Macrina, "is the guide in our motion forward and memory follows upon the motion effected by hope. If hope leads the soul to what is beautiful by nature, the motion of choice imprints a bright track upon our memory."[77]

Hope reflects the expectation that the deficiency or lacking of the soul can indeed be fulfilled. Without such possibility, however, the desire, deep though it may be, is ultimately futile; such futility breeds only frustration and despair. Nyssen's grief in the dialogue reflects both a longing for Basil and a desire not to lose the goods of this life. Beset with doubts about the immortality of the soul, however, his frustrated desire has produced only petulance. He can overcome this *pathos* only once his errant judgment about the soul's mortality is corrected. It is not until the hope of eternal life is restored to him through Macrina's arguments for the resurrection that his intellect is freed from unconstructive passions for the deeper examination of Christian anthropology and eschatology.

The Second Solution to Passion: The Correction of Errant Belief

So far I have described Nyssen's depiction of the passions according to the Platonic model as the impulses of our nonrational nature, which by virtue of their innate orientation toward the sensual stand in frequent conflict with the intellect's pursuit of higher goods. Therefore, Nyssen's solution to this conflict was sublimation; that is, since the emotions are an inescapable and necessary component of the soul, the best an individual can do is keep them under the constant control of reason, which harnesses their power and directs them toward those lofty goods befitting the rational soul. Thus the emotions (*hormai*) are transformed from passion (*pathos*) in the pejorative sense into virtue. In the case of passion understood as emotional disturbance in the soul resulting from a flawed judgment or belief, the solution lies in the education of the soul through the elimination of the errant judgment and the training of the intellect. For all teachers, Christian and non-Christian alike, the aim of education was training the soul to distinguish the good from the bad and so choose the good. For the Stoics this meant training the student to distinguish between that which is within one's power and that which is beyond one's control. It also meant knowing the difference between mere social convention and the law of nature. For a Christian theologian and pastor, like Nyssen, errant judgment was corrected through instruction in the theological virtues. In the case of grief, which results from the doubts about the immortality of the soul, the mistaken beliefs about the soul can be purged and the order of the soul restored when it is grounded in the orthodox hope of the resurrection.

The argument Macrina employs to persuade her brother of the hope of the resurrection places more emphasis on the need for hope than it does on understanding the mechanics of resurrection. Rather than appealing to Scripture and the apostolic witness to Christ's own resurrection, she argues for the importance of hope purely in terms of its practical implications for the moral life. Hope stands in contrast to the materialist view of the finality of our present bodily existence. Without mentioning the

Epicureans by name, Macrina tells Nyssen to dismiss the pagan views that are ultimately antithetical to the pursuit of virtue. By eliminating any possibility of life beyond death and the enjoyment of goods other than the immediate one, the pagans necessarily promote a *carpe diem* hedonism.[78] Hope is indispensable for virtue; in fact hope is the source of virtue's "superiority" (*to pleion*). By this she means that the hope of eternal goods provides one with that perspective on life necessary to achieve those eternal goods. In other words, sacrificing the certain goods of the present life for remote and improbable goods would be foolish. Without a real hope of attaining some future good, one would have no reason not to seek, first and foremost, the pleasures of this life. There would be scant warrant for self-sacrifice. In contrast, the hope of attaining greater goods in an eternal existence drastically relativizes the goods of our present existence.

Thus the pursuit of virtue, which for Macrina prepares the soul for the eternal enjoyment of the intelligible goods by means of ascetic discipline and self-denial, is superior to the short-sighted pursuit of inferior and transient goods. Disbelief or doubt militate against the requisite discipline and striving needed to achieve virtue. Nyssen himself recognizes Macrina's meaning: "I myself perceive that virtue is deficient unless some unequivocal belief on this subject prevails in us. How can virtue have a place among those who assume that the present life is the limit of existence and that there is nothing to be hoped for after that?"[79] In Abraham, Nyssen finds the exemplar of Christian hopefulness. Commenting on Jesus' parable of the rich man and Lazarus, Macrina explains that the "bosom of Abraham" is a symbol for the "good state of the soul" because Abraham was the first of the patriarchs to have centered his life around the pursuit of the future goods promised by God rather than to be content with the present comforts of hearth and home.[80] Thus Abraham's life as an alien sojourning in strange lands is paradigmatic for the Christian's sojourn in the present life. The "bosom of Abraham" symbolizes the soul's heavenly resting place as well as that orientation of the soul which is centered upon the eternal goods of the age to come.

Similarly in *De Vita Moysis*, Nyssen identifies hope as a necessary condition for the pursuit of virtue. In this biographical allegory, Nyssen uses the story of Exodus as a type for the Christian journey. Egypt represents the Christian's former life. Canaan, as the land of promise, is heaven. And the journey through Sinai corresponds to the disciple's life of purgative preparation for entry into heaven. Nyssen acknowledges that the journey through the wilderness at first seems hard and even bitter

because the Christian finds quite difficult the separation from the pleasures to which her appetites had become habitually accustomed.[81] The
mystery of the resurrection and its concomitant hope of good things to
come — both of which have their origin in the wood of Christ's cross —
are prefigured in the wood with which Moses purified the bitter waters
of Marah (Exod. 15:23–25). For the hope of the resurrection and of the
glorious life to come minimizes both the sweetness of the pleasures of
Egypt that one has abandoned and the hardships of one's initiation into
the life of virtue.[82] The hope of eternal blessedness acts as a counterweight to the memories of past pleasures that make the ascetic life seem
unbearable;[83] therefore, hope is necessary for the Christian to endure the
seeming hardships of the life of virtue and so achieve her end.

Hope not only aids the novice who must endure the process of being
weaned from the excesses and immoderate appetites of her pre-Christian
lifestyle, but it continues to assist those already committed to the life
of virtue. Commenting on human freedom, Nyssen explains that God
assists our freedom beginning with our birth and through the struggles
and contests of our mature life. He speaks of this assistance as taking
the form of a good angel who, by means of reasoned demonstration,
reveals the goods to be enjoyed by those who pursue virtue. These goods
are grasped by the intellect guided by the revelation of hope granted to
those who live upright and virtuous lives (*tois katorthousin*).[84] Moreover
through hope, not only is the Christian encouraged to stay the course, but
the character of her soul is actually transformed by this vision of hope.

When the soul resists evil and turns toward the good things for which
it hopes, it then undergoes a metamorphosis in which, as a mirror, it
begins to bear the image of the virtues it desires and contemplates.[85]
Given his assumption that one must become holy like God in order to
know and to participate more fully in God's goodness, Nyssen must
also assume that there is a direct correspondence between the future
goods hoped for and the virtues needed to attain them. In other words,
the goods of which the soul hopes to partake in heaven are intelligible
goods proper to the supreme beauty of God's goodness. Since God is
incorporeal, his beauty obviously does not take the form of physical
comeliness. Rather it is to be contemplated in the sheer perfection of
God's virtues.[86] Therefore, when the mind is set upon the virtues of God
and contemplates their supreme beauty, the soul begins to take on the
divine virtues. Thus it is through the theological virtue of hope that the
soul begins to participate in the virtues of God's holiness and so enjoy
the blessings proper to that end for which one is striving.

Conclusion: The Distinctiveness of Nyssen's Solution to the Passions

I have argued that Nyssen shares with the Stoics and Aristotle the be-lief that passion and sin are ultimately the product of errant judgment or mistaken belief. For Nyssen the healing of the soul's passion comes from instruction in the orthodox faith and the cultivation of the theo-logical virtues. Yet Nyssen's appeal to the theological virtues illustrates how different his Christian solution is from that of pagan philosophical schools. By making hope the principal precondition for virtue, Nyssen radically separates the Christian understanding of virtue and its causes from that espoused by certain Stoics. Seneca acknowledged the symbi-otic relationship between desire and hope. But concomitant with hope, he contends, is fear — fear that one may not gain what one desires or that one's present goods may be lost. Writing to his friend Lucilius, he observes, "though they [i.e., hope and fear] do seem at variance, yet they are really united. Just as the same chain fastens the prisoner and the soldier . . . each alike belongs to a mind that is in suspense, a mind that is fretting by looking forward to the future. But the chief cause of both these ills is that we do not adapt ourselves to the present, but send our thoughts a long way ahead."[87]

The passion or suffering of anxiety comes from concerning ourselves about a future over which we have no control. Our destiny as determined by fate cannot be altered; to hope for some good that may never come to pass only creates the greater likelihood of future disappointment.[88] Con-sequently, in the present we are disturbed by the fear or anticipation of disappointment. Under the delusion of hope, men act contrary to nature in the futile effort of gaining mastery over their destiny. For many Stoics, the virtuous life as a life in conformity with nature and fate accepts one's present condition and circumstances without regard to regrets about the past or without looking to the future, which is beyond the scope of our control.[89] Here a critical point should be made. Both the Stoics and Nyssen view the future as in some sense determined. The future for the Stoics ultimately ends in death followed by the cosmic conflagration that results in the absorption of the individual's spirit, or *pneuma*, into the cosmic *pneuma*.[90] Thus the individual loses her discrete subsistence and consciousness. Instead of being anxious about the inescapable cy-cles of the cosmos, the sage frees herself from the emotional disturbance of worry and instead is resigned to the transient nature of her life. For Nyssen, as well, the future in an ultimate sense is determined. Yet it is determined because it is subject to the sovereign sway of a God who wills the redemption and blessedness of all creation—a redemption that has already begun with Christ's incarnation and resurrection. Hope, therefore, does not mean for Nyssen the self-deluded optimism that tempts one to resist one's irresistible fate, as it does for Seneca. It is, rather, confidence firmly founded upon God's sure and benevolent economy.[91] Thus to be motivated by hope is, for Nyssen, to act in conformity with our divinely ordained destiny.

Nyssen's critique of the passions bears a marked similarity to the critique offered by his Christian and non-Christian predecessors. For this reason he gladly appropriated the language of Greek philosophical schools to articulate this problem that he saw as the chief cause of sin. Yet Nyssen cannot be classified strictly as a Platonist or a Stoic or an Aristotelian. Although he borrows the terminology and imagery from all three schools, he never uses their language in a manner fully consistent with their system of thought as a whole. Nyssen's theological and soteriological concerns, especially his understanding of the *imago Dei* as well as the role of humanity in the completion of creation, so shape his anthropology and psychology that his ultimate account of the passions cannot be dismissed as baptized Platonism. While on the one hand Nyssen's theory of the soul's development from the vegetative soul of an embryo to the rational soul of an adult does not allow him to speak of the soul as tripartite as does Plato, on the other hand, his concern for the tension between the conflicting orientations of the appetitive and rational faculties prevents him from having a strictly unitary view of the soul, as does Chrysippus. Consequently, his account of the passions as both arising from our sensually oriented impulses as well as from mistaken judgments about the Good and the Real reflects both traditions.

Ultimately Nyssen's solution to the problem of the passions rests upon a highly unified doctrine of the soul in which the intellect functions as the *hegēmonikon* that harnesses all the soul's powers into an alliance enabling its ascent to God. As was illustrated in his discussion of the role of hope in the training of the soul, Nyssen maintains that the intellect that is grounded in the theological virtues is both free from mistakes of judgment about man's true nature and destiny and is strengthened in its grip over the soul's appetitive drives. For it is the understanding of our place in the divine economy as apprehended through the theological virtues that enables the soul to reevaluate the objects of its desires and so turn from the sensual and mundane to the intelligible and eternal goods of God. The theological virtues, which rest upon belief in that vision of God, human nature, and the eschatological end of creation and history revealed in Scripture, transform the soul's intentional awareness (*orexis*) of the world from which all emotions come and so reorient the drives (*hormai*) of the soul toward the Divine. Thus even though virtues admired and encouraged by Nyssen may be almost identical to those admired and recommended by Seneca and Plato, Aristotle and Posidonius, the judgments and assumptions that inform the soul's *orexis* are decidedly different for Nyssen.

So far we have seen that Nyssen offers two solutions to the problem of the passion in this life: (1) the sublimation of the soul's impulses and (2) the elimination of errant judgment through adherence to the claims of orthodoxy. Yet the questions lingers: what part do the emotions play in the eschaton? After all, Nyssen, in Macrina's modified view, maintains that emotions lie on the borderland of the soul rather than being a part of man's essential nature. From this reasoning he concludes that the emotions are morally neutral and can be a vital ally of the intellect if controlled by reason. At the same time, this view leads him to conclude that the emotions are necessary for moral action in the present life in which the soul is beset with the attraction of conflicting goods. But in the eschaton where no such conflicts exists, the soul will not need virtues like courage or the godly grief. Moreover, given Nyssen's view of the essential nature of humanity and its actualization in the eschaton, what will happen to the *hormai* of the sentient faculties when the soul is restored to that passionless state proper to the divine image that God intended for us before our creation? This is the question that will concern the remaining exploration of this book.

CHAPTER FOUR

Satiation and Epectasy

In the present age, the problem of the nonrational impulses of the soul or passions can be solved, according to Nyssen, in two ways. First, the power of the emotions can be harnessed and used to aid the soul's ascent to God when they are fully controlled by reason. Second, the intellect controls the emotions and eliminates the negative character of *pathos* when the judgments of the intellect itself are informed by the church's teachings and the theological virtues. When the intellect is trained to see the world through the lens of the Catholic faith, it is able to make right judgments about those goods worthy to be sought above all else, those transitory goods to be pursued with moderation, and those things to be avoided. Yet this right ordering of the emotions by no means constitutes an end in itself; it is simply a necessary step in order for the soul to enter into contemplative union with God. Nor does the transformation of the passions mark the full restoration of the divine image that the Triune God intended for us in his deliberative creation of the *plērōma* of humanity. *Metriopatheia* does not entail a transformation of human nature sufficient for our full participation in God. After all, Nyssen never repudiates Macrina's claim that the emotions lie on the margin of the soul serving humanity's present needs but are not a part of human nature as God intended it in the beginning.

That leaves several important questions about Nyssen's soteriology that must be answered. If the sublimation of the emotions is the best man can hope to achieve in the present age, what must happen to the soul in order to achieve a purer and more profound union with God in the eschatological age? How is the image of God perfected in the soul so that it is equipped for intimate eschatological union with God? Must the soul ultimately be freed from the impulses of man's nonrational nature? Is there a place for the passions in the paradise to come? These questions will occupy the remaining pages of this book. The thesis I will argue is that divinization of the soul is the result not primarily of a change in human nature, but of the soul's eschatological relationship with God. In other words, in the age to come God will be present to the soul in a way very different than God is at present. This transforming relationship of the soul with God is summed up in Nyssen's theory of epectasy — the soul's eternal movement into God's infinite being.

"Epectasy" is the term coined by Jean Daniélou from the verb *epekteinomai*.[1] It appears only once in the New Testament where Paul in Philippians 3:13 describes his pressing on toward perfection as "forgetting what lies behind and straining forward [*epekteinomenos*] to what lies ahead." Although Nyssen himself uses the term only once in a mystical sense, for Daniélou it aptly describes the essence of Nyssen's soteriology: the soul's eternal process of moving into and partaking of God's infinite goodness. Epectasy applies to the soul's participation in God in both this life and the age to come. In the present age, epectasy describes the unending struggle that accompanies the sublimation and moderation of the appetitive impulses in ascetic discipline and the contemplative life. When epectasy is applied to the soul's eschatological union with God, it includes the transformation of erotic desire *(epithymia)* for God into perfect, passionless love *(agapē)* and at the same time preserves the dynamic character of communion with the Divine when the soul finally shall enjoy the immediate vision of God's glory.

Through the first half of *On the Soul and Resurrection,* Macrina refined her notion of the emotions. The emotions, instead of being inherently the cause of evil, are morally neutral in character. Given by God to humanity among all animals for the sake of survival, the appetitive impulses, which are forms of *epithymia* and/or *thymos,* can become virtues necessary for the soul's ascent to God. When the passions are uncontrolled by reason, they follow their natural orientation toward sensual or mundane goods. However, when the principal drives of man's irrational sentient faculties are steered by reason, which apprehends the highest good, then *epithymia* takes on the character of love, a longing to be united with God. And *thymos* takes the form of courage, which reins in the drives of the lower impulses for lesser goods of the transitory, material realm. Moreover, passions, such as grief, that are not primarily responses to sense stimuli, can be overcome when the intellect is rightly informed by the tenets of Christian orthodoxy, which grounds the soul's judgments of this life in the context of Christ's incarnation, death, and resurrection.

In the eschaton, however, the soul experiences a significant change in the character of its communion with God and consequently a corresponding change in the character of its love for God. Unlike the present

age in which the life of the Christian resembles the pilgrim, the soul in
the age to come has already arrived at his place of rest, the bosom of
Abraham. No longer is one's experience of God mediated by the church
and the sacraments; rather one then enjoys immediate beatific union with
God. When our knowledge of God changes from that of faith, which anticipates some distant and future goal, to the uninterrupted communion
characterized by immediate participation in the life and nature of God,
then the character of our love will be changed. This eschatological transformation of *epithymia* Nyssen describes as *apolausis*. I will argue that
this new character of *agapē*, as described in *On the Soul and Resurrection* corresponds with Nyssen's doctrine of epectasy developed in *The
Life of Moses* and his *Commentary on the Song of Songs*.

Origen's Theory of Satiation

The doctrine of epectasy can be understood as the Cappadocian cor-
rective to Origen's account of the intellect's satiation with the divine
beauty and subsequent fall from God.[2] Origen's theory of the fall of
the preexistent rational beings (*logikoi*) and God's subsequent creation
of the material universe is constructed around two related loci of concern: theodicy and the righteousness of Christ's creation. His concern
for theodicy is not the larger issue of why a powerful and benevolent
God allows evil to thrive. Rather his worry is with instances of apparent
suffering *built into* the order of creation. The case of an infant who is
blind from birth is the paradigmatic instance of created evil.[3] Moreover,
such anomalies are only the most extreme examples of inequality which
pervades the cosmic order. Angels, human beings, and demons, each of
which occupies a different rung of the hierarchy of rational beings, is
allotted an unequal degree of blessedness or misery.

Even among human beings, individuals are born into very disparate
situations of advantage and disadvantage. Some are born into enlightened Greek culture while others are the children of benighted barbarians.
Some are endowed with a high degree of intellectual aptitude; others lack
strength in body as well as intellect. Unlike the accounts of either Mar-
cion or various Gnostic sects that attribute such created evil to the work
of a lesser god or an ignorant and foolish demiurge, Origen insists that
all creation including the material world is ordained and fashioned in
Christ's wisdom. This tenet of his thought creates for Origen the per-
plexing conundrum: how to reconcile the *disparity* between and among
rational beings with the *righteousness* of Christ's plan of creation.[4] Such
inequality seems incongruous with a sense of divine justice inherent in

the righteousness of Christ in whom all things were made. The unequal portions of suffering and blessedness, privilege and poverty can, for Origen, be reconciled with Christ's righteousness only if this diversity is the reward or punishment merited by each individual prior to being assigned to their particular station or niche within the hierarchy.[5] Origen, therefore, is led to posit a twofold process of creation.

In the beginning, Christ created the full complement of rational beings. All were fashioned *equally* after the image of God. In other words, all were endowed with an equal share in the rational nature of the eternally begotten Logos who is the Image of God the Father. Thus each intellectual being, or *nous,* shares with the Divine an incorporeal, immaterial, and incorruptible rational nature so that it may enjoy the blessedness of contemplative union with God the Father through the mediation of his Word and Wisdom. Origen describes this contemplative communion with the Father in terms of the participation in the knowledge and grace of God as mediated by the Son and the Holy Spirit.[6] The second stage of creation comes with Christ's fashioning the material world following the fall of the rational beings from their state of blessedness.

According to Origen all rational beings, except the *nous* that will eventually become the soul of Jesus, turn away from God in varying degrees. The result is a loss of holiness and blessed union with God. The separation of the *nous* from God Origen characterizes as a fall from the heavenly realm due to the cooling of the intellect's love for God. In this cooling the *nous* becomes a soul, *psychē;* for, he observes, *psychē* is derived from the verb *psychesthai,* which means "to become cold."[7] As a remedial punishment for the fall, Christ creates the material cosmos. Into this material existence the souls fall. Within this world of material embodiment, each soul is situated according to the degree of its own particular "coolness" toward the divine goodness. Those souls that were faithful to God were given celestial bodies to rule the heavens.[8] Some angels were given aerial bodies. The most rebellious, the demons, entered bodies of darkness. Those souls who were neither as faithful as angels nor as rebellious as demons assumed the coarse material form of human beings.[9] Although the soul's state of embodiment was designed to be painful and the source of hardship, such suffering is not the visitation of God's purely punitive punishment. Rather the pain and discomfort of the soul's material existence are in God's plan ultimately a redemptive suffering. For bodily suffering, Origen says, rekindles the soul's lost love for God by arousing a longing for the blessedness of its original, graced union with God.

Origen's theory of the soul's preexistence, though obviously influenced by the Platonic concept of the transmigration of souls,[10] entails problems not faced by his classical predecessors. Even as Origen used his theory of preexistence and the fall to explain the inequalities among people, so too Plato before him had used the transmigration of souls to justify the social hierarchy of *Republic* and to explain the different degrees of aptitude or apprehension of the forms or eternal goods in *Phaedrus*.[11] Origen's theory of the rational being's preexistence differs from that of the Platonic scheme on a number of levels. But Origen's most significant point of departure is his explanation of the fall of rational beings. While the souls for Plato are given a partial and thus imperfect vision of the Good and Beautiful, each *nous* according to Origen enjoys a perfect vision of the divine goodness. With an incomplete vision of the Good as well as a flawed recollection of that vision, Plato's souls fall into error as a result of ignorance. For Plato there is a direct correlation between our knowledge of the good and the choices we make. However, because Origen's intellectual beings are created in a state of blessed union with God and so enjoyed uninterrupted and unhindered contemplation of the perfect image of God the Father, the fall of the *logikoi* cannot be explained, as with Plato, in terms of either an obstructed and imperfect vision of the Good[12] or the training of the soul in some prior state of existence.[13] Therefore Origen's account of the fall must explain how rational beings could ever turn away from the one who is supremely beautiful and so who is to be desired above all things.

Origen's answer begins with a traditional assertion about the metaphysical conditions for humanity's fall from holiness. Unlike God, who is holy in his immutable and eternal nature, rational beings are holy only by virtue of participation in God's holiness. The holiness for created beings is derived from and contingent upon the intellect's union with the Divine, which is perfectly holy. Our holiness, therefore, must be thought of as an accidental rather than an essential component of our constitution. Thus holiness in creatures lacks the permanence that it has in God's nature and so has the potential to be lost.[14] Here Origen seems to be saying that the only essential feature of our nature is that since we were created from nothing we are inherently unstable and subject to change. Although the innate mutability of created beings establishes the possibility of the loss of holiness, such a falling away is not an inevitable or necessary consequence of our mutability. The constancy of devotion and fervor exhibited by the *nous* of Jesus illustrates the capacity of created beings to preserve their union with God.[15]

Participation in the divine virtues is voluntary. The mind is created with the capacity for free participation in the good so that the good of which it is capable may be fully internalized.[16] Rational beings, therefore, are free and responsible for their participation in the Divine. Origen explains that the loss of holiness springs from carelessness or from inattentiveness to participation in God. The lapse or falling away from God, therefore, is the result of sloth or a lack of vigilance on the part of the intellect.[17] In Rufinus's Latin translation, Origen emphasizes that the intellect's degree of participation corresponds to "the movements of the mind and will."[18] This double movement of the intellect and the will is suggested by Origen's later remark that "sloth and weariness of taking trouble to preserve the good coupled with disregard and neglect of better things began the process of withdrawal from the good."[19] It would be anachronistic to impute to Origen a faculty of will clearly delineated from the faculty of reasoning (as one finds in the Western tradition after Augustine). When Origen speaks of "the will" (*propositum*), the term simply denotes the mind's choices. Nevertheless, in this passage he seems to distinguish the attitude of indifference for the good, which is related to the intellect's judgment or discernment of the good, from the moral weakness of sloth or weariness in participation, which is associated with the realm of moral choice or determination of actions.

What is significant for Origen's understanding of the righteousness of Christ's ordering of the cosmic hierarchy is that the ranking of the rational beings and their conditions within the threefold order of angels, human beings, and demons reflects their degree of participation in the Good. Given its etymology, Origen contends, the word "soul" inherently connotes blame since *psychē* denotes a cooling of the intellect's fervor of righteousness due to its withdrawal "from its participation in the divine fire."[20] This suggests, first, that union with God the Father through participation in the grace mediated by the Word and the Spirit enables the rational being to share in the divine virtues, especially love. But second, this blessed communion is sustained by the rational being's reciprocal love of God's goodness. Thus participation in the Good is the cause of the intellect's holiness, which can be understood principally as the intellect's holy love of the Good. When Origen speaks of complacency and indifference toward the Good as a lack of fervor, he implies that the intellect's love of the Good has waned. In fact, he explains that human beings are separated from God, not because they have lost the power to return, but because they have so "abandoned themselves to wickedness" that they do not possess the ardent desire necessary to return and cling to the Good.[21] Yet this correlation only begs the question: if the love of the

Good is the result of participation in the Good, how could the intellect, which is created in a state of blessed communion with God, ever become indifferent or uninterested in the beauty of God's perfection?

The source of the rational beings' indifference, Origen explains, is in Greek *koros* or in Latin *satietas*. There are two important passages in which Origen appeals to the notion of *satietas* or *koros* to account for the fall of intellectual beings. The first instance occurs in a passage not directly about the fall itself, but about the restoration of the intellect to its blessed life of union with God. Commenting on 1 Corinthians 12, Origen explains how the restoration of the intellect is achieved by the work of the whole Trinity. Once sanctified by the Holy Spirit one is able to receive Christ afresh and so receive the gift of wisdom. Likewise, participation in Christ by sharing in his wisdom, knowledge, and holiness enables the soul to advance to higher degrees of perfection. Through participation in the Holy Spirit the soul gains that holiness and purity which characterize the life worthy of God's original intention. Such a life of holiness God rewards with the power of eternal life such that one may enjoy the highest degree of blessedness, that is, that we "may be unceasingly and inseparably present with him [i.e., God] who really exists."[22]

Even when such blessed communion is achieved, Origen says that "we ought so to continue that no satiety of that blessing may ever possess us" but that "the loving desire for it [i.e., blessedness] deepen within us, as ever our hearts grow in fervor and eagerness to receive and hold fast the Father, Son, and Holy Spirit."[23] The implication is that *satietas* causes the intellect to turn away from the highest blessedness. Moreover, in this passage he seems to suggest that such *satietas* might be a recurring phenomenon.[24] Yet by way of offering hope, he observes that "if at anytime satiety possess the heart of one of those who have come to occupy the perfect and highest stage," the fall is "a decline by slow degrees" so that we may recover quickly and not face utter ruin.[25] The second passage comes at the beginning of chapter 4 of book I, immediately on the heels of the preceding discussion. Here Origen illustrates his theory of the gradual fall of the *logikoi*. It is comparable to a man who after having acquired complete knowledge of a science such as geometry or medicine gradually loses his knowledge of the discipline when due to lack of interest or *satietas* he neglects his study of the science. The loss of knowledge is slow and therefore easily retrieved if the mind is once again set on its study.[26] By such neglect the intellectual beings eventually sank into the mire of material bodies.

How should one translate *koros* or *satietas?* Brooks Otis understands *koros* to refer to the intellect's satiation with God's goodness. It is not enough, he contends, to explain the fall in terms of free will. For neither Origen nor any Greek could conceive of anyone's knowingly choosing evil, which in Origen's context meant turning from the greatest good to a lesser good. Rather such satiety is principally the result of acquiring an exhaustive knowledge of God. Origen's explanation of the fall rests upon the theological assumption that God, as an object of knowledge, is exhaustible or limited (*peperasmenēn*).[27] Otis's claim that Origen conceives of God as finite is derived from two passages. The more explicit of the two is a Greek fragment preserved in Justinian's *Epistula ad Mennam.* In this passage, Origen claims that God created only a finite number of intellectual beings. For, since God's power is finite, he could create only as many beings as he could control. The critical point is Origen's explanation for the finite character of God's power. Were God's power infinite, that is, without bounds or limitations, it would of necessity be incomprehensible even to God himself since that which is infinite cannot be circumscribed by intellectual faculties.[28]

Here Origen's argument rests upon a logical fallacy. That which is infinite cannot be the object of comprehension if "to comprehend" means to get one's mind completely around the object of one's thoughts. If, however, the thinking subject is itself infinite, then the infinite object of thought could be matched at every point by the infinite thinking subject, especially if the former is *derived from* the latter. Hence understanding would not be a matter of the mind circumscribing the object of thought; but, as one infinite plain resting upon another, the mind would extend infinitely touching upon every point proper to the infinite object of its meditation. What is most important, however, for Otis in this passage is Origen's assertion that the divine power is comprehensible. By claiming that God's power is finite and therefore comprehensible, Origen has allowed for the principal condition for a thinking subject to become satiated with it object. In other words, even if God's finite power is exceedingly vast, over the course of infinity the intellectual beings could come to understand the full extent of God's power.

Having fully charted the bounds of God's vast power, they might become satiated with their contemplative exploration. Indeed the second significant passage lends support to this view. In Origen's illustration of the fall at the beginning of chapter 4 of book I, the doctor or mathematician is described as having advanced so far in his studies as to have come "up to the point of reaching perfection, having trained himself for a long

time by instructions and exercises so as to acquire *completely* the knowledge of the aforesaid art."[29] The logic of Origen's analogy is that even as
the scholar loses interest in his study because he has learned all there is
to know about it, so too the intellectual beings become indifferent and
neglect their contemplation of God because they have gained complete
knowledge of God. Such loss of interest is due to the finite nature of the
object of their contemplation.

One possible solution to the question of God's finite or limited power
is to construe Justinian's term *dynamin,* which may not actually be Origen's exact word but that of his disciples in the fourth and fifth centuries
against whom Justinian is writing, as actually referring to God's activity and not to his potential activity.[30] If this is the case, what is limited
is God's creative enterprises. This limitation of his activity need not be
anything other than a self-imposed limit, rather than an inherent limit on
the potential scope of his power. In other words, God chooses to create
a finite cosmos. If this is the case, one cannot easily conclude that the
self-limitation of God's creative energies implies that God's nature itself
is finite.

Henri Crouzel, however, contends that *koros* or *satietas* refers to the
boredom of contemplation that often is analogous to the phenomenon
of "accidie" experienced by Eastern contemplatives who lose interest in
their prayer and then in the contemplative life itself. Here he relies on
Marguerite Harl's argument that Origen's writings must be read in the
context of his concerns about spirituality.[31] Since his writings would have
been read by monks centuries after his death, Origen was understood
by these monks of the fourth and fifth centuries to be employing an
analogy drawn from the hard experiences of contemplative retreat to
illustrate how the *logikoi* might turning from their contemplation of
God. The problems faced by earnest contemplatives of the third century,
who often succumbed to the fatigue of long hours of prayer and so were
not properly attentive to God in their meditation, provided Origen with
an analogue to which his readers could relate.[32]

Rejecting Otis's reading that Origen's God is fully knowable, Crouzel
contends that Origen's God is infinite and therefore cannot in himself
be the source of satiation for the *logikoi.* Rather than seeking a mechanistic explanation for the turn from God, Origen's principal point,
Crouzel maintains, is that the rational beings in their freedom turn
from God because they voluntarily succumb to the temptations of boredom.[33] Here we see the principal difference between Crouzel and Otis.
By emphasizing the negligence of the rational creatures, Crouzel seeks
to avoid the highly mechanistic account suggested by Otis's emphasis

upon *koros*. Given Origen's concern for the relation between God's just ordering of the cosmos based on the rational creature's use of freedom, Crouzel's reading conveys the relationship between the rational creatures' responsibility and their situation, which better fits within Origen's larger speculative theory of creation.

Otis is correct that one possible implication of Origen's two descriptions of *koros* or *satietas* in *On First Principles* presupposes that God can be fully known and thus is in some sense finite. Yet such inferences do not stand up to other selections from Origen's writings in which he explicitly asserts that God is infinite. In his *Commentary on John*, Origen, when explaining that the richness of God's nature is incomprehensible to human beings, says that God seems utterly inaccessible to the intellect: "God is enveloped in darkness, for no one can formulate any conception rich enough to do him justice. It is then in darkness that he has made His hiding-place; he has made it thus because *no one can know all [agnoeisthai]* concerning him who is *infinite [achōrēta]*."[34] Initially his argument is that God appears to us as darkness because God is so radically different from his material creation and because the intellect, since it derives its categories of thought from the created order, has no analogues in its experience to enable it to think about or describe God's nature accurately. Yet the veil of darkness that separates the intellect from full understanding is God's infinite nature, which prevents our knowing him exhaustively. Moreover, in Rufinus's Latin translation of *On First Principles* Origen appeals to God's incomprehensibility to created being in order to defend the divinity of the Logos by distinguishing his knowledge of God from that of the *logikoi*. God, he writes,

> made creatures worthy of himself that is, creatures capable of worthily receiving him, whom he also says he has "begotten as sons." But he made all things by number and measure; for to God there is nothing either without number or measure. For by his power he comprehended all things, while he himself is *not comprehended by the mind of any created being*. For that nature is known to itself alone. The Father alone knows the Son, the Son alone knows the Father, and the Holy Spirit alone searches out even the depths of God.[35]

This passage is significant for two reasons. First, his argument presupposes that the creatures can be comprehended because they are finite, corporeal beings delimited in number and measure; God who is incorporeal and not circumscribed by number or measure is not comprehensible to any but himself. The Father and the Son can comprehend the other because only that which is infinite can comprehend another infinite being. But second, even Origen had not thought through the implications of God's infinite nature. Origen in this passage explicitly rejects any suggestion that finite creatures can have exhaustive knowledge of God precisely because God is infinite. The explicit evidence supports Crouzel's interpretation.

Although boredom and satiety are related phenomena, each is distinct in that each locates the principal cause of indifference or sloth in a different source. *Koros* as boredom implies a waning of interest because one is tired of the same old thing. *Koros* as satiety, on the other hand, is the result of having too much of a good thing — more than one can hold.[36] The latter rendering of *koros* implies that the cause of indifference lies with the limitations of the contemplator who is unable to absorb or digest the vastness of the object of contemplation. *Koros* as boredom, however, suggests that while the cause of indifference may reside in the limitations of the object of contemplation, it may just as well result from the limited stamina or intelligence of the contemplator. In the first case, the object of contemplation is either not sufficiently important and interesting to sustain one's interest or is so finite and simple as to be fully understood. When one's contemplation of an object has been exhaustively covered, the object of contemplation ceases to be sufficiently interesting to arrest one's attention for all eternity. In the second instance, boredom may arise out of a limitation on the part of the rational being when it is incapable of sustained interest due to fatigue or a lack of discipline. Boredom may also arise because an individual lacks either sufficient understanding or interest to remain focused on his contemplation. In such cases, one's intellect is unable to gain new insights and so becomes bored.

To adjudicate whether boredom for Origen arises principally out of a limitation on the part of the object of contemplation or the subject who is doing the contemplating it helps to remember the model Origen employs to describe the rational beings' participation in the divine goodness. It is the metaphor of the heavenly classroom presided over by the greatest of teachers. Given this model, it is hard to imagine that Origen is going to place the blame on the teacher rather than the student. Although *koros* as satiation might explain why the *logikoi* are unable to maintain concentration and so, feeling overwhelmed, lose interest; such satiety does not excuse the intellectual beings for their lack of love for the goodness of God. It is this loss of love or desire for God that, for Origen, is the principal cause of the cooling transformation of the *logikoi* into *psychai*.

Ultimately, the argument between Otis and Crouzel as to whether or not Origen himself actually held that God is finite does not determine how we read Gregory of Nyssa. First, although Nyssen never explicitly mentions Origen in his treatment of satiation, satiation was such an essential feature of Origen's theory of the fall that Nyssen must have had Origen in mind when he argued that the soul's love of God is insatiable. Second, regardless of Origen's own understanding of satiation, the fundamental presupposition of Nyssen's doctrine of epectasy, as will be shown in the next chapter, is that satiation results when the intellect's contemplation reaches a definitive end or limit. *Koros* settles upon the soul when its forward progress is brought to a halt either by the limitation of the object of meditation or by a limitation of the contemplative subject's intellect or will. Nyssen's position on satiation, whether it corresponds with Origen's own views on the matter, is that man's finite intellect could never gain such mastery over God's infinite goodness and being that it could ever cease to be filled with both intellectual fascination and rational desire for a greater share in the Divine.

Indeed this, I will argue, is the key contribution of Nyssen's account of epectasy. For even though there is convincing textual evidence supporting Crouzel's claim that Origen thought that God is infinite.[37] Origen, nevertheless, does not seem to have recognized the bearing this tenet of his thought would have on his own theory of satiation. As Andrew Louth has observed, "Only rarely does he [Origen] raise the question of the implications of God's infinity.... In *De Principiis* (2.4.1; 4.4.8) he definitely seems unhappy with such an idea."[38] It was, therefore, left to Gregory to work out the soteriological and eschatological implications of Origen's own theological position. In other words, Nyssen had to demonstrate that Origen's theory of satiation is incompatible with his own doctrine of an infinite God. For although Nyssen rejects Origen's theory of the preexistent *logikoi* and the related doctrine of creation as the result of the fall, he is still haunted by Origen's explanation for the fall. For the problem of satiation does not vanish once one jettisons Origen's theory of the soul's preexistence. Rather the question "Can one become bored or satiated with God's gracious fellowship after having seen him 'face to face'?" poses a serious challenge for all Christian theories of eschatological redemption.

Nyssen's Reply: The Incomparable Eschatological Vision

Nyssen's solution to the conundrum of satiation bequeathed by Origen begins with his rejection of Origen's fundamental assumption that the soul's present contemplation of God is analogous to the eschatological contemplation. Nyssen contrasts man's incomplete knowledge of God in the present age with our perfected vision of God in the eschatological consummation of God's creation, thereby disallowing Origen's comparison between the contemplative participation of the intellectual beings in God's holiness and the contemplation of ascetics battling the problems of *koros*. By denying Origen's notion of the preexistence of the souls Nyssen, in a manner similar to Irenaeus, presents the eschaton as the fulfillment of God's original intention for his creation. Thus in perfected creation of the eschaton the soul is allowed union with God unlike its present imperfect experience. Although Origen too sees the end as the perfection of the soul's participation in God's holiness, this eschatological perfection nevertheless entails a restoration of the blessedness that the *logikoi* lost when they turned from God.

Although Gregory appropriates Origen's term *apokatastasis*, thus speaking of our eschatological redemption as a "restoration," he parts company with Origen on the question of *what* is restored. For Nyssen what is restored is not the soul's original state of blessed union with God, but God's original design for human beings, the *imago Dei,* which God augmented with the introduction of gender distinctions in anticipation of the need for procreation after the fall. Even though Origen's notion of *apokatastasis* is not merely a restoration of the beginning, but an enhancement and perfection of that original state of blessedness, nevertheless, the beginning serves as a model or precedent for thinking of the soul's contemplative reunion with God. For Nyssen, by contrast, the soul's eschatological union with God is wholly without precedent. Consequently, his eschatology allows him to create a sharp contrast between our soul's highly limited vision of God now and its far fuller vision of God in the new Jerusalem. The latter vision will prove so much more vivid and thus so much more attractive to the intellect that the soul will be inseparably bound in its love for God by virtue of the compelling nature of the beatific vision. Consequently, Nyssen argues, the *koros* experienced by Christians engaged in contemplative prayer will not enter into the experience of the soul's eternal contemplation of the beatific vision. This contrast between our present experience of God and our eschatological vision is found principally in Nyssen's accounts of the soul's mystical encounter with God in *The Life of Moses* (*De Vita Moysis*) and in the eleventh homily on the Song of Songs (*Commentarius in Canticum Canticorum*).

Nyssen's view of the soul's spiritual ascent follows the traditional threefold cycle of purification, illumination, and unification. Purification begins when the soul's appetitive faculties are turned by the intellect from their innate orientation toward the sensible goods of the world and are filled with longing for the intelligible goods of heaven. The first step in this process is the renunciation of vice and the acquisition of moral virtue. This purification is followed by the illumination that enables the believer to see that the created order is "vanity of vanities," i.e., contingent upon God, and that the created order is filled and informed by God's *presence,* but not his being. As the objects of the soul's affection change, the medium through which God is contemplated changes as well. No longer does the soul meditate upon the material creation as evidence of God's activities,[39] but now the soul seeks to know God as the One who transcends the material creation. Thus the soul seeks a knowledge of God beyond the level allowed by language. Yet even this higher experience of God offers a very limited understanding that ultimately proves unsatisfying. Nyssen illustrates the point by contrasting our present experience of God with the face-to-face vision promised in 1 Corinthians 13.

Commenting on Moses' ascent of Mt. Horeb and his encounter with the burning bush, Nyssen observes that Moses was led up the mountain by the mysterious light of the unconsumed bush. This light, representing the grace by which God reveals himself, draws him, not into a face-to-face encounter with the Lord, but into an encounter only with God's voice.[40] Nyssen makes a similar observation when commenting on Song of Songs 5:2, where the bride hears the voice of the bridegroom at the door of her chamber entreating her to open and receive him. The bride, he observes, has gained that state of moral perfection necessary to be joined to the one who is perfectly holy. Yet even before she opens the door she is almost overpowered by the strength of his voice. This illustrates that even when one has achieved moral perfection, one still encounters God, not face to face, but in the mystery of his invisible voice. This side of the resurrection, the soul is capable of receiving only the voice of the bridegroom promising that he will eventually reveal himself. But when God fulfills his promise, Nyssen asserts, "he will be seen as has not yet been beheld by human eyes."[41] Two points should be noted. First, although the soul has gained moral perfection, it is not yet capable of receiving a revelation beyond the guidance of the Bridegroom's voice, i.e., the divine Logos. But second, Nyssen seems to be suggesting that the beauty of the Beloved when seen face to face far exceeds the beauty apprehended by the soul's experience of the divine voice. In other words, God's eschatological revelation is categorically different from the revelation that is afforded to the soul in the present age.

The voice of God that Moses encounters on the slopes of Mt. Horeb and that calls to the bride in her chamber represents in both cases the

limited view of God that we mortals can have this side of the eschaton.
Paradoxically, however, it also represents, for Nyssen, a truer way of
conceiving of God than when we, at a less mature stage of the Christian
life, conceived of God largely in corporeal terms. Indeed the theophanies
on Mt. Horeb and Mt. Sinai represent two distinct phases in the development of one's understanding of God's nature. On Mt. Horeb, Moses
encounters God in the form of light. By contrast, at Sinai's summit Moses
is enveloped in a thick cloud of smoke. Far from seeing the two metaphors as incompatible, Nyssen follows the tradition that views each as
reflecting different stages of one's encounter with God. The light of the
burning bush is the divine illumination that shows us the erroneous concepts about God that have heretofore dominated our thinking. Thus in
a sense we leave the darkness of theological error and enjoy the light
of proper knowledge of God as transcending the created order and the
world of the senses.[42] Yet having matured and become perfect in virtue
by the time he ascends Sinai, Moses encounters the divine voice speaking to him through the medium of a dark cloud. Clement of Alexandria
viewed Moses' encounter with God in the cloud as a sign that Moses
had come to recognize that God *kat'ousian* was remote and inaccessible
(*eis tas adytous*) to either the senses (*aeideis*) or the unaided intellect.[43]

Thus the dark cloud represents Moses' apophatic experience of God.
Although God is not properly speaking either darkness or a cloud, the
amorphous and indescribable character of a cloud more nearly corresponds to Paul's experience of being caught up into the third heaven
and encountering God, who spoke to him through unutterable words
(*arhrēta hrēmata*) that cannot be approximated by human language
(*ainissomenos*). Again Clement says that the bosom of God the Father,
which John says the Logos alone has beheld, is that invisible (*aopraton*)
and ineffable (*arhrēton*) repository (*bathyn*) that contains all things, yet
is inaccessible (*anephikton*) in its boundlessness (*aperanton*).[44] Similarly,
Nyssen explains that Moses' ascent to Sinai's summit far beyond the view
of the Israelites encamped in the valley below serves as a model for those
seeking friendship with God. In order to enjoy intimate association with
God, one must lift one's mind beyond all the material categories of form
and color, quantity and quality and accept that a true knowledge of God
is beyond the normal categories of human understanding.[45] Even as one
who enters a cloud becomes insensible to all dimensions and forms and
anything outside of the cloud's encompassing presence, so too the soul
must leave behind the categories of cognition and all attempts to make
comparison with all that is accessible to human nature. The soul, therefore, is left only to contemplate the invisible and incomprehensible.[46]

This is not to say that in the apophatic moment one experiences nothing. Quite to the contrary; for the bridegroom, who speaks to the bride from out of the darkness of night beyond the veil of the bridal chamber door, is perceived by the soul, not in a clear and distinct form readily apprehended by the intellect, but simply as an invisible but palpable presence.[47]

Although the apophatic is a higher form of the soul's contemplation of God, in this age the soul will never completely transcend the corporeal images to conceive of God. Gregory of Nazianzus observed that, while God is indeed incorporeal, unchanging, and incorruptible, these negative attributes do not reveal or contain God's essence. Moreover, in order for these attributes to be meaningful we need to have an adequately developed impression of the object to which to attribute these characteristics. The eager soul, he contends, will not be content to stop at simply enumerating what God is not; instead it desires to make some assertion about what God is.[48] This is why, Nazianzen says, we turn to Scripture. For although we speak of Scripture as containing absolute knowledge of God, in truth it has only relatively superior sources and is but only "a small effulgence from a greater light."[49]

Nyssen, commenting on the Song of Songs 5:2, shares the older bishop's view of Scripture. The kinsman who knocks at the door is Christ the incarnate Word; for as the Word who fully assumed our nature, the Logos is our kinsman as well as our Bridegroom. The door to the bridal chamber is a type for our "intuitive (*stochastikē*) understanding of things inexpressible."[50] This image of the kinsman knocking from without conveys the idea that the truth that the Word brings to us is only partial because it is external to our nature and thus provides only "hints" of the greater unseen glory. And the dew that falls from the kinsman's locks onto the bride represent the subtle and barely discernible knowledge of God that comes from the prophets, evangelists, and apostles who, like the locks of hair, absorb as much of "the dark, hidden, and invisible treasures," revealed by the Word's inspiration. Yet like Nazianzen, Nyssen remarks that although this knowledge is so partial as to be nothing more than dew drops in contrast with the potential flood of knowledge that awaits one in the kingdom, nevertheless, when compared with our scanty knowledge of God, these dew drops seem to deluge us with manifold and profound treasures.[51]

The soul's knowledge of God's positive attributes is derived from two sources. The first is God's activities, or *energeia*. Arguing from a doctrine of divine simplicity, Clement of Alexandria reasoned that as the eternal first principle God is indivisible, lacking parts (*merē*) or members into which he can be dissected and explained by being broken down into his constitutive parts. Moreover, as the One from whom all else derives its existence, God is unique and so cannot be categorized along the lines of genus and species. Since naming, in any scientific sense, entails a process of classifying a thing in accordance with the similarity and dissimilarity of its parts or features to other comparable creatures, God in his simplicity and uniqueness is without a knowable form (*aschēmatiston*) and so is without a name. Even titles such as One or Absolute Being or Father or God are not truly proper names for God. Rather they function as place holders that signify God and so enable us to have a clearer point of reference or object of reflection. But, while, each name by itself is not expressive of God's nature, taken altogether the sum (*hathroōs*) of the names indicates the truth of God's omnipotence.[52]

The Cappadocians, during the struggle with the Neo-Arians, who asserted that God could be named and that from these names he could be known in his essence,[53] expanded upon Clement's notion of God as unnamable. More importantly, they elaborated upon his notion that as a whole the names attributed to God in Scripture and philosophy denote God's omnipotence. Since God's manifold powers are manifest in his various activities or actions in the world, the Cappadocians contended that what is truly knowable about God, this side of the eschaton, is his *energeia*. Responding to the question, "Do we know the God whom we worship and adore," Basil explains to Amphilochus that the faith in God by which we gain salvation arises out of our encounter with God's activities. His greatness (*megaleiotēta*), power (*dynamis*), and pastoral providence (*tēn pronoian hēi epimeleitai hēmōn*) we have experienced; these we can claim to know. Although he descends to us and reveals his presence with us through his activities (*ek tōn energeiōn*), his essence (*hē ousia*) remains exalted, unapproachable, and wholly beyond our knowledge.[54] Nazianzen, without speaking of God's activities directly, asserts even more strongly that in mystical experiences, such as Moses' upon Sinai's summit or Paul's rapture into the third heaven, we encounter, not God's "unmingled nature," but only his back-parts. These back-parts are reflections or shadows of the transcendent cast upon the earth to accommodate the weakness and impurity of our soul, which cannot bear the full strength of the light of divine nature.[55]

Nyssen, in his explanation of Song of Songs 5:4, "My kinsman has put his hand through the opening [of the door]. My belly has cried out for him," relates the distinction between essence and activities to the effect upon us of the revelation of God's nature in the Incarnation. This is a curious passage. For the Bridegroom has come to the door of the bridal chamber to receive his bride; yet instead of opening the door, revealing himself, and fully embracing his bride, he continues to stand outside extending only his hand through a small window in the door. In the freedom of this speculative work of *theōria,* Nyssen gives two different yet related explanations for the Bridegroom's eccentric behavior. First, the bride sees no more of her beloved than his hand because, in spite of achieving moral perfection, all of her exertions and concentration of her mental faculties still afford her only a limited view of God. The hand of the Bridegroom that the bride glimpses obviously symbolizes the divine activity (*energeia*) that descends to us and that we discern in the world.[56]

The second possible significance of the passage plays on the first view of the workings of God in the cosmos. In the light of the Christ event, the hand might also represent the Father's agent of creation, the Word "by whom all things were made." At the Incarnation, the Word enters the world, represented by the bridal chamber, by "contracting itself" to circumscribed human nature. In the unique event of the Incarnation God's *energeia* is the grace of the Gospel.[57] It is interesting that Nyssen seems to make a distinction here between the hand as a type of God's *energeia,* namely, the power of grace that was manifest in the works of Christ, and the hand as a type of the agent or bearer of grace, the incarnate Christ himself. Just having equated the hand with the activities of God in the first interpretation, Nyssen appears reluctant to turn around and say that the hand also denotes Christ himself. The reason: he does not want to confuse epistemological claims about the Godhead with ontological claims about the incarnate Word. In other words, the point of the first interpretation of the hand coming through the door's window is that God's works, countless though they are, disclose only a small fraction of God's immensity. The point of the second interpretation is that God enters our world through the *kenōsis* of the Incarnation. When he shifts the allegory from a description of our knowledge of God through his work of creation to our knowledge of God through his self-revelation in Christ Jesus, Nyssen wants to avoid any suggestion that the one who comes to us is not "the one in whom the fullness of God was pleased to dwell" but only God in part.

Thus Nyssen makes the point that the hand of God in Incarnation is God contracted to the dimensions suitable for human apprehension. In his condensed form, Christ performs the works of grace that reveal the greatness of his power. He also makes a distinction between Christ of the Incarnation and Christ's glorious heavenly form, which he laid aside when he assumed our form. For he says that through God's activity among us as one of us, the Incarnate Christ draws our thoughts beyond the narrow confines of the bridal chamber to the world on the other side of the door. Here the door represents the vortex between this world and the transcendent heavenly realm where we shall encounter "the pure and immaterial beauty of the Bridegroom, of the Divinity of the Word, and of the radiance of true light." Thus for the sake of Nicene orthodoxy, Nyssen is careful to separate the Word as the *agent* of the divine *energeia* — the agent who is fully God — from the *work* Christ accomplished, which in no way is exhaustive of God's power or being. Consequently, he is explicit that, although the one who is revealed to us in the Incarnation is "true God from true God," his incarnate form does not reveal the beauty of his transcendent nature, which we shall behold in the eschaton. Therefore, the loveliness of Christ's grace revealed in his lowly, embodied form directs our thoughts beyond the corporeal world to consider the greater beauty of his incorporeal being. Thus Nyssen preserves a high Christology while at the same time asserting the highly limited character of our knowledge of God through the Incarnation. In other words, there is still a sense that the knowledge we have through the witness of Scripture or even that of the Apostles' direct face-to-face encounter with the Incarnate Lord is inferior to the immediate knowledge we shall gain from our eschatological union with the Godhead.

The highly limited character of our knowledge of God arises as much out of the finitude of our present constitution as it does from the mysterious and transcendent character of the divine nature. The bride sees only the hand of her beloved because the opening at the threshold of the bridal chamber is but a tiny hole. The bridal chamber does not simply correspond to the world that we inhabit, but more importantly the world of human thought and understanding. The small chamber represents the finite capacity of human cognition. As will be shown in chapter 5, Nyssen believes that the soul has the capacity for infinite growth so that it may grow in understanding and resemblance to the virtues of the God in whom it participates. Such growth at present is impeded by human sin and impurity, which are the principal causes of the intellect's finitude.

Yet Nyssen implies that there is a structural, as well as moral, impediment to the soul's apprehending God's greater beauty. Although by achieving moral perfection she has the power to open the door, i.e., "drawing back the veil of her heart...[and pulling] away from the door the veil of flesh," the door turns out to have but a tiny opening. Here Nyssen's point seems to be that even when we have attained the moral purity that enables us to transcend the limiting categories of the material world and conceive of God in incorporeal terms, still the finitude of our nature and our categories through which we contemplate the Divine provide only the smallest of apertures through which we may apprehend God. Nyssen is even more understated in this passage than in his earlier comment about the dew falling from the Bridegroom's locks. In that text, the dew, representing the knowledge of God via the prophets and the apostles, seems to us to contain vast information about God but in reality represents only the droplets of an infinitely greater reservoir of knowledge. Here, however, Nyssen says that from our encounter with God's *energeia* we know only that these are the words of our Beloved, whom we long to know more profoundly.[58]

By placing responsibility for our very limited knowledge of God on the inability of our *present* finite nature and condition to receive the vastness and complexity of God's transcendent otherness, Nyssen creates the possibility that the eschatological transformation of human nature will equip us with a newfound capacity of apprehending God barely imaginable in our present situation. Commenting on the soul's ascent to God in this life, Basil articulates the premise that will guide the Cappadocian conception of the condition for the soul's union with God in the life to come. When the intellect is "tempered with the divinity of the spirit," the mind turns from its dialectical inquiry, and the scope of its speculations (*tōn megalōn theorēmatō*) is elevated so as to apprehend the beauty of divine truth. Such contemplative ascent is enabled by two conditions: first, the empowerment of grace (*hoson hē charis endidōsi*), and second the constitution of the intellect (*hē kataskeuē autou*).[59] Although the recognition of God is derived from a purely gracious act of self-disclosure by the Holy Spirit and so not automatically the result of the intellect's having attained a certain level of purity, Basil suggests that the very Spirit that raises up the intellect to gain a clearer glimpse of the Divine has already been at work transforming the intellect in preparation for a profounder and more intimate knowledge of God.[60]

This transformative work of the Spirit is divinization for the Cappadocians. For Gregory of Nazianzus, the consummation of this divinizing process is achieved only in the eschaton.[61] Trying to explain Paul's enigmatic words from 1 Corinthians 13, "Now we see as through a glass dimly, but then ... we shall know even as we are known," Nazianzen says that while God's nature and essence have remained beyond discovery in the present age, in the age to come such a discovery will be within our reach. We will know God as we are known, that is, immediately, because that godlike feature of out nature, i.e., our intellect, shall have ascended to its archetype, the Word, and so is "mingled with" that source of all reason and wisdom.[62] Here Nazianzen places primacy on elevation of the soul as the source of that participation whereby we are able to achieve a far higher degree of illumination than is possible with our present degree of participation in the divine Logos.

Nyssen concurs with both Basil and Nazianzen. Our eschatological knowledge of God, he contends, will be radically different from our knowledge because of the transformation of human nature and of the world that we will inhabit. In the present age we know God through his creative activities manifest in the material universe that surrounds us. But once heaven and earth pass away, he observes, we will be transported from the realm of appearances to that realm that transcends sight and sound. Then we shall no longer conceive of God with inadequate corporeal analogies; rather we shall apprehend God's "ineffable blessedness" in a way beyond our present capacity of verbal representation. The principal reason for our inability to apprehend God's sublime nature is that at present we cannot "receive within ourselves the infinite and uncircumscribed nature."[63] Here is Nyssen's strongest statement to the effect that the character of the soul's encounter with God in the age to come will be qualitatively and quantitatively different. For all the vagueness with which he speaks of the character of the soul's perception of God in the age to come, he is clear that our encounter with God in the present age and that of the age to come are so unlike each other as to be beyond comparison.

In summary, the Cappadocians maintain that our eschatological contemplative participation in God's goodness is radically distinct from our present experience of contemplation in two significant ways. First, the soul's apprehension of the beatific vision is *immediate* and *uninterrupted*. In other words, though Paul exhorts us to "pray without ceasing," the soul's present contemplation of God is often thwarted by competing impulses arising out of the nonrational orientation of the vegetative soul to the needs of the body. Moreover, unlike the present age, where our knowledge of God is mediated by the text of Scripture, in the eschaton God will reveal himself more directly. How God can be the constant object of the mind's meditation will be discussed in chapter eight.

Second, he asserts that God will appear to us in a vision of such unprecedented glory that the soul will not turn from its contemplation of such magnetic splendor. This being the case, the present contemplative life and our experience of *koros* can in no way serve as an analogue for the soul's future contemplation of the beatific vision. However, this twofold assault upon Origen does not by itself eliminate the problem of satiation. For one might counter by saying that the intellect could still become satiated with or inured even to a maximally delightful object of contemplation if, as Otis's reading of Origen suggests, God's power is finite. For even the wonder of God's enormous, though still finite, power when contemplated over an infinite span of time eventually becomes fully known and understood and so ceases to hold the intellect's interest. When the intellect has gained true mastery of a subject and has answered all questions, its interest wanes. As intellectual curiosity is satisfied, the intellectual passion cools as well, and the mind wanders to new objects of exploration. On the other hand, if satiation stems from the finite soul's inability to "take in" the beatific vision, then the soul is overwhelmed by this unprecedented vision of God's glory.

Nyssen's solution to the problem of satiation, therefore, must isolate some property of the divine nature and beauty that by its very nature would be able to sustain the interest of the rational soul over the course of eternal contemplation. And he must explain how finite creatures can participate in the divine nature without being overpowered by God's mystery and beauty to the point of saturation. In other words, Nyssen is confronted with two challenges, one theological and the other anthropological. His theory of epectasy, I will argue, addresses both of these problems. In the next chapter I will examine the theological presumptions of epectasy that provide a partial solution to the view of satiation developed by Otis. I will also consider the anthropological foundation of epectasy as I explore his theory of the soul's capacity for infinite development and his understanding of how the participation of human nature so transforms our faculties as to enable the soul a degree of participation in the Divine.

CHAPTER FIVE

The Infinitely Wondrous Being of God and the Eternal Becoming of Humanity

In our earlier examination of the problem of the passions, we saw that the Cappadocians embraced an ascetic piety in order to reorient the soul's desire from the mundane things of this life to the eternal goods of God. At the same time that the discipline of self-denial breaks the desire that binds us to the material world, Nyssen maintains, asceticism allows us to enjoy the contemplative life in the present as a foretaste of our contemplative union with God in the eschaton. In other words, the angelic life is not a wholly future reality, but one in which we participate now. In Nyssen's eyes, Macrina's life of contemplative service enabled her to transcend her present human nature, becoming almost angelic. The ascetic life of detachment from the cares of worldly excess allows the Christian to enjoy proleptic participation in and enjoyment of the blessedness that is humanity's eschatological destiny. Yet, as we saw in the previous chapter, Nyssen and the other Cappadocians were conscious that the present age should never and can never be confused with the age to come. However much the Christian may strive to order her life according to the life that awaits her, she can never in this life fully transcend her mortal nature and put on the incorruption of the resurrection. For in the resurrection, our participation in God shall be radically different than it is now. The divine object of our vision and desire shall be immediately and vividly present to the soul. It is a contemplative participation characterized by epectasy, the soul's eternal movement into God.

Thus Nyssen concluded that one should not assume, as Origen did, that our heavenly contemplation of God is so similar to our contemplation in this life that it contains even the possibility of our satiation with God. Yet, if Nyssen's theory of epectasy is to prove definitive in its answer to the problem of satiation, Nyssen must explain how such an eternal movement into God is possible. In this chapter, we shall examine

Nyssen's understanding of both the God in whom the soul participates and the soul that is eternally growing into the likeness of God. What is the characteristic of the divine nature that makes it eternally interesting and eternally desirable? Why could the soul never grow bored with God? How can the soul's love for God "grow" eternally? To answer these questions, this chapter must lay out the theological and anthropological foundations of Nyssen's theory of epectasy.

In the first part of this chapter I will argue that Nyssen's solution to the problem of satiation begins with his understanding of God as infinite. God shall be for the soul eternally wondrous and awe-inspiring because God in his infinite nature is incomprehensible and yet still accessible to the soul through God's self-disclosure in the distinct persons of the Trinity. Then in the second part, I will examine how Nyssen's account of the soul's relationship with the body illustrates his view of the rational soul as having the capacity for infinite growth or eternally becoming like God.

The Nature of the Infinite

Nyssen's understanding of God as infinite (*apeiron*) was not altogether groundbreaking but nevertheless marked a development in classical theism. Prior to Plotinus, the terms infinite (*apeiron*) or indefinite (*aoriston*) were not used as primary attributes of the Divine. Anaximander, the Miletian philosopher of the sixth century B.C., said that the First Principle was The Unlimited because it was quantitatively inexhaustible, being the source of unlimited potentialities and thus not reducible to any one element such as air or water. Although Aristotle speaks of Anaximander's Unlimited as the Divine,[1] there is nothing transcendent about the Unlimited. For it is the corporeal principle from which all things come and into which all things are resolved.[2] For Aristotle, *apeiria* and *aoristia* are applied to quantities, such as time, space, and distance, and absolute potency as proper to prime matter. Given infinite space and infinite time, an object's movement can be infinite.[3] Moreover, since being is thought of in terms of action the movements of which have a particular form, that which is actualized has form and therefore limit. That which is pure potentiality is wholly without form and therefore is without limit (*apeiron*).[4] Aristotle does not, however, say that God, the Prime Mover, is infinite. Since the Prime Mover is perfect, it is fully actualized and thus has definite form. But Aristotle does say that God's *power* is infinite, meaning that the first mover has the power to cause motion that is temporally unlimited. When we turn to the theology of Neoplatonism, Plotinus's God, the One, is describe as being infinite.

Plotinus, like Aristotle, ascribes to the divine One infinite power since the One is the cause of an infinite possibility of effects.[5] Yet Plotinus pushes beyond Aristotle. The One is the source of all things and yet is not any one of them nor is it the sum of all beings.[6] It is the condition of all things yet is itself unconditioned by anything external. Thus the One cannot be said to have form that would condition the nature of the One. In other words, although the One is simple and itself lacks from, it is the source of all forms. Since form gives being or essence to a thing distinguishing it from other beings, the One must be devoid of any formal determination and so transcends being.[7] Consequently the formless One is infinite in that it is uncircumcised.[8] Moreover, for Plotinus, in contrast to Aristotle, the One's transcendence of form and being is a mark of the One's perfection. For only by transcending form and being can the One be the source of all beings. Thus Plotinus's theology was radically innovative. Divine perfection was not to be equated with ideal form (à la Plato's The Good) or with fully actualized being (à la Aristotle's Prime Mover), but with divine transcendence, unity, and simplicity, which are necessary for the One's infinitely productive power.

The description of the One as infinite also has implications for Plotinus's understanding of the rational soul's love of the One. Since God is infinite and simple, God cannot be loved in the same way that the soul loves objects possessing form. Since the One is without form it cannot properly be the object of the mind's contemplation as long as the mind thinks about the divine Beauty in material and formal terms. Proper contemplation of the One entails the mind's transcendence of the realm of being and form. It is an apophatic ascent. Likewise, the soul's love of the One must be an apophatic love that transcends the love of beautiful form. Although the mind's inward turn begins with an appreciation of the beautiful form of material things which turns the mind toward the consideration of the beauty of the rational soul,[9] the soul is able to love the One precisely because the One communicates its love for the rational soul. We are drawn to the One by the beauty of the One's love for us. The glory of the One is a beauty beyond beauty for it is the source of beauty in all things.

Since the beauty of a particular thing is constituted by its particular form, the source of all beautiful things cannot have a particular shape. Otherwise it would not be universal beauty but a particular instantiation of beauty. Therefore the Beautiful must be itself a formless beauty.[10] The love of this formless One grows only when our love turns from particular beautiful objects apprehended by the senses toward that beauty which is beyond both sense and understanding.[11] How the soul can love formless beauty is, Plotinus acknowledges, beyond our understanding. The key insight at which Plotinus arrives is that the rational soul's love of the One corresponds to the nature of the One who communicated to the soul its love for us. The implication of this insight is that the soul's love of the infinite One is itself an infinite love.[12]

The beauty of an object lies in its form, and the love of that beauty is inherently limited even as the beauty of the object is limited. In other words, love for finite objects of beauty is itself limited because the love corresponds only to the specific form that is inherent in the finite object. For example, Plotinus would say that one's love of the splendor of a sunset over the Grand Canyon is limited because the beauty of that sunset is a form of visible beauty, but not a form of beauty associated with the sense of touch or taste or sound. Thus the soul's love of the sunset is limited to the sphere of visual beauty. And the same would be true of one's love of Handel's *Royal Fireworks,* which has a beauty confined to the sphere of sound. Likewise, justice has a beauty that belongs exclusively to the sphere of moral beauty. All of these instances of beauty are limited expressions or forms of beauty. By contrast, the beauty of the One transcends all particular forms of beauty; yet as the source of all beauty, it encompasses all forms of beauty.[13] Thus the beauty of the One is unlimited and consequently the soul's love for that transcendent beauty is unlimited.[14] Moreover, Plotinus suggests that there is something in the apophatic nature of the soul's experience of the One that makes the soul's desire for the One infinite. Because the One cannot be fully grasped by the mind, its goodness and beauty are elusive. The elusive character of the One's beauty makes it more desirable to the soul. Consequently, the soul's love is infinite in the sense that it is ever desiring the elusive One.

Among Christian thinkers, Nyssen was hardly the first to speak of God as "infinite" (*apeiron*). Clement of Alexandria derived his understanding of God as infinite from his theory of divine simplicity. Having argued that God, as the First Principle, is utterly unique and therefore beyond classification in terms of *genus* and *differentia,* he concludes that God cannot be known in the way that things of the created order are known. As the Father of all things (*tōn holōn patēr*) whose greatness necessarily exceeds and envelops his creation, God is called the All (*to holon*). Yet paradoxically the All is also called the One (*to hen*) because, having no constitutive parts, God is not divisible (*adiaireton*). Such simplicity, Clement asserts, necessarily implies that God is also infinite, being without dimensions (*adiastaton*) or limits (*mē echon peras*) by which he might be circumscribed in place and time.[15] Although Clement's appellation "the All" risks blurring the line between Creator and creation, the important point is that God's simplicity necessitates God's being infinite. For that which is utterly simple, according to Clement, lacks both components, by which God might be classified and given a name, and form, which presupposes some substance made to conform to certain dimensions of height, width, and depth. Since, however, God is incorporeal, he is composed of no material substance that might be circumscribed. Thus by virtue of his lacking dimension, God is unbounded or infinite.

Nazianzen makes this point explicitly. Form and limit are attributes of bodies. Were God corporeal, he would cease to be eternal and impassible. For every body is circumscribed and has form because it is composed of elements into which it may be — and always is — broken down. The capacity for division and fragmentation is the source of the strife and dissolution. Had God such limitations he would not be worthy of worship.[16] Being incorporeal, God possesses no material substance upon which limits may be imposed. Therefore, God's spiritual nature knows no limits. Nyssen makes a slightly different argument but to the same effect that God's incorporeal nature precludes the possibility that God can be delimited. Were God not infinite, he would necessarily be enclosed by something, just as the sea which surrounds the fish is itself surrounded by land. Moreover, since that which surrounds a thing controls or determines the character of that which it envelops, a circumscribed God would be ruled by that other which surrounds him.[17] The logic of his point is that even as the sea is in some sense prior to the fish which depend on the sea for survival, so too that other entity that enveloped God would in some sense be logically prior to God. Consequently, God would be dependent upon that which contained him. Were God surrounded by something he would cease to be in any ultimate sense the one "in whom we live, in whom we move, and in whom we have our being"; for he himself would live and move and have his being in some other thing. That which enclosed God would be God's environment on which God would be dependent.[18]

The doctrine of divine simplicity proved problematic for the Cappadocians and their defense of the Nicene doctrine of the consubstantiality of the Father and the Son. How can a thoroughly simple God be a trinity? Curiously though, Eunomius opens his position to attack by claiming that the Father, Son, and Spirit are necessarily distinct from one another because the *ousia* of each is "unmixed, simple [*aplēs*], and absolutely one."[19] Each is distinguished from the other by differing activities that follow from their distinct beings. These activities establish an ontological hierarchy between the beings. Nyssen responds that it is appropriate to make a clear ontological distinction between the persons in order to avoid the error of Sabellius's nominal distinction of Father, Son, and Spirit as but modes of God's self-revelation.[20] Seizing upon Eunomius's description of the persons as "simple" or "single," Nyssen argues that there cannot be three beings that are utterly simple and yet can be ordered hierarchically. His reasoning is this: beings can be ordered in a hierarchy only when there is some deficiency in one being which makes it less in some way than another being. One being can be inferior to another being because it is lacking in size or wisdom or goodness or power. Yet the divine nature, which transcends all thought, is simple and therefore is without form or shape or size.[21] Therefore the simple nature of the persons of the Trinity cannot be differentiated one from another by degree of difference.[22] Moreover, borrowing from Plotinus's doctrine of divine simplicity, which equates simplicity and infinity with the absolute aseity of the One, Nyssen argues that what is simple does not derive its qualities from any source. In other words, for Plotinus the One, as "the unconditioned condition," is wholly autonomous and self-sufficient. Since the One is not conditioned by anything external to it nor is it reducible to any set of parts or limited by form or external boundary, it is, therefore, simple and infinite.

Such simplicity is necessarily a sign of the One's perfection. Likewise, for Nyssen, God's nature is simple and infinite in that it is neither derivative nor circumscribed. Nor is there a limit to its goodness and wisdom.[23] Therefore, the divine nature does not possess wisdom or goodness by virtue of participation in some other source. Rather it simply is good and wise. Since simplicity and infinity imply self-sufficiency, therefore, Nyssen reasons, if Eunomius admits that Father, Son, and Spirit are simple, then their being is identical with their goodness and wisdom. That is to say, if each is simple then each must be infinite; and therefore each is self-sufficient and perfect. If a being is simple and infinite, it cannot experience any diminution.[24] Since, however, there can be no deficiency in that which is perfect, infinite, and simple, there can be no difference whereby one is deemed superior and another inferior.[25] Consequently, Eunomius cannot claim that Father, Son, and Spirit are separate simple and infinite beings whose activities reflect a hierarchy between them. There can be only one simple and infinite being, not three. Thus the Father, Son, and Spirit, being consubstantial, are infinite in goodness, power, and wisdom and so cannot be separated hierarchically.

An important corollary to divine infinity is Nyssen's conception of temporal interval or spatial extension (*diastēma*).[26] *Diastēma* gained great theological currency during the Arian controversy. One of the theological slogans employed by the Arians was "there once was when he [i.e., the Logos] was not." This formula denied that the Logos was eternal. Arius's opponents countered that there was *diastēma* within the Godhead. That is, there is no interval or gap when the Father was alone prior to the generation of the Son and the procession of the Holy Spirit.[27] Out of this dispute about the Trinity, the term *diastēma* came to be one of the signposts distinguishing the creature from the Creator. Contrasting the uncreated divine nature and all created natures, Nyssen comments, "Vast and insurmountable is the gap by which the uncreated nature is separated from the created nature. The latter is circumscribed; the former has no end point [*peras*] . . . [and] infinity [*apeiria*] is its boundary. The latter stretches itself out along intervals [*diastēmatikē*] and works in time and space; the former transcends all known intervals [*diastēmatos*]."[28]

Since God is infinite and eternal Being, there can be no interval in God's being. There can be no "time" when God is one thing before he is something else. An interval is a moment within the process of becoming; but God eternally is. Because uncreated nature is infinite, there is no deficiency in God in need of being filled. Therefore, the divine nature need not be moved in order to become something else. Created natures, by contrast, are bounded by time and space. They come into existence in time and move toward an end. This movement is measured by intervals of becoming, i.e., changing by degrees from what it is in its beginning to what it shall be at its end. God, however, is immediately and eternally what he is. Unlike the Father's generation of the Son, which entails no interval, *diastēma* is a necessary mark of creation of the world since the world itself has not always been but has a set beginning point.[29]

Nyssen's use of *diastēma* to establish an absolute boundary between the transcendent God and creation is a break with the monism of Neoplatonism. Plotinus's cosmology does not have room for a theory of creation in the Judeo-Christian sense. There is moment in which the Divine fashions a world that is ontologically distinct from himself. On the contrary, according to his theory of emanation, all things that come from the One are but eternal reflections of the One. Insisting that the eternal One is unmoved and unmoving, Plotinus says that the One generates the cosmos by neither an act of will (*boulēthentos*) or of inclination (*prosneusantos*), but in a manner analogous to the way that sun radiates the light that forever surrounds it. "How did it [i.e., the cosmos] come to be then," he asks, "and what are we to think of as surrounding the One in its repose? It must be a radiation from it while it remains unchanged, like the bright light of the sun which, so to speak, runs round it, springing from it continually while it remains unchanged."[30]

Since the cosmos is simply an eternal projection or extension of the One, there is no temporal interval separating the One and the world: "the One and the cosmos are totally continuous."[31] For Nyssen, however, the world is not a hypostasis of God, but is something other than God created by God. Far from being eternal, the world came into being; unlike the Plotinian cosmos, there was a time when the world was not. Thus *diastēma* denotes for Nyssen the divide between God, who is eternal, infinite, and necessary Being, from creation, which is finite and contingent becoming. Here we see Nyssen's contribution to the subject of divine infinity. While he and Plotinus insist that God himself, and not simply God's power, is infinite, Nyssen breaks with Plotinus in two respects. First, the infinite God is not beyond being (à la Plotinus), but as the great "I AM" God is infinite Being. Second, Nyssen derives a distinctly Christian conception of *diastēma* from the Plotinian concept of divine infinity in order to be faithful to the depiction of God in Exodus as supreme Being yet at the same time as transcendent Being. Thus from God's infinity, Nyssen articulates an account of the Creator-creature distinction central to Christian thought.

Nyssen builds upon this ontological foundation in his account of the infinite character of God's moral attributes and of the soul's participation in God. In the preface to *The Life of Moses*, Nyssen argues from God's perfection to the infinite character of God's virtue. The perfection (*hē teleiotēs*) of corporeal beings, he says, is generally conceived in static terms that suggest some boundary or limit determined by its beginning and its end.[32] Presumably, the static model of perfection Nyssen has in mind is Aristotle's. According to Aristotle, a thing is said to be perfect when its potentiality is fully actualized. When perfection is achieved, all motion ceases; for it no longer has any unfulfilled potential. For it no longer has any unfulfilled potential. This static notion of perfection is reflected in Aristotle's theory of motion.[33] When an object such as a rock has reached its proper place in the universe, its movement ceases and the object is at rest.[34] There is no further movement because there is no need to move. Following the axiom that like is attracted to like, Aristotle explains that an object comes to rest because it is united with those things of like nature. There is no other group of like objects to which an object is attracted. Thus the end, or *telos*, establishes an ultimate boundary for an object's movement. Beyond that locus, nothing more can be gained.

For Nyssen, the term "perfection" when applied to virtue, however, takes on a very different character. In the Platonist tradition, all virtue is derived from participation in the Good; therefore, moral perfection implies conforming to the Good. That is, possessing all the qualities proper to the Good. Yet since the Good is incorporeal, its limits can be thought of only in terms of its opposite, as one might say of light bounded by darkness. But the Good contains within its nature nothing which is contradictory to its essence. For the only limit to virtue is its opposite, evil. Since the divine nature admits no alloy with evil, God's goodness is without limits.[35]

The Cappadocians recognized that the theological view that God is infinite had significant implications for how we understand the soul's participation in an ultimate union with God — implications that seriously undermined Origen's hypothesis about the soul's satiation. Initially, the Cappadocians realized that, as the One who is infinite Being, God is beyond our comprehension. Nazianzen observes that, although the intellect can reason back from the visible creation to the existence of its invisible creator,[36] it is unable either to apprehend or accurately conceptualize the nature of the Creator. Even allowing for the distinction between God's unknowable essence (*ousia*) and his goodness perceptible in his activities (*energeia*), Nazianzen implies that at either level the divine nature proves unfathomable because it is infinite. Were God finite, he could be comprehended. For "comprehending," Nazianzen says, is a form of circumscribing the object with the powers or categories of the intellect. Since, however, God is an infinite being, he is beyond our complete understanding.[37] For as far as the mind penetrates the boundless Divine, it will never reach a point at which it can grasp God in God's totality. This is the critical point from which the Cappadocian refutation of Origen's theory of satiation begins. Origen had suggested that falling away from God was analogous to a doctor who having learned all there is to know about his specialty fails to continue studying and so loses his mastery of the subject. The implication is that the intellect's boredom comes when the intellect has so thoroughly studied God's nature that there is no new knowledge to again; and so the intellect loses interest in God.

This at any rate is Otis's reading of Origen. Since, however, God is infinite in nature, he is an inexhaustible source of new knowledge. God will always be revealing further partial knowledge of himself, which both satisfies the soul and yet arouses further longing for him. Thus the Cappadocians' insight solves the problem of satiation at two levels. On one hand, if satiation is the product of God's finitude as Otis's reading of

Origen suggests, the claim that God is infinite eliminates the principal cause of satiation. On the other hand, if satiation is the result of the inability of finite, created intellects to understand the Divine, then God's accommodation of our finite minds' limited capacity for apprehension overcomes the problem of satiation. The paradox that God is both incomprehensible and yet at the same time can be apprehended reflects the relationship between the immanent and the economic Trinity in Nyssen's theology. God who is in essence one and therefore incomprehensible becomes knowable because he exists in three distinct modes of being by which he reveals himself to human beings. Because the divine being revealed in the persons of the Trinity is, by virtue of its simplicity, infinite, the content of God's self-disclosure is also infinite. Therefore, the divine nature is the bottomless wellspring of virtues that are the cause of the soul's insatiable wonder and desire. This point Nyssen develops more fully in his eleventh homily on the Song of Songs.

The central thesis of these homilies is that although the soul's eschatological apprehension of God's goodness will be far clearer than it is now, nevertheless we, like Moses, will never behold the full face of God. As shown above, our situation at present is at best analogous to that of the eager bride who knows only the disembodied voice of her beloved. Our clearest knowledge of God comes primarily from the word of Scripture, which affords us only a sense of the far greater goodness of God's nature that is concealed in mystery. Thus our present knowledge of God's activities related in the testimony of Scripture give us such a fragmented glimpse of God's great goodness that it serves only to awaken in us desire and hope for the greater vision to come. Nyssen illustrates the contrast between our imperfect vision of God now and our fuller vision in the age to come by comparing the bridegroom's partial self-disclosure to the fountain of limitless water (Gen. 2:6), which in the antediluvian age irrigated the whole earth. Looking at the spring from above ground, one could claim indeed to have seen the water and in some sense to have knowledge of the spring. Yet one could not claim to have seen all the water since much is still concealed in its subterranean aquifers. Even if one were to watch the upwelling of the spring for a long time, one would be just beginning to contemplate the water that gushes forth in a never ending flow. Similarly, Gregory says, when one contemplates the divine beauty that is infinite (*aoriston kallos*), one is always seeing things that are yet newer (*kainoteron*) and more surprising (*paradoxoteron*).[38]

This passage from his *Commentary on the Song of Songs* marks Nyssen's refinement of his account of the soul's participation in God's infinite nature—an account that refutes either of the two possible readings of Origen's satiation theory. First, Nyssen recognizes that it is not enough for God's goodness to be infinite in order to be eternally interesting and attractive; it must also appear infinitely *new* and *fresh* to the contemplating subject. God's infinite nature does not in and of itself preclude the possibility of the soul's becoming bored. Since, as Clement contends, divine infinity is a necessary corollary of divine simplicity, an infinitely simple nature might create the condition by which the soul might become tired of contemplating God.[39]

Perhaps God's infinite simplicity is best illustrated by the cloud that enveloped Moses atop Sinai. To be sure, the dark cloud on Sinai represents to the fathers, including Nyssen, the mystery of the divine nature that utterly transcends the categories of the senses. But the cloud is also an apt model for God's utter simplicity, for being undifferentiated by variation in color, components, dimension, or shape, the cloud possesses that uniformity approximating that which is truly simple. Yet such uniformity, even of pure and absolute goodness, is static. In order to stave off the intellectual entropy of boredom, the soul must be engaged dynamically with its object of contemplation. In other words, as the soul moves into the utterly simple God, as through a thick cloud, which is infinitely the same for all eternity, the soul might easily become bored. For a perfectly simple God is exactly the same to the contemplating intellect in the first moment of contemplation as it will be in every subsequent moment. Even maximal goodness or blessedness, which lacks variation or development, could become the source of boredom. Nyssen solves this objection by arguing that the soul's contemplative participation in God's boundless goodness will not reach a point of satiation because the infinite beauty that God discloses to the soul is not the same thing over and over. Rather God's beauty appears to the soul in an ever new (*kainoteron*) and ever more curious and captivating (*paradoxoteron*) form.[40] This is the first essential qualification Nyssen makes with respect to God's infinite being. God's goodness seizes and holds the attention of the contemplative soul for all eternity because it is *eternally novel*. In other words, as Clement's All, God's beauty is not static but contains an infinite array of forms of beauty that match God's infinite activities, both actual and potential. Thus the soul's movement into God's goodness is sustained by its eternal encounter with new qualities or aspects of God's nature that will forever provoke new curiosity.

The second nuance that Nyssen adds to the idea of God as "the Infinite" is that God's goodness and beauty will appear progressively more desirable with each successive revelation. Nyssen repeatedly employs the

comparative form of the adjective to describe the soul's experience of
God's infinite novelty. With each new vision of God's splendor, the soul
beholds, not simply a new dimension or quality of God's goodness, but a
facet of the divine nature that proves more curious (*paradoxoteron*) and
more awe-inspiring (*megaloprepesteron*) than the one before it.[41] The
eternally novel manifestations of God's beauty that the soul will apprehend arrest the soul's interest because each new revelation of the Good
is *progressively* more beautiful and therefore ever more attractive and
desirable.

Gregory's account of God's ever unfolding revelation of his infinite
goodness and glory in ever new and more spectacular visions establishes
a dynamic relationship between the soul and God — a dynamic that
explains how the soul's eternal participation in God's infinite being can
be conceived as an unending journey of insatiable intellectual fascination.
Gregory's discussion of God's limitless beauty in his homilies on the
Song of Songs and his account of God's boundless and inexhaustible
perfection in *The Life of Moses* are not unrelated. For God's beauty
(*kalos*), according to Nyssen, is a predicate of God's virtue (*aretē*).[42]
Even as the Good and the Beautiful are identical for Plato, so too are
they for Nyssen. Since, therefore, the divine beauty is identical to God's
infinite and perfect goodness, God's beauty is infinitely splendid as well.
Thus as the soul participates in God's goodness by contemplation and
imitation, the attraction of God's great beneficence is ever fresh and new
to the soul. The infinite glory of God's virtues, like the eternal wellspring
of Eden, cannot become stagnant to the mind inasmuch as it provides
the mind with every new marvel for the intellect's consideration.

Nyssen explains then how God's infinite goodness and beauty draw
the soul into a perpetual participation in the divine by depicting our
intellectual contemplation of God as motivated by an aesthetic attraction to and desire for God. This enables Nyssen to described the soul's
penetration of the divine mystery in terms of the dynamic between the
appetitive and intellectual faculties of the soul described in *On the Making of Man* and *On the Soul and the Resurrection*. Desire (*epithymia*),
as we saw earlier, is the principle of movement in the soul. It is desire
which rouses the soul from the lethargy of its present contentment and
satiety, setting the person moving toward some goal. The unfolding of
God's endless goodness presents to the soul new and ever more enticing
stimuli that perpetually arouse the appetitive faculty to desire God all the
more. Consequently, the eternally new and progressively more splendid
theophanies that endlessly stimulate the soul's highest appetites keep it
in a state of perpetual motion.

For this reason in his *Homilies on the Song of Songs,* Nyssen speaks of the soul's desire (*epithymia*) as being limitless. As the soul loves the object of its contemplation, it changes and expands in response to each encounter with some new facet of God's beauty. Moreover, since the more the soul experiences a new source of amazement as it moves further into the Divine, the soul actually anticipates the beauty that is yet to be unfolded. The soul proves insatiable in its desire (*oudepote . . . histatai tēs tou idein epithymias*) for the more splendid (*megaloprepesteron*) visions lying deeper within the Divine (*Theioteron*). Therefore, Nyssen concludes that the soul's present amazement (*aei thaumazousa*) and wonder (*ekplēttomenē*), like the bride hearing her beloved's voice, eternally stimulate the soul's speculative curiosity (*oudepote . . . histēsi tou theōroumenou*).[43] In this way, the beauty of God's goodness has the effect of attracting or drawing the soul to communion with the Divine.

By expressing the soul's unquenchable attraction to the divine beauty in terms of both the soul's appetitive reaction (*epithymia*) and its intellectual reaction (*theōria*), Gregory provides a solution to the problem of satiation in two ways. First, because God's nature is infinite, the soul will never come to a point when it has so comprehended the Divine that all its questions have been answered. Second, because the infinite goodness of God's being eternally presents itself to the soul, not in a single vision, but in an eternal succession of visions each more awesome than the last, God's infinite beauty never ceases to evoke wonder and love. Since God's beauty is boundless, the soul's desire itself has no stopping place but extends eternally outward.[44] This never-ending cycle of questioning and exploration is an expression of the soul's intellectual desire for the intelligible goods of God. The eternal novelty of God's self-disclosure, Nyssen claims, has the paradoxical effect of filling the soul to capacity yet leaving it desiring more.

This paradox Nyssen develops in *The Life of Moses,* where he comments upon Moses' ascent to Sinai's summit. Although Moses by virtue of his striving and straining to participate in the good (represented by all his activities in Egypt and during his sojourn in the wilderness) made much progress and became great (*aei meizō*), he did not grow complacent (*mēdamou histasthai*) but kept on climbing.[45] Although these many experiences, including his encounter with God in the cloud on Sinai, served to fill him as far as was allowed him (*dia pantos kat'exousian enephoreito*), they nevertheless left him as strong in his desire for the good as if he had never partaken (*hōs mēpō meteschēkos tychein deetai*) of God's goodness.[46] This explains his seemingly presumptuous request to be shown God's glory. Nyssen's conclusion is that the soul's desire, which initiated its ascent to God, far from being satisfied by its vision of the Divine, actually expands in proportion to its progress (*synepketeinetai*) into the divine mystery.[47]

The perpetual movement of the intellect will always follow a dialectic between wonder and curiosity. It is an immersion in the immediate and yet the eye of the soul is ever looking ahead in hopeful anticipation. That is, the wonder of the immediate vision of God's beauty is the source of the highest degree of blessedness the soul has thus far experienced. Yet since the latest vision has surpassed all previous visions in beauty and blessedness, the soul's desire is stirred by the confident expectation of even greater blessedness. Commenting on the impetus behind Moses' steady and unwavering ascent of Sinai, Nyssen finds the explanation in Moses' hope of seeing greater beauty. "Hope ever draws [the soul] from the beauty which is seen to that which lies beyond [*pros to hyperkeimenon*] [our immediate vision], through that which is always perceived [hope] ever kindles the desire for that which is hidden [*pros to kekrymmenon*]."[48] Nyssen's vague reference to "that which lies beyond" and "that which is hidden" has two layers of meaning. Since in *The Life of Moses* he is speaking about the soul's earthly journey to God, the object of desire is that which is beyond the realm of the senses, i.e., the intelligible and heavenly realm that are imperfectly mirrored in the created world. Yet in the context of a doctrine of epectasy, this statement conveys a more general principle that in God's infinite being the soul expects to receive even greater visions of God's wonderful goodness.

Nyssen's aesthetic language and the corresponding language of aroused desire has an erotic element from which one could mistakenly assume that he urges on the struggling Christian with a spiritually hedonistic vision of heaven. Yet one must remember that, although Nyssen uses an erotic motif to describe the dynamic motivating the soul's ascent to God, the divine beauty that affords the soul maximal blessedness corresponds with God's *agapē*. Because the goods that constitute God's *aretē* are intelligible goods, the wonder that excites the soul's desire corresponds to an intellectual fascination manifest in its contemplative questioning and experiencing of the divine. This is certainly conveyed by Nyssen's description of the soul's desire for the good as arising out of its ceaseless amazement (*aei thaumazousa*) and wonder (*ekplēttomenē*) at the divine beauty that is simultaneously curious (*paradoxoteron*) and awesome (*megaloprepesteron*).[49] Nyssen's language of ever-expanding intellectual desire is evocative of two images. First, the soul's desire for God can be imagined as the beam of an infinitely strong flashlight lying at the fringe of an infinitely long and wide piece of black construction paper. The flashlight's conical projection of light spreads out across the paper ever widening as it moves further from its starting point.

The second image is of a ship sailing toward an horizon dotted with the silhouettes of distant islands. Yet when the ship reaches the islands, the horizon has receded yet again bearing dark outlines of yet more islands arousing new curiosity and a new impulse to explore further.[50] Clement of Alexandria speaks of the soul's contemplative movement toward God and God's concomitant self-disclosure as a process of ebb and flow. God seems to condescend to us with revelation but then recedes (*exanachōroun aei ... porrō aphistamenon tou diōkontos*) from the mind's presence.[51] It is unclear if God's receding from the beckoned soul is, for Clement, the result of his description of God as boundless. But it is certainly the dynamic Nyssen has in mind when he observes that the beatific vision never fully exhausts the soul's desire. For the soul's immediate apprehension of God's goodness always rekindles his desire to see more. His conclusion is, therefore, that the soul's desire never suffers satiation with God's beauty because its desire is never abated.[52]

Yet the theory of epectasy cannot rest simply on the power of God's infinite goodness and beauty to sustain the soul's interest for all eternity. While God's infinite being explains why the soul will never become bored with God, it does not by itself explain how the soul can contemplate God's immensity for all eternity without experiencing the satiety, not of boredom, but of saturation. How can a finite mind contemplate the goodness of God without being overpowered by the vastness of God's infinite beauty? How can the finite eternally "take in" the infinite? The answer lies in Nyssen's account of the nature of the soul as eternal becoming.

The Soul's Capacity for Eternal Growth

Nyssen's understanding of the soul's capacity for infinite growth is grounded in his account of the psychosomatic unity of the person. He continues to speak of the soul as distinct from the body and to hold that the soul, prior to the resurrection, is able to transcend the body in death. Yet the soul never exists without being united with the body. Even in death the soul remains attached to the particles of the body at the same time that it rests in Abraham's bosom. While all discussions of anthropology in classical and late antiquity acknowledged the reciprocal influence of soul and body, for Nyssen psychosomatic unity is not merely descriptive of a temporary coexistence of the immaterial and intellectual with the material. Rather the soul and body are together from conception into eternity. The history of the soul is inseparable from the history of the body.[53] This is most apparent in Nyssen's rejection of what is commonly, though imprecisely, called Origen's theory of the "preexistence of souls."[54] According to this view, God created the earthly body as the locus of punishment and rehabilitation for the rational beings who fell from their heavenly contemplation of God.

Two theological concerns led Origen to adopt this theory. First, he wanted to preserve the biblical distinction between the Creator and the creature, which, he recognized, is often obscured in Greek depictions of the soul as divine.[55] Second, he sought to defend the justice of God's material creation against the claim of certain Gnostics that the material world fashioned by an ignorant demiurge is the cause of ignorance and evil. This he does by locating the origin of evil in the spiritual realm of rational beings prior to God's creation of the material world. That is, all rational beings were created equal in the beginning and equally enjoyed communion with God the Father through the Son and Spirit. The unequal positions of rational beings in the world created after the fall is the result of the varying degrees of disobedience on the part of each of the rational beings.[56] The unfortunate implication of this suggestion is that the material creation is the result of evil. The physical universe becomes the locus for the soul's convalescence after the fall and so prepares it for restoration to the ethereal realm. The body, therefore, serves a vital function in God's redemptive economy. Ultimately, however, the body and all things material are epiphenomena that, though not evil, are not intrinsically good. For while the material body may be vital for God's postlapsarian strategy for reclaiming fallen rational beings, it is not an essential element of the soul's life in God and so will in the end pass away.

This, for Nyssen, is a troubling implication of Origen's thought. For he recognizes that Origen's epiphenomenal view of the body fails to do justice to the sense of worth imputed to the material world in Genesis, "God saw everything that he had made and indeed it was good" (1:31). Another troubling consequence of this theory of the preexistence of the souls is that the soul does not change or develop substantially together with the changes or developments of the body. The only development is its appreciation of the goodness of God about which it had grown complacent. Therefore, Origen's anthropology lacks a sufficiently dynamic view of the soul necessary to explain its participation in God's nature. I will argue that Nyssen's conception of the dynamic character of the soul emerges from his understanding of the organic relation of the soul to the material body.[57]

Nyssen's Alternative to Preexistence

Nyssen's alternative anthropology holds that the material body is not an epiphenomenal appendage to the rational soul. Rather he contends that the soul actually grows and develops together with the body from the moment of conception. Having rejected the hypothesis that the soul exists prior to the body, Nyssen is left with two other possibilities: that the soul is added after the body has been fashioned or that the soul and the body come into existence at the same time. The former option, also called the "creationist" theory,[58] Nyssen discounts on the grounds that it is used by its proponents to demonstrate that the flesh is more noble than the soul, which was created for the service of the body.[59] Appealing to Christ's declaration in the Sermon on the Mount that man was not made for clothing but clothing for the good of the body (Matt. 6:25), the advocates of this position extrapolate that things second in order of creation are intended to serve the needs of that which precedes them.[60] Nyssen disputes this inference from Genesis 2 by shifting the focus to the order of creation recounted in chapter 1. Here the chronology contains, he claims, a "hidden doctrine" about the hierarchy of the created order. Created on the sixth day, man is the climax of God's creative purpose; for human beings as the union of the vegetative, sentient, and rational soul are the perfection of bodily existence since in man reason functions as a principle of order and harmony for the inherently chaotic and formless matter.[61] Exegetical issues aside, the creationist position is nonsensical to Nyssen because it exalts the body above man's intellectual nature in which principally the image of God is manifest.[62] By process of elimination, therefore, Nyssen concludes that the soul and body come into being simultaneously.

The unity of the soul and body from conception, however, is not a conclusion at which Nyssen arrives merely by process of elimination. There are both biological and theological reasons driving his theory. According to Aristotelian biology, which he employs from time to time, the soul in its most basic form is the animating principle of the material body. No body is able to move by itself without the soul. Since movement and growth, two basic activities of the soul, are indisputably present in the womb, Nyssen concludes that the soul is responsible for the vegetative functions of ingesting and processing nutrients for growth from the beginning.[63] It is interesting that in recognizing that the sperm that enters the womb is already possessed of animus[64] Nyssen seems to adopt a tradutionary theory of the soul. He comes close to making this claim in comparing the human cycle of procreation to that of corn. Even as the seed of corn contains within itself the power, i.e., the vegetative soul, which merely takes the nutrients from the ground, so too "what is taken (*apospōmenon*) from man (*ek tou anthrōpou*) for the producing of a human being is also itself in the same way a living thing, the animate (*empsychon*) coming from the animate, and the nourished from the nourished."[65] In this respect he is not following an Aristotelian theory of conception whereby the male contributes the soul, which is the formal cause that orders the material cause provided by the female. Instead he may be following a Stoic model according to which an individual's nature is derived wholly from the father while the mother simply provides the womb in which the male's seed grows.[66]

Nyssen's promotion of a tradutionist theory of the soul is connected to his concept of the *plērōma* of human nature. As shown in the passages above, he has suggested that human nature derives its being entirely (i.e., both soul as the animate principle and the initial matter of the body, i.e., the semen, in which the soul is present from the beginning) from the father while the mother's body provides the nutrition by which the body increases in mass and size. In *On the Soul and Resurrection*, having adopted the principle that "living proceeds from the living," he concludes that "reason necessarily foresees an end [*stasin*] to the increase [*auxēseōs*] in the number of souls."[67] For reason apprehends that "the nature does not flow [*hreoi*] forever [*diapantos*]," but is "becoming used up [*tou elleipontos*]" as new beings are born. The flow of our nature will cease when "mankind reaches the point of its own fulfillment [*eis to oikeinon plērōma*]" for "all intelligible nature consists in its own fulfillment."

Assuming that the *plērōma* mentioned here corresponds with the *plērōma* of humanity fashioned in the beginning mentioned in *On the Making of Man*, the point is that procreation will cease when the *plērōma*, i.e., the full number of human beings that God willed prior to the fall, becomes actualized or born. Once this threshold is crossed, the resurrection will occur. He describes it this way: "When our nature has completed its planned sequence, in keeping with the periodic movement of time, this flowing motion will stop going forward in its succession of births. When the sum of everything no longer goes on to a greater increase, the whole complement of souls will return." He seems to suggest that our nature's sequence refers to the gradual increase of its number until the preordained number has been reached. Hence "our nature" is identical with the *"plērōma,"* which is identical with the "sum" of human beings. This critical mass necessary for the resurrection extends beyond human beings only inasmuch as he speaks of the "the sum of everything." What is less clear but possible is that, given his account of human nature as flowing from one generation to the next and his earlier suggestion that the individual (body and soul) proceeds from the father in seminal form, he implies that the whole of humanity, i.e., the *plērōma,* existed seminally in Adam. Thus the members of the *plērōma* are derived from that nature which "flows forth" from each generation of fathers.

The immediate implication of his theory of the soul's origin is that the soul, far from being static in nature, is subject to growth and development. According to Nyssen's theory, the soul and body exist together from the beginning in a mutually informing relationship. The soul acts as the formal cause of the body, organizing its material and giving it form. Commenting on the puzzle of how the material can come from the immaterial, Nyssen argues that the body consists of the unity (*henōsis*) of qualities (*theōroumenai*) such as figure, color, weight, dimension, and quantity; such qualities are ideas which are grasped (*katalambanontai*) by the mind, not the senses. Thus the sensible qualities are derived from (*katergasasthai*) the mind (*noēmata*), which unites them, fashioning the body.[68] In other words, the mind gives structure to the nutrients received from the mother so as to give the body the qualities common to all human beings as well as those features distinctive of the individual.

At the same time that the mind gives form to the body, the form of the body influences the character of the soul. That is, the structure of the human body allows for both the development of the soul's rational potential as well as the expression of its intellectual nature. In Nyssen's comparison between the development of the soul and a seed of wheat, he observes that the seed does not become an ear of corn immediately upon germination. Rather the young shoot must grow until the plant has reached maturity or perfection. Even so with human beings, "the power of the soul also appears in accordance with the condition of the body."[69] Nyssen rejects the Platonic tripartite soul in favor of the Aristotelian view of a single soul with distinct powers, i.e., vegetative, sensual, and rational. Each set of powers develops in accordance with the needs and capabilities of the body being formed in the mother's womb. From the beginning the soul has the minimal vegetative powers of ingestion, respiration, digestion (*threptikos*), and growth (*auxētikos*) necessary to sustain any animate being. Then once the child is born and enters the world of light, which Nyssen treats as representative of the sensible world, the sensual faculties (*aisthetike*) of the soul emerge. Ultimately, in accordance with the body's present mode and limitations (*metriōs*) the soul exhibits its rational faculties (*logikē dynamis*).

In addition to the horticultural metaphor, Gregory also borrows an image from music. He often speaks of the body as an instrument through which our reason expresses itself.[70] Like an unfinished flute or lyre that cannot produce a wide range of tones, an infant's or small child's under-developed and untrained muscles in the eyes, limbs, and vocal cords both limit the soul's capacity to make rational judgments and also prevent it from expressing its needs, desires, and thoughts. The development of the rational powers of the soul is dependent upon the body, because the implanted mind (*ho enkeimenos nous*) relies upon sense data for knowledge about the world. The soul pervades the body like a field of force stretching throughout the body which, like a city with many portals, receives sense data from the outside world through the senses. The mind, like a guard at each entrance to the citadel, immediately experiences the world through the senses and simultaneously renders judgments about the perceptions.[71] If, however, the sense organs were underdeveloped or damaged, the mind would not have access to the sense data about the world upon which rational judgment could be made.[72]

This image is significant because it shows how closely Nyssen conceives the reciprocal relationship between the development of language skills and the cultivation of the soul's rational powers. In fact, drawing on Aristotle, he argues that the distinctive form of the human body, especially the hand, enables human beings to possess a face the configuration of which allows for the development of speech and reason.[73] Although the hands serve many useful purposes, Nyssen claims that their primary purpose is the service of reason. If human beings had paws which cannot easily carry food to the mouth, then the face would have been equipped with a mouth that protruded like the snout of a dog. Such a form, however, would not allow for articulate speech, but only grunting or bleating or barking.

As it is however, we are able to transport heavy items in our hands and arms rather than in our jaws; and we can tear our food into small pieces with our fingers instead of relying primarily on our incisors to rip meat off the bone. Consequently, the mouth of man can be constructed for more specialized tasks associated with speech and reason. Nyssen does not in detail develop a theory explaining how a capacity for speech allows the rational nature of the soul to develop. In fact, his assertion that the form of the body is intended as an instrument for the service of our *logos* is confusing.[74] On one hand, he has spoken generally about the whole person; the body's configuration bears features that assist man's regal nature. On the other hand, here he specifically draws the correlation between the hand, mouth, and *logos*. The general former principle suggests that *logos* can refer to the capacity for both language and reason. Yet he may also be suggesting that the discursive powers allowed by the command of language do indeed aid the development of our intellectual faculties.

To summarize, both human nature generally and the rational powers of each person individually require certain formal conditions of the body be met in order to develop in its embodied existence. It is not the case that the soul is already rational from its generation and must wait for the body to develop to the point that its rational faculties can be expressed. Nor is it the case that the rational faculties are infused in the soul.[75] Rather rationality is an acquired power that comes from nothing but the transformation of the soul in accordance with the body's development. Even as the entire form of a stalk of corn preexists in the seed only potentially, so too the soul in the male's seed is only potentially rational. And that rational nature gains actuality and is manifest through the unfolding of a natural sequence of bodily development. Nyssen supports this claim with an epistemological analogue from theology. Even as the mind deduces the existence of the invisible God from his activities in creation, so too the invisible soul is known by its "manifest activities" in the body. Therefore, since one cannot discern activities related to rational judgment in a newborn infant, one cannot conclude or assume that its soul is yet capable of rationality. Rather we observe that such powers are manifest concurrently with (*symproiousa*), and not before, a "necessary sequence of events" in the body's development.[76]

Since the growth and development of the body is directed by the soul, which is responsible for setting in motion the bodily activities, the soul seemingly contains a *paradeigma* of intelligible concepts that it imposes on matter to give the body a form suitable for aiding our rational nature. Poetically, Nyssen speaks of the soul "preparing for itself a proper dwelling place by means of the implanted matter," which is like wax onto which the signet imprints its distinctive mark.[77] Hence, although the soul does not acquire its rational nature until the body has been suitably formed, the soul contains a template or code that, though not by its own deliberation, organizes the body's material cause into that necessary form through a set process of maturation.

Nyssen's theory of the co-originate character of the soul and body necessitates viewing the soul, not as static, but organic in nature. Perfection for the soul means *growing into* its rational nature and *maturing in* its rationality. The growth of the soul in accordance with the changes in the body has definite implications for Nyssen's conception of the soul's relationship with its glorified body at the resurrection. But of more immediate concern for my argument is that Nyssen's theory of psychosomatic unity establishes the dynamic nature of the soul whereby it is able to adapt to and grow in its capacity for participation in the divine nature. As I will argue in the next chapter, Nyssen's organic soul can be so adapted to the divine nature in which it participates eschatologically that it is able to grow forever in communion with God without being satiated.

This study of Gregory of Nyssa's psychology began with the problem of the passions. The appetitive drives of the sentient soul and the specific emotions that proceed from them are naturally oriented to the sensual goods of the material world and are not inherently regulated by reason. This habitual orientation of the soul's desires for mundane goods is, for Nyssen, the chief character of sin that compromises the soul's divine likeness to God and its participation in God. Humanity is delivered from the passions by a reorientation of the soul's appetitive drives toward the intelligible goods of God and by the subsequent transformation of the soul's emotions into virtues.

Nyssen describes this transformation in terms of *epectasy*, the eternal process of growing into God's likeness. In this chapter we have seen how the Nyssen's conception of the divine nature as infinite Being and human nature as perpetual becoming sets the conditions for the soul's unceasing growth through eternal participation in the Divine. God as infinite Being can never be comprehended and so is the source of inexhaustible amazement and curiosity for the soul's contemplation. At the same time, the soul is by nature elastic. From the seed it is the source of the basic vegetative functions of any organic life form. Over time its faculties develop and its capacities expand as the body develops until it acquires the rational faculties necessary for contemplative participation in God. The human soul, far from being static in nature, is hardwired for dynamic development. Thus it is capable of the change requisite for life in a body that is to be transformed in the resurrection, but also that can grow as the character of its participation in God changes. The dynamic transformation of the appetites is central to Nyssen's soteriology. How can the desires be steered by reason beyond the pleasures and pains of the material world that constantly bombard the soul? What is the nature of the soul's participation in the transcendent goodness of God? These are the questions to which we must now turn.

CHAPTER SIX

Purgation and Illumination:
The Dialectic of Salvation

Plotinus maintained that the soul's love of the One can be infinite because the One itself is infinite. As we have seen, Nyssen used this axiom as the basis for his theory of epectasy with which he challenged Origen's account of our turning from God. Since God is infinite, the glory of the Divine is an ever unfolding source of wonderment and curiosity for the mind, whose intellectual desire for even greater visions of God's goodness is insatiable. Epectasy is Nyssen's account of the soul's dynamic participation (*metousia*) in God, which is the heart of his soteriology — the solution to the problem of the passions and the fulfillment of God's plan for the soul. As we saw in the first two chapters, in his two major treatises on anthropology Nyssen depicts humanity as created with a rational nature that is the image of the divine nature, by which human beings are capable of participating in the Divine. The image of the divine archetype is compromised by the habitual orientation of the soul's appetitive faculties toward the mundane goods of the sensual world.

Rather than being embodied angelic creatures — as God intended — sustained solely by their participation in God, human beings share with the beasts the drives of the spirited and appetitive faculties common to the beasts. The powers of the intellect, rather than controlling the spirited and desiring faculties, serve the lower impulses of the soul in determining the means to attain the objects of their desire. At the same time, in both *On the Making of Man* and *On the Soul and Resurrection* Nyssen establishes the basic principle that governs his account of salvation, namely, that the soul's spirited and desiring faculties can be directed by the intellectual faculties from the sensual goods to the eternal and intelligible goods of God. Thus the impulses and emotions that spring from these faculties are transformed from base passions into virtues. The drives of the soul's lower faculties, therefore, are not to be quashed. Rather their power must be harnessed and put to the service of the intellect if the soul is to rise above the temptations of this world and ascend to God.

This relation between the intellectual and nonrational faculties of the soul remains the governing dynamic in Nyssen's subsequent accounts of the soul's journey into God. Yet his accounts in *On the Making of Man* and *On the Soul and Resurrection* describe the process *anthropologically.* That is, he outlines the inner dynamics of the human soul to explain psychological mechanisms necessary for the transformation of the passions; but in these works he does not offer a narrative description of the ascent — the intellect's turning of the lower faculties toward the Divine. Perhaps the closest he comes in his early works to providing such a description is in his hagiographical writings.[1] In his last great works, *Homilies on the Song of Songs* and *The Life of Moses*, Nyssen finally offers a picture of the ascent to God through the interplay of reason, spirit, and desire. The *Homilies on the Song of Songs* is a masterwork of allegory in which he works out the meaning of the soul's desire and pursuit of an infinite God. In *Life of Moses*, his speculative interpretation of the Exodus story, he depicts for his readers the process of the soul's transformation as it moves further into the Divine. Here the reader sees, not simply a diagram of the soul's structure as in *On the Making of Man* and *On the Soul and Resurrection,* but those dynamics at work in response to God's self-revelation. This is the full picture of Nyssen's soteriology, for *The Life of Moses* brings together his anthropology and his theology to describe the divinizing process of our participation in God.

Soteriology for Gregory of Nyssa is essentially an account of man's participation (*metousia*) in God. It is our fellowship (*koinonia*) with the One who is the source of life and all its concomitant goods in which we take delight. His soteriology emerges as the confluence of his theology and his anthropology; for it seeks to explain how our flawed and finite nature can ascend to the beatific union with God's holy and infinite nature. The story of salvation that emerges from his speculative renarration of the Exodus story[2] turns out to be a process of transformation and perfection that follows a cyclical dynamic of purification, illumination, and union with God. One of the elements foundational for understanding the logic of this dynamic participation is Nyssen's notion of perpetual motion. He recognized that human beings are, by virtue of being creatures, in a perpetual state of movement and change — a movement that inevitably becomes movement into God's nature and change into greater and greater degrees of likeness to his glory. Such an implication leads Nyssen to redefine the church's conception of the soul's perfection imputing to it a dynamic rather than a static character.

There is, I will argue, a second important implication of Nyssen's "Being-becoming" distinction for his theory of epectasy. By claiming that the principle of change is inherent in the character of our created nature, Nyssen is able to use the doctrine of the *imago Dei* both to provide a basis for the soul's communion with the Divine and at the same time to preserve the distinction between us and God. By saying that God on the one hand is infinite Being and we on the other hand are finite creatures in the state of perpetual becoming, Nyssen is able to conclude that despite our unending imitation and appropriation of God's virtues humanity will never acquire all the divine virtues and thus parity with God. In this way Nyssen is able to articulate a thoroughly orthodox *theōsis* soteriology. Although his *Homilies on the Song of Songs* is thought to have been written first, I want in this chapter to focus on *Life of Moses* and examine how he characterizes this process of growing in godliness. While it will be appropriate to touch upon passages in *Homilies on the Song of Songs* that may prove illuminating for our reading of *Life of Moses,* I will postpone our discussion of the transformation of desire in *Song of Songs* until the final chapter.

Humanity's Perpetual Becoming

As a narrative account of the soul's eternal ascent to God and growth in virtue, *The Life of Moses* presupposes that "change" and "becoming" are necessary corollaries of our creaturely nature. In contrast with God's uncreated nature, which is eternally the same, immutable, unchanging, and without variation, man's nature is created and so subject to change. Since it came into being out of nonbeing, by definition, it has an innate tendency to change and to be changed.[3] Thus Nyssen baptizes the classical Greek distinction between Being and becoming, applying it to the Judeo-Christian distinction between Creator and creature. Commenting on Genesis 1:26, "Let us make man in our image," he says that an image is not identical with its archetype. Despite all its similarities, the image differs at some level or in some degree from the original. Man's created and ever changing nature, therefore, is at best an image of God's uncreated and eternally unchanging nature.[4] Having characterized our created nature as ever changing and always becoming, Nyssen must explain what we are becoming and where we are going. His answer is that we are moving either toward and into God's goodness or in the opposite direction. Either we are being perfected in virtue or we are suffering the deterioration and regression of moral entropy. For we are always in motion; God alone is at rest.[5]

Since our virtue is derived from our imitation and contemplation of the perfect virtue of the One who is absolute Being, then the pursuit of vice entails a turning from Being toward nonbeing,[6] from life to death.[7] Thus the ontological and the moral spheres are linked. Nyssen speaks of God's Being as permeating the whole of creation and thereby giving life to all. For no creature could continue to exist without "remaining in 'The Being.'" Nevertheless, the life of sin he characterizes as being "outside" of God. Therefore, to live in the true and proper sense is not a mere existence but existence in communion with God from whose Being the rational creature derives goodness and life.[8] Nyssen does not, however, conclude that the soul's movement from Being to nonbeing results in complete privation of the goodness of existence. The way of evil ends, not in oblivion, but in a return to the Good.[9] Moreover, since the Good into which we move is infinite, our movement in the Good is unending. He writes, "Now that which is always in motion, if its progress be to the Good, will never cease moving onward to what lies before it, by reason of the infinity of the course to be traversed — for it will not find any limit of its object such that when it has apprehended it, it will at last cease its motion."[10] This movement into God's infinitely good nature involves a "continual change...for the better."[11] Here Nyssen articulates the essential soteriological implication of epectasy: the soul's unceasing contemplative movement into God's infinite goodness entails the soul's unending progress in virtue.

The Life of Moses is devoted to the examination of the *process* that is not merely a movement toward perfection but that is the life of perfection itself. The topic of perfection was not new to Nyssen's thought. Earlier he had written a shorter work entitled *On Perfection,* in which he explains that bearing the name "Christian" means nothing less than embodying Christ's perfections. This work is principally an exhortation to believers to take seriously the Lord's command, "Be ye perfect." It does not, however, offer a model for the life-long process of growing in virtue nor does it attempt to incorporate the elements of mystical illumination. *The Life of Mosses* explores these dimensions of perfection. The state of blessed intimacy, which is the prize for those who like Moses achieve perfection, is summed up for Nyssen simply as "friendship" with God.[12] This intimacy is conferred on the soul that has attained the Levitical holiness of a "servant of God" (*oiketēs theou*)[13] who waits upon the Lord in the Heavenly Tabernacle.

Following the tradition of Alexandrian Christianity, Gregory's soteriology is essentially a theory of divinization, or *theopoiēsis*. Divinization

for Athanasius meant purification of the soul for the purpose of rendering the body incorruptible. While Nyssen agrees that the deliverance
of his soul from passion frees the body from corruption and decay,[14]
his principal concern is with the conditions whereby the soul may attain union with God (*anakrasis*). The relation between *theopoiēsis* and
anakrasis is understood in terms of the twin axioms of Greek theories of
movement and attraction: "like is known by like" and "like is attracted
to like." In Patristic thought these principles translated into two fundamental tenets: (1) the soul could not know God unless it possessed some
likeness to God, and (2) the greater the soul's likeness to (and consequently knowledge of) the Divine the stronger its desires to know him
more intimately. While being made in the image of God established in
our nature the structural capacity for such knowledge, the soul, nevertheless, will not know God until that capacity is actualized when the
soul achieves moral likeness to God. That is, the soul must bear the likeness of God's holiness and purity if it is to have immediate and intimate
knowledge of God. Nyssen presupposes that there is a certain threshold
of purity that must be achieved before the soul can experience mystical union with God — that union which constitutes true friendship with
God. Yet, as I will argue below, he does not maintain a rigid view of the
stages of spiritual ascent.[15]

Nyssen's theory of the soul's ascent to God is patterned after Origen's
three stages of spiritual ascent. Origen appropriated from the Hellenistic world the threefold curriculum of ethics (*to ēthikon*), physics (*to
physikon*), and enoptics (*to enoptikon*), reinterpreting each stage of
pagan *paideia* in Christian spiritual terms. The three stages paralleled
the subject matter of the books of Solomon's trilogy: Proverbs, Ecclesiastes, and the Song of Songs. Proverbs, as ethics, is the moral science.
Ecclesiastes, like the science of physics is a meditation on "vanity of
vanities" from which the soul learns that the whole of creation is not
in and of itself of ultimate significance. Rather creation's existence and
value is contingent upon the God whose presence fills the cosmos. Thus
the soul learns not to esteem the visible creation more than the invisible
but omnipresent Creator. And even as enoptics, which is concerned with
metaphysical judgments about what is real, the Song of Songs instills in
the soul a love for and a reliance upon the Divine, who alone is real
Being. It is a love born in the intimate knowledge that my beloved is
mine and I am his.

In the moral *paideia* of Proverbs, Origen envisions the stage of purification. The exhortation of Ecclesiastes to forsake the vanity of the
world corresponds to the stage of illumination. Here the contemplation

of the world is not ultimately an attempt to discern God's fingerprints on creation, but to see the corporeal world as its is, namely, a painful prison that only serves the soul by filling it with the desire to be free.[16] Thus the ethical stage of purgation and the contemplative stage of illumination entail the subjugation of the body and its impulses so that the soul may be free from the sensual for the union with God described by Solomon in the Song of the Bride awaiting the moment of conjugal union with the Bridegroom. Having mastered the desires of the body and seen the vanity of the transient world, the soul has become singleminded in its love and desire for union with God. In this mystical stage, the soul has achieved the blessedness of contemplative (*theōria*) union with God in which one enjoys the vision of the Beautiful.

The elements of purgation, illumination, and unification are ubiquitous themes in Nyssen's spiritual and mystical writings. However, while they represent for Nyssen the logical order of the unfolding life of spiritual ascent, he does not present them as perfectly distinct stages through which the soul passes in succession from the first to the second, and finally on to the third. Jean Daniélou and Andrew Louth are certainly right that these are not so much "stages" through which the soul passes but "moments" in the life of the soul.[17] In Nyssen's allegory of spiritual ascent, *Life of Moses,* Daniélou identifies the purgative with moments such as Moses' encounter with God in the burning bush. With this revelation the soul learns to distinguish true Being from non-Being and so gains mastery of the passions (*apatheia*) and boldness (*parrēsia*) to persevere. Moses' entry into the Cloud atop Sinai corresponds to the soul's illumination through contemplation of God as the Logos, i.e., how God manifests himself to us through his divine activities (*energeia*). Thus contemplation is not of God *in se*, but God as revealed in his *oikonomia.* Because of the ontological chasm between the uncreated, eternal Being and the creatures of the realm of becoming, the moment of the soul's union with God entails passing beyond the cognitive categories of contemplation. As the bride in the darkness of her wedding night, the soul does not see the unknowable God, but rather feels with its spiritual senses only his loving presence.

While I agree with Louth and Daniélou that purgation, illumination, and unification are not discrete stages, I do not believe that it is enough simply to say these represent different "moments" in soul's journey. If they are moments, then they are moments linked together in an ever-ascending spiral in which the soul advances toward and into God by moving through a dialectical cycle of purgation and illumination. In other words, there is, for Nyssen, a logical necessity for the purification of the passions before there is sufficient order in the soul to engage in the contemplative life and to be illuminated by the knowledge of God's benevolent economy. Yet he never suggests that the soul must be totally purified before there is illumination. Instead, the soul advances in its understanding and enjoyment of God in proportion to its growth in moral likeness to God.

The greater one's degree of purity the greater one's knowledge of God's goodness and consequently the greater one's experience of blessedness. This greater knowledge of God further purifies the soul's desire for God and so contributes to the soul's moral perfection. Thus this revelation of God's goodness serves to sanctify the soul. Following the Greek axiom "to know the good is to do the good," Nyssen assumes that the soul's union with God's goodness informs the character of the soul. The vision of God's goodness purifies the soul, thus making it more suited to receive a greater revelation of God's goodness. Nyssen's cyclical understanding of the ascent of the soul provides the dynamic principle behind his theory of epectasy. That is, because the soul's knowledge of God and enjoyment of his goodness is proportionate to its holiness, the soul ever strives to gain a greater and greater share of God's virtues so that it may know ever more profound states of bliss. In *The Life of Moses,* one can see three cycles of ascent marked by the dialectical pattern of purification and illumination. Each cycle builds upon the progress made in the previous one as Moses' participation in God moves him on to the higher moments of mystical fellowship with the Divine. The three identifiable cycles in Nyssen's speculative reflection on the spiritual meaning of Exodus are, first, the cycle of moral and intellectual purification; second, the cycle of kataphatic illumination; and third, the cycle of mystagogy.

Cycle One: Moral and Intellectual Preparation

The first cycle of purgation and illumination that begins the soul's spiraling ascent to God could be described as the phase of preparation through education and discipline. Nyssen's comments in *The Life of Moses* suggest that Moses' preparation for the theophany on Horeb begins much earlier in the narrative. Quite independent from the instruction of the church, Nyssen assumes that the freedom (*ek proaireseōs*)[18] inherent in the structure of human nature enables the individual to give birth to a virility of the soul characterized by austerity (*to katesklēkos*) and strength in virtue.[19] The birth of this virile constitution is aided by education in various disciplines, which like the ark in which the infant Moses was placed, saves one from being drowned by the battering waves of passions.[20] Nyssen does not suggest that this education resembles the illumination that will come from the soul's contemplative speculation; rather it corresponds to education in the moral sciences, i.e., basic training in virtuous living, as was fundamental in pagan education.

Yet he counsels against reliance on the barren wisdom (*tēs agonou sophias*) of profane philosophy (*tēn eksōthen philosophian*), represented by the childless daughter of Pharaoh, who raised Moses. Instead, Nyssen says that even as Moses was suckled by his own mother, so too the secular education received by a Christian should be supplemented by instruction in the church's customs (*ta ethē*) and observances (*ta nomima*).[21] For these, like Moses' mother's milk, nourish the soul, training it in virtue and right belief, thereby enabling it to make its way to God.[22] Indeed, Nyssen describes the purification as a healing of the passions of the soul's basc naturc. Commcnting on thc plaguc of frogs in Exodus 8, Nyssen says that the passions are "unnatural" (*atopos*) and "frog-like emotions" (*tōn herpēstikōn kinēmatōn*),[23] which are manifest "in the sordid [*ton hryparon*] and licentious [*akolaston*] life ... born out of clay and mire and ... through the imitation of the irrational."[24] The passions constitute an illness with which the dignity of rational human nature is corrupted. For under the influence of the passions the soul is no longer fully and purely human, bearing the image of God, but is amphibious (*to amphibion*) or bipolar (*epamphoterizon*) in nature.[25] The church's teachings aid in healing and purifying the soul of the alloyed form of its nature, Nyssen says, when the soul looks upon Christ, who stretched his arms out upon the cross as Moses killed the frogs by stretching out his arms holding the staff of virtue.[26]

The struggle between the profane wisdom of the pagan world and the church's true religion becomes a struggle within the soul. This is represented by the fight between the Egyptian and the Hebrew. A similar conflict exists within the church between orthodoxy and heresy as symbolically illustrated by the dispute between the two Israelites that Moses attempts to mediate. These conflicts, even when one is in the right, can hinder the soul's progress and prevent its contemplative illumination. Thus one facet of the soul's purification that prepares it for contemplation is a withdrawal from the world depicted in the Exodus narrative by Moses' departure from Egypt and entry into a life of retirement in Midian. Even as Moses had left the land of slavery and toil to live alone in Midian, so too by our living the solitary life (*eph'heautōn idiasomen*) we are free from entanglements with adversaries. Nyssen is not counseling his readers to follow the pattern of the Egyptian monk who sought a life of complete withdrawal from society. For he goes on to say that living among like-minded people, our soul is free to be "shepherded" by reason.[27]

The form of monasticism with which Nyssen was most familiar was the communal style practiced by his sister Macrina at their family estate in Pontus and those communities formed by Basil.[28] Against this background, the solitude being praised is not the life of near isolation but simply the withdrawal from distractions of social entanglements that accompanied life in the world.[29] Thus Nyssen speaks of this life of solitude as "the teacher of lofty learning" (*didaskalon tōn hypsēlōn mathēmatōn*). For the solitary life acts as Moses' teacher because it frees the soul of more mundane distractions, allowing more time for reflection and learning. Thus set on higher and ethereal matters the soul is ready for illumination: "It is upon us who continue in this quiet life and peaceful course of life that the truth alone will shine, illuminating the eyes of our soul with it own rays. This truth, which was then manifested by the ineffable and mysterious illumination [i.e., the burning bush] which came to Moses, is God."[30]

Here Nyssen adopts a standard convention common to Hellenistic philosophy and Christianity of antiquity, namely, in order to pursue the philosophical life of contemplation one must remove oneself from worldly distractions. The lofty learning (*mathēma*) that Moses gained during his retirement in Midian prepared him for the theophany on Mt. Horeb. For Nyssen comments that Moses' understanding (*ten dianoian*) was *consequently* enlightened by the light from the burning bush.[31] Although revelation is needed to give fulfillment to understanding, the understanding originating in the *mathēma* of contemplative retirement provides the discipline and elementary knowledge that God's light enables to grow into more profound understanding. He hints at this when he offers a backhanded complement to philosophy: "So whoever applies himself in quietness [*di'hēsychias*] to higher philosophical matters [*tais hypsēlais emphilosophēsas meletais*] over a long period of time will barely [*molis*] apprehend what true being is [i.e., God]."[32] In other words, however limited the understanding one gains from the quiet of philosophical retirement, nevertheless, the discipline of being alone with one's thoughts makes the mind predisposed to receive the revelation that the divine light will ultimately provide. In the context of the Exodus narrative, Nyssen's point is that Moses is not ready for the illumination that he will receive on Mt. Horeb until he has purged his soul of the worldly distractions that rob the soul of the quiet and peace that is necessary for illumination.

Before Moses may advance to the level of right reflection and meditation upon God's splendor, his preparatory purgation must be completed by the revelation of the light of truth that reveals to him what philosophy by itself could not. While all that has led up to the theophany on Horeb has been an anticipation of Moses' act of symbolic purification, i.e., removing his sandals; nevertheless if Moses is to gain true knowledge of God and ultimately come to know God as the unknowable, his understanding at its most basic level must be set right. Specifically his very conception of reality must be purified. Nyssen construes God's disclosure of his holy name, "I am that I am," to be a revelation of God's nature as true Being (*alēthōs to on*). Such knowledge is foundational for gaining further insight into the subtle "dimensions" of God's character. In simplest terms, if one is to grow in knowledge of the truth, one must first be able to distinguish between appearance (*ho en tōi dokein monon einai*) and reality, between Being and nonbeing.

As implied in God's name, true Being is essential to his being,[33] i.e., existence itself is proper to his nature (*tēi heautou physei*).[34] Since God alone has autonomous subsistence, "nonbeing" refers to that which derives its sustained existence from one who truly possesses being. This distinction is critical because it establishes absolutely the ontological division between the Creator (*aitias tou pantos*) and the creatures. From this insight, the soul's understanding is purified at two fundamental levels. First, at the epistemological level the soul now recognizes that God alone is true Being while we abide in the realm of becoming. Because we the perceiving subjects and the created objects of our perception are in a constant state of change, neither possesses the permanence proper to the True and the Real. And knowledge, as distinguished from ignorance, is of that which is true and real. Since creatures of the realm of becoming are subject to flux, we cannot assume that our perception of the world at any given moment possesses the firmness and certainty of what is real and true. Such permanence and certainty can be ascribed only to True Being. Therefore the individual soul, as a perceiving and judging subject, is not the standard of truth. Man is not the measure of all things. If further knowledge of the truth is to be gained, it must come from our apprehension (*hē katanoēsis*) of God.[35]

The second level at which our understanding is purified is our religious understanding — an understanding of God, not as a metaphysical reality or the remote object of philosophical reflection, but as the One with whom humanity was made for relationship. The ontological division between Being and nonbeing teaches the soul the principle of participation, which defines our relationship with God. It is our unilateral dependence upon the Divine. In other words, since God alone possesses being and has existence in his very nature, our existence and subsistence are purely derivative from him. We exist by virtue of participation in God's being. This establishes the principle of absolute dependence of all creatures (*aph'hēs exēptai to pan*) upon the Creator, not just for life at its inception, but for all subsequent existence as well.[36]

Nyssen is explicit that purgation of the soul's actions and understanding is a necessary condition for advancing in knowledge of God.

> That light [*para ekeinou tou phōtos*] teaches us what we must do to stand within the rays of the true light [*entos tōn aktinōn tou alēthinou phōtos*]: sandaled feet cannot ascend that height where the light of truth is seen, but the dead and earthly covering of skins, which were placed around our nature at the beginning when we were found naked because of disobedience to the divine will, must be removed from the feet of the soul. When we do this [*houtōs epakolouthēsei*], the knowledge of the truth will result and manifest itself. The full knowledge [*hē epignōsis*] of being comes about by purifying our opinion [*tēs hypolēpseos katharsion*] concerning nonbeing.[37]

Yet a close inspection of this passage causes one to wonder whether illumination from God is not in some sense prior to and thus the cause of the soul's purification. To speak anachronistically, does Nyssen have a notion of the prevenience of God's grace, as in Augustine's thought, or does he hold that the gift of illumination is predicated upon our own initial efforts to order our lives according to virtue? Would he subscribe to the Franciscan maxim, *"Facere quod in se est?"*[38] At the beginning of the passage, Nyssen distinguishes between "that light" which by its teaching prepares the soul for illumination from the rays of "the true light" (*tov alēthinou phōtos*), which confers true understanding upon the soul. The former light corresponds to the light from the burning bush, which is a type for the divine light of God and specifically Christ,[39] while the latter light refers to the revelation of God's goodness, which the soul receives by the immediate experience of coming into God's presence. In other words, in this passage Nyssen tells his readers that their spiritual interpretation of the burning bush (i.e., the first light) should teach them the necessity of purifying themselves of the passions so that they may come to know God intimately (i.e., to receive the revelation of the true light). Yet in the context of the narrative being interpreted, the light whose command instructs Moses what he must do in order to approach closer and enter more fully into God's presence is the divine Logos himself.

Thus it is the divine light that by its own instructions prepares Moses for illumination — illumination that purifies the soul of its mistaken opinion about Being and nonbeing. Similarly, God prepares the Christian's soul to receive from him "full knowledge" (*epignōsis*) of the truth of his Being. Moreover, Gregory's phrase *houtōs epakolouthēsei toutōn hēmin*, which Malherbe and Ferguson translate "when we do this" does not anticipate the sense of the Franciscan maxim *facere quod in se est* because the verb *epakoloutheō* conveys the sense, not simply of "doing what is in our capacity as creatures bearing the image of God," but of "following" or "obeying." (As we shall see with his interpretation of Moses' vision of God's "backside," "following" becomes for Nyssen the primary rubric for the Christian's participation in God.[40]) Thus our action of putting off the passions is our obedient response to God's prior instructions. Nyssen's view of the relationship between providence and free choice helps to clarify the point. God's providence is not only the context in which we make our choices but is also what elicits from us our choice of the good. Providence, however, does not determine our choices. Rather, our choices determine the effects that providence will have upon us. Right choices enable providence to benefit us. Wrong choices cause it to have punitive effects, but the punishment is always remedial and educative.

The soul's recognition of God as absolute Being and of our dependence upon him for our existence marks a gestalt in the soul's understanding that helps cast off the passions. For Nyssen explains God's hardening Pharaoh's heart by saying that God hands over to the self-destruction of the passions everyone who does not acknowledge him.[41] Recognition of God as true Being and ourselves as contingent beings wholly dependent upon God is the foundational understanding the soul requires in order to be reoriented from its attachment to the sensible goods of the world to its proper love of the intelligible goods of God. Hence the logic of Nyssen's interpretation of Exodus 3 implies the priority of God's condescending illumination by which the soul is purified. Although the education Nyssen recommends offers the soul a more rudimentary understanding of the Divine than is achieved in *theōria*, nevertheless, in this stage of preparation the dialectic between the cognitive training and the moral discipline rightly orders the soul's orientation toward the cosmic hierarchy that is requisite for its higher stage of illumination.

Cycle Two: Kataphatic Contemplation, or *Theōria*

The next cycle of purgation and illumination after that of elementary preparation entails the illuminationof the soul through the contempla-

tion (*theōria*) of God's *oikonomia*[42] by means of spiritual interpretations
of Scripture. While the first cycle is purgative in that it disciplines the
soul's understanding and behavior so that it is inclined toward the intelligible goods, i.e., true Being, of which it has but an inkling, the soul
is by no means close to that purity of heart or likeness to that divine
virtue requisite for intimate union with God. Therefore, the process of
purgation continues. This second cycle, however, is driven by a vision of
God's goodness and beauty apprehended in the contemplation of God's
works, the most compelling of which were accomplished during the Incarnation of the Logos. Louth and Daniélou identify this moment with
Moses' entry into the cloud atop Sinai. For the cloud represents "true
reality" or "intelligible reality," which, corresponding to the forms in
Plato, transcend the realm of sensible knowledge. As Louth says, *theōria*
at this level has as its object not just the principles or forms (*logoi*) behind the objects of the sensible world, but the arch-principle or reason,
The Logos, which not only created but became incarnate to redeem the
world.

Yet, as they acknowledge, Nyssen speaks of the cloud's darkness
(*gnophos*),[43] which is suggestive of the final moment of mystical union
when the soul passes completely beyond the realm of knowing proper
to *theōria*. The darkness represents that true apprehension of the divine:
"the seeing that consists in not seeing [*to idein en tōi mē idein*], because
that which is sought transcends all knowledge [*eidēseōs*], being separated
on all sides by the incomprehensible [*akatalēpsiai*] as by a kind of darkness."[44] This merely illustrates, they contend, that the three ways are not
"strictly successive."[45] In this latter claim they are certainly correct; yet
two further nuances should be added. First, to the extent that entry into
the cloud is a component of *theōria,* it is a markedly different form of
contemplation than the contemplation of God's *oikonomia* as revealed
in the concrete images of Scripture, particularly in the activities of Moses
and Jesus. For the form of contemplation suggested by Moses' entry into
the cloud is apophatic.[46] Thus, second, it is more appropriate to place
the kataphatic contemplation of the images of Scripture and apophatic
contemplation of God's ineffable mystery in distinct cycles. This is not
to suggest that once one attains the apophatic knowledge of God one
abandons the images of God taken from the life of Christ. Rather the
distinction is appropriate because of (1) the degree of purity required to
enter each cycle and (2) the degree of purity that the soul has achieved
when it emerges from each cycle.

The kataphatic cycle is represented by the Israelites' sojourn in the
wilderness — from their departure from Egypt to their encampment

at the base Sinai. In this segment of Nyssen's *Life of Moses* (I.30–42 and II.102–151), the focus is on Moses' leading the Israelites' pursuit of virtue. Here Moses or Moses' actions become a types for Christ or Christ's works, and the Israelites represent the soul struggling in the life of virtue. Having gone through the cycle of preparation in which the soul has been purified of its errors about what is real and what only appears to be real, the soul is now properly oriented toward that which is real. It has also come to realize that its true place of rest is not with the fleshpots back in Egypt, but in the promised land of Canaan. To put it simply, now that the soul knows what is real it knows on what it should set its thoughts. It knows that its proper object of contemplation is not the transient world of apparent being, but the eternal and true Being that is God. Through such contemplation the soul undergoes a far more extensive purification of the passions, which, having become ingrained habits in the soul, still cling and so must be purged.

This purgation comes by meditating upon Christ as prefigured by Moses. In a passage reminiscent of his treatment of the plague of frogs, Nyssen likens the passions to the poisonous serpents that infested the Israelites' camp (Num. 21). Even as Moses healed those bitten by the serpents by instructing them to look upon a bronze serpent lifted upon a stick, so too Nyssen instructs his readers to look upon Christ lifted up on the cross to heal them of their passions. His construal of the bronze serpent as a type of Christ, who healed us by taking on the form of human nature and being raised up on Golgotha's cross, is a common interpretation in the early church.[47] Our interest, however, is Nyssen's repeated instructions that the soul may be cured of the passions by "looking to the cross." Initially, the command "look to" does not refer to an act of contemplation of the cross. Rather it refers to the repeated Pauline trope of "dying with Christ," or "putting sin to death,"[48] as an imitation of Christ's crucifixion: "Looking to the cross means to render one's whole life crucified [*estaurōmenon*] and dead to the world no longer moved or enticed to any sin.... The nail would be the self-control [*hē enkrateia*] that holds the flesh."[49] Our participation in Christ's passion, through which salvation is gained, consists in imitating his ultimate act of obedience and self-control, subduing the soul's fleshly desires for comfort and ease.

At the same time, Nyssen also implies that "looking to" the cross has a cognitive dimension as well — a *recognition* that Christ's death is in itself salvific. He observes, "[Moses] keeps the bites [of the passions] from causing death, but the beasts [i.e., *epithymiai*] themselves are not destroyed.... For although the evil of death which follows [from our sins and passions] does not prevail against those who look to the cross, the fleshly desire [*epithymia*] which exerted pressure [*enkeimenē tēi sarki*] against the spirit has not completely ceased to exist."[50] Unlike the bold statement that "looking to the cross" entails putting the passions to death, here Nyssen is explicit that the passions are not fully extinguished in the soul of the individual, only in their effect, i.e., death. Two meanings are possible. First, he might well mean that although the impulses, such as lust, remain, they do not bring death because we have put them to death in the sense that we do not act upon them. As Christ was obedient to the will of the Father rather than yielding to the impulse of self-preservation, we too put the drives of the body to death in the sense of subduing them rather than succumbing to their enticements.

The second possible meaning, which is not exclusive of the previous interpretation, is that Christ's death on the cross became a ransom (*eulēpon*) for us from the power of the devil, i.e., death itself.[51] In the latter case, "looking to the cross" means that we are given strength to resist the passions by realizing and considering that Christ has saved us from the ultimate consequence of passion, namely, death. Therefore, we need not be slaves to the passions any longer. Yet Nyssen suggests our contemplative action of "looking to the cross" equips the soul with the self-control necessary to subdue the impulses of the flesh. He writes, "The person who looks to the one lifted up on the wood rejects passion [*pathos*], diluting [*diaxeas*] the poison with the fear [*tōi phobōi*] of the commandment as with a medicine [*pharmakōi*]."[52] Although exactly what "the fear of the commandment" means is not crystal clear, the general sense is that when we think on or contemplate Christ's death upon the cross this meditation is medicinal in its effects. That is, it elicits an emotion of fear that exerts a counterforce to the drive of the passions.

Nyssen clearly assumes that there is a correspondence between the character of the object of one's thoughts and the emotions generated in the soul. For example, he warns his readers about the dangers of looking at erotic frescoes, which "by their artful pictures inflame the sensual passions [*empathous hēdonēs*]...[since] through the eye passion pours in upon the soul from the dishonorable things which are seen [*ek tēs atimias tōn theamatōn*]."[53] For this reason, he counsels that the soul should set its thought upon the cross for such an image arouses virtuous emotions that help to hold the passions in check. While it is doubtful that "looking to the cross" in a moment of weakness or temptation constitutes *theōria,* the image of Christ upon the cross dilutes the drives of baser passions because one has already meditated upon Christ's death and so grasped its spiritual significance. For it is out of this understanding of Christ's sacrifice that the emotion of godly fear arises.

Nyssen seems to be operating under the Aristotelian principle that the object of one's thought informs the character of the soul. One meditates upon the life of a figure like Moses, who has achieved perfection, in order to become perfect like Moses. For as our thoughts are fastened upon his virtuous life we internalize those virtues, i.e., we come to know the good and so begin to act in accordance with that knowledge. At the end of *Life of Moses,* Gregory summarizes the aim of this biography,

> ...concerning the perfection of the virtuous life [*tou kat'aretēn teleiotētos*]...we have briefly written [*hypotithetai*][54] for you tracing in outline like a pattern of Beauty [*en morphēi kallous*] the life of the great Moses so that each one of us might copy [*metagraphein*] the image of the beauty [*kallous ton charaktēra*] which has been shown to us by imitating [*dia mimēseōs*] his way of life.... Since the goal of the virtuous life was the very thing we have been seeking and this goal has been found in what we have said, it is time for you, noble friend, *to look to* that example [*pros to hypodeigma blepein*] and by transferring to [*metapheronta*] your own life what is contemplated through spiritual interpretation [*di'hypsēloteras anagōgēs theōrēthenta*] of the things spoken literally [*peri tōn historikōs*],[55] to be known by God and to become his friend.[56]

Moses' life so fully participates in God's virtues that it reflects the beauty of God's moral perfection. Bearing the image or character (*morphē*) of God's goodness, Moses becomes a medium through which we on earth apprehend the form of God's heavenly beauty. As such he provides the soul with a pattern of virtue that the intellect can apprehend and then imitate. When Nyssen employs the term *charaktēr* to describe Moses as a pattern for our imitation, he uses the same language to describe our perception of Moses' virtue that he does to describe the soul's apprehension of the world through the senses.[57] By his participation in God's virtues, Moses bears the stamp of God's beauty. Thus even as the senses imprint upon the soul the sensual images retrieved from the world, so too the one who contemplates Moses' virtuous life receives the impression of his likeness upon the wax tablet of her soul. Moreover, because Moses' virtues are a reflection of the divine beauty, his life arouses in the soul's appetitive faculty the desire to be virtuous so that we may enjoy the supreme blessing of friendship with God. When the soul "looks to the exemplar" (*to hypodeigma*) of virtue, its meditation not only points it in the direction of the good, but actually sets it in motion toward the good. Nyssen intends his biography of Moses to provide just such a tool for the contemplative transformation of the soul. From an examination of the details of the historical or literal sense (*historia*) of the exodus narrative (Book I), the intellect begins the contemplative (*theōria*) exercise (Book II) reflecting on the higher, spiritual (*hypsēlotera*) meaning revealed in the Pentateuch.

The purification of the soul that comes by casting a contemplative eye either to the cross of Christ or to the example of Moses' virtue reflects Nyssen's conception of the divinizing dynamic of prayer. In his early treatise *On Perfection*, perfection is operationally defined as living up to the one name shared by the baptized, "Christian." Being a "Christian" means embodying all the qualities that Christ himself possessed. Here, Paul, not Moses, is the Christian exemplar because Christ lived within him (2 Cor. 13:3) and was visible through him; Paul was "imitating [Christ] so brilliantly that he revealed his own master in himself, his own soul being transformed through his accurate imitation of his prototype."[58]

Perfection as *imitatio Christi* does not mean for Nyssen simply "doing" what Jesus did. Rather the transformation of the soul into the image of Christ manifest outwardly in our actions is the result of an indwelling of Christ's power *through prayer.* Commenting that the road to the divine life, i.e., the life of virtue, is "knowing what the name of Christ means," Nyssen offers an extended commentary on the names associate with Jesus, for these names are to be the objects of our prayerful meditation. The first two names to be considered must be "power" and "wisdom." Since in prayer, the object of our contemplation is drawn into the soul, prayerful reflection of Christ as the power of God and the wisdom of God imprints these dual qualities upon our soul. Thus with Christ's power dwelling in us, the Christian is empowered to resist sin.[59] Through the contemplation of Moses, Paul, and the Gospel accounts of the passion of the incarnate Logos, the image of Christ is mediated to the soul; and through the image Christ, the sanctifying power of the Logos, is imbued into the soul. Thus contemplative prayer is key to our transformative participation in the Divine.

Cycle Three: Mystagogy

Purity of Soul as Precondition for Mystagogy

Moses' actual ascent of Sinai, his entry into the cloud, and God's disclosure of his back parts represent a phase of the soul's journey distinct from that represented by his earlier travels across the plateau of Sinai's wilderness. This is the cycle of apophatic contemplation, or mystagogy (*mystagōgia*). Complete mastery over the passions is a prerequisite for the soul's penetration of the divine mystery represented by the cloud. As the Israelites are encamped at the foot of Sinai, they are instructed to purify themselves of defilements of the body or soul by ceremonial cleansing and sexual abstinence. Free of all passions, i.e., all appetitive impulses not controlled by reason, the soul has so transcended the appetites of the body that it is ready for initiation (*aporrētoteras myēseōs*) into the mystery of the One who transcends the realm of sense and thought.[60] In this situation, passion refers, not to the errant judgments about real being that have already begun to be banished from the intellect (represented in the theophany at Horeb), but to the soul's appetitive orientation toward the sensible goods of the body. Thus the soul must gain such holiness with respect to its desires that it can enter God's holy mountain. Indeed Moses has achieved such mastery over his emotions. For Nyssen tells us that when the summit became so "darkened that the mountain became invisible, wrapped in a dark cloud," Moses, unlike the timorous Israelites waiting below, was without fear[61] as he entered the cloud.

Moses' self-mastery extends even to the emotion of anger. In *On the Soul and Resurrection*,[62] Macrina holds up Moses as the example of one whose rational faculties bearing the divine image so control his appetitive impulses that he does not respond in anger to any provocation. On account of his meekness (*dia praiou*), Moses is described as *aorgēton* or not prone to anger. Macrina goes on to explain that his meekness is because the irascible impulses of the soul are alien to him (*tēn pros ton thymon allotriōsin*). Here Nyssen gives no narrative examples from Scripture from which this conclusion might be drawn. His repeated reference to Moses' meekness, or *praotēs,* is likely an allusion to the description of Moses in Numbers 12:3 (LXX) as being *praus*. In *Life of Moses*, Nyssen explicitly recounts Moses' advocacy of Miriam before God as an example of his mastery over his anger.[63] According to Numbers 12:1–15, God afflicted Miriam with leprosy when she and Aaron turned against Moses because they resented his marriage to a Cushite woman and were envious of his being God's spokesman. Rather than being enraged at their pretensions, Moses interceded on their behalf with God and the leprosy was removed after Miriam's seven-day exile from the camp.

Nyssen comments that Moses exhibited great patience with his sister's jealousy because he was firm in his nature (*ischyroteran tēn physin*) against the impulses of anger (*tēs orgēs*). Has Nyssen softened his account of the emotion of anger between *On the Soul and the Resurrection* and *Life of Moses?* In the former work, his comment that Moses was nonirascible because his *tēn pros ton thymon allotriōsin* suggests that the emotion of *thymos* was not a part of his soul's constitution.[64] In the latter work, however, Nyssen does not suggest that Moses felt nothing, but rather that he exerted such strength or self-control over his nature that the emotions arising from the soul's irascible faculty never developed into the outward, violent emotion suggested by the term *orgē.* Indeed, in his *Homilies on the Beatitudes*[65] Nyssen explicitly excludes the possibility that meekness (*to praon*) can be virtuous if it suggests a lack of spirit resulting in softness or slowness.[66] Rather than being the elimination of *thymos,* meekness must be viewed as the mean or balance between either sluggishness on the one hand and impetuous, rapid action on the other hand.[67] Gentleness, therefore, appears as slow, restrained movement on those occasions where one's actions might easily slide into evil; but rapid when one is making the ascent to the heavenly goods of the rational soul.[68]

Nyssen uses the classical term *apatheia* in *Life of Moses,* as he did in earlier writings, to describe the soul's purity. Yet the meaning of *apatheia* that he intends in *Life of Moses* is not the extreme that denotes a total suppression of emotion, but rather refers to the intellect's restraint of inappropriate impulses. In this respect, Nyssen followed the move among middle Platonists, such as Antiochus of Ascalon and Plutarch, who shifted from *apatheia* to *metriopatheia,* i.e., moderation.[69] Yet, unlike the Middle Platonists, Nyssen retains the term *apatheia* though now carrying the sense of moderation.[70] Nyssen's emphasis on moderation rather than the elimination of emotions is explicit in the second homily on the Beatitudes. The emotions are inherent in the material existence humanity shares with animals; "all emotion [*pathos*] has an impulse that is quick [*okseian*] and not easily held in check [*akatascheton*] for the fulfillment of its desire."[71] Since for embodied creatures the elimination of passion (*apatheia*) is impossible, Christ makes meekness (*praus*), the moderation or reorientation of these impulses, the standard of virtue.[72]

Interestingly enough, Nyssen describes moderation in strong ascetic language. He writes, "Not to be swept away like a torrent by the surge of passion, but manfully to resist such an effect, and to *drive off* [*apōsasthai*] passion with reason, that is the work of virtue."[73] Thus although the passionate impulses cannot be eliminated, they are to be "driven off" by the power of reason. In what sense is "driving off" or "rejecting" the passions, both equally good translations of *aposasthai,* different from eliminating the passions? How is his notion of moderation different from *apatheia?* In this context, reason has a moderating effect on the emotions and the impulses of the appetitive faculties of the soul because it holds the impulses in check. By reigning in the passionate impulses, reason eliminates the most dangerous aspect of the passions, namely, the quickness or rashness (*oxeian*) of the impulse and its resistance (*akatascheton*) to reason's control. Thus for Nyssen reason brings moderation because it eliminates by way of disciplined control the impulsive tendency of the soul's appetites and emotions. This has no minor bearing on his view of *epektasis*. For he comments that *apatheia,* understood as the extreme and absolute elimination of emotion, is unhelpful in the pursuit of virtue precisely because it would render desire (*epithymia*) impotent, lacking that kinetic force (*to akinēton*) necessary for moving the soul toward virtue.[74]

Although Nyssen explicitly repudiates the term *apatheia* in his *Homilies on the Beatitudes,* he retains it in his description of virtue in *Life of Moses.* Explaining the spiritual meaning of the miraculous plagues that beset Egypt, Nyssen says that "true doctrine" is received differently depending on the disposition of the soul of the hearer. The word in itself is the same to all. But to the one who is favorably disposed it brings enlightenment. Conversely the same word brings only darkness to the one who is obstinate and not open to the Gospel.[75] The Hebrews, though living as strangers, "remained unaffected [*apathe*] by the evils of the Egyptians (*tōn Aigyptiōn*)."[76]

Later in his discussion of the Israelites who had sexual relations with the women of Moab (Num. 25:1), Nyssen describes *apatheia* as mastery of the most dangerous of passions, pleasure (*hēdonē*). The narrative's account of Israelites who survived the Egyptian cavalry and were victorious in battle against the Amalekites and Midianites and yet who allowed themselves to be seduced by women of Moab is evidence, for Nyssen, of the power of pleasure to corrupt even those who are virtuous.[77] He writes, "By vanquishing by her *very appearance* those who had not been conquered by weapons, pleasure raised a trophy of dishonor against them. . . . Pleasure showed that she makes men beasts. The irrational animal impulse [*hē ktēnōdēs kai alogos hormē*] to licentiousness made them forget their nature; they did not hide their excess but adorned themselves with the dishonor of passion."[78] Two points need to be made here. First, Nyssen equates pleasure with licentiousness, which is impulses of the appetitive faculty aroused visually. The great danger of pleasure is that it is not like a weapon or external threat against which one can guard. As an impulse of the soul, it is an internal threat that seizes control of the soul. Second, *pathos* here is not being used in a morally neutral sense. For the appetitive drives can cause rational creatures to "forget their nature"; meaning, the desire for pleasure so dominates the soul that reason is overpowered and the person ceases to act rationally.

The therapeutic pedagogy for curing the "disease of pleasure" is, for Nyssen, living a Spartan existence in which "we conduct our lives as *far away* from [pleasure] as possible." After paraphrasing Proverbs 6:27–28, "Can fire be carried to the bosom without burning one's cloths? Or can one walk on hot coals without burning one's feet?" he concludes, "it is in our power to remain unaffected by passion [*en apatheiai*] as long as we stay *far away* from the thing that enflames. If we come close enough to step on this burning heat, the fire of desire will burn in our breast."[79] The caution Nyssen offers is the avoidance of the material object that itself arouses the desire for sensual pleasure. In the specific instance of fleshly pleasures, Nyssen maintains that *apatheia* is both possible and desirable. It is possible because the desire for pleasure can be purged from the soul when through ascetic discipline the object that excites the passion is removed from one's life. *Apatheia* is spiritually desirable because the desire for pleasure is so quick and so forceful that when it seizes the soul, reason cannot control it once it has been excited. This does not contradict his discussion of *apatheia* in *Homilies on the Beatitudes*. Rather the liberation of the soul from the "disease of pleasure" is a necessary precondition for reason's control and moderation of the other emotions.

Although Nyssen generally follows the Middle Platonic shift from *apatheia,* as the absolute elimination of emotions, to *metriopatheia,* as moderation, he retains the term for its theological and Christological significance. As we saw in chapter 1, Nyssen's anthropological works emerged during his dispute with Eunomius. In order to defend the consubstantial relation of the Father and Son, he must resist Eunomius's charge that the generation of the Son from the *ousia* of the Father would have resulted in passion within the Godhead. Passion, for theologians of the fourth and fifth centuries, is synonymous with change, which is usually degenerative. Passion within the divine *ousia* would mean that God is not eternal and immutable, but capable of change and corruption.[80] *Apatheia* was necessary for God's freedom and autonomy morally as well as ontologically. Not only is God sovereign in the aseity of his being, but is perfect goodness; the Triune God of Christianity is not capable of lapses into the passions, as were the gods of the Homeric epics.

In his brief comment on Christology in *Life of Moses,* Nyssen insists that the Son did not forfeit the impassibility of his divine nature in the Incarnation. Nor did the Incarnation introduce suffering and change into the Godhead. Rather humanity was perfected when corruptible humanity took on divine impassibility.[81] The theological and Christological importance of *apatheia* carried considerable currency in Nyssen's anthropology. As shown in chapter 1, *apatheia* is one of the central moral qualities that God conferred upon human nature when it was fashioned in the divine image.[82] Thus *apatheia* is proper to human nature as God intended it from the beginning, as it was transformed in the Incarnation, and as it shall be in the eschaton. It is for this reason that Nyssen never abandons *apatheia*.

Although Macrina's description of Moses in *On the Soul and Resurrection* implies that he has achieved *apatheia*, Nyssen never attributes this virtue to him in *Life of Moses*. Moreover, he says explicitly that even when the allure of pleasure is suppressed, the Christian is not invulnerable to other forms of passion.[83] Nevertheless, Nyssen assumes that a certain degree of purification is necessary in order to enter into the mystical darkness of Mt. Sinai's summit. At the beginning of his speculations about Moses' encounter with God on Sinai, Nyssen reminds his readers that they can take Moses as their guide in the quest for virtue only if they have achieved a certain degree of purity. He then offers a litany of moments of purification:

> Whoever looks to Moses and the cloud, both of whom are guides to those who progress in virtue... who has been purified by crossing the water, who has put the foreigner to death and separated himself from the foreigner, who has tasted the water of Marah (that is, the life removed far from pleasure)... who has then delighted in the beauties of the palm trees and springs (which were those who preached the Gospel, who were filled with the living water which is the rock), who received the heavenly bread, who has played the man against the foreigners, and for whom the outstretched hands of the lawgiver became the cause of victory foreshadowing the mystery of the cross, he it is who *then* [*tote*] advances to the contemplation of the transcendent nature.[84]

In this passage, Nyssen lists purgative trials and moments of purifying illumination by building subordinate clause upon subordinate clause, finally ending with the main clause declaring that the follower of Moses is ready for the ascent. In all the subordinate clauses, verbs are in the perfect tense, which denotes, not simply a past action, but one that has been completed. Among the purgative experiences, the Christian has, in tasting the waters of Marah, removed herself from the life of pleasure. This ascetic withdrawal from the sensually pleasant life of comfort and

ease is the very discipline Nyssen recommends in order to achieve the
apatheia necessary to achieve moderation of the soul's emotions. In fact,
her soul, which has turned from sensual pleasures, has also received
the delights offered by teachers of the Gospel. Thus the soul's desire
has been shifted from the attractions of sensual delights to the beauty of
loftier goods revealed in the Incarnation. At the end of the litany, Nyssen
says that such a person is *then* ready to advance into a higher form
of contemplation, which entails an encounter with the "transcendent
nature." This, Nyssen says, is the *telos* to which the purity of moral
discipline has led. Only when such purity has been achieved can one
begin the contemplative ascent into the transcendent mystery.

To emphasize the point, he asserts that the majority of people never
reach the foot of Sinai in order to begin the ascent.[85] Obviously, the litany
of purgative moments does not represent a precise series of moments that
one must follow in an exact order. Nor is he suggesting that some state of
sinless purity or transcendence of the material world has been achieved
in order to progress into the mystical moment that awaits. Complete
freedom from passions is not assumed. Nevertheless, Nyssen is declaring
that the mystical experience of God is not simply one moment among
many that may occur at any given point along the Christian's journey or
to any Christian. Rather the wondrous entry into mystical communion
with God comes only *after* the soul has been suitably purified.[86]

Moment of Mystical Darkness

The cycle of mystical fellowship with God begins with Moses' entry into
the cloud at Mt. Sinai's summit. Once in the cloud, Moses did not see
God, but heard only the harsh voice of God speaking with the force
of blaring trumpets,[87] revealing to him the divine ordinances for the
covenant with Israel. The blackness of the cloud represents for Nyssen
to adyton which suggests a private and secluded sanctuary where one
encounters God intimately (*syneinai tōi theōi*) and so acquires a mystical knowledge of God (*tēs theias mystagōgias*). Such initiation entails
putting behind all visible or sensual representations of the Divine. In this
transcendental encounter the soul comes to know God as invisible (*to
aoraton*) and incomprehensible (*to akatalēpton*).[88] The divine teachings
(*ta theia prostagmata*) that are revealed to Moses instruct the soul both
in moral virtue and in the highest virtue that is reverence for God expressed in fitting conceptions (*tas prepousas hypolēpseis*) of the divine
nature.

Paradoxically, the moment of illumination when the soul comes to a right understanding about God's nature is actually a moment of darkness. All the soul's knowledge at that instant is experiential rather than conceptual; for it is an awareness that the divine nature "transcends [*hyperkeitai*] all cognitive thought [*gnōristikou noēmatos*] and representation [*hypodeigmatos*] and cannot be likened to anything which is known," nor can it be classified with respect to quantity, quality, or mode of being.[89] The entry into the cloud denotes a shift from illumination through kataphatic contemplation to the apophatic moment. Once again Nyssen depicts such moments of revelation as being purgative as well as illuminating. For the revelation of the transcendent and incomprehensible character of the divine nature also entails the experience of God as beyond representation and understanding. Thus the intellect is purged of its material representations and analogues by which it formally had conceived of God. Such purity of thought is essential in order for the soul to advance to the next step of intimate union with God represented by Moses' entry into the Heavenly Tabernacle, including the holy of holies.

Although at times Nyssen seems to speak of the cloud itself as the holy of holies, ultimately however, he views Moses' entry into the Tabernacle as a more advanced moment of mystagogy than the prior experience. He writes, "With his mind purified by these laws, as it were, he was led to the higher initiation, where a tabernacle was all at once shown to him by divine power."[90] Nyssen's description of Moses' experience inside the Tabernacle is strikingly different from his experience in the cloud. Whereas in the cloud Moses' faculties of perception and comprehension were rendered impotent by the darkness of the cloud, now in the Tabernacle Moses beholds sights of manifold splendor. To be sure, he does not behold God's face; but he apprehends vividly the dwelling place of God in all its glory. In fact, the beauty of the Tabernacle is beyond description, not because the senses and the intellect are silenced by the darkness as in the cloud, but because of the manifold diversity of its splendid features (*en dysermēneutōi tini poikiliai to kallos*).[91]

The image here suggested is that of an elaborate tapestry embroidered with such an interweaving of different colored threads and patterns that its intricate details cannot be easily enumerated.[92] Nyssen nevertheless speaks of Moses' apprehending the wonder of the Tabernacle through sensible forms, e.g., draperies, curtains, pillars, a candlestick, various altars. Although Moses does not see God's glory directly through a "face-to-face" encounter, his experience of God's splendor represented

symbolically by the ornate features of the Tabernacle is quite different from the sense-numbing experience of the featureless darkness of
the cloud. Thus in this highest cycle of ascent the soul moves beyond
the purely apophatic experience of the divine. This is not to say, however, that Moses' experience in the Tabernacle represents a return to the
kataphatic knowledge of God proper to the cycle of *theōria*. Rather in
the Tabernacle there is a dialectical synthesis of the kataphatic and the
apophatic. Having passed into the cloud of apophatic experience, the
soul is purified of its tendency to conceptualize the Divine by adopting
analogues from the sensual world. It no longer naively maintains that
these sensual images accurately depict God's nature *in se*. Yet now in the
sensually vivid features of the Tabernacle, the soul no longer contemplates the Divine in his absolute simplicity as represented by the cloud.
Rather it discerns God's presence and knows God *indirectly* through the
glory of the sanctuary. While God in his essence remains unseen, as when
the face of the sun is obscured in a full eclipse by the moon, nevertheless,
the glory of God's activities, his *energeia*, like the glow of the penumbra
around the eclipsed sun, is visible.

   Although Nyssen employs details of the earthly Tabernacle to depict — for the purposes of *theōria* proper to Part II of *Life of Moses* — the
heavenly Tabernacle not made with hands, the soul that enters the Tabernacle does not "see" lampstands and altars, but senses the multiplicity
of virtues revealed in God's excellent *energeia*. For in this dialectical synthesis the divine penumbra is not contemplated in the sensual analogues
of the cycle of *theōria*. Instead the glory of the God who is beyond sensible and intellectual representation is apprehended as transcendent spirit
through the spiritual senses. In his eleventh homily on the Song of Songs,
Gregory alludes to the spiritual senses by which Moses beholds the splendor of the Tabernacle. Commenting on the bride's encounter with the
Bridegroom in the darkness of their wedding night, he observes, "But
how may that which is not seen appear in the night? It confers on the
soul perception [*aisthesin*] of its presence, but it escapes clear and distinct
intellectual grasp in being concealed by the invisibility of its nature."[93]
As in Moses' experience in the Tabernacle, God remains unseen (the remaining feature of the apophatic moment), but the supreme goodness of
his *energeia* derived from his ineffable *ousia* is unmistakably *felt*.

Priesthood: Height of Purity and Intimacy

Moses' entry into the Tabernacle marks the highest degree of intimacy
with God extended to creatures. By virtue of his passage from the cloud

into the Holy of Holies, Moses is consecrated into the holy priesthood. Such initiation presupposes that the priest has achieved moral perfection, i.e., complete mastery over the passions.[94] Indeed the priesthood and its concomitant blessed intimacy of friendship with God is not merely the highest, but the single ambition of each rational creature. Summarizing the lessons to be drawn from his *Life of Moses*, Nyssen says the reader should realize that her life has but one purpose: to be addressed by God as "servant of God because of the character of her life" (*dia tōn bebiōmenōn*). Then Nyssen summarizes the labors of Moses' spiritual ascent by which he came to receive this highest of accolades. The climax of the ascent is being "taught the mysteries of the Tabernacle and the dignity of the priesthood" (*to tēs hierōsynēs axiōma*).[95] Such noble actions made him worthy of the lofty name "servant of God" (*oiketēs theou*).[96] The title "servant" obviously refers to the office of the priest who waits upon the Lord in his holy house. The source of the priest's dignity is holiness. For it is his holiness that sets him apart and makes him suitable to act as mediator between God and Israel. Holiness, therefore, is the precondition for intercourse with God. Such dignity corresponds to the virtues that, as marks of our likeness to God's goodness, denote our royal sonship.[97]

The correlation between the royal dignity of human nature described in *On the Making of Man* and the dignity of the priesthood alluded to in *Life of Moses* is seen more clearly in Nyssen's emphasis on the priest's chief virtue, self-control (*enkratē*). For *enkrateia* is the principal fruit of the priestly life that stands in contrast with the life of indulgence (*tryphē*) in sensual pleasures.[98] In *On the Making of Man*, Nyssen explains that inasmuch as God made human beings to have dominion over the earth[99] the divine architect fashioned his nature "for the work of royalty." In order for human beings to rule the lower creatures of the earth, they must be equipped with the capacity for self-governance (*autexousion*) and freedom from compulsion through the sovereignty of their wish or intention.[100] This notion of autonomy is, Nyssen says, the precondition for the soul's possession of the other virtues that are characteristic of the image of God. Even as God's sovereignty over the cosmos is the result of his freedom from necessity, so too if human beings are to exercise royal dominion over the earth they must be free from any necessity or from any compulsion imposed on them by the forces of nature.[101] Although Nyssen does not list *enkrateia* among the virtues proper to the image of God, it is clear that self-control is the active operation of the soul's capacity for freedom from the impulses and drives of the material world and the body in which the soul dwells.

The priesthood for which the soul labors is not attained solely by one's personal zeal and merit; rather it is conferred *graciously* by God. Nyssen observes that this priesthood does not devolve upon the moral elite who exhibit great effort in subduing the passions so that they might be exalted above lesser men who are slaves to their desires. Such "lofty arrogance" (*en tōi hypsōmati tēs hyperēphanias*) ironically is itself a passion that causes the soul to fall. For it is a form of worldly ambition, and thus is characteristic of a soul that is oriented toward the earthly and the mundane (*ton hypogeion*) instead of the heavenly.[102] Rather, he writes, "The law teaches in this manner that the priesthood is divine, and not human."[103]

By saying that the priesthood is divine and not human, he implies two things. First, the character of the priest is like a nut the hard outer shell of which belies the palatable meat concealed within. Even as God's virtues are hidden so too the excellence of the priest's life does not conform to the outward appearance of the good life. Second, the priesthood is divine in the sense that it is not ultimately gained by human effort, but by divine election. While moral purity is a necessary condition for the priesthood, it is not a sufficient condition automatically meriting friendship with God. Nyssen does not believe that the illumination that Moses received was ultimately the product of his own efforts. To illustrate the uniqueness of their friendship, Gregory cites God's words to Moses in Exodus 33:11–12: "I have known you more than all others." In this instance, being "known by God" does not refer to God's general knowledge of his creatures resulting from his sovereign omniscience. The expression, rather, is suggestive of intimate contact of God's own initiation. For this reason Nyssen points out that the title "friend of God" is bestowed on Moses by God himself.[104]

Although moral perfection is requisite for this highest cycle of illumination and intimate union with God, this cycle of illumination purifies the soul even further by giving it a singularity of orientation it had not acquired in the preceding cycles of purgation. The earlier stages of the soul's ascent, represented by the Israelites' trek through the wilderness after leaving Egypt, were particularly hard because the pleasures of their former life were very fresh in their memory. Thus the pilgrims had to be coaxed on by the hope of the greater goods of the promised land. But by gradually stripping life of sensual pleasures and comfort and by being drawn upward by successively greater episodes of illumination, the soul gains a greater degree of detachment from the earthly goods.

Finally, the one who attains the perfection proper to a "friend of God" becomes locked on the trajectory of ascent into God. Nyssen writes,

"For he who elevates his life beyond earthly things through such ascents never fails [*ouk ēporēse*] to become even loftier [*hypsēloteros*] than he was until as I think, like an eagle in all things, his life may be seen above and beyond the cloud whirling around the ether of spiritual ascent [*noētēs anabaseōs*]."[105] In this passage Nyssen hints at the dialectic between ascetic purification and illumination. The more removed one is from worldly distractions the weaker the soul's appetitive attachment to the world. As the soul's focus is shifted from the beauty of the sensual and the mundane to the greater beauty of God's goodness, the soul's interest in the sensual diminishes and its desire for the divine goodness increases. In this respect Nyssen is following Plato's description in *Symposium* of Socrates' initiation into the mysteries of *erōs* through the tutelage of Diotima. As Socrates is led up the heavenly ladder of being, he discovers not only the beauty that is shared by all material, beautiful things, but also the greater beauty of the soul and the intelligible virtues of the soul. The recognition of the superior beauty of the invisible, intelligible realities "quickened in his heart a longing for such discourse as tends toward the building of a noble nature" (210b). The vision of the greater intelligible beauties stimulates a desire for further contemplation, drawing Socrates even higher.

Having meditated upon the beauty of the laws and political institutions (which embody the virtues of justice and moderation) and the sciences, he finally reaches the rung of philosophy, where he beholds the single form of knowledge, the Beautiful (210d). The soul's vision of the "everlasting loveliness which neither comes nor goes, which neither flowers nor fades" (211a), which is beyond body, word, and knowledge (211b) is so splendid that Socrates is no longer impressed or attracted to the lesser bodily forms of beauty. As Diotima tells him, "You will never be seduced again by the charm of gold, of dress, of comely boys" (211d).[106] Similarly in *Life of Moses,* as the soul's vision of God's goodness becomes progressively more splendid, the soul's desire for the good becomes more intense. Nyssen observes that even as falling objects descend ever more rapidly unless they face resistance, so too the soul once free from its attachment to the mundane ascends more easily and more quickly to the celestial heights.[107] Although being freed from the bounds of earth is logically prior to the soul's ascent, Nyssen assumes that the soul, once freed from the passions, ascends rapidly for its "eyes" are fixed upon the Good and thus subject to the powerful, attractive force. For the appetitive faculty is now directed by the intellect from the lesser beauty of the world to the greater beauty of the Divine. Since each higher level provides the soul with an even more glorious vision than the stage before, the soul's desire virtually runs ahead of itself in anticipation of the greater good to come.[108] This explains, Nyssen says, why after having beheld the glory of God reflected in the Tabernacle, Moses impulsively makes the presumptuous request to see God's glory. The vision of the Tabernacle, far from leaving Moses satiated, arouses a bolder desire to see deeper into the divine beauty.

This illustrates a critical difference between Nyssen's and Plato's conception of the encounter with the Good. For Plato, the elevated soul experiences the Good as pure Being; for Nyssen, however, the soul experiences the Divine as a redeemed becoming. That is not to say that God *in se* is in process or is still developing. Rather the insight of epectasy is that God's infinite being is, from the perspective of the human soul, eternally unfolding Being. Given his notion of the soul's perpetual progress into the Good, Nyssen seems to be saying that the soul's entry into the Holy of Holies is the end of the soul's quest *toward* God and yet paradoxically is merely the port from which soul begins its voyage *into* God. In other words, once the soul has gained mystagogical communion with God, it has achieved that ideal vantage point from which it can rightly know God. In this account of Moses' encounter with God in the Tabernacle, Nyssen begins to reveal his conception of dynamic perfection.

The Prize of Perfection

Nyssen's explanation of God's irresistible attraction for the soul and hence the soul's perpetual movement in the Good is illustrated by his treatment of Moses' return to the Israelites encamped at the foot of Sinai. Following the ascent-descent motif of Plato's philosopher in the "Myth of the Cave," Moses descends Sinai to reveal the Law and the earthly pattern of the heavenly Tabernacle to the Israelites. However, Moses' repeated exposure to God's brilliance has extinguished his desire for the things of the world. So completely uninterested is Moses in the world and so fixed is his desire for the immediate presence of God that he gladly forgoes seeing his life's labor — leading Israel into the land promised to Abraham — to its completion. "After all these things," Nyssen writes, "he went to the mountain of rest. He did not set foot on the land below for which the people were longing by reason of the promise. He who preferred to live by what flowed from above no longer tasted earthly food."[109]

The contrast between the focus of the Israelites and that of Moses illustrates the character of true perfection for Nyssen. The Israelites are

still driven by desire directed by *hope* for the fulfillment of God's promise of a "land flowing with milk and honey." By contrast, Moses, who
has experienced God's goodness *intimately,* has leaped beyond hope's
distant goal. For now Moses' singular desire is for the God who has
been immediately present to him. He loves God, not because he hopes
for wondrous goods that God promised. Rather his love for God is perfect; for to Moses God is an end in himself and not merely a means to
gain the promised goods. God is loved, not as the benefactor bestowing
great treasures, but as the One who, as the supreme Good, is himself the
soul's greatest prize.

One could argue that since participation in God's goodness provides
the soul with the greatest degree of pleasure and happiness, God is still
loved because he is the source of our happiness. Such an argument assumes that the soul's real *summum bonum* is the happiness found in
God. Thus the soul's love for God is not a disinterested love at all; in
point of fact God is still valued as a means to our happiness. Nyssen,
however, depicts the disinterested character of perfect love in his account
of the soul's chief incentive in striving after holiness. At the very end of
Life of Moses, Nyssen writes,

> This is true perfection: not to avoid a wicked life . . . for fear of pun-
> ishment, not to do good because we hope for rewards. . . . [Rather]
> disregarding all those things for which we hope and which have
> been reserved by promise, we regard falling from God's friendship
> as the only thing dreadful and we consider becoming God's friend
> the only thing worthy of honor and desire.[110]

Although he does not explicitly employ the distinction between servile
fear and filial fear, Nyssen is in this passage drawing on Jesus' distinction in John 15:15 between the obedience of a servant and that of a
friend. Moses is not driven to seek virtue out of a fear of divine retribution. Nor is he looking for the rewards of his virtue and labor. Instead
Moses' desire for virtue is grounded in a love for God growing out of
his knowledge of God's gracious activities and his visions of God's glory.
Moses, therefore, knows that God is supremely good and therefore alone
worthy of adoration and worship. Consequently, he seeks to be counted
acceptable to God. Even more than our enjoyment of that greatest reward, i.e., beholding God's beauty and partaking of his goodness, the
perfected soul is driven by its desire merely to be so esteemed by God as
to be deemed worthy of his intimate friendship.

Thus although Moses had already achieved purity of desire prior to
entering the holy presence of God in the Tabernacle, the vision of God's

incomparable beauty and goodness at Sinai's summit perfected Moses' love for God. After his dwelling in the Holy of Holies and seeing God's backside, Moses' appetites are wholly reoriented from the temporal to the eternal, from the sensual to the immaterial, from the mundane to the celestial. God has become for Moses the single object of his longings. As will be discussed in great detail in the following chapter, Moses' single-mindedness on the eve of his passing anticipates Nyssen's conception of the soul's eschatological orientation toward the Divine as "the all in all."

The Nature of Perfection

When this dialectic of purification and illumination is coupled with the Cappadocian doctrine of God's infinite nature, Nyssen offers his strongest refutation of Origen's theory of satiation. The perfection, which Moses ultimately achieved and for which all Christians should strive, is not a static state of being at all, but is a state of unceasing striving to imitate God's perfect goodness. For as the soul grows in its resemblance to God, it comes to know God at an even more profound level and so enjoys the even higher degree of blessedness that fellowship with God affords. In *Life of Moses,* God's perfection is important primarily because of its consequences for the Christian's spiritual journey in her present life. Paul in Philippians 3:13 describes himself as never ceasing to "strain toward those things that are to come." From Paul's words, Nyssen concludes that the life of the faithful disciple is not one of rest or ease, but of an ongoing struggle in which she is ever striving toward the good. Such a life is characterized by a continual climbing up-ward and straining forward toward some distant goal because the goal is nothing other than becoming like God and so enjoying the greatest form of blessedness, fellowship with God. That is, we become virtuous by participating in God's goodness and virtue. Since, however, God is perfect and therefore infinite, our imitation of his excellence never at-tains a maximal degree of godlikeness. The soul never becomes fully like God. Thus human actualization of divine perfection in virtue is a state never fully achieved (*to epibēnai tēs teleiotētos*) in this life or in the life to come.[111]

Far from abandoning the concept of perfection, Nyssen wants to re-tain Jesus' solemn injunction from the Sermon on the Mount, "Be ye perfect." To do this, he must reconceive the notion of perfection in a way that is compatible with God's infinite nature and the principle of our perpetual becoming. Therefore, he must distinguish between two senses of perfection: the absolute perfection of God's Being on the one

hand and the perfection of our becoming on the other. The latter I will
call "participatory perfection" for perfection in the realm of becoming
can be construed for Nyssen only as perfect participation in God. In
other words, perfection in virtue comes by our eternal participation in
and subsequent growth in God's virtue. God, who is the great "I Am"
as well as the "Alpha and the Omega," is eternal Being; human beings
who are created in time and space belong to the realm of becoming.

Perfection, therefore, if thought of in the Aristotelian sense,[112] is not
attainable since we cannot fully mirror the infinite virtues of God's perfection. Nor does Nyssen believe that by some act of divine fiat we
acquire them in a moment of instantaneous sanctification. Rather the
virtues come to us gradually by progressive participation in God's goodness. Since God's virtues are limitless, we will never cease to acquire new
virtues. Thus we will never achieve a perfect likeness to God; for God
alone has eternally possessed the infinite sum of virtues simultaneously.
It is, therefore, logically impossible for us to be perfect as God is perfect.
Yet when confronted with Jesus' explicit command, "Be ye perfect even
as your heavenly Father is perfect" (Matt. 5:48), Nyssen cannot dismiss the language of "perfection" (*teleios*). Reasoning that Christ would
never bind his disciples to an impossible command, Nyssen asks himself in what meaningful sense can creatures be perfect. He begins by
drawing a distinction between God's perfection and the perfection that
Christ requires of his disciples. The former is understood in terms of both
God's eternality and his immutability. First, God's perfection is inherent
in his essence, and not derived by participation in some other source of
goodness. Second, in his essence God is both eternal and unchanging.
Therefore, the syllogism concludes, God's perfection is the sum of his
infinite virtues which he has had and will always have for all eternity.

Yet when "perfection" is applied to human beings who are virtuous,
not according to their nature, but by their participation in God's virtues,
"perfection" cannot be an eternal state of being as it is for God. Nor is
it a state of resemblance to the Divine that will ever be reached. Therefore, "participatory perfection," as applied to human beings and as that
condition demanded of us by Christ, refers to (*a*) the soul's orientation
toward God and (*b*) its unceasing movement into God. By perfect "orientation" I mean that the soul is oriented or focused with respect to its love
wholly upon God and God's goodness. The soul is perfect in its human
sense when God has truly become its "all in all." When God becomes
the "all in all," the soul's life is lived out fully *within* the One, whose
goodness it desires and seeks to imitate (*hoson an endon tou zētoumenou*

chōrēsōmen). Thus the perfection of human nature is not static perfection but comes through growth in God's goodness (*aei ethelein en tōi kalōi to pleon echein*).[113]

Nyssen's notion of the soul's movement or progress within an infinite God is the paradox at the heart of his discussion of God's instructions to Moses, "You must stand on this rock" (Exod. 33:22). Having denied Moses' request to reveal his face, God places Moses in the cleft of a rock and passing by shows Moses the divine backside. Nyssen concedes that at this point his allegorical reading of Moses' ascent of Sinai as a representation of the soul's ascent to God breaks down. For, he concedes, one who makes progress into God does not stand still; yet Moses' clearest vision of God comes not as he is climbing Sinai, but as he is staying put. Nyssen's solution takes the form of a paradox: "The firmer [*hosōi pagios*] and more immovable in the good [*ametathetos en tōi agathōi*], the more one progresses in the course of virtue."[114] His point is that the orientation of the soul, i.e., whether it is fixed upon the good, determines its hope of making progress in virtue. In other words, when the soul is firmly planted within God, its desire and intellectual reflection are single-mindedly focused on the Divine.

When the soul's desires and meditations are fastened on the material and transient goods of the world, the soul is not likely to grow in its knowledge of the Good. For created goods, like shifting sand, lack either permanence or clarity in representing the good. By contrast, the soul that is completely focused on the One who is perfect and unchanging goodness has a clearer and more certain knowledge of the good. Having truly apprehended the Good, the soul can more accurately conform its thoughts and desires to the likeness of the Good, and thus is able to make greater progress in becoming virtuous. Moreover, when the rock in which the soul anchors itself is Christ (1 Cor. 10:4), the soul is able to make greater progress in the good because he who is consubstantial with the Father is archetypal goodness (*hē pantelēs aretē*), that is unchanging and eternal. Thus on the principle that one is able to make greater progress in virtue the more one knows of and possesses the good, the soul which participates in Christ's goodness more nearly mirrors the divine goodness and so is able to grow in its sure knowledge of God.

Here we see how Nyssen's theory of epectasy grows out of the integration of his anthropology of psychosomatic unity with the mystical spirituality that underlies his soteriology. As was established previously, from his tradutionist theory of the soul's origin Nyssen develops a theory of psychosomatic unity that necessitated formulating an organic model of the soul that could grow and adapt to the changes of the body with which it was bound. Because the soul is intelligible and therefore un-dimensional, its growth is not analogous to that of physical entities that expand and contract.[115] Yet he speaks of the rational soul metaphorically as a vase whose elastic properties allow it "always [to] become larger [*to aei meizon*] because of what is additionally being poured into it [*tēi prosthēkēi tou eischeomenou*]."[116] In this way the nature of the soul is constructed for its final cause, participation in God.

Nyssen says that our rational nature was designed and given to us by God so that we might share in the goods proper to God's own nature. Specifically the soul's deliberative faculty (*tina proairetika tōn psychōn*) is the vessel that allows for the soul's expansion in its participation in God. At the same time he suggests that growth is enabled, not only by the elastic nature of the rational faculty of choice, but also by the object in which the soul participates, i.e., the divine nature itself. Nyssen gestures at the reason behind the correlation between the rational soul's elastic nature and divine nature that promotes eternal expansion, "For participation in the divine good is such that it makes larger and more receptive that in which it exists. It is accepted by the recipient for the purpose of increasing power and size so that what is being nourished always grows and never ceases to grow."[117] Hence participation in God does not mean that the soul dwells in God in the same way that God, who permeates his creation, dwells within the soul, fostering its growth from the inside. Rather the divine nature in which the rational soul participates and which fills the vessel of the soul promotes this growth in two ways. First, the divine nature itself is infinite in magnitude,[118] never lacking goods with which to fill the vessel of the soul. Second, because the Divine is supremely good, it is so strongly attractive to the soul that the deliberative or choosing faculty of the soul is ever desirous of more of God's goodness. The soul increases in "power" in that, as it partakes of the divine goodness that is understood as the divine virtues, it has the power to partake of more of the divine nature inasmuch as its likeness to God increases.[119] Thus the greater the soul's likeness to God the greater its power or capacity to participate more deeply and receive more of the divine goodness. The soul's increase in "size," as was said above, is purely metaphorical. The size here simply refers to the soul's sharing in the divine qualities and the expanse of its desire for more. Nyssen actually speaks as if God's abundance itself increases, "The two are reciprocal; the capability [of the soul] increases as it is nourished by the abundance of goods, and the nourishing agent abounds with the increased growth."[120] Greater understanding begets, not satiation, but greater and greater questions. Thus God abounds as the ever unfolding object of our ever expanding curiosity and adoration.

To summarize, *Life of Moses* is not primarily a treatise on eschatology. It is an exhortation to Christians to imitate Moses' perseverance and progress in virtue. Yet in this work, Nyssen presents his doctrine of epectasy in the vivid image of Moses' sojourn in the wilderness and his subsequent ascent of Sinai. For the final point of this commentary on the Exodus is that Moses, though achieving perfection in virtue, never reaches the end of his journey to the promised land. He must, rather, be content with the highest reward of human perfection, intimate friendship with God. Nevertheless, Nyssen's concept of perfection establishes a principle that easily translates to the soul's eschatological participation in the divine goodness. From Nyssen's understanding of the dialectic between the soul's purgation and illumination and unification, Nyssen assumes the soul will grow in its knowledge of God's goodness as it grows in virtue and so becomes more like God. Simultaneously, the more it knows of God the more it wants to be pure so that it can receive an even greater share of God's goodness. Since, however, God's goodness is perfect and therefore limitless, the soul even in the eschaton will never reach a point where it fully embodies all of God's perfection and enjoys all of the blessings of God's goodness.

Although the basic dynamic of *epektasis* does not differ in the present age from the age to come, Nyssen is conscious that the eschaton will bring changes both to human nature and to humanity's relationship with God — changes that will alter the character of the soul's eternal participation in God. Specifically, Nyssen's description of the soul's ascent to God in the present age is an ascent driven by a sublimation of the appetitive impulses proper to the sentient soul. These faculties, he explained early in *On the Making of Man* and *On the Soul and Resurrection,* serve the animal needs of the present but are alien to the divine image that God intended in the beginning and that will be restored in the eschaton. Does the eschatological transformation of humanity and the restoration of the *imago Dei* change the erotic dynamic between reason and desire? And if so, how does Nyssen explain the soul's eschatological participation in God?

CHAPTER SEVEN

"When God Shall Be All and in All": Erōs and Agapē in the Eschaton

Gregory of Nyssa's vision of the Christian life stands out, especially in contrast with Augustine's, for its realized eschatology. He has a confidence in the Christian's ability to achieve in this life a holiness that resembles the purity of heart and intimacy of communion with God that is the Christian's eschatological hope. *Life of Moses,* with its interpretation of the exodus, provides a narrative of the soul's ascent through the cyclical dialectic between purgation and illumination culminating in mystical union with God. Eschatological union is the end of the soul's journey but not the end of desire; entrance into beatific fellowship is merely the beginning of an even deeper longing. This progressive process of growing in virtue Nyssen explains in terms of his theory of epectasy — the soul's unceasing reformation in the divine image through God's unending disclosure of his infinite goodness. It is in essence a narrative of the transformation of the bestial passions into holy desires. Because God is infinite there will be no end to God's self-disclosure and therefore no end to the growth of the soul's love of God. In this transformation lies the solution to the problem of the passions, and therefore the principle of continuity between the eschaton and the present age. Yet for Nyssen the two ages remain distinct. Nyssen has no single vision of the eschaton[1] and his descriptions of the resurrection are as varied as they are contradictory.[2]

In all his various speculations, however, the eschaton brings the consummation of God's creative intention for humanity and the reformation of our humanity corrupted by sin. Within the many aspects of his eschatology, the one on which this chapter focuses is the transformation of the passions. How are human beings freed from the passions in the eschaton if in the resurrection they retain the material body with the appetitive faculties whence the passions come? The basic answer to this question is

183

summed up in Nyssen's description of eschatological love as "impassible desire." Desire is focused on God rather than carnal pleasures. Indeed, the *object* of the desire shapes the *character* of the desire. But in this life, the saint, who, like Moses or Paul or Macrina, has achieved perfection, has replaced fleshly desires with an "impassible desire" for God. Yet the bliss of the saints in the resurrection far surpasses their experience of God in the present. The more subtle question this chapter shall explore is how the change in our *experience* of God from the present age to the age to come when God shall be "all in all" transforms the character of our love God. What will be the difference in the way the perfected saint experiences God now and how she will experience him in the eschaton? How will this different experience of God change the character of the saint's love?

Two strikingly different answers to these questions come in the different accounts of epectasy in *On the Soul and Resurrection* and in *Commentary on the Song of Songs* and *Life of Moses*. In the earlier view of epectasy from *On the Soul and Resurrection* the eschaton brings the purification of the soul through the transformation of passionate desire, or *erōs,* into a pure and passionless love, *agapē.* The key to this transformation is the change in our experience of God summed up in Paul's declaration that God shall be "all and in all." The later view of epectasy contained in *Commentary on the Song of Songs* and *Life of Moses* grounds the transformation of desire in the ontological divide between the finite creature who loves and the eternal and infinite one who is the eternal object of the creature's love. The result is that in these later works, far from asserting that the erotic desire is eliminated, Nyssen insists that the soul's love of God is always a form of *erōs.* This is a tension he never resolves or even addresses. So the question remains open. Are these views in fact mutually exclusive? Or are they simply expressions of different aspects of the soul's relation to God? Even if eschatological love retains its erotic character, how is the character of godly *erōs* altered when the soul enters into eschatological union with God?

To address this question, we first need to examine the classic passages on *epektasis* and desire in *On the Soul and Resurrection* and then those in *Commentary on the Song of Songs* and to a lesser degree in *Life of Moses.* These two sections will lay the historical and textual basis for the constructive theological project of the final section. Here I want to explore the possibilities of integrating these two seemingly contradictory views into a coherent synthesis — a step that Nyssen himself does not take — that may contribute to contemporary discussions of eschatology.

Eschatological Epectasy in *On the Soul and Resurrection:*
End of Time and End of Desire?

Nyssen's early account of the difference between the soul's movement to God in the present age and its perfect eschatological participation in the divine nature is developed in a pivotal passage from *On the Soul and Resurrection*. At the conclusion of Macrina's interpretation of Jesus' parable of the rich man and Lazarus, Nyssen after some initial hesitation suggests that Macrina's reformed view of the emotions and her account of the purification of the soul are in apparent conflict. On the one hand, Macrina has explained that when the appetitive impulses of the soul (*epithymia* and *thymos*) are controlled by reason and directed to that which is good, the emotions are counted as virtues. Moreover, they are necessary for the soul's pursuit of virtue in the present life.[3] Godly desire is the virtue of love that sets the soul in motion pursuing God. Godly gumption or irascibility is the virtue of courage that resists the desire for comfort and ease or the difficulties that might impede the soul's movement toward God.

Yet on the other hand, Nyssen infers from Macrina's immediate discussion of the purification of the soul that the irrational faculties of the soul will eschatologically be eliminated altogether. She has asserted that the appetitive faculties are not proper to the soul made in the image of God, but are faculties lying on the margin of the soul that serve humanity's needs in the present life.[4] Moreover, the eschaton shall bring, she says, a restoration of that humanity as it was in the beginning.[5] Nor does she retract or modify these early claims as the dialogue progresses. According to Macrina, God uses death as an instrument for purifying the soul of the evil that has been mixed with man's simple nature as it was in the beginning — a simplicity that enabled him to enjoy the beauties of paradise.[6] Nyssen takes the soul's "simple" and "unmixed" nature to refer to the pure image of the divine nature prior to the addition of the alien, irrational principles.

Macrina does not in that passage explicitly advocate the purgation of the emotions, only the evil that is mixed with the soul. Indeed in light of the reformulation of her account of the passions, one might think that purging the soul of evil would mean, not the elimination of all emotions, but only the orientation of the emotions toward that which is rightly judged to be evil. But Macrina's reply to her brother's query supports his interpretation of her account of purgation: "Either because of our effort here on earth or because of our purgation afterwards, our soul is freed from its association with the emotions."[7] Therefore, Nyssen draws the problematic conclusion: "Since every irrational impulse [*alo-gou kinēseōs*] in us is removed after purgation, the desiring faculty will no longer exist, but, if this is so, there will be no inclination toward what is better [*hē tou kreittonos ephesis*], since the soul will no longer have a desire for the good."[8] Nyssen recognizes a fundamental conflict between Macrina's anthropology and her soteriology. First, if the appetitive faculty is purged from the soul in this life, then we shall seemingly lose that mechanism by which the soul acquires virtues which enable it to participate in the good.

Second, it conflicts with his doctrine of epectasy. Although Nyssen has not developed his idea of *epektasis* in *On the Soul and the Resurrection* to the extent that he does ten years later in *Commentary on the Song of Songs* and *Life of Moses*, even in the works written shortly after Basil's death he already has the essential theological building blocks and has begun to fit them together to articulate an early form of epectasy. In *Against Eunomius*, he has already articulated the conclusion that a God who is infinite cannot be known fully or essentially.[9] In *On the Soul and Resurrection*, Nyssen uses this principle of divine infinity to critique Origen; our love for God will never be satiated because the object of our love is infinitely beautiful. Macrina says,

> Wanton satiety [*koros*] does not touch the truly beautiful. And, since the habit of loving the beautiful is never broken by satiety, the divine life, which is beautiful by nature and has from its nature a love for the beautiful, will always be activated by love. Nor does it have a limit of its activity of love, since we assume that beauty has no limit [*horon*] which would cause love to cease when beauty comes to an end. The beautiful comes to an end only through its opposite. Its nature is not to accept anything inferior and it continues to an unending [*aperanton*] and boundless [*aoriston*] good.[10]

Nyssen focuses on two arguments to explain why we will never be satiated by God's beauty. The general assumption behind both arguments is that the love ends only when the beauty that first excited the amorous feeling ceases to be appealing either when one experiences a defect in it or because the soul grows tired of the finite character of the beautiful object. Yet, for Nyssen, the divine beauty is not finite either qualitatively or quantitatively. First, since the beauty of God's goodness will be without limit, the soul's love of God will also be without limit. Second, because the divine love is essentially and perfectly beautiful, the soul will never find any defect in the love that would make the soul dissatisfied with its beauty and hence feel anything but admiration for God. Earlier in

On the Soul and Resurrection, Nyssen's question to Macrina (89A) —
How can the soul be inclined to the better if the appetitive faculties and
their impulses are purged in the eschaton? — suggests that he already
has (*a*) a sense that the soul's eschatological participation in God entails
some movement (Macrina certainly answers his question in terms of the
soul's movement) and (*b*) a sense that the movement is to that which is
progressively better.

Yet this theory of epectasy appears at odds with Macrina's account of
the eschatological purification of the soul. If the soul is purged of its appetitive drives in the eschaton, then the principle of movement whereby
the soul eternally moves deeper and deeper into the infinite being of
God is lost. If the soul's capacity for desire is removed, how will the soul
be drawn into the Divine? If Macrina's conception of the purified soul
indeed reflects Nyssen's own thought, then his anthropology and his eschatology are incompatible. In other words, his eschatology insists that
the soul must be purified of the irrational impulses in order to achieve
that likeness to the supremely rational and passionless God necessary for
perfect communion with God. Yet his theory of the soul's participation
in the Divine relies upon the very elements of his anthropology, i.e., the
appetitive faculties, that his eschatology insists be purged. Freedom from
the passions for communion with God is the supreme *end* for humanity — the climax of God's salvation history begun with his deliberative
act of creation — that his soteriology seeks to describe. Yet by claiming
that the soul is purged of the emotions proper to its irrational, appetitive
faculties, wherein lies the soul's *mechanism for movement* toward that
end, he seems to have eliminated the principle that explains how the soul
grows into perfection. As a creature belonging to the realm of *becoming,* humanity requires a principle of movement that explains the changes
and motions of the soul. In the context of Nyssen's soteriology, which
upholds both a theory of perpetual growth in the good and the principle
of freedom, he must explain how the soul freely and willingly acquires
the divine virtues and so actualizes its potential to bear the likeness of
God. The immediate task that Nyssen faces is to articulate a principle
for the soul's dynamic participation in God that is not dependent on the
appetitive faculties.

First Solution: Purely Intellectual Movement

Macrina responds to her brother's concern with two observations:
one anthropological and the other eschatological. Initially, she reminds
Nyssen that the human soul, although equipped with vegetative and
sensual faculties that animate the body, is chiefly endowed with the

"godlike" (*theoeidos*) faculties of reason that confer the powers of contemplation (*theoretikon*) and of adjudicating between goods (*diakritikon*). These movements of the intellect are independent of the body's mediation. That is, through the rational faculties the soul can apprehend the intelligible goods of God's nature that are wholly beyond the grasp of its faculties of sense. Through its contemplation of the divine virtues, our intellect judges such qualities to be supremely beautiful and attractive. And as was shown in the previous chapter, the more the soul reflects the beauty of the divine likeness the more the soul is capable of discerning the beauty of God.[11]

Macrina's point is, fundamentally, that Nyssen is wrong to think of the appetitive faculties as the sole cause of movement in the soul. Rather the human soul, with its threefold hierarchy of powers, is itself the source of discrete types of movement, not all of which are derived from the appetitive faculties. For example, the activities of ingestion, respiration, and growth, i.e., the functions of our vegetative faculties, are movements internal to the body that more often than not occur without conscious deliberation or intention or desire. Similarly, the intellectual faculties that apprehend intelligible goods and are capable of making judgments about the relative worth of a variety of goods produce movements in the soul that are not necessarily informed by the senses. Moreover, as was shown in chapter 1, Nyssen distinguishes between the ends for which God intended the intellectual faculties proper to the rational soul and the appetitive faculties proper to the sensual soul. The latter are necessary for the moral and active life; the former for the life of contemplation.[12] Thus the appetitive faculties exhibit utility in a context where the soul is torn between competing goods, those that gratify the senses and the needs of the body as well those that prove fulfilling for the intellectual soul. For example, the pursuit of ascetic piety is dependent on our ability to override the sensual inclinations of the body with a stronger impulse of desire for holiness and purity. Thus the redirecting or sublimation of the appetitive drives under the command of reason establishes a necessary counterweight to desires of the flesh thereby preventing the soul from being distracted from its spiritual pursuits.

By contrast, in a situation where there would be no conflict between the needs of the body and those of the intellect — a setting where the soul would be free to meditate on loftier goods without interruption — the soul would have no need of faculties to act as a counterforce in order to resist the urges toward lesser goods. In such a context, the soul's only movement would be the analytical and speculative activities of the rational soul. On the basis of her threefold hierarchy of the soul's faculties,

Macrina has established anthropologically that there are other forms of movement, such as a movement of pure intellect, that are not driven by desire. Thus she is suggesting that if the soul can behold the intelligible, immaterial goods of God's nature and judge them to be supremely beautiful, then one can think of these judgments as representative of a form of purely intellectual attraction. Therefore, even if the appetitive faculties were expunged from the rational soul, one should not assume, as does her brother, that we would no longer have a mechanism to draw us to God.

Second Solution: A New Experience of God

The second part of Macrina's reply describes how the eschatological setting changes the way God is present to the soul and therefore the nature of the soul's movement in God. The essence of her argument is that while *epithymia* is the driving force behind all the soul's actions in "our present life," it is not a characteristic of "the nature beyond thought" of which we shall partake and in whom we shall live eschatologically.[13] In its present state of affairs the soul is perpetually in motion, choosing between a variety of goods. The frenetic activity of making choices is driven, she says, by desire that waxes and wanes according to a constant dialectic between hope and memory. The soul may find many types of goods desirable. Some belong to the realm of daydreams and fantasies; others to the domain of an immanently possible reality. The latter is the form of desire Macrina has in mind. For true desire — a desire that is purposeful — is born of the promise of hope. When the prize appears within one's reach, our expectations, aroused by hope, draw us forward in search of that which is beautiful by nature. Should the beautiful object for which we hoped be gained, memory becomes stamped with the imprint of its beauty; this impression on our memory becomes the substance of future hope. But should our hope prove unfounded either with respect to achieving the object of our hope or to being satisfied with the object's actual beauty, our memory is imprinted with the emotions of shame and grief, shame at having been deceived and grief over following an imprudent impulse.

For Nyssen the cases of hope disappointed are more commonplace than hopes fulfilled. For Macrina observes, "But in us nature, because it is impoverished [*dia to ptōchēn*] of beauty, always aims at what is needed [*aei pros to endeon*], and the desire for what is lacking [*hē tou leipontos ephesis*] constitutes the desiring disposition [*hē epithymētikē diathesis*] of our nature, which either makes a mistake because of the vagueness [*di'akrisian*] of the truly beautiful, or happens upon it by chance."[14] In this pregnant sentence, Nyssen makes two significant claims about the relationship between desire and the activities of the soul in this life. First, the desiring faculty is motivated by its *need for* the *beautiful* because of our nature's inherent *deficiency of* beauty. In other words, our soul's beauty is lacking in two respects. First, because our nature is only a reflection of the divine nature that is supremely beautiful, its own splendor is imperfect. Second, because our nature has been corrupted by evil, its already imperfect beauty has been marred even further. As was demonstrated in the previous chapter, the former deficiency will never be completely overcome since we can never fully embody the beauty of God's infinite goodness.

However, here Nyssen is suggesting that the soul is driven in search of the beautiful both because the soul's proper orientation is toward that which is supremely beautiful and also because it hopes that by seeing and partaking of that which is lovely it may share in the object's beauty and so regain its own original beauty. Yet in this life, the search for beauty is often frustrated because the soul is confused and deceived as to what is truly beautiful. Thus Nyssen's second point is that the soul's frequent failure to grasp what truly satisfies its longing is the result of being easily led astray by misplaced hopes in "some false image of beauty." For by its nature beauty is nebulous (*akrisia*).

To summarize, out of the deficiency of one's own beauty, the soul is set in constant motion by the desire for some object of beauty to satisfy or supplement its own inadequacy. Yet because true beauty in the world has no clear form that the soul recognizes with ease and certainty, its elusive nature often makes it the source of frustration and an unsettled disposition. With such an account of the desire, Nyssen is casting the soul's movements in the language of classical Greek conceptions of *erōs* reflected in Plato's *Symposium*.

Epithymia *and* Erōs

Even as Nyssen characterizes *epithymia* as arising out of some deficiency or need, Plato initially describes *erōs* as a desire for that which one lacks. In Pausanias's speech from *Symposium,* love is the emotion of a youth who in the poverty (*ho deomenos*) of his experience and of his wisdom desires to be made better. So he seeks to acquire virtue through a liaison with an older and more experienced lover.[15] Likewise, in Aristophanes' myth of the hermaphrodites, he describes *erōs* almost tragically[16] as the momentary but frenetic rushing together and separation of bodies in an attempt to heal an incomplete and wounded nature. "Therefore each of us," says Aristophanes, "is but a portion [*symbolon*] of a man, like the flat-fish appearing to have been cut into two from one fish. Each forever seeks his other half [*symbolon*]."[17] Thus *erōs* is a longing (*epithymia*) and pursuit (*diōxis*) for the wholeness of our original form — a desire arising from the incompleteness or brokenness of our nature (192d-193a). Similarly, according to Diotima's account of the birth of Eros, he was the offspring of Poverty (*Penia*) and Resource (*Poros*) (203c). The poverty from which love is born, Diotima claims, is not satisfied, as Aristophanes suggests, by a sense of wholeness through union with "one's other half," but through achieving immortality through one's progeny. Immortality can be sought through two types of progeny: first, the progeny of the flesh, i.e., one's children in whose memories one transcends death, and second, the progeny of the spirit, which are the virtues, especially justice and moderation, begotten from a life devoted to the search for wisdom (207a-209a).[18] Thus whether love's particular object is virtue to rectify a deficiency of one's character or the companionship of a soul-mate who fulfills a want of the soul or immortality to supplement the finitude of our nature, *erōs* is always seeking to attain an elixir that will satisfy some want or privation of our being.

Although the dialogue between Macrina and her brother derives its impetus from Gregory's fear of death and desire for immortality, Nyssen does not, like Plato, try to explain all desire in terms of a longing to secure immortality. Nor does he offer a deconstruction of love that traces all love back to any single universal inadequacy in human nature. To be sure, one might make a convincing case that Nyssen does believe that human nature is inherently oriented toward the source of all goodness, God. Yet, because he identifies love with the appetitive faculties of our irrational nature, he characterizes the universal object of desire only in the most general terms — terms descriptive of irrational animals as well as rational human beings — as "that which is beautiful."

Erōs, for Plato as for Nyssen, directed toward the beautiful arises out of the deficiency of one's own beauty. Poetically Diotima says *Erōs*, being conceived on the day of Aphrodite's birth and so drawn to her great beauty, is thus the chief servant of the goddess of love (203c). Yet contrary to the assertion of Agathon's eulogy of Love, *Erōs* has the greatest happiness (*eudaimonestaton*) because it is the most beautiful.[19] Socrates argues that our desire for the beautiful can be explained as a desire to enhance or complete the beauty of one's surroundings or one's soul. Equating *erōs* with *epithymia*, Socrates asks Agathon whether the object of love and desire is something that the lover possesses or lacks; Agathon concedes that one has desire for only those objects one does not already possess (200 A–B). Socrates even argues that when one who is presently in good health or very wealthy speaks of desiring health or wealth, he is thinking not of his present condition but of his future state of physical or financial well-being (200D). In point of fact the present object that the athlete or the rich man is presently lacking is not wealth or health but the certainty that his current state of strength or affluence will continue into the future.

Since, therefore, the principal object of love is that which is beautiful, Socrates concludes that one longs for the beautiful, not because he already possesses it, but on the contrary because he sorely lacks it. Socrates is quick to qualify this conclusion lest we mistakenly think that the lover of beauty is wholly bereft of that quality. Recounting his initiation into the mysteries of love at the hands of Diotima, he explains that the nature of love can best be understood by comparing it to opinion. Even as opinion (*doxa*) is a middle form of knowledge between understanding (*phronēsis*) or wisdom (*sophia*) and their opposite, ignorance (*amathia*), love is a middle term referring to a state between the extremes of wholly lacking beauty on one hand and possessing it fully on the other.[20] *Erōs* is the hunter who is ever seeking and yet whose prey even when captured is never his for long.

The true significance of this analogy between *erōs* and *doxa* is that Plato locates love with opinion in the realm of change, the realm of becoming; for both the lover and the object of his love are themselves in constant flux. Love that seeks to possess the goodness and immortality of beauty is wholly a form of "becoming," never gaining the permanence of "being." The intermediary status of love and *doxa* is illustrated in Socrates' ideal lover — the philo-sopher. The philosopher is the greatest lover because she alone loves that which is most beautiful, namely, wisdom itself.[21] At the same time, however, the philosopher is truly wise precisely because she knows the limitation of her own understanding. Yet she is not wholly ignorant or stupid; for she possesses enough knowledge to recognize the supreme value of wisdom. Hence the philosopher's desire for wisdom emerges from the dialectic between her present partial apprehension of the Good, the True, and the Real and her awareness of the inadequacy of her understanding. Neither the student who, having just finished one of Plato's dialogues with all its loose ends, is perfectly content with her understanding nor the one who skeptically assumes she has learned nothing is Plato's lover of wisdom. For the philosopher recognizes both what she has learned and what she has yet to learn and so devotes herself with greater ardor to the quest for wisdom. As will be shown later, it is principally this understanding of love as the principle of motion proper to the realm of becoming that becomes reformulated in Nyssen's theory of eschatological epectasy so that it is transformed into a passionless love.

Macrina's complaint that the quest for the beautiful object often ends in disappointment because of beauty's inherent vagueness parallels Plato's view that the soul's desire for beauty in this world is often frustrated and rarely satisfied because of its ephemeral nature. At the climax of Socrates' initiation into the mysteries of love, philosophical discourse leads him to discover the one "single form of knowledge, the knowledge of beauty" (210d). In this last stage comes "the final revelation . . . [when] there bursts upon him a wondrous vision which is the very soul of beauty" (210e). This vision is of a beauty possessed of "an everlasting loveliness which neither comes nor goes, which neither flowers nor fades . . . the same then as now, here as there" (211a). While his erotic ascent of the "heavenly ladder" began with his attraction to particular material examples of beauty, the vision awaiting him at the final rung is of that eternal, immaterial beauty that can be grasped by the intellect alone. Having beheld the highest form of beauty, Socrates regards the beautiful objects lower on the chain of being as but imperfect reflections that hold very little attraction. Diotima tells Socrates, "you will never be seduced again by the charms of gold, of dress, of comely boys" because their beauty will no longer seem so appealing in comparison with the Beautiful itself. There will be a lessening of interest in meat and drink. The vision of true beauty inspires the initiate to pursue virtue through our participation in the Good and the Beautiful. For when the soul participates in the supreme beauty of virtue the soul will be immortal (212a).

It is interesting that Plato does not say explicitly that Socrates' vision is of the highest form of beauty — that beauty greater than which none can be imagined. Rather by speaking of it as "the very soul of beauty" he stresses its eternal nature. Even as the human soul is immaterial, immortal, and survives the decay and death of the body, so too its beauty endures the corruption of material bodies. In Plato's thought their is an assumed correlation between the eternal and the perfect. The vision of unchanging beauty enables Socrates to discern the inferiority of material forms of beauty because he now recognizes their ephemeral nature. Gold, fine wine, and comely boys are no longer as enticing or as desirable precisely because their loveliness is fleeting and so is neither stable nor reliable. The unstable beauty of material objects does not immediately suggest that their beauty is vague or unclear, as Macrina suggests. For an object may indeed appear lovely and desirable at any given moment.

Yet for Plato, since sense perceptions are no more reliable than the fluc-
tuations of the material object perceived, the judgments based on sense
perception are equally unreliable. Thus one cannot trust that an object
that appears beautiful at one time and under one set of circumstances
will appear just as lovely at another time and under other circumstances.

There is a second sense in which beauty can be thought of as vague:
in the moral realm of human beings, the outward appearance may belie the inner beauty of the soul. Consequently, the conflict between the
immediately apparent external form and the concealed inner subject is
evident in Plato's contrast between Socrates and Alcibiades at the end of
the dialogue. For in its truest form, beauty is found, not in the seductive
and handsome form of the corrupt Alcibiades, but beneath the satyr-like
visage of Socrates (216a), who is truly worthy of love. Yet because the
virtue and wisdom even of Plato's paragon of philosophers, Socrates, is
imperfect, beauty remains elusive. Because the philosopher is always in
the process of seeking wisdom and virtue without ever fully attaining
them, her desire is never fully satisfied.

Desire Transformed and the "All in All"

This erotic love, though an apt model of the soul's quest for God in the
present age, ceases to be descriptive of the Christian's love of God in the
eschatological context. For, according to *On the Soul and Resurrection*,
Christ's parousia ushers in a fundamental change in the soul's participation in the divine nature — a change of relation that also alters the
character of love. Erotic love is a form of desire born out of want or poverty; yet in the age to come, we will know neither want nor poverty, but
only the abundance of God's goodness. Once the soul has been purged
of evil, it abides exclusively in the midst of the divine beauty. For then
the soul will be united with the divine nature to which it is similar.[22]
Thus the purified soul abides in God and experiences God as "the all
in all."

The soul's union with God is, for Nyssen, the end of a long period of
purgation either by the mortification of the flesh in this life or through
its involuntary and painful separation from sensual goods in the life to
come. The principal objective of this purgation is to restore the primordial "simplicity" (*monoēides, haplous*) proper to the nature of one made
in the image of God. Simplicity in this sense is synonymous with moral
purity; a simple nature, like God's, admits no admixture of contradictory
qualities or impulses. Purgation restores that freedom from the corruption that God conferred on human nature in the beginning, but which
we forfeited through our evil choices.

The result of our evil choices is that the soul is subject to the domi-
nation of the passions — subject in the sense that the natural impulses
of our appetitive faculty become habitually attached (*prospatheia*)[23] to
the sensual goods of this life. Nyssen compares the habitual attachment
of the passions to nails that rivet the soul to the material goods of the
world, preventing its ascent to God. In her remarks on the parable of
the rich man and Lazarus, Macrina explains that the rich man's request
of Father Abraham to send someone from the dead to warn his family
reflects how, even in hell, his mind is fixated on the things of his previous
life. His passionate orientation toward the sensual, Macrina says, acts as
"fleshly glue" (*tēs sarkōdous kollēs*) bonding his soul to the world and
preventing his ascent to God.[24] Such habitual attachments to the world
explain, she says, why some souls in spectral form can be seen in ceme-
teries lingering in this world rather than passing on to their life among
the dead.[25] This habituation to the comforts and ease of the worldly life
becomes a sort of debt in the sense that for the sake of a present enjoyment of transient pleasures we have assumed for ourselves a future
hardship that must eventually be paid.[26] The cumulative effect of our
evil choices is that our preference for the lesser goods of the material
world instead of the intelligible goods of God has become fixed in our
appetitive disposition like layers upon layers of mud embedded in the
fibers of a rope.[27] Consequently as the soul is drawn to God, its alloyed
nature must be purified. The habitual attachments to the world, like the
layer of dried mud, must be scraped off.

Once the soul is purified of its habitual attachments to the world, it is
no longer bound to the world and so experiences the freedom (*eleutheria*)
that God bestowed upon humanity from the beginning. For such freedom is the capacity for self-governance (*autokrates*) and independence
(*adespoton*) from the constraints of necessity that result from subjection
to the world through the passions.[28] By speaking of freedom in terms
of autonomy and freedom from necessity, Nyssen employs the same
language that he employs in *On the Making of Man* to speak of the
distinctive capacities given to creatures whose nature is fashioned in the
likeness of the king of the universe. That nature which was made for the
work of royalty (*eis basileias energeian*) is equipped with the superior
advantages of autonomy.[29] The beauty of our august nature is denoted
in us, as it is in God himself, in the form of the chief virtues of purity
(*katharotēs*), impassibility (*apatheia*), blessedness (*makariotēs*), and freedom from evil (*kakou pantos allotriōsis*).[30] Freedom understood rightly
as self-governance is preeminent among the virtues which characterize
the likeness of our nature to the Divine, for it is the precondition for all

other virtues.[31] When our nature has been purified of its evil habitual affections and the freedom of godlike simplicity has been restored, then our nature is able to share in the life of virtue.

The process of purgation enables us to reclaim the virtues that befit our likeness to the divine archetype. For Nyssen explains that the pregnant phrase "in the image of God" is simply Scripture's way of saying "that [God] made human nature participant in all good; for if the deity is the fullness of good [*plērōma agathōn*], and this is His image, then the image finds its resemblance to the Archetype in being filled with all good."[32] Such "perfect godlikeness" (*akribōs theoeikelos*) enables the soul to apprehend God's simple and incorporeal nature (*aulon*) and to esteem him as the sole object of adoration (*to monon ti agapēton kai erasmion*). When the soul realizes that God alone is truly lovable, it unites (*prosphyetai synanakirnatai*) itself with God through movements of love (*dia tēs agapētēs kinēseōs te kai energeias*).[33] By our imitation of God we make the divine nature our dwelling place (*entōi mimeisthai pōs tēn hēmeteran zōē'n*). When the soul by its imitation of God's goodness is united to the divine nature, God becomes the sum of the soul's existence — its "all in all."[34]

Nyssen explains Paul's eschatological communion with God as "the all in all" in three ways. First, once the soul is purified of all evil, it possesses nothing except goodness and virtue. And since all goodness and virtue are derived from the divine nature, the divine nature completely permeates our whole being. There is nothing in the soul's life that is not of God. God has become everything to the soul. Second, the divine nature becomes the single source of our sustenance. In contrast with the present life in which we tend to think of our needs as being satisfied by a variety of goods, in the age to come our lives will be so thoroughly sustained by the divine nature in which we will participate that we will have no need for any form of physical sustenance.[35] In other words, in the resurrection we will have no need to eat, or drink, or sleep. In this respect, our life, sustained solely by the divine life rather than by foods, resembles the angelic life.[36] The divine nature even replaces sunlight as the source of warmth and energy.[37] Third, the purification of human nature means that we will experience the ubiquity of God's presence so that the soul can never turn away from God. Our participation in God's life and our incorporation of the divine virtues into our nature will be so thorough that were the soul to turn from God to itself, even there it would behold in its own nature the reflection of the beauty of the divine archetype.[38] Thus the idolatry, the tendency to love the creature more than the Creator, is overcome. When God becomes "all and in all" the soul will be so fully conscious of God both as the source of all goods that sustain life and in the way in which God's beauty is reflected in the entirety of the redeemed creation, that the soul will never be able to look at the eschatological creature and not also be conscious of the presence of the Creator in the creature.

The principal implication of Macrina's account of God's becoming "all in all" is that the soul's erotic longing is eliminated. Macrina's reasoning is straightforward. When we shall make our home in the One who is the fullness of all goods (*tōn agathōn ousia to plērōma*), we abide in a state that admits no deficiency of any good.[39] Where there is no want or privation, there cannot be erotic desire in the Platonic sense. Because we dwell within the divine fountainhead of goods, there is never a need to go in search of any good. For in God in whom we dwell all goods are immediately accessible to us (*to aei katalambanomenon te kai heuriskomenon*).[40]

Thus the soul never experiences God and the goods of God as things that are removed or stand off at a distance. Rather, since all goods in God are immediately present to us, we experience no sense of lack or poverty out of which emotions of desire arise. Nor can the soul experience the frustration of having been attracted to some vague and fleeting representation of beauty; for the One in which the soul participates is beautiful, not by virtue of participation, but in its very essence (*ousia hē tou kalou physis*).[41] As the essence of beauty from which all others derive their beauty, the divine nature is perfect and eternal goodness. Thus, unlike our present frustrated experience of the transient reflections of beauty in the material world that so often have disappointed the soul, in the age to come the soul will never find the divine beauty diminished or unsatisfying. Thus our eschatological love for God loses its tragic or disheartening character as described in Aristophanes' speech from *Symposium*.

When God becomes for us the "all and in all," he is *immediately* and *eternally* present to the soul. The result is the transformation of erotic desire into a holy enjoyment of God. When the soul is intimately united with God and all the goods of the divine nature are immediately present to it, the erotic longing of *epithymia* is replaced with an intellectual enjoyment (*apolausis*) of God's beauty that Nyssen identifies with *agapē*. Put simply, when the soul participates fully in the bounty of the divine nature, it has everything and so lacks nothing that it possibly could desire.[42] Since the soul wants for nothing, neither does it long for anything. Macrina observes, "The one who lives in darkness has a desire for the light. If he comes into the light, the enjoyment of it follows upon the desire and the power of enjoying makes the desire useless and foolish."[43] The soul no longer separated from God by its corrupted nature now experiences intimate union with God's supremely beautiful nature. Thus it is no longer that distant and elusive object of frustrated longing. The soul does not need to search out the beautiful, for it is surrounded by true splendor. In such a setting, Macrina asserts, when the good sought is at hand, one is filled, not with longing, but with satisfied enjoyment.

The End of Desire and the End of Time Consciousness

Time and desire are closely related in Nyssen's thought. As a subjective reality, time is a state of consciousness that arises out of desire. Time exists both as an ontological reality and as a subjective reality, that is, a product of our consciousness. During the dispute with the Arians and later the Neo-Arians, time became the defining characteristic of a creature in contradistinction from the Creator. God is eternal because God, who revealed himself to Moses as the great I AM, is true and absolute Being (*ontōs ōn* or *autozōē*).[44] Creatures, unlike God, who does not derive his existence from some other source, derive life and goodness entirely from God. The creature exists by participation in God's life. God exists because he is life itself. Because God absolutely is, he is eternally. That is, there is no becoming or change in the Divine.

If there is no change in God, there is no coming to be or passing away which characterizes the life of creatures in time. For such passing away, creates an interval of separation, or *diastēma*, for the creature between the past and present.[45] God, who contains all within himself such that nothing is lost to him, experiences no interval of separation. For temporal beings, the things of the past are lost; they cease to be.[46] For God who knows no change and so transcends time, nothing is lost; all is present to God.[47] In the context of the Arian controversy, the pro-Nicenes insisted that the Father's begetting the Son contains no interval. The Son is begotten *adiastatōs*, without a temporal interval. Thus time, understood as *diastēma*, is inherent in the existence of finite creatures subject to becoming and passing away.[48] Nyssen's concern to preserve the Creator-creature distinction leads to a theologically informed conception of time that gives it the status of an ontological reality. Unlike Aristotle, for whom time had no substantial existence but was an accident of coincidental movements, Nyssen makes time constitutive of creatureliness.[49]

Time is also a subjective phenomena; it is the consciousness of the interval between moments of becoming and ending. Time is subjective in that the mind's consciousness of temporal separations is shaped by one's desires. Desire arises from the dialectic between hope and mem-\ ory. The recollection of something desirable in the past inspires hope that we might once again enjoy the object of our desire. In this way, desire is produced by memory and hope. At the same time, however, our recollection of the past and our hopeful anticipation of the future are activities prompted by desire, which itself arises from our dissatis-faction with the present. In other words, the intellect looks beyond the present moment either because it lacks some good in the present or fears the immanent loss of a present good. For example, the adolescent living under her parents' roof looks with hope to the future day when she will leave home and will enjoy the freedom and new experiences that await her. Conversely, the old widower remembers the vitality of his youth and the joy of his wife's company because he now has neither. Desire results when we are conscious of some present deficiency and the *diastēma,* or interval of separation, between us and the object of our desire.

The consciousness of this separation is time consciousness. Where there is no separation between us and the object of desire, there is neither desire nor time consciousness. This shall be the case, Nyssen says, when God is "all and in all." When all goods in God are immediately and eternally and perfectly present to us in the eschaton, the soul has no need for hope that looks beyond the now to some good that it does not currently enjoy.[50] In this context, time ceases to have meaning for the mind because there is no disjuncture between what we want and what we have. Precisely because we shall live fully satisfied with the abundance of God's riches, our life in God will be one eternal now. In other words, since all goods are found in God, who is immediately present to us, we have no need of hope, which moves only "toward that which is not present" (*pros to mē paron*).[51] Nor does the soul need to be directed by memory (*mnēmoneutikē*) of past encounters so that it may know what goods to seek and what phantasmal beauties to avoid.[52] Rather the soul is united with God in one continuously satisfying moment of fellowship.

Because the soul's concentration on its present enjoyment of God's goodness is uninterrupted (*ascholia*), its thoughts are not diverted to rec-ollections of the past.[53] For one is lost in nostalgic thought principally when we miss some good — a good that is superior to the present goods of our present experience — which we once had but no longer enjoy in the present. The uninterrupted experience of God's perfect goodness leaves no room for a fissure in our consciousness between our past and present experience of the good. Thus in the all-consuming now of our eschatological participation in God's being, the soul dwells in eternity.

Nor is there a conscious regard for the future; for there is no imperfection, no defect or inadequacy in God's goodness that would produce a feeling of dissatisfaction in the present that turns one's thought in hope to some preferred state in the future. Moreover, since God's perfection is eternal, there is no fear that the soul's present blessedness will be lost some time in the future. Neither hope nor memory have any significance in the eschatological now.[54] Since, therefore, desire is the progeny of hope and memory, the soul — so entranced with the beatific vision that it has regard for neither the past nor the future — ceases to experience the emotion of desire. Moreover, since all other emotions are derivative of *epithymia,* they too will cease. In their place is left only love (*hē agapētikē*) and the only movement of the soul motivated by eschatological love is a clinging to and growing with (*prosphyomenēs*) the beautiful.[55]

Macrina's account of desire and time consciousness addresses a serious point of conflict between Nyssen's anthropology and his soteriology or eschatology. The conflict is between his model of the trichotomous soul and his insistence that our bodies in the resurrection are not ethereal but the same material body of our earthly sojourn. Soteriologically, he is concerned that human nature be purified of all that is alien to it and so distorts the soul's likeness to God, which hinders our beatific union with the divine nature. At the same time, Nyssen's anthropology so fully integrates our irrational and rational natures that the appetitive faculties, which are alien to the divine nature, nonetheless appear to be an inextricable feature of human nature. The problem is that under his threefold structuring of the soul's faculties the appetitive faculties are inherent in our sensual nature. Thus the soul could become free of the emotions alien to God's impassible nature only by being freed from the material body.

This is the solution adopted by both Plato and Origen. Such a solution is not acceptable for Nyssen; the body of the resurrection must be a material body for two reasons. First, it does not go far enough to stress the intrinsic goodness of God's material creation. If the body of the resurrection must shed its material fabric and become ethereal, the assumption is that our material body has only an epiphenomenal value. Second, Gregory wants to uphold the Pauline doctrine that Christ's resurrected body serves as the paradigm for our resurrected body. Hence even as Christ's body in the resurrection was the same body that suffered upon the cross, so too our bodies in the final resurrection will be the same material bodies with which our soul has been united since its beginning. Yet, if the soul is to retain its union with the same body in the resurrection that it had before its death then it also retains with the body the faculties of its sensual nature and its capacity for the passions. How, therefore, can the soul gain a godlike impassibility while it retains the sensual faculties from which the emotions are derived? Nyssen's solution lies in his reconception of desire, not principally in anthropological terms of the sensual faculties, but as an emotion tied to time consciousness.

In other words, erotic desire is an emotion that grows out of a tension between our present lack of goods and the goods either recalled from our past or sought for in the future. Therefore, based on his explication of the Pauline eschatological vision of God as the "all in all," Nyssen is able to explain how the soul exists in a state where neither the past nor the future have any meaning for the soul. The emotions derived from our sensual nature are not purged by way of altering human nature per se, but are transformed by changing the soul's consciousness. Satisfied by its experience of God in the present, it loses consciousness of time, of the past and future. Abiding in a fully satisfying now, the soul will not experience the frustration with its immediate situation out of which the conflict of emotions grows. This understanding of the transformation of the emotions in the soul's experience of the beatific now enables Nyssen to explain how our human nature can retain its physical nature in the resurrection and yet overcome the irrational emotions alien to the divine nature.

To summarize, Macrina's speech (89B–96C) has enabled Nyssen to answer one question, at least in part, about the compatibility of his soteriological aim of purifying the soul of the passions and his theory of epectasy. As Gregory posed the question (88C–89B), since *epithymia* and *thymos* are necessary for the soul's ascent to God, how can the soul be eternally drawn into God's infinite being—the argument Nyssen uses to counter Origen's theory of the soul's satiation with God's goodness— if the soul is purged of its irrational faculties, including *epithymia* and *thymos*, which are alien to the divine nature? Thus far, Macrina's argument has reestablished the compatibility of her theory of the soul's purification and the theory of epectasy on two levels. First, she made the case that there are activities of an individual, such as ingestion, digestion, and respiration as well as intellectual movements, which are not dependent upon the appetitive impulses. Therefore, the soul's participation in the divine nature might be driven by faculties of the soul other than those of our irrational nature. Second, by her account of the soul's eternal participation in the God who, as the fullness of all goods, shall be immediately present to the soul, Macrina explains how the soul can participate in the divine nature without relying on the erotic dynamic of desire to draw the soul to God.

There is a problem with this account of the transformation of desire: is not the idea of God being immediately present to the soul incompatible with God's being infinite? If God is infinite and creatures are finite, then the infinite can never be fully present to the soul. This is the conflict inherent in Nyssen's early account of epectasy in *On the Soul and Resurrection*. God's perfection may not be the source of dissatisfaction, but God's infinite goodness means that there will always be more of God's goodness yet to be experienced and therefore to be desired. God's infinite nature presents to the soul a boundless horizon of infinite goods to explore. This image of the soul's movement into God's nature assumes (1) that the soul does not enjoy the totality of God's goods immediately, (2) that the soul is kept moving further and further into the divine nature because it *anticipates* or *hopes* for the discovery of some more glorious good that is just beyond its immediate experience, and therefore (3) that the soul's dynamic relationship with God is driven by a form of love that in fact has the erotic character of *desire*. Can the metaphor of the ship's unending voyage upon the boundless ocean[56] be reconciled with the image of the soul's *desire* for dawn during the dark of night being replaced by its *enjoyment* of the light of the sun's first rays?[57]

Epectasy in *Commentary on the Song of Songs:* The Dialectic of Enjoyment and Desire

A decade or more after writing *On the Soul and Resurrection*, Nyssen composed the homilies that make up his great mystagogical text, *Commentary on the Song of Songs*. Whereas epectasy was already a feature of Nyssen's thought in his earlier writings, it is arguably the central motif in his account of the soul's mystical ascent to and ultimate union with God as developed in the *Commentary on the Song of Songs* and *Life of Moses*. In both of these texts, there is a noticeable shift in his thinking about the role of desire and the nature of the soul's enjoyment of the God with whom it is united. Whereas *On the Soul and Resurrection* dispenses with the erotic model of participation when describing the soul's eschatological movement into God, his homilies on the Song of Songs, while retaining the language of *apolausis* to describe the soul's beatific communion with God, view enjoyment as the beginning of desire, rather than its end. This raises the question: is his treatment of *apolausis* and *epithymia* in the homilies merely a shift of emphasis — an exploration of a new facet of *epektasis* — or does it mark the repudiation of his earlier view of epectasy and of our eschatological participation in the Divine. To answer this question we need to examine generally the theological scope and exegetical approach in the *Commentary on the Song of Songs* and then more specifically his treatment of epectasy by looking at his use of *apolausis*.

Written between 391 and 394, the *Commentary on the Song of Songs* consists of homilies Nyssen preached during Lent at his church in Nyssa.[58] He collected them into a single volume with a preface addressed to a young aristocrat named Olympias, a devout ascetic whom the emperor Theodosius had sentenced to "domestic exile" because she was unwilling to remarry after her husband's premature death in 386/87. Although the homilies were presumably preached to the whole congregation and not simply a select group of the spiritually advanced,[59] Nyssen is explicit that the Song of Songs and the allegorical reading that they require are not for the education of the carnally minded, but for advancement of those, like Olympias, who have such purity or soul and a zeal for the immaterial things of God that they might attain perfection represented by the bride.[60] The Song of Songs is the third and final stage of the Solomonic trilogy intended to guide the soul from its early preoccupation with material delight to the immaterial delights of God. The first volume, Proverbs, aims at equipping the soul with a capacity to know and love God by first training it to desire virtue.[61]

Ecclesiastes prepares the soul to love God by turning it from the pleasures of the sensual realm and grounding it in the insight of philosophy that the world of the senses is the "vanity of vanities." For philosophy teaches the soul the transitory and defective nature of material pleasures and beauty of intelligible goods beyond the senses. Once the soul desires to grasp the unseen world of ideas, then it is ready to pursue with all zeal the immaterial beauty of the God represented by and revealed through the very sensual images that Solomon employs in the Song of Songs. This reorientation of the mind from the sensual to the intelligible is necessary in order for this text to be read allegorically.[62] The text mirrors the order of reality and the images raise the mind to a higher level of reality if we have the patience for contemplation, or *theōria*. The allegorical reading of the Song of Songs entails a shift of consciousness from the obvious to the not-so-obvious, from the "virtual reality" of the material world to the "absolute reality" of God's eternal Being and economy.[63] Nyssen speaks of the soul's study of the Song as analogous to Moses' entry into the Holy of Holies. Its external appearance is plain, but its interior is glorious.[64] This is a curious description of a text whose images, which are external figures representing the One beyond sense and thought, give its rhetoric a rich, sensual texture. Yet Nyssen's point is that as evocative as the images of the text are, the transcendent or inner reality to which they point is so splendid as to make these images of the text seem plain.

Here we begin to see the paradoxical nature of the book. For the soul's experience of God in the Holy of Holies *is like Moses' encounter with God* in the Dark Cloud of Sinai, the God who cannot be grasped by the senses or by the intellect. The entry into the Holy of Holies is an entry into apophatic communion with God. Yet the very book that leads the soul into the apophatic is not free of sensual images at all, but virtually overpowers the soul with images built upon images.[65] How can a text whose vivid metaphors demand an engagement of the intellect in careful contemplation (*theōria*) lead the soul to the apophatic? Nyssen's homilies carry the contemplative soul into the apophatic through their use of paradox. The homilies unpack the meaning of the Song with paradoxical language: "passionless passion" and "knowing of unknowing." Paradox is a verbal negation of language. By juxtaposing or conjoining words of antithetical meaning the author breaks down our traditional understanding of their meaning; for the words cease to refer to the same concept. With Nyssen's use of paradox in the homilies one is left, not with incoherence or no meaning whatsoever, but with a palpable sense of divine qualities that push beyond our simplistic concepts of God. The riddle of the Song awakens the intellect's desire for God and the riddles are "resolved" only in the oxymoronic assertion of Nyssen's paradox. Thus Nyssen's paradox is a verbal similitude of the apophatic.

Although *Commentary on the Song of Songs* belongs to a different genre of writing than *Against Eunomius* or *On the Soul and Resurrection,* it is no less theological than these treatises. It expresses many of the same themes first articulated in these earlier works, but now in a different style.[66] For example, Nyssen's notion of persons of the Trinity, though distinct hypostases, work economically in a unity of operation. In homily six, Nyssen expresses this unity of operation in his interpretation of the metaphor of the archer from Song of Songs 2:5–6. The archer is the Father who sends the Son, i.e., the arrow, who gives the soul the Spirit, represented by the liquid in which the arrow is dipped, which infects the soul with transforming love for God.[67]

Another critical theological similarity between these homilies and Nyssen's earlier writings is the emphasis on the soul's preparation for entry into the Holy of Holies through the attainment of *apatheia.* While Proverbs trains the believer to love with "the lustful, passionate, even obsessive love which the Greeks called *erōs*,"[68] Nyssen says the entry into the Holy of Holies entails a passionless love: "Let not any passionate [*empathēs*] and fleshly person [*sarkōdēs*], who still gives off the deadly stench of the old Adam, drag the meaning of the inspired ideas and words down to the level of the brutish irrationality. No, let each depart from himself and get outside the material cosmos and ascend somehow, by way of impassibility [*di'apatheias*], into Paradise, having by purity been made like God."[69] Yet the passionate *erōs* taught by Proverbs is not in conflict with the *apatheia* that Nyssen counsels. For the impassible soul is not devoid of desire. Rather its desire is no longer for the base and fleshly, but for God. It is *erōs* because it is the most intense and pleasurable of all passion. At the same time it is an "impassible love" because its orientation is not that of the bestial passions of our lower nature.[70]

Because it is a passion for the incorporeal, *erōs* is viewed as dispassionate.[71] The reorientation of desire is not so much the elimination of *pathos* as it is the purging of *orexis*, the drive for pleasure, glory, and wealth.[72] Nyssen uses paradoxical language to describe this sanctified desire. *Apatheia* could be translated "lacking material passion." When one's desire is directed toward God, the passionate impulses that arise if one is focused on transitory material goods do not stir in the soul set upon eternal goods. In homily fifteen, Nyssen interprets Paul's radical claims in Galatians 2:20 that Christ "lives in him" and Philippians 1:21 "to live is Christ" to refer to a soul purified of such base emotions. He writes, "Paul cries out that no human, material passions [*hyilkōn pathēmatōn*] live in him, neither pleasure, grief, anger, fear, timidity, strong passions, pride, rashness, ill will, jealousy, vindictiveness, love of gain, nor any such habit that ruins his soul.... [He is saying] 'I do not have anything in myself which is not Christ.'"[73]

Yet this does not mean that one does not feel suffering and its accompanying emotions. Commenting on the Song's description (6:5) of the bride's virtues, "Your hair is as flocks of goats which have appeared from Galaad," Nyssen observes that hair, unlike another part of the body, lacks sensation; "its uniqueness [is] feeling no pain from burning or cutting." He therefore concludes, "The bride's hair teaches us that those persons seen around the bride's head must be of greater value than the senses, for they conceal sensation with wisdom.... The wise do not judge beauty by sight, not the good by taste; neither is assessment of beauty entrusted to smell, touch, or any other sense organ. When each sense is dead, the soul alone lays hold of and stretches forward to the good with respect to the mind."[74] He then explains that such a person even if thrown to the beasts or burned at the stake for the faith will endure the pain as if with the "insensitivity of the hair." Nyssen's point is not that the martyr feels no pain, but that the mind so controls soul and body that it is unaffected or unmoved in its faithfulness by the pains of the body.

Desire turned upon God undergoes transformation in two ways. First, the shift of orientation from the material to the Divine changes the moral quality of the desire. It ceases to be morally suspect and becomes a virtue. Humanity was created to "fall in love" with Wisdom. Second, desire has God as its sole object; the soul's habitual orientation toward the sensual realm and the habitual emotions that accompany that orientation are subdued. They begin to lose their power over the soul. Yet is the desire for God simply *erōs* sanctified? Are all the qualities of *erōs* common in the most intimate human relations transferred to the soul's relationship with God? Or is *erōs* itself radically altered, changed by the very nature of the God who is its object? In order to appreciate Nyssen's conception of this transformation, we first need to examine his understanding of the relation of desire and enjoyment.

Enjoyment and Holy Desire

Enjoyment (*apolausis*), in *Commentary on the Song of Songs,* is used differently than in *On the Soul and Resurrection* because of its close association with desire. In its most basic sense, *apolausis* is a form of *epithymia,* that is, it is a passion or emotion that refers to the satisfaction and fulfillment of one's desire.[75] Initially, *apolausis* is used in the pejorative sense as a base emotion associated with greed[76] and ambition.[77] The life of the Christian who strives after virtue is incompatible with one devoted to the pursuit of pleasure and *apolausis* in the present. Rather the virtuous life is represented by the pomegranate the exterior of which is hard and protected against thieves by thorns. One, therefore, cannot enjoy its fruit prematurely but must wait for the opening of the pod in its due season. So too the fruit of the virtuous life is not enjoyed in the present life but only in the fullness of time. Therefore, he concludes, "We must hear [the bride's] words and not become soft by indulgence and enjoyment of this present life. Rather, we should choose a life that has become toughened by continence. Thus virtue's fruit is inaccessible to thieves."[78] Ultimately the fruit of the virtuous life is the blessedness of beholding God's glory. Even as the bride is made to wait for the consummation of her marriage to the bridegroom until she is ready, so too the Christian must wait for the beatific union until she has achieved maturity or perfection. Nyssen explains that God intentionally does not reveal his great glory to one who is immature or a novice in the life of virtue. Rather, by delaying the vision, God makes the novice more and more eager for her goal. Thus the postponement of the soul's enjoyment (*hē anabolē tēs apolauseōs*) of God's great goodness serves pedagogically to bring the imperfect one to that perfect or suitable desire in which God and God alone is the object of one's longing.[79]

Although Nyssen in his interpretation of the pomegranate metaphor seems to relegate "enjoyment" of God to the age to come, he elsewhere in the homilies suggests that even in this life our desire for God arises, not out of total deprivation of God's goodness, but in part as a response to the joyful experience of God in the midst of our present circumstances. Commenting on the bride's description of the bridegroom in Song of Songs 1:9–14 as "a cluster of cypress in the vineyards of En-Gadi," Nyssen assumes that the "cluster of cypress" refers to the vines outside God's house (Ps. 127:3), heavy with the blossoms that will in time become the ripe grape and in turn become the wine that gladdens the heart (Ps. 103:15).

Reading this passage in the light of Jesus' own metaphor of the vine and the branches (John 15), Nyssen explains that the vine is Christ, the bridegroom, whose loveliness is manifest to the Christian in varying degrees corresponding to her maturity. To one who is new to the life of virtue, Christ is the blossoms; to one already made perfect in virtue, he is the wine. The latter revelation is the source of greater delight (*apolausis*) than the former stage.[80] Yet even in her immaturity, the novice derives no insignificant degree of enjoyment from Christ as the blossom: "A faith firm in a grace we hope for becomes a delight for us who wait in patience."[81] Although we do not experience the fullest degree of intimate communion with Christ our beloved until we are completely purged of corruption, we still experience enjoyment proleptically in the confident anticipation of the fulfillment of our hope. Our joy derives from two sources: (1) the expectancy of the greater blessedness to come but also from (2) the glory and beauty of the divine nature that the Incarnate Word reveals to us now. Hence Christ incarnate provides the soul a foretaste of a more glorious vision that awaits those who are patient and persist in the way of virtue.

The enjoyment that we derive from our experience of Christ through the Scriptures not only gives us a foretaste of the blessed communion to come, but it enables us to be inured to the lure of the sensual goods so that we might steal ourselves for the ascetic preparation for the joy to come. In his tenth homily on Song of Songs, Gregory comments on the bride's prayer at the end of chapter 4. She asks that the winds from north and south blow through her garden, allowing the beloved to come into the garden and enjoy the spice and the ripe berries. Not only is her petition fulfilled, but the bridegroom confers on her more blessings than she originally requested. For myrrh is mixed with spice, bread with honey, and wine is added to milk. For bread provides greater health than berries alone and even the berries are made into the more valued wine. Thus Gregory exclaims, "Oh blessed gardens, whose plants smell with such fruit and are transformed into every kind of nourishment according to the desire of those who enjoy them! To be enjoyed along with the fragrance of the bride's fruit is myrrh combined with spices. They mortify our earthly members and make a pure, fragrant life from the varied, different spices of virtue."[82]

This passage is significant for two reasons. First, the transformation of the berries into wine and the addition of the more nutritious bread with its sweet honey suggest that God answers our prayers by conferring on us grace that provides the nourishment necessary for perfection. Moreover the nourishing grace comes, not in the form of the bitter herbs that represent the Law, but as "the bread of gladness sweetened by the honey of the command."[83] Second and more importantly, the last clause explains how the enjoyable nature of grace assists the soul's growth in virtue. The grace, represented by the fragrant spice and the sweetened bread and the wine, enables us to mortify our members in the process of ascetic training in the ways of virtue. Nyssen seems to imply that the delight we take from the grace conferred makes the soul all the more resolved to do whatever is necessary, including the mortification of the flesh, so that we might gain that greater degree of enjoyment when we are purified and made ready to be united with Christ.[84] This description of our enjoyment of God is not in tension with his account in *On the Soul and Resurrection.*

The real conflict, however, is his view of the relation of *apolausis* and *desire*. In the homilies, *apolausis* is not a static contentment; rather Nyssen speaks of our *apolausis* of present goods as the source of *epithymia* for more and greater goods. In his first homily on Song of Songs, Nyssen explains that in the life after the resurrection we shall gain an angelic freedom from the passions, which he explains in terms of the absence of conflict between the passions and the mind. Our resurrected nature will be free from such corruption because both our flesh and our spirit will have one spirit.[85] Then immediately on the heels of this discussion of our resurrected nature he says that once the soul has learned that God alone is truly desirable (*alēthōs glykyte kai epithymēton kai erasmion*) and worthy of love, its "eternal enjoyment becoming a starting point of greater desire [*meizonos epithymias*] is intensified or expanded with respect to its desire for participation in God's goodness."[86] Because of his interjection of an exhortation to live in the present in anticipation of our life in the resurrection,[87] one is not clear whether the soul's recognition of God's supremely loveable nature comes in this life or after the resurrection. Nevertheless, the phrase "eternal enjoyment" suggests that he conceives of our eschatological participation in God as being driven by a dialectic between enjoyment and desire.

The same erotic dynamic that explains the soul's ascent to God in this life applies to his description of the soul's eschatological participation in God. In the twelfth homily, Nyssen describes this dialectic: "When she [i.e., the bride] hoped, like Moses, that the king's face would appear to her, the one whom she desired escapes her grasp. She says, 'my beloved has passed by' but he did so not to forsake her soul's desire, but to draw her to himself."[88] Instead of revealing his face, i.e., his full glory, to the soul, God reveals only his backside, i.e., a partial glimpse. He does so because it is impossible for the soul to comprehend the fullness of God's infinite nature. Yet God uses the limitations of our capacity to comprehend his infinite being for the soul's ultimate redemption by drawing the desire-filled soul into communion with him.

We see this dynamic at work in Gregory's metaphor of Christ as both the blossom on the grape vine and the blood of the grape, wine. The glimpse of God's glory revealed in the Incarnation provides the new Christian with such a foretaste of the greater beauty to be experienced at the consummation of Christ's kingdom that her soul is filled with desire for the greater vision yet to come. From her early meditation on the image of Christ's goodness portrayed in Scripture an incipient desire for God is born that sets her soul in motion, ever seeking the object of her desire. In this respect Nyssen treats Moses' unquenchable desire for God as paradigmatic of all who share his deep love for God. Even as Moses "sought God as if he had never seen him," so too those who share his ardor, "never cease to desire, but every enjoyment of God they turn into the kindling of a still more intense desire."[89] Thus our present enjoyment, incomparable though it may be to the soul's delight at the beatific vision to come, arouses and intensifies our desire for God. Since our knowledge of God is a knowledge gained not principally by encountering God face to face but by following the one who reveals himself, God uses our desire born of *apolausis* to entice the soul to follow him. Following him the soul sees and enjoys more of the divine beauty and so grows in its yearning to share in God's virtues and enjoy the blessing of more intimate communion.

Nyssen employs the dialectic between *apolausis* and *epithymia* to describe our eschatological participation in God because, contrary to the account of God as the "all in all" in *On the Soul and Resurrection*, the

Bridegroom is not immediately present to the soul. In the passage cited above, the bride is not a novice but has achieved the perfection in virtue by which she is made ready for the consummation of her marriage. For he says of her, "Whoever dies to good lives for evil, and he who dies to evil, lives for virtue. Thus the bride's hands are correctly shown to be full of myrrh; by her death to all sin she rises to make an entrance for the Word. The Word whom she admits is life. [Thus] the soul looking towards God is raised to this sublime height."[90] The bride's hands are covered with myrrh, which iconographically denotes her death both with respect to sin and the soul's separation from the body. Her passage into life eternal is marked by her opening the gate of the kingdom, at which she expects to find her beloved bridegroom waiting for her. Instead she but sees him running past her. Thus he explicitly says of the bride, "Once the soul has risen through death and has been filled with myrrh, it places its hands on the door's bolt by means of good works and hopes that the desired one will enter within. Then the bridegroom passes by and the bride exits; she no longer remains in the place where she had been, but touches the Word who leads her on."[91]

The reason Nyssen is not always clear as to whether he is describing the bride in this life or in the life to come is precisely that the soul's communion with God after the resurrection mirrors the process of the soul's ascent to God in this life. He writes, "I believe that we are taught that the person desiring to see God can behold the desired one by always following him. [For] the contemplation of God's face is a never ending journey toward him accomplished by following right behind the word."[92] Thus he implies that the process of contemplation which is begun in this life by imitation of God's virtues and by meditation upon God's likeness revealed in Scripture will not cease once we enter the kingdom. It will not cease precisely because we never fully comprehend the one on whom we meditate. Rather we are filled with desire to see even more.[93] Even when Gregory speaks of the soul as being united to God by the bonds of love, he is explicit that the enjoyment derived from that union is never so complete as to be an unsurpassable height of joy.[94] For the more we cling to the words of the bridegroom that are spirit and life, the more we become spirit.

So far, Nyssen's account in *Commentary on the Song of Songs* of the soul's enjoyment of communion with God in the life to come is fundamentally at odds with the descriptions of our eschatological participation in *On the Soul and Resurrection*. Yet even in the homilies on the Song of Songs, Nyssen qualifies his account of *epithymia* and *apolausis* by

suggesting that the desire that drives the soul in its eschatological participation is not identical to the desire that propels the imperfect soul in
the present age.

Although the present age and the age to come have as a common
characteristic the soul's endless contemplation of God, Nyssen acknowledges that the model of erotic desire that characterizes our present love
of God will be outmoded in the eschaton. In his eleventh homily on
the Song of Songs he writes that in the age to come when heaven and
earth have passed away and our knowledge is not as it is now, "we will
fully comprehend the form of the ineffable beauty according to a different mode of enjoyment, the nature of which has not yet entered man's
heart."[95] There are several things that are striking about this passage.
First, his allusion to 1 Corinthians 13 assumes that our knowledge now
is limited but that in the eschaton it will be full. Were Nyssen to take the
idea of *full* comprehension literally, he would be contradicting one of
the central claims of his doctrine of epectasy, articulated not only in the
eleventh homily but in all the homilies.[96] If Nyssen's comment is at all
consistent with *epektasis,* one must conclude that he uses the hyperbolic
language of Paul to convey the sense that God will be present to us in
an immediate manner, rather than indirectly through a dark glass as he
is now. This immediate experience of the divine will enable us to know
God with a certainty and clarity not characteristic of our experience of
God through faith as in our present circumstances.

Second, he speaks of our "comprehending" God's beauty through
"enjoyment." The implication is that we shall experience God's immediate presence not principally through our cognitive competence, but
affectively. Our "knowledge" of God's ineffable beauty, therefore, is not
something arrived at by sheer force of our contemplative efforts. Rather,
as with Moses standing in the rock, we experience the immediate presence of God who reveals himself to us. Our joy is serendipitous. Every
new feature of the divine nature that he reveals surprises us, for each new
revelation discloses a splendor beyond our imagination or expectation.
This reflects a change in the nature of *erōs* in the eschaton. Whereas one
of the chief features of *erōs* in the present life is that it seeks to seize,
possess, and control the beloved, such is not the case when the Beloved
is an infinite God. Nyssen is conscious that this change in *erōs* is characteristic of those who are ready to study the Song of Songs. Whereas the
soul under the tutelage of Proverbs seeks to possess the divine virtues for
its own uses, as an impetuous young man seeks to possess a beautiful
maiden, the soul in Song of Songs is now the bride. While not passive, the
soul of the bride has sufficiently grown in wisdom to know that it cannot

presume to possess or control the divine Beloved. Rather the soul's love is not that of masculine adolescence, but of feminine receptivity.[97]

Third and most important for our immediate purposes, Nyssen says explicitly that our mode of enjoying God is unprecedented in our present situation. It is unprecedented because it is based on an experience of God unlike any we have known before. His key assumption is that the character of *apolausis* is determined by the nature of our knowledge of God. And since our eschatological consciousness or knowledge of the divine possesses an immediacy and a clarity that is not typical of our experience in this age, the manner of our enjoyment will also be different than it is at present. The significant conclusion to be drawn is that even in his sermons on the Song of Songs Nyssen is conscious that his model of *apolausis* and *epithymia* must be modified to fit the different character of God's presence to the soul in the eschaton.

Does he convey any sense of *what* that new mode of enjoyment might take? In homily twelve, after describing the bride's passage from this life into life eternal, he begins to describe the soul's feeling of futility as its chases after the One whom it tries to follow. In accordance with his account of Moses in the dark cloud (*Life of Moses*), the soul, represented by the bride, experiences God as the one who is beyond sense and thought. "After the soul has gone out at her spouse's word, she seeks him who cannot be found. She calls him who cannot be comprehended by any name, is taught by the guards that she loves him who is unattainable, and goes after him who cannot be seized."[98] According to Nyssen's allegory, the perfected bride may have hoped that upon opening the gate of the kingdom her waiting would be over and at last she would be able to draw her beloved to her and hold him in her arms. But even in the kingdom the soul never *possesses* the God in whose nature it participates and from whom all its sustenance and delight are derived.

This is problematic inasmuch as he has already said using the metaphor of the blossoms and the grapes that the mature soul's eschatological enjoyment of Christ the bridegroom is like partaking of the vine and not merely looking at a lovely bloom. The metaphor seems to suggest that the delight of the immature soul is the proleptic joy of one who sees ever so partially the joy that awaits him. The delight of the pure soul comes from drinking in Christ's goodness. Drinking suggests partaking of the divine goodness in a more immediate way than merely looking at its external beauty. Yet in the passage from homily twelve, God seems anything but near at hand. Not only is there no sense of "drinking in" the Divine, but there is also no sense that the bride catches much of a glimpse of the bridegroom. At best she is able to touch only his robe as she follows where he leads her.

What is more, Nyssen describes the bride's futile pursuit of her beloved in even more dower terms. He explains the violent episode in Song of Songs 5:7 ("The watchmen . . . in the city found me. They smote me, they wounded me; the keepers of the walls took away my veil from me.") as a painful epiphany through which the soul must pass in its transition from life in the present age to life in the age to come. On one hand this moment of transition is violent because, from our perspective, our desire for God will be satisfied in the Kingdom but satisfied in a way incomparably more wondrous than the joy of the present age. In other words, according to the *erōs* motif, our desire is satisfied when we obtain and possess that for which we have been longing and which we have been pursuing. Even though, as Aristophanes' myth makes clear, the satisfaction is short-lived, there is still the sense that even if for a brief time our longing is fulfilled and we are satisfied in holding the object of our desire. At the climax of the soul's quest, the frenetic impulses of *epithymia* subside, and the soul momentarily rests in the enjoyment of its beloved. Yet the rest of satisfaction is truly fleeting. For soon the soul becomes discontent with its prize due to the imperfections in its likeness of true beauty. Driven by a renewed longing it sets off in search of a higher form of beauty. Thus the violence inflicted on the bride represents for Nyssen the shock our soul receives when we realize that our enjoyment of God's nature is not as we imagine now; for our expectations of *apolausis* are predicated on an outmoded model of desire and fulfillment. Consequently, he writes of the bride, "Because the desire for her beloved is frustrated, her yearning for his beauty cannot be satisfied."[99]

On the other hand, however, the same epiphany that casts the soul into disappointment brings the soul to a profounder form of satisfaction and fulfillment. For at that moment when the bride is set upon by the guards the veil falls from her eyes. Then she recognizes that her eschatological experience of God's infinite being bestows upon her a higher form of *apolausis*. He writes, "But the veil of despair is removed when the bride learns that the true satisfaction of her desire [*hē alēthēs tou pothoumenou apolausis*] consists in always progressing in her search and ascent: when her desire is fulfilled, it gives birth to a different desire (*heteran epithymian*) for the transcendent."[100] Desire finds its true satisfaction — its true enjoyment — in the realization that the goods of God will never grow old but will continue to excite the soul and eternally arouse desire for more. Here the bride has undergone a gestalt. She now sees that God's infinite and therefore incomprehensible nature is not the cause of despair or frustration of unsatisfied desire, but is the very hope of our eternal enjoyment of God. With this realization, the soul surrenders the erotic impulse that seeks to possess God for its own. Its desire is satisfied in waiting to receive God's newest self-disclosure. Our enjoyment comes as we recognize that our desire for God will never wane. Moreover, this satisfaction of desire is eternally progressive. Earlier in the same homily, Nyssen comments on the activity of the bride in light of Jesus' metaphor of the good shepherd who is the door of the sheepfold through whom the sheep go in and out (John 10:9): "She never ceases going in nor going out, but always enters into that which is above through progress and always begins from what she has already apprehended."[101] The soul, like the sheep in the fold, is in constant movement; but unlike the sheep who go in and out of the safe confines of the sheepfold, the soul's movement is always movement within God. It is a movement of progress that always has as its starting point the soul's "prior" experience of God. The ascent of the soul, therefore, parallels Moses' journey into God, which Nyssen immediately recounts. Although these passages are describing the soul's ascent to God in this life rather than its eschatological communion, this view of enjoyment as unending progress can equally describe the eternal enjoyment of God in the eschaton.

Our enjoyment of God's transcendent goodness is progressive precisely because all progress is made *in God*. Arguably the heart of *Life of Moses* lies in Nyssen's extended commentary on Moses' request to see God's face and instead being shown God's backside (Exod. 33:12–32). Here he presents his final view of *epektasis*. If the soul has shed its attachments to the mundane and material pleasures and looks to the one who is the Good, "the soul rises ever higher and will always make its flight yet higher — by its desire of the heavenly things *straining ahead (synepekteinomenē) for what is still to come*. "[102] The ascent is unending because the soul's desire increases in intensity[103] as it seeks God's beauty, which is without limit.[104] Nyssen observes that Moses made the greatest progress in God while he was standing still firmly planted in the cleft of the rock in the shadow of God's hand. "In another Scriptural passage the soaring progress [*dromos*] is a standing still [*stasis*], for it says, *You must stand on the rock*. This is the greatest paradox [*paradoxotaton*] of all: how the same thing is both standing still [*stasis*] and moving [*kinēsis*]. For he who ascends certainly does not stand still, and he who stands still does not move upwards. But here the ascent takes place by means of the standing still [*hestanai*],"[105]

Moses receives the vision of God's glory, i.e., God's backside, and so progresses in his knowledge of God only when he is standing still.

The paradox is that the soul's movement in God comes only in a *stasis*. While Nyssen gives a moral interpretation of the scene as an exhortation to be firmly planted in Christ and not give in to doubts that may cause regression,[106] he goes on to explain that Moses sees the glory of God by standing in Christ because "since Christ is understood by Paul as the rock, all hope of good things is believed to be in Christ, in whom we have learned all the treasures of good things to be. He who finds any good finds it in Christ who contains all."[107] Thus progress in the knowledge of God is made in Christ because Christ, as the only begotten of the infinite God, contains all the divine goods that the soul ever could desire. Moses' standing in Christ, in whom the fullness of God dwelt, is a type for the soul's eschatological life in the "all in all." Christ is also the hand of God that covers Moses in the rock and that discloses God's back. This divine hand is "a help to the person who has joined himself close behind God . . . and who waits in the rock upon the divine voice and prays that he might follow behind."[108]

Here Nyssen applies to Moses his description of the bride who follows after the Bridegroom. For Moses' seeing God's backside signifies that we can never see God's face; we can only follow behind him. The moral meaning is that progress is made only when we follow Christ looking in the same direction as he.[109] Nyssen is also making an epistemological judgment. The soul cannot behold the full glory of God directly. The image of the backside represents the partial vision of the infinite God we are capable of receiving. Christ as the "place" where Moses beheld God is the soul of the Christian, "the 'place' in which infinite desire 'runs,' i.e., the transcendent world where we will follow God — but only see his 'back.' "[110] Moses' request to see God's glory was satisfied as he gazed after God from the rock. As he stood in the rock, his desire soared, wanting to see even more divine wonders.

In Moses' "soaring *stasis*" and the Bride's enjoyment of progress there is a parallel of which Nyssen himself is conscious, for he comments, "In a similar way [to the bride's experience], the Lord's face passed Moses by, and thus the lawgiver's soul kept going out of that state which it had attained, ever following the word who went before him."[111] The passage about the bride's fallen veil and the passage alluding to the good shepherd are important because they help to define the eschatological character of *apolausis*. In the former passage, he says that *alethes apolausis* consists in "ever progressing" while in the latter he says that the soul makes progress only while being immovably fixed *in* the self-disclosing Word. The idea of "soaring *stasis*" does not in and of itself reconcile the views of eschatological epectasy in *On the Soul and Resurrection* and *Commentary on the Song of Songs*. Both the homilies and *Life of Moses* insist that enjoyment leads to an eternal increase in desire whereas *On the Soul and Resurrection* views the eschatological enjoyment of God as the end of desire.

Yet the description of our eschatological participation in the eternal God using the oxymoronic language of "soaring *stasis*" or "impassible love" challenges our conventional ways of speaking of desire and eternity, of change and permanence. Nyssen's paradox awakens intellectual desire to resolve the riddle by reconsidering the compatibility of two incompatibles. In order for oxymoronic expressions to be true paradoxes, i.e., *apparent* contradictions, and not simply outright contradictions in terms, the ideas must be compatible in some way. A paradox is a synthesis of concepts in which one term negates and yet adds to the other term some nuance in a way that they do not cancel out each other but create a new way of viewing reality. In this instance, the project is not to give exegetical analysis of "soaring *stasis*" or "impassible love." Rather the question is whether Nyssen's description of the soul's experience of God as the "all in all" can be integrated into his view of God as the object of endless desire. In the eschatological consummation of creation, is there a sense in which desire is replaced by beatific enjoyment and at the *same time* that enjoyment leads to a renewal of desire? Following the logic of Nyssen's early view of epectasy in *On the Soul and Resurrection* and his later view in *Commentary on the Song of Songs* and *Life of Moses*, this is the synthesis toward which hs eschatology leads.

A Constructive Synthesis:
Epectasy as the Transformation of the Erotic

There is no simple integration of Nyssen's early and late views of epectasy. This in many ways reflects his approach to theology. Nyssen, while a careful thinker at many levels, was not a systematic theologian in the modern sense. Nyssen's eschatology in general and specifically his treatment of the resurrection cannot be spoken of in the singular; he has not one eschatology, but many eschatologies. Nor does he feel any compulsion to reconcile them.; for they are but speculations and insights of a reality seen as through a glass dimly. The works themselves are also stylistically different. *On the Soul and Resurrection* is an imitation of Plato's *Phaedo* and therefore has a philosophical character, whereas the homilies of *Commentary on the Song of Songs* employ vivid images that engage his listeners rather than careful philosophical distinctions.[112]

Nevertheless, both works offer a theocentric account of the eschatological transformation of humanity. Although the transformation of the resurrection occurs by divine fiat, the change in the soul's love is directly related to the nature of the God in whom humanity participates. More to the point, eschatologically humanity's love of God will be different, not primarily because our bodies will be different, but because our experience of God will be different. Nyssen's early and late views of epectasy each emphasize a different aspect of God's nature. These different dimensions of the Divine, I would suggest, draw out different dimensions of the soul's love of God.

The eschatology of *On the Soul and Resurrection* is shaped by two concerns: explaining how the pure nature of the *imago Dei*, which has been obscured by the passions of our bestial nature, is restored eschatologically and at the same time describing how the soul's participation in God can be conceived of as an eternal progress in the Good. The easy solution would have been to extend Macrina's revised account of the passions and argue that reason so controls the appetitive impulses that they are no longer like those of beasts — ever directed downward to the sensual and mundane — but are holy desires for God and God alone. Instead, Nyssen followed a harder line of reasoning. First, by distinguishing between multiple types of movement in the soul, Nyssen is able to describe the soul's participation in God as an intellectual movement set in motion by curiosity and wonder rather than by desire. This segregation of the rational and irrational faculties is actually at odds with his own organic view of the soul, which assumes that love is essentially the reaction of the appetitive faculties to the intellect's apprehension of the beauty of the intelligible realities.

Second, his argument that the soul's experience of God as "all and in all" changes the character of our love from an erotic desire (*epithymia*) to a holy love (*agapē*) characterized by enjoyment (*apolausis*) that does not look to the past or future out of some dissatisfaction with the present. While Nyssen's asceticism assumes that there is a greater continuity between the life of the saint in the present and the life of the resurrection, his position here makes a conscious distinction between our experience of God in the present age and in the age to come. This more subtle position focuses explicitly on the eschaton whereas neither *Commentary on the Song of Songs* or *Life of Moses* make a clear distinction between their description of the present and the life of the resurrection. In fact, given the rhetorical and pedagogical purpose of these texts, they are more concerned about the former than they are the latter.[113] What aspect of the Divine does Nyssen's account of God as "all in all" emphasize? It is

that God is the locus of the soul's perfect fulfillment. God is the source
and sum of all goods that the soul could ever desire. In the perfection
of God's limitless beauty, the soul will never experience any defect that
would mar its enjoyment of God. God as the "all in all" is the end of
desire in the sense that the soul need look nowhere else for its joy.

The *Commentary on the Song of Songs* must be viewed first and foremost as a Lenten sermon series the chief aim of which is to inspire a
love so pure and single-minded that his parishioners may become like
the bride and so ready for the celebration of Easter, which points not
simply back to Christ's resurrection but to the final resurrection[114] when
they, like the bride in Song of Songs, shall be united with Christ, their
Bridegroom. The key rhetorically to this exhortation to perseverance
on the upward way is to explain the frustrating points along the soul's
journey where, for all of the soul's disciplined striving, it has not come
to "possess" the Beloved whom the soul seeks. He addresses this issue
by emphasizing the progressive nature of the soul's journey to God and
by depicting the process itself as a glorious movement into God who,
as it turns out, can never be possessed. Behind this pastoral concern is
Nyssen's own theological agenda. Namely, he seeks to work out how
a finite creature, who by the nature of her creatureliness is marked by
diastēma and so is forever located in place and time, participates in the
life of a God in whom there is no *diastēma* but whose eternal being encompasses all times and places. Because God is infinite, he is inherently
beyond the comprehension of finite creatures.

This is the theological explanation behind the pastoral concern for
the persevering saints. How can the finite and extended enter into the
life of the infinite and unextended? How can we come to know the unknowable deity? The language of the Song of Songs and the Pentateuch's
account of Moses' life provide with him with the images — following
behind the Bridegroom, beholding God's backside, seeing the Beloved's
finger, touching his robe — that shift Christian epistemology from the
Greek and Pauline language of "seeing" God "face to face" to sensing
the presence of God who is simple and infinite. Because God is simplicity, he is unique and beyond human language and thought, which
understand and classify by way of analogues (none of which can apply
to God). Because the Divine is infinite he can never be comprehended
or fully known. Because *Life of Moses* and *Commentary on the Song of
Songs* focus on the ultimate incomprehensibility of God as well as his
perfect goodness, they describe the soul's enjoyment of God as an enjoyment of the very *process* of experiencing a God who, as ever new and

progressively more wondrous, is the cause of unending and ever inten-sifying desire. Even as God's perfection is manifest in his being infinite, the perfection of humanity is recognized in its infinite growth in love for the infinite God.

Nyssen's later doctrine of epectasy makes two necessary corrections of *On the Soul and Resurrection*. First, the homilies challenge the view that the intellectual movement into God can be made independent of desire. To be sure, pure love is "impassible love," which is distinct from carnal desire, i.e., desire not directed by the intellect to God but led by the senses or the co-opted intellect to sensual or mundane goods. Yet Nyssen in the later works recognizes that there is not intellectual move-ment that is not accompanied or driven by desire. The contemplative curiosity that propels the soul through its study of the Songs of Song to God is *epithymia* informed by the intellect's apprehension of the Divine in the images of Scripture. The dialectic between purgation and illumi-nation seen in the soul's ascent in *Life of Moses* is a dynamic synergy of the intellect and desire. The soul experiences God with the intellect and the affections together. The intellect is capable of receiving greater revelations of God because the appetites predispose the intellect to study and contemplate more earnestly.

The second correction is an immediate consequence of the first. If there is not intellectual movement unaccompanied by *orexis*, then desire is an essential component of our participation in God, in this life and in the eschaton. The provocative language of the Song of Songs provides the perfect context in which to reintroduce the erotic to his account of epectasy. Yet *On the Soul and Resurrection* adds a nuance to erotic love missing in the homilies precisely because they lack a clear distinc-tion between the present age and the eschaton. This is the synthesis: eschatologically, *erōs* is retained but also transformed.

Although Nyssen forthrightly speaks of love as *erōs* in the homilies, this *erōs* is not identical with the *erōs* motif of Plato's *Symposium*. Ac-cording to the Platonic tradition that incorporated the view of love articulated in Aristophanes' speech, *erōs* is inherent in the unstable and uncertain realm of becoming. The sensible realm is always in flux. Change follows a pattern of birth, decay, and death. *Erōs* is born amid the unceasing cycles of acquisition and loss, blossom and fade. In such a world where the beloved is neither perfect nor lasting, the lover never knows complete satisfaction. Along the way in its quest for beauty the soul that has ascended the heavenly ladder may experience the beatific vision of the very soul of beauty. Such moments constitute the high-est experience of joy for the rational soul. Yet such episodes are short lived. For the philosopher must return to the streets of Athens to turn the educable souls from their illusions to the real and the true. In a realm where there is neither permanence nor perfection the individual lives in a state of lacking. The goods she does possess are not without blemish and even the best of these goods is lost sooner or later. In Aristophanes' speech, the quest for wholeness through sexual union is emblematic of the individual's labors in life. Yet his tale is a tragedy, for Aristophanes' conclusion is that "sexuality does not produce wholeness. Instead it produces internal division between, on the one hand, a drive towards a meaningless, fleeting wholeness...and, on the other, an activity that results in genuine human survival."[115] Because man, in Aristophanes' view, can never transcend the body, which represents the flux of life, he lives "within the self-contradictory dimension of desire and satisfaction: self-contradictory because [it is] perpetually cyclic."[116]

Socrates' model lover, the philosopher, illustrates Plato's reworking of the Greek *erōs* motif by introducing the notion of love as a characteristic of human nature, which is incomplete and eternally in process. The love described by Agathon is the love of reciprocal admiration of the perfectly beautiful for the perfectly beautiful. It is the esteem of equals. It is the love characteristic of the realm of eternal being that admits no deficiency of beauty or excellence. Naturally Agathon's conception of love accords with Nyssen's account of the love shared between the persons of the Trinity. Yet Plato's concept of love (as expressed in the words of Diotima and Socrates and illustrated in the ideal of the philosopher) is a love proper to "becoming" — that mean between complete privation or nonexistence and perfect actuality. It is the love of creatures who participate in the Beautiful and so possess enough beauty in themselves that they may discern the loveliness of others as well as the perfect beauty of the Good. At the same time, they also recognize the partial nature of their own beauty. Thus the desiring character of love is born out of an awareness of the lack of perfection in one's own beauty and the beauty of those things that surround us. Although creatures, for whom the diastemic change is inherent in their creatureliness, will never attain a godlike wholeness and completeness either in this life or the next, nevertheless, the becoming that characterizes this life and that proper to the eschaton are decidedly different.

In the present age, there is no union between the soul and God in which the soul experiences God as "all in all." In large part this is the result of our current state of embodiment. Our appetitive faculties are naturally oriented toward securing the material needs of the body. Even though the ascetic life tries to wean the soul away from its attachments to the material world, freeing desire for movement toward God, the body's simplest needs must be met and protected. Because the soul's appetites will always be divided between seeking the material goods for the flesh and striving after God, maximal union with God in this life cannot be achieved.

Even the virtue of courage — *thymos* controlled by reason to serve the pursuit of the Good — is a necessary diversion of consciousness and emotional energy to the task of keeping in check the impulse of fleshly desire and temptations from the Devil. These internal conflicts and external threats from the adversary hinder sustained communion with God. Even for a Christian who through ascetic discipline has mortified the flesh completely — someone such as Macrina — the body's pains and ailments prevent an entry into the felicity of union with Christ. In his depiction of Macrina's last days, Nyssen is clear that she had so transcended love for the things of this life that she experienced a proleptic joy in anticipation of her union with her Bridegroom. Yet this joy was not sustained, but repeatedly interrupted by the painful decay of her body. Therefore, in this life we who lack full and sustained union with God desire that fellowship which we do not have, and in hope and longing we stretch our mind toward the day of uncompromised fellowship with God. Out of our current lack of union with God, our love is *erōs*, a longing for that which we do not as yet enjoy. Unlike the *erōs* of Aristophanes which is tragic and will never be perfectly satisfied, the passionate longing analogous to hungering and thirsting for God is a *hopeful* desire because it is confident that God himself will one day be our food and drink. In the resurrection, when the body shall put on incorruption and we shall be like the angels, God will be "all and in all" because we will be sustained entirely by communion with God. Therefore, Christian love, in this age, is a hopeful, rather than a tragic, *erōs*.

How does the experience of God as "all in all" change the character of the hopeful *erōs* of the present age? The desire and hope for God is born, not out of lack, but out of the experience of God's *immediate* and *ubiquitous* presence. When God is "all in all" the Divine pervades all our thoughts so we are fully conscious of his sustaining presence. God is immediately, perfectly, and uninterruptedly present to the soul. Therefore, the soul's love of God does not resemble Aristophanes' *erōs*. For the soul never lacks the goods of the divine nature that are ubiquitous, accessible, and without defect. In such a context, the soul, even if it cannot experience all of God's goodness all at once, cannot be said to experience the poverty or want (save in comparison with the divine nature itself) that breeds the *frustrated longing* of *erōs*. Even if one were to view the soul's eschatological state as lacking the boundless goods that the soul in some sense desires to have, the desire of which Nyssen speaks in the homilies on the Song of Songs is free from the futile striving and disappointment often characteristic of desire in the present age.

Erōs in the pagan Greek sense sprang from the unstable and uncertain soil of the realm of flux. For Nyssen, the soul's erotic movement is necessarily a form of creaturely becoming. But it is a perfect becoming. For it is a becoming that occurs *in* the presence of God whose perfection and eternity establish a stability and certainty to our becoming that does not exist in the present age. Therefore because the soul's enjoyment is of that which is infinitely perfect in its beauty, the soul has no fear or anxiety about being disappointed "some time down the road" because God's beauty has somehow diminished or been found wanting "with the passage of time."

Even when God is "all in all" our love always retains an erotic hue. Because God is eternal Being and we are finite, the ontological gap between us and God can never be overcome. Eschatologically, God may be the object of our thoughts and our spiritual senses, but he will always be an *object*. For our union with God is the union of *koinōnia* or communion with, rather than absorption into, the Divine. Nyssen's depiction of the bride chasing after the Bridegroom who is hastening on ahead is a poetic representation of the unbridgeable ontological gap between God's Being and our becoming. God, therefore, will always be the *Other*. So our love reaches to him as Other. Yet when God is "all in all" the Divine will be the Other who is *near at hand*. While our experience of God is always only partial such that there is always some aspect of the Divine that is a distant horizon, eschatologically we are never at a distance from God. When God is "all in all," the soul never shall experience *Deus absconditus*. Therefore the soul's erotic movement in God is, as Paul Plass puts it, a " 'motionless motion' that is always at the 'place' to which it is 'going.' "[117] The *erōs* of this life is a striving *toward* God whose revelations refresh us, ever drawing us to him; the *erōs* of the age to come is a rapacious enjoyment of being *fully within* the embracing presence of God. Since this embrace is by an infinitely wondrous God, the soul will be eternally excited, ever seeking insight into God's goodness. This eschatological *erōs* is a "soaring *stasis*." It is soaring because it is ever ascending. It is *stasis* because the soul is perfectly situated in God's presence. Is this *stasis* comparable to Augustine's restless soul that finally "rests in" God?[118] If by rest we mean that the soul ceases all activity and passively receives God's blessings, then the answer is no. But if by rest we mean peace in fellowship with God when the struggles of this life that attend our that quest for God are ended and we are content to live in the presence of the supremely Beautiful, then, yes, rest must be a dimension of eschatological epectasy. God fills our life completely, but we are not full. We are eternally satisfied by God's goodness, yet we never become satiated. The soul's eschatological movement in the ubiquitous and eternal God replaces an anxious sense of "longing after the beloved who is far removed" (typical of Greek *erōs*) with a hopeful desire for more of God that is in some sense serene and peaceful because it is confident that the God who is with us will presently reveal more of the wonders of his goodness. This is the difference between desire born of enjoyment (*apolausis*) of God and Aristophanes' *erōs*, which futilely seeks to fill the void of the self's isolation and separation from the one who would make her whole.

Does the eschaton bring an end to time consciousness? In *On the Soul and Resurrection* Nyssen is explicit that people do not hope for a present good that they immediately enjoy. Yet in *Life of Moses* he revives the language of hope. Since time consciousness is born of desire, our eternal desire for more means that we will forever have an eye to further revelations. Time as an ontological reality inherent in our creatureliness is an unalterable reality. But does *erōs* of the eschaton produce time consciousness? A synthesis of Nyssen's early and late theories of epectasy that retains the erotic in its transformed form as satisfied but insatiate desire should do two things. First, it should preserve the sense of our ecstatic enjoyment of God in which we lose self-consciousness and its corollary, time-consciousness. Second, this synthesis should preserve the "forward looking" aspect of desire summed up in the word "hope." Yet any account of hope must be grounded in the soul's enjoyment of God rather than discontent with the present.

What would such a synthesis be like? The analogy I would use is that of reading an intensely engaging book, such as a superbly crafted mystery, in which the plot's unfolding draws the reader along to its conclusion or resolution. Reading such a book, we may become so absorbed in its details and the author's gradual provocative disclosure of clues that we lose track of time. Hours pass with scarcely a thought. We may even be so enthralled that we do not want to put the book down to attend to activities outside of the world of the book. Yet as absorbed as we are in the book, thoroughly pleased by the author's skillful storytelling, our mind is ever active *looking forward,* not out of boredom, but in anticipation of where the present details direct the plot. In this scenario, the reader is both fully enjoying the book and at the same time looking ahead. This "looking ahead" takes place within the "timelessness" of reading. The enjoyment of the book means that one is uninterested in anything outside of the world of the book; this is what it means to lose track of time while reading. At the same time, the desire to know what happens next arises from our enjoyment of the book. In fact, the more we enjoy the book the greater our desire is to know what happens next. Our curiosity is driven by our desire.

In the same way, one could imagine that loving God and enjoying his goodness so completely one had no desire to be anywhere else but in God's presence. Such unalloyed satisfaction means that one was lost in the love of the Beloved. (This is similar to the experience of young lovers who lose track of time because they are hopelessly enthralled with each other.) Yet as each of God's successive revelations stirs the intellect's sense of wonder, the intellect in its contemplation might well leap ahead or press forward in eager anticipation of what God will reveal next. As a creature marked by *diastēma,* man can never cross the ontological divide between ourselves and God, and so enter God's eternity. As such our lives, both now and in the eschaton, cannot escape becoming or desire. Yet unlike the dialectic of desire and enjoyment in the present age, which is episodic and sporadic, the desire flowing from an eternal enjoyment of God's infinite goodness is uninterrupted. The unending progression of our becoming and our desire follows God's ceaseless self-disclosure of his infinite being. This eschatological freedom from interruption must, in some sense, be free from distractions and dissatisfactions which make us time conscious.

One brief word needs to be said about the role of the apophatic experience of God and the transformation of *erōs.* The soul's movement within the presence of God is expressed most evocatively in Nyssen's account of the apophatic moment. As with Moses' entry into the great cloud, apophasis entails a negation of the rational faculties in that the soul surrenders the move by the intellect to conceptualize God because the soul discovers that God is beyond knowledge. Yet the paradox is that this unknowing brings the highest knowledge of God. The knowing of unknowing is not an agnostic experience. On the contrary, it is the moment of greatest knowledge because the soul apprehends with absolute certainty the presence of the One who cannot be mastered by any name. The soul senses God's presence rather than sees God's face. This apophatic experience is the *immediate* experience of God and his mystical goodness, which fills the soul with such confidence that it feel itself separated from God. In the cloud of unknowing, we see both the inherently erotic nature of humanity and the distinctly Christian character of that *erōs.* On the one hand, we are aware of the ontological gulf between the creature and its God. In the cloud, God appears to the soul radically other than when he is the object of intellectual speculations. Therefore, our love possesses the ecstatic qualities of *erōs*. On the other hand, in its experience of God as wholly Other, the soul realizes the futility of the erotic impulse to possess the Beloved. Moreover, because the soul is enveloped by the sure presence of the supremely good God, it feels neither the poverty of lack nor the dissatisfaction of imperfection that characterizes Aristophanes' *erōs*. The soul is at rest in the cloud in that it does not desire to be anywhere else. Yet it is full of desire for the God it is enjoying.

Conclusion

At different points in Gregory of Nyssa's corpus, he explores different implications of God as the Infinite. In *Against Eunomius* he first asserts that God as infinite being cannot be comprehended. In the anthropological writings, e.g., *On the Making of Man* and *On the Soul and Resurrection,* composed at roughly the same time, he reasons that if God's goodness is infinite then there can be no end to our love of God. His theological insistence on the impassibility of the Godhead informed his conception of human nature as being made in the image of God. The passions arising from our kinship with the beasts appear to Nyssen incompatible with our higher nature that bears the likeness of the Divine *Logos.* Consequently, his conception of the eschatological fulfillment of God's intention for humanity entails a purification of humanity from the passions. Therefore, he seeks in *On the Soul and Resurrection* to articulate how the soul's eschatological love of God is different from the desire proper to the nonrational faculties of the soul. The character of the rational creature's love of God must be qualitatively different from a lion's desire for a mate. The transformation in our love of God he explains, not primarily as a change in human nature, but as the result of a change in our experience of God as the "all in all." He, therefore, places emphasis on God as the source of the soul's perfect fulfillment. Our desire "ends" because we desire none other than the One in whose presence we dwell. This is an account of love that is psychological and relational.

When Nyssen turns to his exegesis of the Song of Songs and the exodus story, his account of epectasy advances an ontology of desire grounded in the ontological difference between Creator and creature. Based on his conception of the Divine as infinite (i.e., being without end) and eternal (i.e., being without extension in place or time), he concludes that the finite creatures, for whom temporal extension is inherent in their being, are always ontologically separated from God. Therefore, God is the *Other* who lovingly condescends to us and to whom we in the eternal extension (*diastēma*) of our becoming reach out. Because of the ontological distance between ourselves and God, our love is inherently ecstatic and therefore has the character of *erōs*. The ontological distance between the eternal Creator and the extended creature is never overcome. Even eschatologically when the omnipresent God becomes ubiquitously present in our consciousness, the ontological gulf remains.

Even as extension is inherent in human nature, our creaturely love is inherently erotic. Inasmuch as epectasy is an account of the finite and extended soul's love of the infinite and unextended God, epectasy must include an account of human love, born in the context of our extension, as *erōs*. *Commentary on the Song of Songs* and *Life of Moses* restore "desire" to the soul's eschatological participation in God, which he had sought to eliminate in *On the Soul and Resurrection*. Epectasy, as an account of love and participation in God grounded in his ontology of the temporal creature and the eternal Divine, subsumes within its judgment the eschatological. The conclusion of his later theory of epectasy is that there is no transformation of human love that can eliminate its inherently erotic nature. Nyssen's ontology of *erōs* leads to epistemological conclusions that influence his psychological account of *erōs* in these later works. Because God is infinite and therefore inherently incomprehensible to finite creatures, our love of God is partly the product of our partial knowledge of God. Therefore the epectasy of love — that straining forward to what lies ahead — has the psychological character of *erōs*. For there is always some lacking in that knowledge of God from which our desire is aroused.

The synthesis I have proposed at the end is a constructive theological proposal rather than a historical judgment of what Nyssen actually thought. The synthesis, however, rests upon historical judgment. Whereas the discussion of epectasy and desire in *On the Soul and Resurrection* is a *psychological* account of the soul's eschatological love of God, *Commentary on the Song of Songs* and *Life of Moses* build an *ontology* of desire. The accounts make *categorically* different claims about love and, therefore, need not be viewed as mutually exclusive theories of epectasy. The synthesis, which I summarize using with Nyssen's paradox of "soaring *stasis*," holds that while Nyssen is correct that love as desire neither can nor should not be absolutely eliminated even eschatologically (as in the case of *Life of Moses and Commentary on Song of Songs*), he is also correct that the change in the soul's consciousness of God as the "all in all" (as in the case of *On the Soul and Resurrection*) changes at the psychological level the nature of Christian *erōs* or, to put it another way, the erotic nature of *agapē*. The eschatological transformation of our relation with and consciousness of God also transforms the way we desire God. Even the soul's sense of lack characteristic of its incomplete knowledge of God is a different type of lacking when it is experienced when we are fully immersed within the divine presence. The logic of his theories of epectasy leads me to the conclusion that for Nyssen eschatological *erōs* is more than "impassible desire." It is more than the transformation of carnal desire into a spiritual desire for God. It is a desire that proceeds from the ceaseless and undiminishing enjoyment of the One whose infinite and perfect goodness cannot be fully contained in any simple moment of joy. The certainty of the presence of the eternal God gives to our desire an impassible stasis unlike the episodic vacillations and undulations of even godly desire in the present.

Nyssen's ontological distinction between the Creator and creatures provides continuity between the present age and the eschaton. But his discussion of God as "all in all" preserves the critical division of the two ages. Even as the creature can never be absorbed into the Creator, neither can the eschatological Kingdom be conflated with the present age. The proposed synthesis of Nyssen's thought preserves this distinction and so requires that any use of "the erotic" in theology must be a fully baptized notion of *erōs* conspicuously different from the *erōs* of Aristophanes. For Christian *erōs* in the present can be hopeful "Mid toil and tribulation, And tumult of her war" because it is confident that "with the vision glorious, Her longing eyes are blest, And the great Church victorious Shall be the Church at rest." Nyssen does not abandon the idea of eschatological "rest"; it is simply reconceived within the dynamics of epectasy. *Erōs* can be hopeful, rather than tragically fateful, because it looks proleptically to abiding in the security and surety of the One who is the impassible Rock and in the ubiquity and blessedness of the One who is the ineffable Cloud. The *stasis* of our love and enjoyment is grounded in the eternal being of God who is our "all in all" — the God whose infinite wonder calls the soul to soar within God's presence. This eschatological vision fuels the hope that is the source of the holy desire in which we persevere.

Notes

Introduction

1. Although Basil had died two years before the Council of Constantinople was summoned, his writings and ecclesial diplomacy (especially with respect to Basil of Ancyra and the Homoiousian party) greatly contributed to the success of the pro-Nicene party at Constantinople.

2. See Raymond Van Dam, *Kingdom of Snow: Roman Rule and Greek Culture in Cappadocia* (Philadelphia: University of Pennsylvania Press, 2003), and *Families and Friends in Late Roman Cappadocia* (Philadelphia: University of Pennsylvania Press, 2003).

3. See Raymond Van Dam, *Becoming Christian: The Conversion of Roman Cappadocia* (Philadelphia: University of Pennsylvania Press, 2003).

4. For a discussion of Basil's work among the poor of Cappadocia, see Susan R. Holman, *The Hungry Are Dying: Beggars and Bishops in Roman Cappadocia* (Oxford: Oxford University Press, 2001).

5. Although Basil of Caesarea occasionally used the term *hypostasis* as a synonym for *ousia*, he at the end of the day crafted an understanding of *hypostasis* that was a distinctly Christian understanding of the relation of the Persons of the Trinity which, unlike the modalism of Sabellius, treats each as discrete from the others. At the same time, he was clear that the three *hypostases* of the Godhead in no way corresponded to the three arch hypostases of Plotinian metaphysics. Moreover, Basil originally was in the camp of Basil of Ancyra, rather than Athanasius; therefore he was not committed to the absolute necessity of using *homoousios*. Eventually, however, he came to hold that if *homoousios* were rightly understood, it meant that the Son was unalterably (*aparallaktōs*) like the Father at the level of essence (*homoiousios*). By explaining that *homoiousios* and *homoousios* are synonymous, Basil satisfied the objections of the Homoiousians, thereby effecting a *rapprochement* with the pro-Nicenes. For a fuller description of Basil's contribution to the Trinitarian formula, see R. P. C. Hanson, *The Search for the Christian Doctrine of God* (Edinburgh: T & T Clark, 1988), 690–98.

6. For recent discussions Nyssen's Trinitarian theology, see Sarah Coakley, "Rethinking Gregory of Nyssa: Introduction — Gender, Trinitarian Analogies, and the Pedagogy of the Song"; Lewis Ayres, "On Not Three People: The Fundamental Themes of Gregory of Nyssa's Trinitarian Theology as Seen in *To Ablabius: On Not Three Gods;*" Lucian Turcescu, " 'Person' versus 'Individual,' and Other Modern Misreadings of Gregory of Nyssa," in the special Issue of *Modern Theology* 18 (October 2002); and Michel René Barnes, *The Power of God: Dynamis in Gregory*

of Nyssa's Trinitarian Theology (Washington, D.C.: Catholic University of America Press, 2001).

7. See Brian E. Daley, "Divine Transcendence and Human Transformation: Gregory of Nyssa's Anti-Apollinarian Christology," *Modern Theology* 18 (October 2002): 497–506.

8. Ronald E. Heine, "Gregory of Nyssa's Apology for Allegory," *Vigiliae Christianae* 38 (1984): 360–70, and Anthony Meredith, "Allegory in Porphyry and Gregory of Nyssa," *Studia Patristica* (Berlin: Akademie-Verlag, 1985), 423–27.

9. For a detailed account of evolution of Arianism from Arius to Eunomius, see Thomas A. Kopecek, *A History of Neo-Arianism,* 2 vols. (Cambridge, Mass.: Philadelphia Patristic Foundation, 1979).

10. Kevin Mongrain, *The Systematic Thought of Hans Urs von Balthasar: An Irenaean Retrieval* (New York: Crossroad Publishing Company, 2002), 1–12.

11. Hans Urs von Balthasar, *Présence et pensée: Essai sur la philosophie religieuse de Grégoire de Nysse* (Paris: G. Beauchesne, 1942).

12. Jean Daniélou, *Platonisme et théologie mystique: Doctrine spirituelle de Grégoire de Nysse* (Paris: Aubier, 1944).

13. Walther Völker, *Gregor Von Nyssa als Mystiker* (Wiesbaden: Franz Steiner Verlag, 1955).

14. Andrew Louth, *Origins of the Christian Mystical Tradition: From Plato to Denys* (Oxford: Oxford University Press, 1981).

15. Jaroslav Pelikan, *Christianity and Classical Culture: The Metamorphosis of Natural Theology in the Christian Encounter with Hellenism* (New Haven, Conn.: Yale University Press, 1993).

16. Herald Cherniss, *The Platonism of Gregory of Nyssa* (Berkeley: University of California Publications in Classical Philology, 1930).

17. Karl Gronau, *Poseidonios und die jüdisch-christliche Genesisexegese* (Berlin: B. G. Teubner, 1914).

18. Cherniss, *The Platonism of Gregory of Nyssa,* 11.

19. Cherniss, *The Platonism of Gregory of Nyssa,* 1.

20. Of Gregory's piety, Cherniss says, " . . . that he believed the dogma, there can be no doubt; and just here lies the key to his whole mental character. He would be orthodox at any cost of intellectual integrity and, sure if the Church had branded the whole of his reasoning as heretical he would have assisted at the burning of his own work without a murmur" (Cherniss, *The Platonism of Gregory of Nyssa,* 63).

21. Cherniss, *The Platonism of Gregory of Nyssa.*

22. *Dominican Studies* 1 (1948): 113–26.

23. *Dumbarton Oaks Papers* 12 (1958): 29–57.

24. Charalambos Apostolopoulos, *Phaedo Christianus Studien zur Verindung und Abwägung des Verhältnisses zwischen dem platonischen "Phaidon" und dem Dialog Gregors von Nyssa "Über die Seele und die Auferstehung"* (Frankfurt: Peter Lang, 1986).

25. Anders Nygren, *Agape and Eros,* trans. Philip S. Watson (Chicago: University of Chicago Press, 1982), 430–46.

26. Nygren, *Agape and Eros,* 446. For a key example of the confusion, see *De Anima et Resurrectione,* PG 46, 64C–65A.

27. *De Anima et Resurrectione,* in Saint Gregory of Nyssa, *Ascetical Works,* trans. Virginia Woods Callahan (Washington, D.C.: Catholic University of America Press, 1967), 237; PG 46, 89B–C.

28. Werner Jaeger, *Early Christianity and Greek Paideia* (Cambridge, Mass.: Belknap Press of Harvard University Press, 1961), 99.

29. Werner Jaeger, *Two Rediscovered Works of Ancient Christian Literature: Gregory of Nyssa and Macarius* (Leiden: E. J. Brill, 1954), 72. Nyssen's identification of the Christian life with *ho kat'arēten bios,* which is achieved through struggle (*agōn*), hard work (*ponos*), and toiling labor (*kamatos*), establishes the moral heroism of Greek philosophy as the paradigm for thinking about the quest for salvation (85–86). Such a model leads Nyssen to adopt a synergistic view of grace and individual effort and results in an Eastern form of Semi-Pelagianism (89). Focusing on one of Nyssen's last works, *De Instituto Christiana,* Jaeger painstakingly points out the number of times that Nyssen asserts that although human efforts are not sufficient in themselves to bring the soul to perfect union with God, nevertheless grace is conferred on the individual as a reward for her struggle toward perfection. By saying that grace is given to those who have made themselves worthy (*kataxiousthai*), Nyssen has stripped grace of its gracious quality. Thus individual human effort is primary in the process of spiritual ascent while grace is viewed merely as a necessary supplement to our powers.

30. Peter Brown, *The Body and Society: Men, Women, and Sexual Renunciation in Early Christianity* (New York: Columbia University Press, 1988), 285–304.

31. Caroline Walker Bynum, *The Resurrection of the Body in Western Christianity, 200–1336* (New York: Columbia University Press, 1995), 81–86.

32. Teresa M. Shaw, *The Burden of the Flesh: Fasting and Sexuality in Early Christianity* (Minneapolis: Fortress Press, 1998), 92–97, 187–98.

33. Among Harrison's extensive work on conceptions of use of gender in patristic writings are "Receptacle Imagery in St. Gregory of Nyssa's Anthropology," *Studia Patristica* 22 (1989): 23–27; "Male and Female in Cappadocian Theology," *Journal of Theological Studies* n.s. 41 (October 1990): 441–71; and "A Gender Reversal in Gregory of Nyssa," *Studia Patristica* 27 (1993): 34–38.

34. Mark Hart, "Reconciliation of Body and Soul: Gregory of Nyssa's Deeper Theology of Marriage," *Theological Studies* 51 (1990): 450–78; and "Gregory of Nyssa's Ironic Praise of the Celibate Life," *Heythrop Journal* 33 (January 1992): 1–19.

35. Hart, "Reconciliation," 455.

36. Hart, "Ironic," 6–7.

37. Hart, "Reconciliation," 476.

38. John Behr, "The Rational Animal: A Rereading of Gregory of Nyssa's *De hominis opificio,*" *Journal of Early Christian Studies* 7 (1999): 227–46.

39. The logic of Nyssen's psychology, Behr says, leads to the conclusion that "once the mind is free from passion and vice, [there shall be] a restored use of human sexuality, an exercise of sexuality under the full autonomy of reason, in angelic mode, in which the human being fulfills its purpose in creation of uplifting and integrating the life of the body and the sense with reason and the divine" (224).

40. Rowan Williams, "Macrina's Deathbed Revisited: Gregory of Nyssa on Mind and Passion," in *Christian Faith and Greek Philosophy in Late Antiquity:*

Essays in Tribute to George Christopher Stead, ed. L. Wickham and C. Bammel (Leiden: E. J. Brill, 1993), 231.

41. Martin Laird, "Under Solomon's Tutelage: The Education of Desire in the *Homilies on the Song of Songs,*" *Modern Theology* 18 (October 2002): 507–25.

42. Contrary to Hart's assertion that contemplative marriage is for the strong but virginity is for the weak who cannot avoid being sucked into the worldly cares of married life ("Reconciliation of the Soul and Body," 474), Nyssen's portrait of Macrina is of a strong woman whose celibacy enables her to transcend her gender and embrace the angelic communion with Christ that awaits her in the resurrection. See my article "A Just and Reasonable Grief: The Death and Function of a Holy Woman in Gregory of Nyssa's *Life of Macrina,*" in *Journal of Early Christian Studies* 12, no. 1 (2004): 56–84.

43. See my discussion of Williams's reading in "Macrina, Tamer of Horses and Healer of Souls: Grief and the Therapy of Hope in Gregory of Nyssa's *De Anima et Resurrectione,*" *Journal of Theological Studies* n.s. 52 (April 2001): 37–60.

Chapter One: The Imago Dei

1. *De Hominis Opificio* 12.9; NPNF 5 p. 399; PG 44, 161D.

2. Prominent among the writings on Nyssen's treatment of the *imago Dei* are J. T. Muckle, "The Doctrine of St. Gregory of Nyssa on Man as the Image of God," *Mediaeval Studies* 7 (1945): 55–84; A. H. Armstrong, "Platonic Elements in Gregory of Nyssa's Doctrine of Man," *Dominican Studies* 1 (1948): 113–26; Roger Leys, *L'image de Dieu chez Saint Gregoire de Nysse* (Bruxelles: Edition universelle, 1951); Gerhart B. Ladner, "The Philosophical Anthropology of Saint Gregory of Nyssa," in *Dumbarton Oaks Papers* 12 (1958): 61–64; Brooks Otis, "Cappadocian Thought as a Coherent System," in *Dumbarton Oaks Papers* 12 (1958): 97–124; Maryanne Cline Horowitz, "The Image of God in Man: Is Woman Included?" *Harvard Theological Review* 72 (1979): 175–206; Frances M. Young, "Adam and Anthropos: A Study of the Interaction of Science and the Bible in Two Anthropological Treatises of the Fourth Century," *Vigiliae Christianae* 37, no. 2 (1983): 110–40; Rowan A. Greer, "The Leaven and the Lamb: Christ and Gregory of Nyssa's Vision of Human Destiny," in *Jesus in History and Myth,* ed. R. Joseph Hoffmann and Gerald Larue (Buffalo, N.Y.: Prometheus Books, 1986), 169–80; Verna E. F. Harrison, "Male and Female in Cappadocian Theology," *Journal of Theological Studies,* n.s. 41 (1990): 441–71; Johannes Zachhuber, *Human Nature in Gregory of Nyssa: Philosophical Background and Theological Significance* (Leiden: Brill, 2000), 145–73.

3. "But, in the peculiar nature of the image, there is something different from the archetype, for it would not be an image if it were identical with it in all respects." *De Anima et Resurrectione,* Saint Gregory of Nyssa, *Ascetical Works,* trans. Virginia Woods Callahan (Washington, D.C.: Catholic University of America Press, 1967); PG 46, 41B; cf. *De Hominis Opificio* 6.3; NPNF, 392a; PG 44, 140C.

4. *De Hominis Opificio* 4.1; NPNF 5, 390b; PG 44, 136B.

5. *De Hominis Opificio* 5.2; NPNF 5, 391a; PG 44, 137C.

6. Nyssen's actual characterization of *autexousia* that I have translated "free will is" *idiois thelēmasin autokra torikōs dioikoumenēn* (*De Hominis Opificio* 4; PG 44, 136C). The autocratic will (*thelēmasin autokratorikōs*) describes the autonomous character of *proairesis,* which simply refers to a choice the free character of which arises from the reason's capacity for critical deliberation about the good.

7. Albrecht Dihle, *The Theory of Will in Classical Antiquity* (Berkeley: University of California Press, 1982), 119.

8. In works representative of Augustine's mature thought, such as *City of God*, Augustine seems to distinguish three senses of the will: *liberum arbitrium* refers simply to the power to choose; *voluntas* denotes, not a separate faculty of the soul, but a wish, want, or inclination of the soul; *libertas* is the freedom to love God rightly. After the fall, man's *voluntas*, no longer possessing the *libertas* of being rightly oriented toward God and the good, is corrupted by the self-serving will to power, *concupescentia*, that rebels against the intellect and God. See Rowan Greer, "Augustine's Transformation of the Free Will Defense," *Faith and Philosophy* 13 (1996): 471–86. Nyssen makes a distinction between autonomy (*autexousia*) and the "wills" which are exercised autonomously. But these "wills" (*thelēmasin*) appear to be choices by which our autonomy is actualized. Consequently, it seems unlikely that Nyssen makes any distinction between *thelēmasin* and *proairesis*.

9. Nyssen is not consistent in his terminology. In *De Hominis Opificio* he lists the qualities of the rational soul that bear the likeness to the divine nature as *logos* and *dianoia* (137C) and in *De Anima et Resurrectione* as *theōrētikē, diakritikē*, and *epoptikē* (57B). I understand *logos* to refer either to speech or to the capacity to make calculations regarding ends and means. Nyssen uses *diakritikē* to refer to the analytical judgments that may concern either practical or theoretical activities. The terms *dianoia* and *theōrētikē* are used almost interchangeably to refer to the higher speculative activity of the intellect related to the soul's contemplative ascent into the Divine. Although *epoptikē* might be used to describe the soul's contemplative union with the God, it all but falls out of usage in *De Anima et Resurrectione*.

10. *De Hominis Opificio* 16.11; NPNF, 405b; PG 44, 184B.

11. *De Hominis Opificio* 16.11; NPNF, 405b; PG 44, 184B.

12. *De Anima et Resurrectione*, Callahan, 212; PG 46, 41B.

13. *De Hominis Opificio* 5.2; NPNF, 391b. Cf. *De Anima et Resurrectione*, Callahan, 211; PG 46, 41A.

14. *De Hominis Opificio* 6.1; NPNF, 391b, and 10.1–3; NPNF, 395b–396a.

15. *De Hominis Opificio* 14.2; NPNF, 403a.

16. *De Anima et Resurrectione*, Callahan, 205–27; PG 46, 25A–33B.

17. *De Hominis Opificio* 10.5–6; NPNF, 396a.

18. Although Nyssen identifies nondimensionality as characteristic of our soul's structural likeness to God (Callahan, 212; PG 46, 41B), its significance is revealed in his discussion of the soul's capacity to be united with the elements of the decayed or dismembered corpse and simultaneously in heaven (Callahan, 213–14; PG 46, 45 A–C). The soul's union with the elements of the body after the separation of the elements of the body becomes the chief principle by which Nyssen explains how the elements are "tagged" and so can be reunited at the resurrection (Callahan, 228–31; PG 46, 72C–77B). Thus it seems that Nyssen recognizes the divine characteristic of nondimensionality as a feature of the human soul from working through the problem of the resurrection.

19. *De Hominis Opificio* 8.2–3; NPNF, 393.

20. *De Hominis Opificio* 8.1; NPNF, 393a.

21. The word *apatheia* had no univocal meaning for classical, Hellenistic, and Christian authors. I will discuss its range of meanings later in the next chapter.

22. Michel R. Barnes, "The Polemical Context and Content of Gregory of Nyssa's Psychology," *Medieval Philosophy and Theology* 4 (1994): 4–5.

23. John J. O'Keefe rightly observes, "It is almost possible to substitute the word *pathos* for sin in much of Gregory's writings." See John J. O'Keefe, "Sin, *Apatheia* and Freedom of the Will in Gregory of Nyssa," *Studia Patristica* 22 (1989): 56.

24. Daniélou commenting on *apatheia* and *katharotēs* says, "elles sont également des désignations de la grâce sanctifiante, une participation à la vie de Dieu qui seul est proprement *apatheia* et *katharos*." See Daniélou, *Platonisme, 55.*

25. *De Hominis Opificio* 5; NPNF, 391b.

26. *De Hominis Opificio* 4; NPNF, 391a.

27. *De Hominis Opificio* 16.10; NPNF, 405b; PG 44, 184A.

28. "There is a great difference between that which is conceived in the archetype and a thing which has been made in its image; for the image is properly so called if it keeps its resemblance to the prototype; but if the imitation be perverted from its subject, the thing is something else, and no longer an image of the subject." *De Hominis Opificio* 16.2; NPNF, 404b. Thus being the image of the archetype is dependent upon our sustained participation in God's goodness.

29. *De Hominis Opificio* 12.9; NPNF, 399a.

30. *De Virginitate* XI, Saint Gregory of Nyssa, *Ascetical Works,* trans. Virginia Woods Callahan (Washington, D.C.: Catholic University of America Press, 1967), 41.

31. *De Virginitate* XII.3, Callahan, 44; SC 119, p. 410.

32. *De Virginitate* XI.5, Callahan, 41; SC 119, p. 392.

33. *De Hominis Opificio* 16.12; NPNF, 405b; PG 44, 184C.

34. *De Hominis Opificio* 16.7; NPNF, 405a.

35. When Nyssen does comment on Col. 1:15 in *De Perfectione,* he is clear that Paul by calling Christ "the image of the invisible God" is referring to Christ according to the flesh (Rom. :5), i.e., the human form that contains "the God over all and the great God." Nyssen writes, "in order that He might again make Himself an 'image of God,' because of His love for man, became Himself an 'image of the invisible God' so that he took on the form which He assumed among you" (*On Perfection,* in Saint Gregory of Nyssa, *Ascetical Works,* trans. Virginia Woods Callahan (Washington, D.C.: Catholic University of America Press, 1967), 109–10).

36. *De Hominis Opificio* 16.7–8; NPNF, 405a; PG 44, 181AB.

37. "That the intellectual element, however, precedes the other, we learn as from one who gives in order an account of the making of man; and we learn that his community and kindred with the irrational is for man a provision for reproduction," *De Hominis Opificio* 16.6; NPNF, 405a.

38. *De Hominis Opificio* 16.10; NPNF, 405b; PG 44, 184A.

39. *De Hominis Opificio* 16.12; NPNF, 405b; PG 44, 184C.

40. "Perceiving before hand by his power of foreknowledge what, in a state of independence and freedom, is the tendency of the motion of man's will . . . He devised for his image the distinction between male and female, which has no reference to the Archetype, but as we have said, is an approximation to the less rational nature." *De Hominis Opificio* 16.14; NPNF, 406a.

41. Responding to the question of whether there would have been procreation in Paradise if there had been no fall, Nyssen makes a correlation between Jesus' remark in Luke 20:35–36 that children of the resurrection shall be "equal to angels" and

his belief that the resurrection constitutes a restoration of our state in Paradise. He comments, "while looking upon the nature of man in its entirety and fullness by the exercise of His foreknowledge and bestowed upon it a lot exalted and equal to the angels." *De Hominis Opificio* 17.4; NPNF, 407b; PG 44, 189C.

42. *De Hominis Opificio* 16.9; NPNF, 405a; PG 44, 181BC. Nyssen proceeds to explain that among the passions that come to human nature by its kinship with irrational animals is the impulse to breed out of a desire for sensual pleasure; see *De Hominis Opificio* 18.2; NPNF, 408a.

43. *De Hominis Opificio* 17.4; NPNF, 407b; PG 44, 189D.

44. *De Hominis Opificio* 18.2; NPNF, 408a: PG 44, 192BC.

45. *De Hominis Opificio* 12.10–11; NPNF, 399a; PG 44, 161D.

46. *De Hominis Opificio* 12.9; NPNF, 405a; PG 44, 161CD.

47. *De Hominis Opificio* 18.1–2; NPNF, 407b–408a.; PG 44, 192AB.

48. "It is the sensual pleasure which precedes human birth that is weakness." *Oratio Catechetica* in *Christology of the Later Fathers*, ed. E. R. Hardy (Philadelphia: Westminster Press, 1954), 293.

49. *De Hominis Opificio* 17.6; PG 44, 189D–192A.

50. *De Hominis Opificio* 3.1; NPNF, 390; PG 44, 133C–D.

51. Gerhart B. Ladner, "The Philosophical Anthropology of Saint Nyssen of Nyssa," *Dumbarton Oaks Papers* 12, 82.

52. *De Hominis Opificio* 16.16; NPNF, 406a; PG 44, 185C.

53. Ladner, "The Philosophical Anthropology of Saint Nyssen of Nyssa," 82–83.

54. Whether or not Ladner is suggesting this, his account needs to add a greater nuanced discussion of the corporate nature of the *plērōma* described in *De Hominis Opificio* 16.17.

55. See *De Hominis Opificio* 28; NPNF 419–20; PG 44, 229B–233C and *De Anima et Resurrectione*, Callahan, 246–48; PG 46, 109B–112C.

56. *De Hominis Opificio* 16.17; NPNF, 406b; PG 44, 185C.

57. Rowan A. Greer, *Christian Hope and Christian Life: Raids on the Inarticulate* (New York: Crossroad, 2001), 74. Here Nyssen is, as is common in his writing, inconsistent in his terminology. In *De Hominis Opificio* 16.7 (181B) he uses *kataskeuē* for God's activities in both stages of creation.

58. Philo of Alexandria, *De Opificio Mundi* II.12.

59. *De Opificio Mundi* II.46–48.

60. *De Opificio Mundi* II.51.

61. Philo's treatment of the *paradeigmata* differs from Plato's view in *Timaeus*. The models from which Plato's *dēmiourgos* fashions the world are eternal and uncreated. The eternal, being unchanging, is perfectly beautiful. A world modeled on something that is not eternal, but created, would reflect its archetype's imperfections (see *Timaeus* 28AB and 28C–29A). Although Philo does speak of the *paradeigmata* as being eternal or unoriginate (*agenēton*) (*De Opificio Mundi* II.12), he nevertheless contends that the patterns were created by God. "For God, being God, assumed that a beautiful copy would never be produced apart from a beautiful pattern.... So when he willed to create the visible world, he first fully formed the intelligible world, in order that he might have the use of a pattern wholly godlike and incorporeal" (IV.16). How the models are both eternal and yet formed by God can be explained

only if one recognizes that they are ideas in the mind of God, who is eternal. Therefore they exist in God who is eternal and outside of time (VII.26). The *paradeigmata* are eternal in the sense that they are the image of the eternal God (VI.25). Whatever Philo's philosophical commitment to Plato, he deviates from *Timaeus* in deference to the absolute priority of God demanded by Jewish theology. For Plato, the demiurge and the paradigms are coeternal principles. For Philo, God is absolutely prior to all things, even his own ideas. Thus although the paradigms are eternal inasmuch as they are images of the Divine, they are, nevertheless, derivative — a product of God's will (*boulē*). By making the paradigms the product of God's will, Philo establishes the gracious character of creation. The world was born, not of necessity inherent in God's nature, but of God's freedom.

62. *Apologia in Hexaëmeron* PG 44, 72B.

63. I am grateful to Rowan Greer for his helpful suggestion of this passage as an illustrative contrast with Philo.

64. *De Infantibus Premature Abreptis* GNO III/II, 77, 4 and 18–20.

65. *De Hominis Opificio* 16.16 in NPNF 5, 406a; PG 44, 185B.

66. *De Hominis Opificio* 16.17 in NPNF 5, 406a; PG 44, 185C–D.

67. Johannes Zachhuber, *Human Nature in Gregory of Nyssa: Philosophical Background and Theological Significance* (Leiden: Brill, 2000), 150, offers an excellent, detailed discussion of the philosophical traditions that are presupposed by Nyssen's theory of "double creation." I am greatly indebted to him for this meticulous work.

68. Aristotle, *Metaphysics* VII.7.

69. See W. K. C. Guthrie, *Aristotle: An Encounter,* vol. 5 of *A History of Greek Philosophy* (Cambridge: Cambridge University Press, 1981), 100–105.

70. Zachhuber, *Human Nature in Gregory of Nyssa,* 151.

71. *De Hominis Opificio* 16.9 NPNF 5, 405a; PG 44, 181B–C.

72. Eugenio Corsini is correct that "double creation" does not refer to two moments of creation, but to the two "orders" in which human nature participates: the divine, which includes the intellect that does not include gender, and the nonrational, which includes our bodily constitution and the division of male and female. See Eugenio Corsini, "Plérôme humain et plérôme cosmique chez Grégoire de Nysse," in *Écriture et culture philosophique dans la pensée de Grégoire de Nysse,* ed. Marguerite Harl (Leiden: Brill, 1971), 116.

73. *De Hominis Opificio* 16.17 NPNF 5, 405a; PG 44, 185C.

74. *De Hominis Opificio;* PG44, 128A. I am grateful to Rowan Greer for pointing out to me the curious order of the Greek, which is wholly lost in the reordering of the passage in the Moore and Wilson translation from NPNF 5.

75. *De Hominis Opificio* 16.6; NPNF 5,405a; PG 44, 181A.

76. *De Hominis Opificio* 2.1; PG 44, 133A.

77. *Oratio Catechetica* 32,GNO III/IV, 76.6ff. Also see Greer's discussion of this point in *Christian Hope and Christian Life,* 79–80.

78. *De Hominis Opificio* 25 and 27; *De Anima et Resurrectione* PG 46, 41C–45C, 137C–145C; *Oratio Catechetica* 8,GNO III/IV, 29.1ff.

79. See T. J. Dennis, "Gregory on the Resurrection of the Body," in *The Easter Sermons of Gregory of Nyssa,* ed. Andreas Spira and Christopher Klock (Philadelphia: Philadelphia Patristic Foundation, 1981), 55–80, and Morwenna Ludlow,

Universal Salvation: Eschatology in the Thought of Gregory of Nyssa and Karl Rahner (Oxford: Oxford University Press, 2000).

80. Philo, *De Opificio Mundi* XXIV.76.

81. *De Opificio Mundi* XLVI.134.

82. Origen, *Homilae in Genesim*, PG 12, 146–262.

83. The phrase that is translated "universal humanity" is *"en pasēi tēi anthrōpinēi,"* *De Hominis Opificio* 22.3 in NPNF 5, 411; PG 44, 204D.

84. See Zachhuber, *Human Nature in Gregory of Nyssa,* 163ff.

85. *De Hominis Opificio* 22.4–5 in NPNF 5, 411–12; PG 44, 205A–C.

86. "For this reason the whole race was spoken of as one man, namely, that to God's power nothing is either past or future, but even that which we expect is comprehended, equally with what is at present existing, by the all-sustaining energy." *De Hominis Opificio* 16.18 in NPNF 5, 406; PG 44, 185D.

87. *De Anima et Resurrectione,* Callahan, 217–18; PG 46, 53A.

88. *De Anima et Resurrectione,* Callahan, 264; PG 46, 145A.

89. *De Anima et Resurrectione,* Callahan, 243; PG 46, 104AB.

90. *De Hominis Opificio* 17.2; PG 44, 188BC.

91. See Nyssen's discussion of the rich man and Lazarus in *De Anima et Resurrectione,* Callahan, 233–34; PG 46, 81Aff.

92. Plato, *Symposium* 189E-190A.

93. *Symposium* 190B and C.

94. *Symposium* 192E.

95. See Wayne Meeks, "The Image of the Androgyne: Some Uses of a Symbol in Earliest Christianity," *History of Religions* 13, no. 3 (1974).

96. Meeks (185–86) explains that among certain rabbis there was known a version of the Septuagint in which Genesis 1:27c reads "male and female he created *him,*" reflecting the influence of Aristophanes' myth from *Symposium.* One saying of Rabbi Samuel bar Mahman seems an obvious borrowing from Plato, "When the Holy One, blessed be he, created the first man, he created him *diprosōpon.* Then he split him and made two bodies, one on each side, and turned them about."

97. Meeks, "The Image of the Androgyne," 189, quotes the Gospel according to Philip 117: "When Eve was in Adam, there was no death; but when she was separated from him death came into being. Again if [she] go in and he take [her] to himself, death will no longer exist." There is no indication that the Gnostic community that produced the Gospel of Philip viewed marriage as a ritual reunification.

98. See the excellent discussion in Maryanne Cline Horowitz, "The Image of God in Man — Is Woman Included?" *Harvard Theological Review* 72, nos. 3–4 (1979): 173–206.

99. Philo, *De Opificio Mundi* LIII.151–52.

100. Cline Horowitz, "The Image of God in Man," 192.

101. Origen, *Homilies on Genesis* 1.14–16, quoted in Cline Horowitz, "The Image of God in Man," 194.

102. The Gospel according to Thomas 114 in *The Gnostic Scriptures,* trans. Bentley Layton (Garden City, N.Y.: Doubleday, 1987), 399.

103. Cline Horowitz, "The Image of God in Man," 192.

104. Cline Horowitz, "The Image of God in Man," 198.

105. Gregory of Nyssa, *De Vita Macrinae,* SC 178, 10.7–8.

106. *De Vita Moysis* II.2–3; SC 1c, pp. 106–8. In this passage, Nyssen makes no explicit reference to the image of God.

107. Philo, *Legum Allegoriarum* III.1.3 and III.87.243.

108. Origen, *Homilae in Genesim* 1.14.

109. Verna E. F. Harrison, "Male and Female in Cappadocian Theology," *Journal of Theological Studies*, n.s. 41 no. 1 (1990): 468.

110. Harrison, "Male and Female in Cappadocian Theology," 470.

111. Elizabeth Clark, "Devil's Gateway and Bride of Christ: Women in the Early Christian World," in *Ascetic Piety and Women's Faith*, ed. E. Clark (Lewiston, N.Y.: E. Mellen Press, 1986), 43.

112. Nyssen explains to his catechumens preparing for baptism that through baptism they participate in the reality of Christ's resurrection, "Seeing then, that the Pioneer of our life died and was buried under the earth in common with our nature, the imitation we make of his death is represented in the allied element. Now after the man from above had assumed a state of death and had been buried under the earth, on the third day he returned to life once more. In the same way everyone who by his bodily nature is united to him and looks to the same successful issue — I mean the goal of life — has water instead of earth poured on him, and by being immersed three separate times reproduces the grace of the resurrection which occurred on the third day." *Oratio Catechetica* 35, in *Christology of the Later Fathers*, 315; GNO III/IV, 88.2–12.

113. *Oratio Catechetica* 32, in Hardy, *Christology*, 310; GNO III/IV, 78.9–17.

Chapter Two: Nyssen's Eclectic Psychology

1. Eduard Zeller, "Eclecticism" in *Encyclopaedia Britannica* (14th edition) quoted in John Dillon and A. A. Long, *The Question of "Eclecticism": Studies in Later Greek Philosophy* (Berkeley: University of California Press, 1988), 3.

2. Pierlungi Donini has demonstrated that while the concept of "eclectic" philosophy was known in antiquity it was not used with the same frequency and scope with which the term is applied today. In fact, after surveying the various usages of the term "eclecticism," he concludes that the term is not very helpful in describing Hellenistic philosophy since it only begs the question why a particular philosopher tries to combine the thought of different systems. See Pierlungi Donini, "The History of the Concept of Eclecticism," in *The Question of "Eclecticism,"* 33.

3. Aristotle, *Metaphysics* I.6.

4. A. A. Long, *Hellenistic Philosophy: Stoics, Epicureans, Skeptics* (Berkeley: University of California Press, 1986), 89.

5. Cicero, *Academica* I.12 quoted in Charles Landesman, *Skepticism: The Central Issue* (Oxford: Blackwells, 2002), 182.

6. R. J. Hankinson, *The Skeptics* (London: Routledge, 1995), 75.

7. Hankinson, *The Skeptics,* 74.

8. John Dillon, *The Middle Platonists, 80 B.C. to A.D. 220* (Ithaca, N.Y.: Cornell University Press, 1996), 63ff.

9. See Dillon, *The Middle Platonists,* 114.

10. In a wonderful example of Plato's use of irony, one of Socrates' interlocutors, Simmias, relates the Thebans' quip, "Philosophers are nearly dead or deserve to be so" (64B). The irony is that the philosopher by turning from the body has already begun that separation from the body that climaxes in death. Moreover, because the

philosopher has purified her soul from the body's corrupting passions, she does in fact deserve the liberation from the body's pains, illusions, and passions that her death will bring (64E).

11. Plato does not develop in *Phaedo* his theory of the transmigration of the souls as one sees in *Phaedrus* and *Republic*. Yet even here his suggestion that the soul comes out of death, i.e., Hades (70D and 71D–E), presupposes some cycle of reincarnation. In the description of the judgments in Hades, Plato does not say that these souls are given new bodies after their sojourn in Hades. Philosophers differ from all of the rest in that their souls are allowed to leave the earthly realm and their bodies in order to enter the beautiful abode that transcends the material world (114B–C).

12. Guthrie observes that Socrates' allegory of the chariot reflects a more mature and less dualistic view of the soul and its relation to the body than in the earlier paradigm introduced in *Phaedo*. In this dialogue, the soul is simple and unitary, as it must be in order to be immortal. Were it not wholly distinct and capable of subsistence independent of the body, the soul could neither survive the flesh in death nor be freed from the pains associated with its embodied existence. All sensations of pain and all forms of desire, therefore, are traceable to the body, which being heavy hinders the soul's search for the True and the Good. In the *Phaedrus*, however, Plato has begun to realize that the soul is not simply *nouj* while the passions are relegated to the body. Rather with the analogy of the chariot, he demonstrates a more complex view of the soul, which is the seat of the appetitive as well as the rational faculties. W. K. C. Guthrie, *Plato: The Man and His Dialogues, Early Period*, vol. 4 of *A History of Greek Philosophy* (Cambridge: Cambridge University Press, 1975), 412.

13. It is worth noting that although the soul's immortality is the implicit conclusion of *Phaedo*, Plato does not make the claim in another dialogue written probably about the same time as *Phaedo*, namely, *Symposium*. Here the soul experiences immortality only vicariously through its children. Ultimately, there is nothing in *Symposium* that denies the soul's immortality. See T. M. Robinson, *Plato's Psychology* 2nd ed. (Toronto: University of Toronto Press, 1995), 125–27.

14. Guthrie, *Plato*, 476–77.

15. W. K. C. Guthrie, *The Later Plato and the Academy*, vol. 5 of *A History of Greek Philosophy*(Cambridge: Cambridge University Press, 1989), 308–9. Guthrie argues that the account of the soul's creation in *Timaeus* articulates a theory of the tripartite structure preciously presented in *Republic* and *Phaedrus*. The significance of the *Timaeus* myth is that it establishes the difference between the soul that is simple, divine, and immortal from the mortal part of the soul, which is the locus of the passions. Thus the nonrational parts of the soul are not the original elements of the soul, but were acquired solely to go along with the body.

16. Charles L. Griswold, Jr., *Self-Knowledge in Plato's Phaedrus* (University Park,: Pennsylvania State University Press, 1996), 80.

17. Quotations of *Phaedrus* are taken from *Plato* I, trans. Harold North Fowler (Cambridge, Mass.: Harvard University Press, 1914).

18. "The natural function of the wing (*pterou dynamis*) is to soar upwards and carry that which is heavy up to the place where dwells the race of gods. More than any other thing that pertains to the body (*peri to sōma*) it partakes of the divine," (246D–E). Clearly Socrates' point is that the soul must be equipped with all excellence of character in order for one to live the life of the philosopher who

rises above the tumult of the unreflective masses and peers into the realm of eternal truth. Yet presumably one cannot achieve such virtue unless one has already seen the essence of justice and temperance — the imitation of which produces beauty, goodness, and wisdom in the soul.

19. That both horses are given wings is an important detail that differentiates Plato's representation of the tripartite soul in *Phaedrus* from that in *Timaeus*. In the latter dialogue, the nonrational faculties are not divine at all, but are secondary powers conferred on the soul for its life in the body. Even if one can reconcile the mythic narratives of the two dialogues, that the human soul's lower faculties have the same wings as the souls of the gods suggests that these lower parts of the soul have the potential for the same movement in the heavenly realm as do the pure souls of the gods.

20. F. Nuyens, *L'evolution de la psychologie d'Aristotle* (Louvain: Éditions du Institut supérieure de philosophie, 1948) cited in W. K. C. Guthrie, *Aristotle: An Encounter,* vol. 5 of *A History of Greek Philosophy* (Cambridge: Cambridge University Press, 1981), 277–78.

21. Of this final stage, Guthrie says that Aristotle makes an explicit (*De Anima* 402b3–5) repudiation of Plato's doctrine of the soul to which he once adhered. Cf. *Aristotle,* 278. Book I 402b3–5, however, simply reviews the range of questions that must be addressed in any examination of the soul; Plato is not mentioned until 404b16 during his recapitulation of previous theories. What he explicitly rejects is Plato's claim in *Timaeus* that the soul's movement of the body is modeled on the movement of the cosmos by the world soul (406b–407b).

22. Thus Aristotle says that the soul is the substance in the sense that it is "the essence of such and such a body" (412b10) in the same way that the essence of an ax is that which makes it what it is. As implied in the example of the ax, there is a level of potentiality already present in the form. This Aristotle already acknowledged (412a) when he said that a thing can be actualized in two ways analogous (1) to having knowledge (*epistēmē*) and (2) to exercising that knowledge in thinking (*to theōrein*). In the former way of being actualized, which can be compared to *epistēmē*, there is an element of potentiality. Perhaps one might say that the first way of being actualized is the formal cause and the second way is its use for its final cause.

23. In *De Anima* book 8, Aristotle distinguishes between two levels of activity. First-level activity is the potency conferred by the soul upon the body such as the eye's ability to see. The second-level activity is the act of seeing itself. He defines the soul as the first-level activity of a body with organs. I am grateful to Marilyn McCord Adams for pointing out this distinction in Aristotle.

24. "The body is that which exists potentially; but just as the pupil and the faculty of seeing make an eye, so in the other case the soul and body make a living creature" (*De Anima* 413a2–4).

25. Aristotle can claim that *nous* is indestructible because he has argued that it cannot be affected. Having said that it is more appropriate to say that the soul is the instrument by which a man is courageous or angered rather than to say that the soul itself is courageous or angered, he says that old age affects the body, not the soul. "Thus the power of thought and speculation decay because something else within perishes, but itself (i.e., the soul) is unaffected" (408b23–30).

26. Guthrie, *Aristotle,* 311.

27. *De Anima et Resurrectione,* in Saint Gregory of Nyssa, *Ascetical Works,* trans. Virginia Woods Callahan (Washington, D.C.: Catholic University of America Press, 1967), 216; PG 46, 49C.

28. "We accuse those forms of argument which strengthen our beliefs, through dialectic and syllogism and analysis, of being weak and suspect for revealing truth. It is clear to everyone that the dialectical method is equally effective for subverting truth and accusing an opponent of falsehood. Even truth itself, when it is advanced with such artfulness, often becomes the object of suspicion on the grounds that cleverness in such matters can mislead us and even divert us from the truth. However, if someone brings forward an argument which is extemporaneous and devoid of such circumlocution, we say that it may be credible and apply it to the theory about these subjects set forth in Scripture." *De Anima et Resurrectione,* Callahan, 217; PG 46, 52B.

29. Commenting on the looting of the Egyptians in the Exodus narrative, Nyssen comments, "It [i.e., Exodus] commands those participating through virtue in the free life also to equip themselves with the wealth of pagan learning [e.g., moral and natural philosophy, geometry, astronomy, dialectic] by which foreigners to faith beautify themselves." These are not only aids in *preparation* for the life of virtue, but they actually prove useful in the soul's higher stages of ascent. He continues, " . . . these things will be useful when in time the divine sanctuary of mystery must be beautified with the riches of reason." *De Vita Moysis,* II.115, Gregory of Nyssa, *The Life of Moses,* trans. Abraham J. Malherbe and Everett Ferguson (New York: Paulist, 1978), 81; SC 1c, 174.

30. *De Anima et Resurrectione,* Callahan, 205; PG 46, 28D–29A.

31. *De Anima et Resurrectione,* Callahan, 215–16; PG 46, 48C–49B.

32. *De Anima et Resurrectione,* Callahan, 201; PG 46, 21A.

33. *De Anima et Resurrectione,* Callahan, 216; PG 46, 49C–52A.

34. William Guthrie sites F. Nuyens's account from *L'Evolution de la psychologie d'Aristotle.*

35. *De Anima et Resurrectione,* Callahan, 216; PG 46, 49C–52A.

36. Earlier in the dialogue (PG 46, 44D–45A) Macrina does defend the immortality of the soul on the basis that it is not composed of parts into which it can be broken down as is the material body.

37. Herald Cherniss, *The Platonism of Gregory of Nyssa* (Berkeley: University of California Publications in Classical Philology, 1930), 12–13, reads Nyssen as sharing with Plato the exact concern for preserving the unitary nature of the soul as a requisite for its being immortal. Yet this is not the driving concern in Macrina's rejection of the model of the chariot. Nor is there anything in either *Phaedrus* or *De Anima et Resurrectione* that suggests that either author feared that the model rendered the soul subject to decay.

38. "Surely, it is agreed that activity connected with anger and desire is characteristic of a nonrational nature." *De Anima et Resurrectione,* Callahan, 218; PG 46, 53A.

39. *Topics* 153a15 and 23; 143b9.

40. "How could part of a nature undermine the definition, since every definition of essence looks to what is proper to the subject? Whatever is outside of the specific difference is rejected as being alien to the definition. . . . But what is characteristic

of something is that which is particular (*idion*) to it." *De Anima et Resurrectione,* Callahan, 217–18; PG 46, 53A.

41. "We base our argument on the inspired Scripture, which decrees that there is nothing in the soul which does not reflect the divine nature. For one who says that the soul is 'the image of God' affirms that what is alien to God is outside the definition of the soul." *De Anima et Resurrectione,* Callahan, 217; PG 46, 52A.

42. *De Hominis Opificio* 15.2; NPNF 403b.

43. *De Hominis Opificio* 16.2; NPNF 404b.

44. Macrina is willing to speak of the faculties, like perception, nutrition, desire, and irascibility, as being "in us" (in the sense that they occupy the margin or borderland of the soul) and yet will assert that "one faculty is present in the soul and the other faculties are not." *De Anima et Resurrectione,* Callahan, 218; PG 46, 53A.

45. *De Anima et Resurrectione,* Callahan, 219; PG 46, 56C.

46. See chap. 3.

47. *De Anima et Resurrectione,* Callahan, 218; PG 46, 53C. Macrina appeals to Moses' example to illustrate that *piqumia* and *qumoj* are not essential to the nature of man's soul. Were they, she argues, Moses could not have been free from them. "Moses, you see, was true to his essence and not involved in desire and anger which are an addition to our nature and not our nature itself" (PG 46, 53C–D).

48. "The ordinary man thinks of anger as a boiling of the blood around the heart. Others look upon it as the desire to avenge injury. As we understand it, it is an impulse to harm someone who annoys you. Nothing of this is pertinent to the definition of the [rational] soul." *De Anima et Resurrectione,* Callahan, 219; PG 46, 56A.

49. *De Anima et Resurrectione,* Callahan, 219; PG 46, 53D.

50. *De Anima et Resurrectione,* Callahan, 221; PG 46, 60A–B.

51. *De Hominis Opificio* 8.4; NPNF 393.

52. *De Hominis Opificio* 8.3–4, NPNF 393.

53. *De Anima et Resurrectione,* Callahan, 221; PG 46, 60C. If the soul itself is the efficient cause of all movements within the body then the appetitive faculty simply refers to the impulse in the soul toward an activity that obtains the essentials for living.

54. Nyssen's categorization of plants as nonsentient life forms is obviously problematic. For it ignores examples in nature, such as the turning of a sunflower toward the sun or the movement of the roots of a tree toward an underground water spring, which suggest that certain plants do have sensual awareness of their environment.

55. *De Anima et Resurrectione,* Callahan, 215; PG 46, 48C.

56. "There is also perceived in its nature much movement connected with the desiring faculty [*epithymia*] and the spirited faculty [*thymos*]." *De Anima et Resurrectione* Callahan, 215; PG 46, 48D.

57. *De Anima et Resurrectione,* Callahan, 221; PG 46, 60B.

58. *De Anima et Resurrectione,* Callahan, 221; PG 46, 60C.

59. *De Anima et Resurrectione,* Callahan, 222; PG 46, 60C–61A.

60. *De Hominis Opificio* 11 and 12; NPNF 396–99.

61. As will be argued below, Aristotle's argument to the contrary is the assumption upon which his belief in the morality of the soul is predicated. Cf. *De Anima et Resurrectione,* Callahan, 216; PG 46, 49C–52A.

62. "The deity beholds and hears all things, and searches all things out: you too have the power of apprehension of things by means of sight and hearing and understanding that inquires into things and searches them out." *De Hominis Opificio* 5.2; NPNF 391.

63. "And what is regarded as the opposite of pain, I mean the sensation of pleasure, is likewise, divided between anger and desire, for pleasure is the guiding force of each of these." *De Anima et Resurrectione,* Callahan, 219; PG 46, 56C.

64. *De Anima et Resurrectione,* Callahan, 219; PG 46, 56B–C.

65. *De Hominis Opificio* 8.5; NPNF 394; PG 44, 145C.

66. Cherniss, *The Platonism of Gregory of Nyssa,* 13.

67. *De Anima et Resurrectione,* Callahan, 219–20; PG 46, 56C.

68. Cherniss, *The Platonism of Gregory of Nyssa,* 14.

69. These Nyssen calls "*tēs psychēs merei.*" *Canonical Epistle* PG 45, 224A–B.

70. *De Vita Moysis* II.96, Malherbe and Ferguson, trans., *The Life of Moses,* 76; SC 1c, 58.

71. *De Beatitudinibus* 2, PG 44, 1216C; *In Inscriptiones Psalmorum* I.8, GNO V ,61; *De Virginitate* 22, PG 46, 404D.

72. Cherniss, *The Platonism of Gregory of Nyssa,* 17–18.

73. *De Hominis Opificio* 8.4; NPNF 393–94; PG 44, 145B. Michel Barnes makes a helpful comparison between Nyssen's taxonomy here and that of Alexander of Aphrodisias, *On the Soul.* See Michel R. Barnes, "The Polemical Context and Content of Gregory of Nyssa's Psychology," *Medieval Philosophy and Theology* 4 (1994): 16.

74. *De Anima et Resurrectione,* Callahan, 221; PG 46, 60A.

75. *De Hominis Opificio* 8.4; NPNF 393–394; PG 44, 144 D.

76. Aristotle, *De Anima* 2. 413a20.

77. *De Anima* 2.2 414a29.

78. Barnes, "The Polemical Context and Content of Gregory of Nyssa's Psychology," 14. To illustrate the nuance added to the doctrine of the soul by viewing it as trichotomous, Barnes quotes Galen's comparison of Plato's doctrine with that of Aristotle and of Posidonius, "Aristotle and Posidonius do not speak of forms [*eidē*] or parts [*merē*] of the soul, but say that there are powers [*dynameis*] of a single substance [*ousias*] which stems from the heart.... Our soul is not simple or uniform [*monoeidē*] in substance but composed of three parts (*merōn*), each with its own form and each having not one power [*dynamin*], but several." *On the Doctrines of Hippocrates and Plato* 6.2.5 and 9.9.22, quoted in Barnes, 15.

79. "He treats each single philosophical view only as a help to grasp the formulae of faith; and the truth of that view consists with him only in its adaptability to that end." William Moore and H. A. Wilson, "Prolegomena," to *Gregory of Nyssa Selected Writings and Letters;* NPNF 5 ser. 2, 8.

80. *De Anima et Resurrectione,* Callahan, 204; PG 46, 28A.

81. *De Anima et Resurrectione,* Callahan, 205; PG 46, 28D.

82. *De Anima et Resurrectione,* Callahan, 409; PG 46, 40A.

83. *De Hominis Opificio* 11.3; NPNF 396b; PG 44, 156A–B.

Chapter Three: The Nature of the Passions

1. *De Anima et Resurrectione*, in Saint Gregory of Nyssa, *Ascetical Works*, trans. Virginia Woods Callahan (Washington, D.C.: Catholic University of America Press, 1967), 219; PG 46, 56B–C.

2. *De Anima et Resurrectione*, Callahan, 218 and 224; PG 46, 64 C–D and 53A. It is worth mentioning that these two passages betray an ambiguity that runs throughout the dialogue and, indeed, throughout Nyssen's writings. On occasions he speaks of the soul as being a single, true human nature (cf. 64 C–D). At other times, the body and soul are treated as if they are two distinct natures (cf. 53A)

3. *De Anima et Resurrectione*, Callahan, 219; PG 46, 56A.

4. *De Anima et Resurrectione*, Callahan, 198; PG 46, 12B–13A.

5. *De Anima et Resurrectione*, Callahan, 217 and 221–22; PG 46, 52CD and 60C.

6. *De Anima et Resurrectione*, Callahan, 219; PG 46, 56C.

7. *De Anima et Resurrectione*, Callahan, 218; PG 46, 53C.

8. *De Anima et Resurrectione*, Callahan, 235–36; PG 46, 88A–B.

9. *De Anima et Resurrectione*, Callahan, 220; PG 46, 56C–57A.

10. Daniel 10:11–12. Nyssen seems to be interpreting *aner epithymion* to mean "zealous man" or "desiring man" (rather than "beloved man") whose passion is expressed in his search for understanding, as explained in verse 12.

11. *De Anima et Resurrectione*, Callahan, 220; PG 46, 57A. Presumably Nyssen is alluding to Numbers 25, in which God tells Moses that he is establishing a covenant with Phineas and his descendants to be his priests for Israel. Yet contrary to Nyssen's portrayal of the episode, *thymos* is a characteristic of God, not Phineas (Num. 25:11). Hence it is not Phineas's *thymos* that is virtuous, but "his zeal [*ezēlōsen*] for God" (Num. 25:13). Perhaps Nyssen's interpretation of Numbers 25 is based on his reading of 1 Maccabees 2:54: "Phineas our father, because he was deeply zealous, received the covenant of everlasting priesthood." However errant his recollection of Numbers 25 was, Nyssen's exegesis stands firmly within a Jewish interpretative tradition.

12. *De Anima et Resurrectione*, Callahan, 219; PG 46, 56B.

13. 2 Corinthians 7:10.

14. *De Anima et Resurrectione*, Callahan, 220; PG 46, 56C.

15. *De Anima et Resurrectione*, Callahan, 236; PG 46, 88C.

16. *De Anima et Resurrectione*, Callahan, 224; PG 46, 65A–B.

17. *De Anima et Resurrectione*, Callahan, 220; PG 46, 57B–C.

18. In the same passage, Nyssen, speaking of Paul's praying that God may sanctify the Christians at Thessalonica (1 Thess. 5:23) wholly in spirit (*pneuma*), soul (*psychē*), and body (*sōma*), identifies these three with the threefold faculties of the soul. *Pneuma* corresponds with the intellect, *psychē* denotes the sentient faculties, and *sōma* refers to the vegetative powers. *De Hominis Opificio* 8.5; NPNF 394; PG 44, 145C.

19. *De Hominis Opificio* 8.6; NPNF 394; PG 44, 148A.

20. Nyssen quotes 1 Corinthians 2:14, 15 to set the natural man apart from the spiritual man: "The natural man does not receive the things of the spirit; for they are foolishness unto him." *De Hominis Opificio* 8.6; NPNF 394; PG 44, 148C.

21. Nyssen does not rely heavily upon the language of grace in his soteriological writings. As will be seen below, he does speak of man's original condition as being

graced; this graced condition also denotes that state to which we shall be returned in the eschaton. See *De Anima et Resurrectione,* Callahan, 270; PG 46, 156C and 157A.

22. *De Anima et Resurrectione,* Callahan, 222; PG 46, 61A.

23. *De Anima et Resurrectione,* Callahan, 222; PG 46, 61B.

24. Although Nyssen is not consistent in distinguishing between *hormai* and *pathē* in *De Anima et Resurrectione* (see 61A, 64 C–D, and 68A); he more clearly identifies the moral character of *pathos* when he observes in *De Vita Moysis* (II.91; SC 1c, 160) that newborn children, being incapable of distinguishing between good and evil, are not capable of passion (*to pathos*)." Also see *De Hominis Opificio* 18.2; PG 44, 192C–D.

25. *De Anima et Resurrectione,* Callahan, 222; PG 46, 61C. Xenophon, after observing that *thymos* in a horse is the same cause of anger as it is in human beings, advises riders not to allow a spirited horse (*thymoeidesteros hippos*) to run at a full gallop lest it get out of control and injure itself, but to check him quietly with the bit and with soothing tones until he quiets down ("The Art of Horsemanship," IX.5–8, trans. E. C. Marchant, in *Loeb Classical Library* (Cambridge, Mass.: Harvard University Press, 1971).

26. While *epithymia* is the primary word Nyssen uses that would be translated "desire" or "longing," he does occasionally use *agapē* to express the same idea. As we shall see, *agapē* comes to refer to *epithymia* transformed in the eschatological context.

27. *De Anima et Resurrectione,* Callahan, 224; PG 46, 65A–B.

28. *De Anima et Resurrectione,* Callahan, 224; PG 46, 65C.

29. "So, also, in us, unless our faculties are directed by reason toward what we need, when emotions govern the mind, man goes from the intellectual and godlike to the nonrational and foolish." *De Anima et Resurrectione,* Callahan, 223; PG 46, 64A. The phrase "what we need" presumably can refer to either bodily needs or those needs unique to his rational nature.

30. *De Anima et Resurrectione,* Callahan, 222; PG 46, 61C.

31. *De Anima et Resurrectione,* Callahan, 237; PG 46, 89A.

32. Commenting on the causes of desire, Macrina observes that the fire of *agapē/epithymia* can be snuffed out by a sense of shame at having been "deluded . . . by some false image of beauty." *De Anima et Resurrectione,* Callahan, 238; PG 46, 92A. Although he does not explicitly define desire as the attraction to beauty, nevertheless, it is implicit in his suggestion that unfulfilled hope produces the shame of being deluded by the false apprehension of beauty. In *De Hominis Opificio* 18.5, however, he is explicit that the object of man's desire, when properly directed by reason, is the Beautiful. When reason rules over our nonrational nature, its emotions, such as the love of pleasure, are transmuted into that virtuous desire for the truly beautiful. Thus he writes, "The high spirit in our character raises our thoughts above the passions and keeps it from bondage to what is base" (PG 44, 193B–C).

33. *De Anima et Resurrectione,* Callahan, 224; PG 46, 64C and 65A.

34. Plato says that justice must be established throughout the *polis,* and its essence is that of doing one's primary task and not meddling in the work that is beyond one's expertise. *Republic* IV, 433A–B.

35. Because the philosopher king is wise, i.e., he knows the Form of the Good that represents the ends proper to the work each class of citizen and the coordination

of those ends to serve the supreme end of the whole, he is able to direct the end that is the good of the whole. *Republic* IV, 428B–D.

36. *Republic* IV, 439D.

37. "The principle of anger sometimes fights against desires as an alien thing against an alien" (*Republic,* IV, 440A). He continues describing the character of this war between the spirited part and the appetitive part of the soul: "when his desires constrain a man contrary to his reason... he reviles himself and is angry with that within which masters him; and... the high spirit of such a man becomes the ally of his reason" (*Republic* IV, 440B).

38. "Whatever lies on the margin of the soul, inclining towards each of the extremes according to its own peculiar nature... these we consider externals because they are not perceived in the beauty of the archetype." *De Anima et Resurrectione,* Callahan, 220–21; PG 46, 57C.

39. In his discussion of the *Imago Dei* Nyssen says that the divine beauty is contemplated according to virtue, meaning that the image is present in human beings to the extent that they participate in the virtues proper to the divine nature. He begins by listing those virtues, e.g., purity (*katharotēs*), freedom from passion (*apatheia*), blessedness (*makariotēs*), and alienation from evil (*kakou pantos allotriōsis*) that God bestows upon us so that we might show forth "his own sovereignty." Then Nyssen enumerates virtues, qualities, and capacities necessary for reflecting the supreme beauty, among them are word (*logos*) and mind (*nous*), the power of apprehension, and love (*agapē*), of which he says, "if this be absent, the whole stamp of the likeness is transformed." *De Hominis Opificio* 5.2; NPNF 391; PG 44, 137C. As Rowan Greer has observed, the reflection of the divine image in the virtues, reason, and love is meant to allude to the three stages of the spiritual life: the ethical or purgative, the illuminative characterized by the study of physics, and the union of the lover and the beloved as described in the Song of Songs.

40. "Intentional awareness" is Nussbaum's translation of the idea of *orexis,* which, as used in Aristotle's *De Motu Animalium,* refers to the "reaching out" or "desire" for some appearance. Aristotle distinguishes between fear and fright (*De Anima* 432b 30). The latter is the instinctual reaction to some phantasia, such as when one is startled by the sudden and violent bang of a car backfiring. Fright, however, is not identical to the emotion of fear because fear entails some *orexis* or judgment that the phantasia is in fact terrible and threatening. See Martha Nussbaum, *The Therapy of Desire: Theory and Practice in Hellenistic Ethics* (Princeton, N.J.: Princeton University Press, 1994), 83–84.

41. Nussbaum, *The Therapy of Desire,*, 81.

42. Aristotle, *Ethics* 119b, 15, cited in Nussbaum, *The Therapy of Desire,* 82.

43. Nussbaum, *The Therapy of Desire,* 95.

44. Seneca, *Epistle* 121.11, quoted in A. A. Long, "Soul and Body in Stoicism," *Phronesis* 27 (1982): 46.

45. Zeno is quoted by Seneca as holding that the Stoic sage experiences *propatheia* that are "certain suggestions and shadows of passion, though he will be free from passions themselves." Thus the sage does not feel nothing, but the *propatheia* are not allowed to gather force by the sage's consent so as to become passions in the morally pejorative sense. See John M. Dillon, *"Metriopatheia* and *Apatheia:* Some Reflections on a Controversy in Later Greek Ethics," *Essays in Ancient Greek*

Philosophy II, ed. J. P. Anton and A. Preus (Albany: State University of New York Press, 1983), 509.

46. *De Ira* II.3.4. Seneca distinguishes the primary passive disturbance of the mind that is the pain and instantaneous flair of anger from "the active impulse consequent upon it [i.e., the passive disturbance], which has not only admitted the impression of injury but also approved it, [this] is really anger — the tumult of a mind proceeding to revenge by choice and determination" (II.3.5).

47. Nussbaum, *The Therapy of Desire,* 374.

48. Quoted in Dillon, "*Metriopatheia* and *Apatheia,*" 513.

49. Chrysippus rejected identifying the passions with our nonrational animal nature because believing that reason can control the passions it was necessary to locate the passion wholly within the intellect itself. Were it not, man would forever suffer under the weight of the passions. See John M. Rist, *Stoic Philosophy* (Cambridge: Cambridge University Press, 1969), 32–33.

50. Dillon, "*Metriopatheia* and *Apatheia,*" 510–11.

51. Rist (*Stoic Philosophy,* 30) argues that Chrysippus held that there was no mental activity unaccompanied by "some kind of emotional colouring." Therefore correct judgments were accompanied by good emotions (*eupatheia*), while errant judgments carried some unpleasant disturbance (*pathos*).

52. Aristotle identifies as a feature of human nature which sets it apart from other animals the fact that man acts on the basis of some judgment while the brutes are moved solely by appearances without critical judgment (*Metaphysics* 980b25–28). See Nussbaum, *The Therapy of Desire,* 374.

53. Seneca does not by any means view the bodily reactions as the chief source of the passions. He explains that the passions grow out of beliefs that are not natural but the product of socialization. Our desires, fears, and anxieties reflect the values and sensibilities inculcated in us by religious, political, and familial institutions. See *Epistle* 22.15.

54. In this respect Nyssen follows a number of Middle Platonists. As Christopher Stead has observed, *pathē* were viewed by Middle Platonists as "unsought interference with the normal current of life, which would indeed convey suggestions of unnatural vice … [or] at best … morally neutral occurrences whose justification depended on their being controlled by intelligence. … Though a distinction existed in theory between the morally neutral *hormē* (impulse) and the morally suspect *pathos,* this distinction was constantly overlooked." See Christopher Stead, "The Concept of Mind and the Concept of God in the Christian Fathers," *The Philosophical Frontiers of Christian Theology: Essays Presented to D. M. Mackinnon* (Cambridge: Cambridge University Press, 1982), 44–45.

55. Although Nyssen never explicitly applies the label *hormē* to the *epithymētikos* in the context of Macrina's discussion of the parable of the wheat and the weeds, her description of the *epithymētikos* immediately follows her description of *hormē.*

56. The Greek reads, *eis pathos hai hormai katastrephontai.* My translation of *katastrephontai* followed by *eis* as "transformed" carries the sense of being changed into something else. But "transformed" does not convey the sense of *katastrephontai* as entailing *violent* change that might be expressed in the metaphor of the chariot destroyed because it has been pulled at breakneck speed and with utter recklessness by out-of-control horses. Regardless of how the verb is translated, the more important

point is Nyssen's contrast of *pathos* and *hormai*. *De Anima et Resurrectione*, PG 46, 61C.

57. "The impulses of our soul [*tas hormas*], each of which, if it works only for the good, produces entirely a harvest of virtue." *De Anima et Resurrectione*, Callahan, 223–24; PG 46, 64C–D.

58. *De Anima et Resurrectione*, Callahan, 222; PG 46, 61A.

59. "If reason ... is in control of the faculties externally imposed upon us then ... none of these faculties within us is activated towards the service of evil." Without the control of reason, however, nonrational creatures "destroy each other, being dominated by rage ... [because] the powerful carnal impulses do not operate for their own good ... nor are they directed with any logic toward anything advantageous." *De Anima et Resurrectione*, Callahan, 222; PG 46, 61C–D.

60. *De Anima et Resurrectione*, Callahan, 225; PG 46, 68A.

61. Rowen Williams, "Macrina's Deathbed Revisited: Gregory of Nyssa on Mind and Passion," in *Christian Faith and Greek Philosophy in Late Antiquity: Essays in Tribute to George Christopher Stead*, ed. L. Wickham and C. Bammel (Leiden: E. J. Brill, 1993), 235.

62. "The attributes [e.g., *thymos, hēdonē, thrasos, deilia*, etc. (192B)], then, human nature took to itself from the side of the brutes; for those qualities with which the brute life was armed for self-preservation, when transformed to human life, become passion (*pathē*)." *De Hominis Opificio* 18.2; NPNF 408; PG 44, 192C–D.

63. Long, "Soul and Body in Stoicism," 47.

64. "Even when the mind contemplates such an object [i.e., something frightful], it does not directly suggest avoidance or pursuit; e.g., it often thinks of something fearful [i.e., *phoberon*] without suggesting fear." *De Anima* 432b 30–32.

65. *De Hominis Opificio*, NPNF 408a–b; PG 44, 193A–B.

66. *De Anima et Resurrectione*, PG 46, 64C–D.

67. *Commentarius in Canticum Canticorum* XI, GNO VI, 323–24.

68. Michel R. Barnes ("The Polemical Context and Content of Gregory of Nyssa's Psychology," *Medieval Philosophy and Theology* 4 [1994]: 14–16) provides an excellent analysis of the similarities between Nyssen's description of the soul in *De Hominis Opificio* and *De Anima et Resurrectione* and Aristotle's ordering of the faculties of the soul. While Nyssen's doctrine of the blending of the rational and nonrational faculties under the rule of the intellect allows for the *possibility* for the moral unity of the soul, as seen in Macrina's chariot metaphor, he does not abandon altogether the Platonic view of competing impulses in the soul.

69. *De Anima et Resurrectione*, Callahan, 198; PG 46, 12B.

70. *De Anima et Resurrectione*, Callahan, 198; PG 46, 13A.

71. *De Anima et Resurrectione*, Callahan, 198–99; PG 46, 16A–C.

72. *De Anima et Resurrectione*, Callahan, 199; PG 46, 17A.

73. Nyssen in *De Anima et Resurrectione* (PG 46, 56A) specifically defines *epithymia* as "a longing to fulfill some need or the enjoyment of some pleasure ... which we are not at the moment enjoying."

74. Macrina says that all desire seeks to satisfy some lacking or deficiency (*De Anima et Resurrectione*, Callahan, 238; PG 46, 92C). Thus *epithymia*, which is ever seeking after elusive beauty but never fully or permanently satisfied, echoes Socrates' description of *erōs* in *Symposium* 203 B–C. Burrus carries the comparison

between *De Anima et Resurrectione* and *Symposium* further. Even as Diotima initiated Socrates into the mysteries of *erōs*, so too Macrina instructs her brother in the
philosophy of love.

75. *De Anima et Resurrectione,* Callahan, 219; PG 46, 56B.

76. *De Anima et Resurrectione,* Callahan, 238; PG 46, 93A.

77. *De Anima et Resurrectione,* Callahan, 238; PG 46, 92A.

78. "To have this attitude toward the soul is nothing else than alienating yourself
from virtue and looking to the pleasures of the moment." *De Anima et Resurrectione,*
Callahan, 200; PG 46, 17B.

79. *De Anima et Resurrectione,* Callahan, 200; PG 46, 20A.

80. For Macrina's purposes, the pursuit of future goods is to a great degree
exclusive of enjoyment of present goods. Sacrifice and the mortification of the flesh
are necessary. "Bereft of everything he had in the beginning of his life, living among
strangers, [Abraham] sought a future prosperity through the present affliction." *De
Anima et Resurrectione,* Callahan, 234; PG 46, 84C.

81. Nyssen explains that the Israelites preferred their bondage in Egypt because
they were tempted to look only at the present pleasures instead of looking to heaven,
which he associates with the freedom born out of the trials of the exodus (II, 59).

82. *De Vita Moysis* II.131–32.

83. The life of virtue in *De Vita Moysis* is characterized by moderation (*sōphrosynē*), rather than by a radically austere asceticism. Yet he explains the disorderly
conduct of the Israelites in the wilderness in terms of by their intemperate appetites
(*hē tōn hēdonōn ametria*), which made them dissatisfied with the manna that God
provided (II, 131–32). The life of virtue, therefore, entails the disciplined elimination
of one's attraction to excess and one's fondness for that which is sensually pleasing
(II, 297 and 302).

84. *De Vita Moysis* II.44–46.

85. *De Vita Moysis* II.47.

86. *De Hominis Opificio* 5.1; PG 44, 137A.

87. Seneca, *Epistle* 5.7–9.

88. While many Stoics, e.g., Zeno, Chrysippus, and Posidonius, equated the
virtuous life, i.e., life according to reason, with "life in agreement with nature,"
Cleanthes suggests that the happiness afforded by the life of virtue comes from an
acceptance of the unfolding of nature and fate without regard to one's own personal
ends. "And virtue, [Cleanthes] holds, is being in harmony [with nature] — desirable
for its own sake and not on account of any fear or hope or anything else external."
Diogenes Laertius, *Lives and Opinions of Eminent Philosophers* VII. 89. Cf. Marcus
Aurelius, *Meditations* IV.1 and Epictetus, *Enchiridion* 2.

89. "For to grumble at anything which comes to pass is to stand apart from
nature of which in part the natures of all things are intertwined." Marcus Aurelius,
Meditations II.16 and X.14. Cf. *Arrian's Discourses of Epictetus* III.17.

90. Marcus Aurelius, *Meditations* III.3, IV.4, X.7, and XI.20. Rist, *Stoic
Philosophy,* 257–61.

91. Jaroslav Pelikan, *Christianity and Classical Culture* (New Haven, Conn.:
Yale University Press, 1993), 265.

Chapter Four: Satiation and Epectasy

1. Jean Daniélou, *Platonisme et théologie mystique: Essai sur la doctrine spirituelle de saint Gregoire de Nysse* (Paris: Aubier, 1944), 298.

2. Brooks Otis, "Cappadocian Thought as a Coherent System," *Dumbarton Oaks Papers* 12 (Cambridge, Mass.: Harvard University Press, 1958), 102–3.

3. Origen, *De Principiis* 1.8.1.

4. Origen, *De Principiis* 2.9.3.

5. Origen, *De Principiis* 1.5.3.

6. Origen, *De Principiis* 1.3.8 and 4.4.9.

7. "If, therefore, the things which are holy are termed fire and light ... and the love of the sinner is said to be cold, we must ask whether perhaps even the word soul, which in Greek is *psyche,* was not formed from *psychesthai,* with the idea of growing cold after having been in a diviner and better state." Origen, *De Principiis* 2.8.3.

8. The matter of the rational beings that occupy the bodies of stars and angels is problematic within Origen's salvation history. On one hand, he claims that the souls of the stars and angels occupy such an exalted place in the hierarchy as a reward for their virtue (Origen, *De Principiis* 1.8.4; 1.7.5; 2.2.2; 2.9.6). Yet on the other hand, his Christology maintains that the soul of Jesus was chosen for the Incarnation because it was the only rational being not to fall away from God (II,6.3). Origen's inconsistency is that in his discussion of freedom and the role of merit in establishing the cosmic hierarchy he assumes that some rational beings other than Christ's soul did not cease participating in God's holiness (II,9.6). See Origene, *Traite des Principes* II, trans. H. Crouzel and M. Simonetti, SC 253, 89, n. 31; 214, n. 9; 218, n. 34.

9. *De Principiis* 1.4.1.

10. While the Myth of Er from *Republic* contains a very developed account of Plato's theory of the transmigration of souls, Plato's description of the fall of souls in *Phaedrus* shares a greater similarity with Origen's account of the fall. Even as Origen describes the intellectual creatures as being made in the image of God, so too Plato describes the souls of mortals as originally possessing divine faculties, symbolized by the wings on the horses (246B and D) that allow the soul to ascend to the vault of heaven and survey the intelligible realities that are the source of true knowledge (247C) even as the souls of the gods do. More significantly, Plato explains the union of the soul and body as "falling" from the heavenly realm into corporeal existence as a result of its corruption by evil (represented by the weakened and ultimately broken wings) (246B–C).

11. *Phaedrus* 248C–D. Unlike the Myth of Er in *Republic,* the account of the fall of souls in *Phaedrus* does not expressly say that the souls choose their destiny. Rather the implication is that each makes those choices in their next life based on the extent of their vision of the heavenly realm prior to the fall. Their individual vision predisposes each soul toward truth and beauty or toward sensual hedonism and self-serving power. The choices reflecting these varied predispositions shape one's life into that of the philosopher or that of the sophist or tyrant. The lowest orders of men who never saw the transcendent, intelligible realities assume the form of irrational animals in their subsequent incarnations (*Phaedrus* 249B). Socrates illustrates this point in *Republic* X, 620A with Ajax's choice to become a lion and Agamemnon's to become an eagle. In *Phaedo* 82A, Socrates again espouses a hierarchical division between human beings and animals.

12. *Phaedrus* 248C and 249E-250A.

13. *Republic* X, 619A.

14. *De Principiis* 1.6.2.

15. Henri Crouzel, *Origen: The Life and Thought of the First Great Theologian*, trans. A. S. Worrall (San Francisco: Harper & Row, 1989), 216. Crouzel argues that, in addition to the evidence of the fidelity of Christ's soul, the logic of Origen's theory of the fall insists that the fall not be inevitable. Were the fall ineluctable, the rational creatures' freedom, which is the central principle of Origen's theory of the righteousness of the cosmic hierarchy, would be greatly compromised. If the fall is ineluctable, the implication is that God only pretends to give intellectual creatures freedom. In that case, either God is the source of the inevitability which is a denial of freedom, or the rational creatures have a destiny beyond the scope of God's sovereignty.

16. *De Principiis* 2.9.2.

17. *De Principiis* 1.6.2.

18. *"pro mentis ac propositi motibus." De Principiis* 1.6.2.

19. *De Principiis* 2.9.2.

20. *De Principiis* 2.8.3.

21. *De Principiis* 1.8.4.

22. *De Principiis* I.3.8.

23. *De Principiis* I.3.8, trans. Butterworth 39.

24. This suggestion is highly suspect because it is at odds with his notion of *apokatastasis* in which all things are ultimately subordinated to the dominion of Christ (*De Principiis* 1.6.1–2). The subjection of all things to Christ is, he says, as it was in the beginning and as it shall be in the end. In this respect the end is the restoration of the beginning. Yet the end is not *identical* with the beginning. On this point Origen is explicit: *semper enim similis est finis initiis* (I,6.2; SC 196). The difference between the eschatological union of the rational creatures with God and their union with God prior to the fall is that eschatologically their contemplative union will not be a state into which they were created. As the result of experiencing the hardships of embodied existence, the complacency born of innocence and ignorance is replaced by a true appreciation of the blessedness of communion with God. Consequently, the naiveté and innocence that characterized their initial union with God will be replaced by a desire for God that has gained stability and firmness of will (*De Principiis* 2.11.7).

25. *De Principiis* 1.3.8, trans. G. W. Butterworth (Gloucester, Mass.: Peter Smith, 1973), 39.

26. *De Principiis* 1.4.1.

27. Otis, "Cappadocian Thought as a Coherent System," 102, n. 11. The participle *peperasmenē* is applied to God's power, not to his essential nature: *peperasmenēn gar einai kai tēn dynamin tou theou lekteon.*

28. *De Principiis* 2.9.1, trans. Butterworth, 129. In Rufinus's Latin text, Origen does not explicitly assert that God's power is finite. Nevertheless, he still claims that the number of creatures must be finite because otherwise they "could neither have been controlled nor provided for by God." The logic here is that God's power must be greater than the number of his creatures; were the creatures infinite in number they would exceed the breadth of his grasp. By implication, then, God's power is not infinite, but finite.

29. "Igitur si sit aliquis qui peritia vel arte, verbi gratia geometriae aut medic-inae, paulatim fuerit inbutus usquequo peruenerit ad perfectum... ut ad integrum supradictae artis assumeret discipliam." *De Principiis* 1.4.1 trans. Butterworth, 40; SC 252, 166.

30. I am grateful to Rowan A. Greer for this helpful suggestion.

31. Marguerite Harl, "Recherches sur l'origenisme d'Origene: la 'satieté' (*koros*) de la contemplation comme motif de la chute des ames," *Studia Patristica* 8.2, ed. F. L. Cross (Berlin: Akademie-Verlag, 1966), 373.

32. Harl, "Recherches sur l'origenisme d'Origene," 397.

33. Crouzel, *Origen: The Life and Thought of the First Great Theologian*, 210–11.

34. *Commentary on John* II, 28; *Griechischen Christlichen Schriftsteller* 85 quoted in Andrew Louth, *The Origins of the Christian Mystical Tradition: From Plato to Denys* (Oxford: Clarendon Press, 1981), 72.

35. *De Principiis* 6.4.8, trans. G. W. Butterworth (Gloucester, Mass.: Peter Smith, 1973), 324. Butterworth also points out that Jerome in *Epistula ed Avitum* attributes to Origen the blasphemy that the Son's "comprehension" of the Father is restricted to knowledge of the Father, "For if the Son knows the Father, it would seem by virtue of this knowledge he can comprehend the Father.... If, however, we mean the kind of comprehension in which one comprehends another not only by understanding and wisdom but in the sense of holding the object of his knowledge under his authority and power, then we cannot say that the Son comprehends the Father."

36. For this reason, Otis's rendering of *koros* does not fit his theological expla-nation for the fall. Indeed the reaction to a finite object of eternal contemplation would be more apt to be boredom rather than the satiation of having more than one can hold.

37. See *Commentary on John* II.28 and *De Principiis* 3.4.8.

38. Louth and Daniélou contend that Origen differs from Nyssen and others who develop an apophatic theology in that Origen's theory of contemplation is not ecstatic. The intellect never needs to go beyond itself. Origen does not want to say that God was ultimately beyond the intellect's understanding. The image of darkness is more the result of our lack of purity. See Louth, *The Origins of the Christian Mystical Tradition*, 73.

39. Humanity's reflection on the nature of God begins principally with a knowl-edge of God as creator of the visible world. From the order of the cosmos the intellect deduces the existence of the creator. *Oratio Catechetica*, GNO III, 4, VI, 18–21.

40. *De Vita Moysis* I.20.

41. *Commentarius In Canticum Canticorum* XI, GNO VI, 321.4.

42. *Commentarius In Canticum Canticorum* XI, GNO VI, 322, 13–15.

43. Clement of Alexandria, *Stromata* 2.2; PG 8, 937A.

44. Clement of Alexandria, *Stromata* 5.12; PG 9, 121A.

45. *De Vita Moysis* I.46.

46. *Commentarius in Canticum Canticorum* XI; GNO VI, 322–23.

47. *Commentarius in Canticum Canticorum* XI, GNO VI, 324

48. Gregory of Nazianzus, *Theological Oration* 28.9.

49. Gregory of Nazianzus, *Theological Oration* 28.17.

50. *Commentarius in Canticum Canticorum* XI, GNO VI, 324.

51. *Commentarius in Canticum Canticorum* XI; GNO VI, 326.

52. Clement of Alexandria, *Stromata* 5.12; PG 9, 121A–124A.

53. See Thomas A. Kopecek, *A History of Neo-Arianism* I and II (Philadelphia: Philadelphia Patristic Foundation, 1979); R. P. C. Hanson, *The Search for the Christian Doctrine of God: The Arian Controversy 318–381 A.D.* (Edinburgh: T & T Clark, 1988), 598–636.

54. Basil of Caesarea, *Epistle* 234.

55. Gregory of Nazianzus, *Theological Oration* 28.3.

56. *Commentarius in Canticum Canticorum* XI, GNO VI, 334.

57. *Commentarius in Canticum Canticorum* XI, GNO VI, 338–39.

58. *Commentarius in Canticum Canticorum* XI, GNO VI, 333. It is hard to believe that Nyssen is suggesting that the knowledge of God we gain through the Incarnation is not really knowledge but only a feeling of confirmation that God is truly loveable and the proper object of desire. Rather at this point in the homily Nyssen is thinking of the hand in the far narrower sense of God's creative activities.

59. Basil of Caesarea, *Epistle* 233. Basil uses grace almost synonymously with the work of the Holy Spirit; for he goes on to comment, "But if it [i.e., the intellect] gives itself up to the assistance of the Spirit, it will recognize the truth and recognize God."

60. Basil, *Epistle* 233. While the intellect of all who achieve this stage of spiritual ascent gain the recognition of the Divine, those who are permitted to recognize God in his infinite nature, Basil says, are a select few.

61. Donald F. Winslow, *The Dynamics of Salvation: A Study in Gregory of Nazianzus* (Philadelphia: Philadelphia Patristic Foundation, 1979), 171–78.

62. Gregory of Nazianzus, *Theological Oration* 28,17.

63. *Commentarius in Canticum Canticorum* XI, GNO VI, 336.

Chapter Five: The Infinitely Wondrous Being of God

1. Aristotle in *Physics* 203b6 comments, "The Unlimited encompasses and governs all things. On this basis the Unlimited is equivalent to the Divine, since it is deathless and indestructible, as Anaximander says and as most physicists who employ the term will agree." Quoted in Philip Wheelwright, *The Pre-Socratics* (Indianapolis: Odyssey Press, 1966), 55.

2. In Fragment 1 Anaximander says, "The unlimited is the first-principle of things that are. It is that from which the coming-to-be [of things and quantities] takes place, and it is that into which they return when they perish" (quoted in Wheelwright, *The Pre-Socratics*, 54). Aristotle construes Anaximander's Unlimited to be the material cause of all things as "one simple unlimited corporeal principle" (*Physics* 204b21).

3. For a sweeping and in-depth examination of classical and medieval uses of *aoristia* and *apeiria* see Leo Sweeney, *Divine Infinity in Greek and Medieval Thought* (New York: Peter Lang, 1998). For Aristotle, see chapter 8 "Aristotle's Infinity of Quantity." Cf. *Physics* III, 207b21–25.

4. *Physics* III, 206a25–33 quoted in Sweeney, *Divine Infinity in Greek and Medieval Thought*, 165.

5. The power (*dynamis*) of the One is derived from its simplicity or unity. Unity is necessary for the production of anything. The power to produce is proportionate to the degree of a thing's being. The One is maximal unity because it is purely simple

rather than being a composite unity. Thus its power is infinite in the sense that it is infinite potentiality. It is also infinite in its productive power as the source of form for an infinite number of things (*Enneads* III.8.10). See Sweeney, *Divine Infinity in Greek and Medieval Thought,* 195–201.

6. "But the Intellect sees, by means of itself, like something divided proceeding from the undivided, that life and thought and all things come from the one, because that God is not one of all things; for this is how all things come from him, because he is not confined by any shape; that One is alone: if he was all things, he would be numbered among beings." *Enneads* V.1.7, trans. A. H. Armstrong (Cambridge, Mass.: Harvard University Press, 1984).

7. The One's indeterminate nature is the essence of its simplicity. It is no being. But it is not nonbeing in the sense that evil is nonbeing. As a privation of some good, evil is a negative i.e., a deficiency or corruption of form. Evil is nothing (see *Enneads* I.8.3–4). By contrast, the One is nonbeing only in the sense that it is not one thing because it is the source of all form and so is necessarily prior to form. But it is not nothing. See III.8.9–10.

8. Sweeney (*Divine Infinity in Greek and Medieval Thought,* 19) says that Plotinus uses *apeiron* and *aoriston* synonymously. The One's power is *apeiron* in that it is potentially the cause of an unlimited number of entities. At the same time, the One that transcends form and being is infinite in the sense of indeterminate (*aoriston*).

9. For a positive account of the body and material beauty in Plotinus's account of the soul's ascent to the One see Margaret R. Miles, *Plotinus on Body and Beauty: Society, Philosophy, and Religion in Third-Century Rome* (Oxford: Blackwell, 1999), 33–83.

10. "You see the beauty which rests upon the very Forms, all of them richly varied. It is beautiful to abide here; but when one is in beauty one must look to see whence these Forms come and whence they derive their beauty. But this itself must not be any one of them; for then it will be one of them and will be part. Nor, then, can it be a shape of any kind or an individual power, nor again all those which have come to be and exist here above but it must be above all powers and above all shapes. The principle is the formless [*aneideon*], not that which needs form [*ou to morphēn*]." *Enneads* VI.7.32. 4–10.

11. "These beautiful things, then, must be measured and limited, but not the really beautiful or rather the super-beautiful (*hyperkalon*).... It must not be shaped or formed.... The experience of the lover bears witness to this, that, as long as it is in that which has the impression perceived by the senses, the lover is not yet in love; but when from that he himself generates in himself an impression not perceptible by the senses [*ouk aisthēton typon*] in his partless soul, then love springs up" (*Enneads* VI.7.33.19–26).

12. Sweeney rejects Norris Clark's interpretation that God's nature is intrinsically infinite because love (for God), which corresponds to the object of the nature of the beloved, is infinite. See Norris Clark, "Infinity in Plotinus: A Reply," *Gregorianum* 60 (1959): 91. Sweeney dismisses this interpretation because it reasons from our love to the intrinsic nature of the beloved. As he summarizes Clark's assumption, "one always loves an object as it is intrinsically in itself; therefore, the object loved is infinite intrinsically — 'in its own inner reality as it is in itself.' " Rather Sweeney argues that Plotinus does not reason from the nature of love to the nature of the

beloved, but from the nature of the beloved to the nature of our love. "The Object loved is somehow infinite; But the object loved characterizes the love; Hence, the love in question also is somehow infinite." See Sweeney, *Divine Infinity in Greek and Medieval Thought*, 225ff.

13. That which participates in beauty is beautiful because it derives its form from the source of beauty. But the source of beauty itself is formless. See *Enneads* VI.7.32.35–40.

14. "Truly, you cannot grasp the form or shape of what is longed for; it would be most longed for and most lovable, and love for it would be immeasurable. For love is not limited here, because neither is the beloved [i.e., the One]" (*Enneads* VI.7.32.25–30).

15. Clement of Alexandria, *Stromata* 5.12; PG 9, 121A–B. One can deduce that God's being is infinite, he says, not from his inscrutability (*adiexēteton*), but because we hold that he is without diminution (*adiastaton*).

16. Gregory of Nazianzus, *Theological Oration* 28. 7.

17. *De Vita Moysis*, 2.236; SC 1c, 268.

18. Nyssen's account of God as unlimited and uncontained reflects the ancient view of Mandate 1 of *The Shepherd of Hermas* 26.1, which argues that as the one from whom all things gain their existence, God "contains all things but is himself alone uncontained (*achōrētos ōn*)."

19. *Contra Eunomium* I.223; GNO I, 91.

20. *Contra Eunomium* I.226; GNO I, 92–93.

21. *Contra Eunomium* I.231; GNO I, 94.

22. *Contra Eunomium* I.232; GNO I, 94.

23. Sweeney, *Divine Infinity in Greek and Medieval Thought*, 483.

24. "It was said, moreover, above that good can be diminished by the presence of evil alone, and that where the nature is incapable of deteriorating, there is no limit conceived of to the goodness: the unlimited, in fact, is not such owing to any relation whatever, but, considered in itself, escapes limitation." *Contra Eunomium* I.236, in NPNF V, 57; GNO I, 95–96.

25. *Contra Eunomium* I.236–37; GNO, I 96.

26. For a detailed account of Nyssen's use of *diastēma*, see T. Paul Verghese, "*DIASTHMA* and *DIASTASIS* in Gregory of Nyssa: Introduction to a Concept and the Posing of a Problem," in *Gregor Von Nyssa und Die Philosophie*, ed. H. Dörrie, M. Altenburger and U. Schramm (Leiden: E. J. Brill, 1976), 243–60.

27. Alexander of Alexandria, who first challenged the orthodoxy of Arius's view of the Logos, described the Father in his seventh letter to the patriarch of Constantinople (PG 18, 557B): "Eternally present to him, he [i.e., the Father] begot the only begotten Son not temporally nor out of that which is extended (*oude ek diastēmatos*), nor out of what was not." Basil of Caesarea used *diastēma* in its temporal sense in his characterization of the Arians in his *De Spirit Sanctum* (PG 32, 177B): "By a temporal interval [*diastemasi*] they distinguish the Father from the Son and the Son from the Holy Spirit." Cyril of Alexandria will come to speak of the Trinity as *tēn adiastatēn triada*. These examples are taken from Verghese, "*DIASTHMA* and *DIASTASIS* in Gregory of Nyssa," 245.

28. *Contra Eunomium* II.70; GNO I, 246.

29. While Aristotle identified time as the mere coincidence of movements and therefore as an accidental property; Nyssen makes time an intrinsic mode of created

substance. See Hans Urs von Balthasar, *Presence and Thought: An Essay on the Religious Philosophy of Gregory of Nyssa*, trans. Mark Sebanc (San Francisco: Ignatius Press, 1995), 31, n. 46.

30. *Enneads* V.1.6.

31. Verghese, "*DIASTHMA* and *DIASTASIS* in Gregory of Nyssa," 248. While Plotinus rejects Aristotle's theory of time and the Stoic identification of time with *diastēma*, he does speak of time as *diastēma* such that Soul "stands apart from" *Nous* in contemplation of the One.

32. "*hoion epi tou posou, tou te synechous kai tou diōrismenou.*" *De Vita Moysis*, Preface 5; SC 1c, 48.

33. "What moves is moveable, i.e., what is potentially in motion but not actually; and the potential progresses towards actuality. Motion is incomplete actualization of the moveable," *Physics* 257b6; quoted in Guthrie, *A History of Greek Philosophy* 6:124.

34. For Aristotle's teleological understanding of movement in nature, see *De Caelo* 310a20–23 and 310a33–b1.

35. *De Vita Moysis*, Preface 7; SC 1c, 50.

36. Gregory of Nazianzus, *Theological Oration* 28.5.

37. Gregory of Nazianzus, *Theological Oration* 28.11.

38. *Commentarius in Canticum Canticorum* XI; GNO VI, 321.18. The point of Gregory's analogy need not be restricted to a comparison between the present age and the age to come. For God is no less boundless in the eschaton than he is in the present. Since God, like Eden's spring, is infinite, his nature cannot be *fully* known in the Kingdom any more than it can on this side of the eschaton. Rather, even in our "face-to-face" encounter with God, he will always be the source of ever unfolding revelation progressively showing us a new profile.

39. Clement himself does not conclude that participation in the simple nature of God leads to satiation. On the contrary, he describes the soul's progress in virtue as an ongoing growth in the knowledge of God until one gains *apatheia*. See *Stromata* VII, 2.10. For a helpful discussion of the philosophical background to Nyssen's theory of God's infinite nature, see Everett Ferguson, "God's Infinity and Man's Mutability: Perpetual Progress according to Gregory of Nyssa," *Greek Orthodox Theological Review* 18 (1973): 60.

40. *Commentarius in Canticum Canticorum* XI; GNO VI, 321.18.

41. *Commentarius in Canticum Canticorum* XI: GNO VI, 321.18 and 21.

42. *De Hominis Opificio* V.1; PG 44, 137A.

43. *Commentarius in Canticum Canticorum* XI; GNO VI, 321.17–25.

44. *De Vita Moysis*, Preface 7; SC 1c, 50. Gregory actually speaks of the desire of the one who participates in God as expanding infinitely, paralleling its movement into God: *tō aoristōi symparateinousa stasin.*

45. *De Vita Moysis* II.227; SC 1c, 262.

46. *De Vita Moysis* II.230; SC 1c, 264.

47. *De Vita Moysis* II.239; SC 1c, 270.

48. *De Vita Moysis* II.231; SC 1c, 264.

49. *Commentarius in Canticum Canticorum XI;* GNO VI, 321.18–25.

50. Nyssen describes the "bosom of Abraham" as the outline of the sea toward which a ship sails. *De Anima et Resurrectione* PG 46, 84B–C.

51. Clement of Alexandria, *Stromata* 2.2; PG 8, 933C–936A. Compare with Origen's statement in his first homily on the Song of Songs 1:7, "The Bride then beholds the Bridegroom; and he, as soon as she has seen him, goes away. He does this frequently throughout the Song. God is my witness that I have often perceived the Bridegroom drawing near to me and being intensely present with me; then suddenly he has withdrawn and I could not find him.... I long therefore for him to come again.... Then when he appeared and I lay hold of him, he slips away once more ... [and so] my search for him begins anew," quoted in Louth, *The Origins of the Christian Mystical Tradition,* 70.

52. " ... *mēte tini korōi ten proodon tes pros to kalon epithymias ekkoptesthai.*" *De Vita Moysis* II.239; SC 1c, 270.

53. Rowen Williams, "Macrina's Deathbed Revisited: Gregory of Nyssa on Mind and Passion," in *Christian Faith and Greek Philosophy in Late Antiquity: Essays in Tribute to George Christopher Stead,* ed. L. Wickham and C. Bammel (Leiden: E. J. Brill, 1993), 244.

54. Origen holds that the term "soul" (*psychē*) refers to the condition of the rational being (*nous*) whose love for God has cooled (*psychesthai*) and therefore has fallen from blessed union with God into a painful material body (*De Principiis* 2.8.3). Origen writes "the nature of bodies is not primary, but it was created at intervals on account of certain falls that happened to rational beings, who came to need bodies; and again, when their restoration is perfectly accomplished these bodies are dissolved into nothing" (*De Principiis* 4.4.8). Thus while the mind preexists its material embodiment, it is not, properly speaking, a soul until its incarnation. Consequently, all individuals (angels or human beings) have a heavenly existence prior to their earthly life in the flesh. At the same time, however, Origen suggests that the rational beings before the fall into material bodies possessed ethereal bodies that are "an essential characteristic of the creature as opposed to the Trinity" (Crouzel, *Origen,* 206). Origen comments, "It is only in idea and thought that a material substance is separable from them [i.e., the rational creatures], and that though this [bodily] substance seems to have been produced for them or after them, yet never have they lived or do they live without it" (*De Principiis* II.2.2). One might, therefore, conclude that the earthly body is not added to the *nous* but that the ethereal body is transformed, acquiring the heavy and rough aspects of our present earthly bodies.

55. Origen appears to be using the distinction between the corporeal and the incorporeal as a way of drawing a line between creatures and the Creator. Of the divine nature Origen says explicitly, "We believe that to exist without material substance and apart from any association with a body is a thing that belongs to the nature of God" (*De Principiis* 1.6.4). God alone is pure spirit and so is incorporeal, uncircumscribed by the finite boundaries of a body. Rational beings in contrast are finite creatures who, unlike the transcendent and omnipresent deity, are fixed in place and time because they exist in bodies. Thus the distinction of *nous* from its body occurs only at the conceptual level. His reason for asserting that corporeality is one of the central markers that delimit the ontological ground of rational beings can only be a point of speculation. The indwelling of *nous* in a finite quantity of matter means that the intellect, despite its capacity for self-transcendence, is in some sense objectively located and confined to a given locus in space and time. God, in contrast, transcends all spatial and temporal boundaries.

56. By locating the fall in heaven before the creation of the world Origen is able to maintain God's just ordering of the cosmic hierarchy based on the proportionate merit or demerit of the rational beings prior to the creation of the material universe. He writes, "Seeing that Christ...is also 'righteousness' (1 Cor. 1:30), it will follow that those things which were made in the Word...have been made in 'righteousness,' which is Christ; whence it will be apparent that in the things which were made there was nothing unrighteous, nothing accidental, but...such as the principle of equity and righteousness demands" (*De Principiis* 2.9.4).

57. For Nyssen's specific arguments against Origen's theory of the preexistence of souls, see *De Hominis Opificio* 28.1, PG44, 229B, and *De Anima et Resurrectione* PG 46, 109A and 112A–113B.

58. This view arose out of strict adherence to the account in Genesis 2, in which God gives life to Adam by breathing the divine spirit into the clay figure that God had molded. Thus according to the creationist view the Genesis narrative provides not only an account of the creation of the first man, but an explanatory model of how all human beings are created.

59. *De Hominis Opificio* 28.1; NPNF 419; PG 44, 229B–C.

60. The creationist could easily have appealed to the order of creation outlined in Genesis 2, in which Adam is made first and all the other creatures including Eve are created subsequently for the purpose of providing Adam with a "suitable partner" to support their principle that what is second in order of creation is made to serve the first. It is hard to imagine that so obvious a point escaped the creationist notice. Nyssen might well have omitted this argument because this particular interpretation of Genesis's creation story runs completely against the grain of Nyssen's construal of the Genesis narrative.

61. *De Hominis Opificio* 8.3–4 NPNF 393; PG 44, 144C–D.

62. *De Hominis Opificio* 29.1 NPNF 420; PG 44, 233D.

63. *De Anima et Resurrectione,* in Saint Gregory of Nyssa, *Ascetical Works,* trans. Virginia Woods Callahan (Washington, D.C.: Catholic University of America Press, 1967), 254; PG 46, 125A and 128A. Cf. *De Hominis Opificio* 29.10; NPNF 422a; PG 44, 237D–240A.

64. Presumably speaking of sperm he writes, "The thing which was implanted by separation from the living body for the production of the living being was not a thing dead or inanimate in the laboratory of nature." *De Hominis Opificio* 29.10; NPNF 422a; PG 44, 240A.

65. *De Anima et Resurrectione,* Callahan, 255; PG 46, 125C.

66. According to von Balthasar (*Presence and Thought,* 58) Nyssen maintains that "in the seeds of all things" are matter and life (*In Hexaemeron* 1, 72 A–B); the soul and body are present and perfectly one. All life was present potentially. In the seed deposited in the womb the person is "potential and not apparent" (cf. *De Hominis Opificio* 29; PG 44, 236C), and the soul in its entirety is to be formed and governs the development of the body. Yet the embryo is incomplete and not yet a man, but a "plastic vitality" that has divine power to become human (cf. C. Apollin. II, 1320A and 1256A).

67. *De Anima et Resurrectione,* Callahan, 255–56; PG 46, 128B.

68. *De Anima et Resurrectione,* Callahan, 254; PG 46, 124C–D.

69. *De Anima et Resurrectione,* Callahan, 255; PG 46, 128A.

70. *De Hominis Opificio* 9; NPNF 395; PG 44, 149B–D and 29.8; NPNF 421b-422a; PG 44, 237C.

71. *De Anima et Resurrectione*, Callahan, 206–7; PG 46, 33 A–B and *De Hominis Opificio* 6.1 (NPNF 391a; PG 44, 137D–140A), 10.3–5 (NPNF 396a; PG 44, 152C–D).

72. *De Hominis Opificio* 15.3; NPNF 404a; PG 44, 177C.

73. "Especially do these ministering hands adapt themselves to the requirements of the reason; indeed if one were to say that the ministration of hands is a special property of the rational nature, he would not be entirely wrong," *De Hominis Opificio* 8.2; NPNF 393; PG 44, 144C.

74. "Now since man is a rational animal, the instrument of his body must be made suitable for the use of *logos*." *De Hominis Opificio* 8.8; NPNF 394b; PG 44, 148C.

75. *De Hominis Opificio* 29.3; NPNF 421; PG 44, 236B–C.

76. *De Hominis Opificio* 29.4; NPNF 421; PG 44, 236C–D.

77. *De Hominis Opificio* 29.7; NPNF 421; PG 44, 237B.

Chapter Six: Purgation and Illumination

1. See *De Vita Macrinae*, PG 46, 959–1000, and *Panegyric on Gregory Thaumaturgus*, PG 46, 893–958.

2. George S. Bebis sees *De Vita Moysis* as evidence that Herald Cherniss's dismissal of Nyssen's theology is misguided. Cherniss complains that Nyssen's thought, filled with all its contradictions, offers neither an improvement on the philosophy of the Platonic tradition nor a faithful use of philosophy to address theological problems in Christianity. Bebis, however, argues that *De Vita Moysis*, which reflects Nyssen's mature thought, "offers him a fine biblical allegory for the place of Greek philosophy in the scheme of the Biblical theology of history." Here Nyssen expresses the theological equilibrium between pagan thought and the wisdom of divine revelation. The genuinely Christian character of Nyssen's thought is revealed in his use of philosophy to explain salvation history. Bebis comments, "The use of philosophical language by Gregory of Nyssa (and the rest of the Fathers) is not a sign of spiritual indigence and improvisation, but on the contrary, it proves a deep sense of 'historicity,' a profound respect for history in which the *Magnalia Dei* (the mighty deeds of God) are intrinsically linked and united in the great design for the salvation of mankind." See "Gregory of Nyssa's 'De Vita Moysis': A Philosophical and Theological Analysis," *Greek Orthodox Theological Review* 12, no. 3 (1967): 374.

3. *Oratio Catechetica*, trans. E. R. Hardy and C. C. Richardson in *Christology of the Later Fathers* (Philadelphia: Westminster Press, 1954), 280; GNO III, 4, 24.3–6.

4. *Oratio Catechetica*, 297; GNO III, 4, 55.17–23.

5. "By reason, then, of its impulse toward change and movement, our nature cannot remain essentially unchanged. Rather does the will drive it toward some end; desire for the good naturally sets it in motion." *Oratio Catechetica*, 298; GNO III, 4, 56.6–10.

6. *Oratio Catechetica*, 279; GNO III, 4.

7. *Oratio Catechetica*, 286; GNO III, 4.

8. David L. Balás, *METOUSIA THEOU: Man's Participation in God's Perfections according to Saint Gregory of Nyssa* (Rome: I.B.C. Libreria Herder, 1966) 118–19.

9. Unlike the Good, which is infinite, "evil does not extend to infinity, but is comprehended by necessary limits" (*De Hominis Opificio* 21.2; NPNF 411). The limits or boundaries of evil are set by the Good itself. Since evil is the privation of good and since the Good is infinite, one might conclude that there is an infinite possibility for privation. Yet Nyssen is no radical dualist. There is no complementary shadow of infinite evil existing side by side with infinite good. In such a dualism, the good would be bounded by evil and so would not truly be infinite. Instead Nyssen portrays the shadow cast by evil; as a momentary eclipse of the sun's light by a much smaller intervening heavenly body. Even as during a solar eclipse the moon casts its shadow over a very limited portion of the earth's surface while the sun's light encircles that small area, so too when the soul reaches the farthest bounds of privation, it encounters the light of God's infinite goodness (*De Hominis Opificio* 21.3; NPNF 411). Phenomenologically, Nyssen's notion that the soul's crossing the boundary between evil and goodness corresponds to the modern pedestrian expression of "hitting rock bottom with no place to go but up." In fact in a passage one might expect to read in Origen, Nyssen writes, "The ever-moving character of our nature came to run its course at last once more towards the good, being taught the lesson of prudence by the memory of its former misfortunes, to the end that it may never again be in like case" (*De Hominis Opificio* 21.2; NPNF 410).

10. *De Hominis Opificio* 21.2; NPNF 410; PG 44, 201B.

11. *Oratio Catechetica*, 286; GNO III, IV, 16–20.

12. *De Vita Moysis* II.320; SC 1c, 326.

13. *De Vita Moysis* II.314; SC 1c, 318.

14. Commenting on the life of simplicity and freedom from evil, Gregory says, "The eye is not dimmed nor does the person age. For how can an eye which is always in the light be dimmed by the darkness from which it is always separated? And the person who by every means achieves incorruption in his whole life admits no corruption in himself...he beautifies his own soul with what is incorruptible, unchangeable, and shares in no evil at all" (*De Vita Moysis* II.318; Gregory of Nyssa, *The Life of Moses*, trans. Abraham Malherbe and Everett Ferguson [New York: Paulist Press, 1978], 136). Although Gregory speaks of the eye, it is not immediately apparent that he is speaking of the eye of the body rather than the soul's spiritual senses. The latter interpretation is suggested by the concluding line. Yet earlier Gregory applies this precise language to Moses' bodily appearance: "Time had not harmed his beauty, neither dimmed his brightness of eye, nor diminished the graciousness of his appearance. Always remaining the same, he preserved in the changeableness of nature an unchangeable beauty" (I.76; Malherbe and Ferguson, trans., 50). While the parallel with Athanasius's *Life of Saint Antony* 14 is inescapable, Nyssen's interpretation (II.318) of his earlier description (I.76) indicates that his main concern is not the deification of Moses' body, but the complete purity of his soul.

15. Ronald E. Heine argues that *De Vita Moysis* is not an account of mystical ascent at all, but instead is simply Nyssen's account of the soul's ceaseless growth in perfection that is part of his anti-Origenist polemic. See his *Perfection in the Virtuous Life: A Study in the Relationship between Edification and Polemical Theology in*

Gregory of Nyssa's De Vita Moysis (Cambridge, Mass.: Philadelphia Patristic Foundation, 1975) 63ff. I will argue below that *De Vita Moysis*, as an account of the ongoing growth in virtue, does not exclude the mystical component of the ascent. I also agree that Nyssen is not giving a strict ladder of ascent. However, regardless of what one means by union with God, the growth in virtue certainly prepares the soul for times when it is ready for God's gracious elevation of the soul into an apophatic experience.

16. Andrew Louth, *The Origins of the Christian Mystical Tradition: From Plato to Denys* (Oxford: Clarendon Press, 1981), 59.

17. Louth, *The Origins of the Christian Mystical Tradition,* 82. Jean Daniélou, *Platonisme et théologie mystique* (Aubier: Édition Montaigne, 1944), 17–18. Daniélou (185–88) sees a progression of these moments, which follows the order of the sacramental life from the purification of baptism in which the soul reclaims the purity of human nature as God willed it and embraces the purity of the eschatological nature that awaits humanity in the resurrection.

18. *De Vita Moysis* II.3; SC 1c, 108.

19. *De Vita Moysis* II.2; SC 1c, 106.

20. *De Vita Moysis* II.7–8; SC 1c, 110.

21. *De Vita Moysis* II.10–11; SC 1c, 110–12.

22. *De Vita Moysis* II.12; SC 1c, 112.

23. *De Vita Moysis* II.79; SC 1c, 152.

24. *De Vita Moysis* II.70, Malherbe and Ferguson, trans., *The Life of Moses,* 70; SC 1c, 146.

25. "Being a man by nature and becoming a beast by passion, this kind of person exhibits an amphibious form of life ambiguous in nature.... For such a man shows his profligacy in everything.... In the house [of the profligate] there are frescoes on the wall which by their artful pictures inflame the sensual passions. These bring out the illness, and through the eye passion pours in upon the soul from the dishonorable things which are seen." *De Vita Moysis* II.70–71, Malherbe and Ferguson, trans., 70; SC 1c, 146.

26. *De Vita Moysis* II.78; SC 1c, 50–52.

27. This passage, *De Vita Moysis* II.18, is curious because in it he speaks of both living a solitary life and at the same time living among like-minded people whom we are teaching. This interpretation seems clearly directed toward people who are already in the church or are living in a religious community and have achieved the office of teacher in that community. Perhaps Nyssen is thinking of the monastic life practiced in the communities begun and supervised by his brother Basil. For according to Nazianzen's Panegyric on Basil, the bishop of Caesarea sought to reconcile the life of contemplation with the life of action. Nevertheless, it does not seem descriptive of the life of the soul at the very beginning of its journey to God. Yet it illustrates that Nyssen's allegory does not follow with precision the order of purgation-illumination-union. Therefore this purgative stage is inclusive of both novices as well as their more advanced teachers.

28. See W. K. L. Clarke, *St. Basil the Great: A Study in Monasticism* (Cambridge: Cambridge University Press, 1913); M. G. Murphy, *St. Basil and Monasticism* (Washington, D.C.: Catholic University of America Press, 1930); J. Gribomont, "Le Monachisme au sein de l'église en Syrie et en Cappadoce," *Studia Monastica* 7 (1965): 7–24.

29. One central component of Nyssen's critique of marriage in *De Virginitate* is that the class pressures to preserve the *dignitas* or social status of one's family lead to the pursuit of power and wealth which divert one from the loftier, spiritual ends. See *De Virginitate* 4.2ff; SC 119, 302–33.

30. *De Vita Moysis* II.19, Malherbe and Ferguson, trans., *The Life of Moses*, 59; SC 1c, 116.

31. *De Vita Moysis* II.310; SC 1c, 316.

32. *De Vita Moysis* II 23, Malherbe and Ferguson, trans., *The Life of Moses*, 60; SC 1c, 120.

33. Balás (*METOUSIA THEOU: Man's Participation in God's Perfections*, 114) rightly observes that while "Real Being" (*to ontōs on*) is how Nyssen repeatedly speaks of God in order to contrast the uncreated and nonderivative nature of the Divine with the created and derivative nature of all else, neither "Real Being" nor "I AM" define the divine essence. They do not name or reveal the content of the divine substance. At most, they demonstrate that the divine essence has no name. For this reason Nyssen does not need to posit God as being "beyond being," à la Plotinus.

34. *De Vita Moysis* II.23; SC 1c, 120.

35. *De Vita Moysis* II.25; SC 1c, 120.

36. *De Vita Moysis* II.24; SC 1c, 120.

37. *De Vita Moysis* II.22, Malherbe and Ferguson, trans., *The Life of Moses*, 59–60; SC 1c, 118.

38. "To do what is within oneself" in the context of high medieval scholasticism rested on the presupposition that since no action has intrinsic merit, God is free to treat any effort on man's part as being worthy of grace. Thus if one did what was within one's natural, though weakened powers to turn to God, God would reward that effort with the gift of grace.

39. Commenting on the light from the burning bush, Nyssen writes, "For if truth is God and truth is light — the Gospel testifies by these sublime and divine names to the God who made himself visible to us in the flesh — such guidance of virtue leads us to know that light which has reached down even to human nature." *De Vita Moysis* II.20, Malherbe and Ferguson, trans., *The Life of Moses*, 59; SC 1c, 114. Since the light from the bush is a type for Christ, then the bush is a type for the Virgin Mary. "The light of divinity which through birth shone from her into human life did not consume the burning bush, even as the flower of her virginity was not withered by giving birth" (II.21). The identification of the Light in the burning bush with the Son was important early for Nyssen in his dispute with Eunomius. Refuting Eunomius's claim that the Son is not the One who is ingenerate Being itself, Nyssen (*Contra Eunomium* III.ix, 35) appeals to the theophany on Mt. Horeb. Since it is the Logos who speaks to Moses and calls himself "I Am that I AM," Nyssen writes, "He who made himself known by the name of 'He who is' was the only-begotten God." Thus "I AM" was not reserved for the Father, but must also be ascribed to the Son. See Balás, *METOUSIA THEOU: Man's Participation in God's Perfections*, 111.

40. See Bebis, "Gregory of Nyssa's 'De Vita Moysis,'" 386. Cf. *De Vita Moysis* II.251–54.

41. *De Vita Moysis* II.75; SC 1c, 150. Divine punishment is the result of our wrong choices (II.86). Yet even Nyssen speaks of this punishment as medicinal (II.87) and remedial (II.82).

42. Daniélou, *Platonisme et Théologie mystique*, 150.

43. *De Vita Moysis* II.169; SC 1c, 216.

44. *De Vita Moysis* II.163, trans. Malherbe and Ferguson 95; SC 1c, 210–12.

45. Louth, *The Origins of the Christian Mystical Tradition*, 86

46. *De Vita Moysis* I.46; SC 1c, 82–84.

47. See Malherbe and Ferguson, trans., *The Life of Moses*, 124 n. 382.

48. When Paul writes in Romans 6:8, "If we have died with Christ [*apethanomen syn Christōi*], we believe we shall live with him also," death with Christ corresponds to the elimination of the sinful activities of one's former life before baptism: "We know that our old self [*ho palaios hēmōn anthrōpos*] was crucified with him [*synstaurōthē*] so that the sinful body might be destroyed" (6:6). He is most explicit in his use of the metaphorical description of baptism as crucifixion with Christ in Galatians 5:24: "And those who belong to Jesus Christ have crucified the flesh with its passions and desires [*syn tois pathēmasin kai tais epithymiais*]." Paul assumes that "putting to death" old sinful ways frees us from the passions: "Let not sin therefore reign in your mortal bodies, to make you obey their passions [*tais epithymiais autou*]" (6:12). Cf. Rom. 8:13 and Col. 3:5.

49. *De Vita Moysis* II.274, Malherbe and Ferguson, trans., *The Life of Moses*, 124; SC 1c, 292.

50. *De Vita Moysis* II.276, Malherbe and Ferguson, trans., 125; SC 1c, 292–94.

51. Nyssen explains the biblical metaphor of Christ's death as a ransom (cf. Matt. 20:28; Mk. 10:45; 1 Tim. 2:6; Rev. 5:9) in terms of God's entrapment of the Devil. Veiled in the familiar and unthreatening form of a mortal man, God allowed the Devil to seize him on the cross where "as with a greedy fish [*tous lichnous tōn ichthyōn*], he [the Devil] might swallow the Godhead [*tēs theotētos*] like a fishhook [*to ankistron*] along with the flesh, which was the bait." Since death cannot contain the One who is life itself any more than the darkness overshadows the light, Christ who is the source of all life completely overpowered death. *Oratio Catechetica* GNO III/IV, 62.2–10; trans. in *Christology of the Later Fathers*, ed. E. R. Hardy (Philadelphia: Westminster Press, 1954), 301.

52. *De Vita Moysis* II.277, Malherbe and Ferguson, trans., *The Life of Moses*, 125; SC 1c, 294.

53. *De Vita Moysis* II.71, Malherbe and Ferguson, trans., 70; SC 1c, 146.

54. *Hypotithetai* carries a stronger sense than merely "have written." As used by Plato (*Politics* 295C) and Aristotle (*Nicomachean Ethics* 105,a,23), *hypotithēmi* in the middle has the sense of putting forward instructions or counsel with the force of a doctor's advice that one is expected to follow.

55. The process of contemplation that moves from the historical or literary sense of the text to its encoded lofty, spiritual meaning follows Origen's threefold exegesis. In *Commentaria in Evangelium Joannis* (Fragment 20, 501.16; and PG 14, 337D) he contrasts the historical or literal sense (*historikos*) of Scripture with the spiritual understanding one gains by contemplation (*theorian noeten*). Likewise Origen (*Commentaria in Evangelium Joannis* 20.10; PG 14, 593B) and Nyssen (*Commentaria in Canticum Canticorum* VI; PG 44, 889C) use the expression *hypsēloteras* to refer to the spiritual meaning of the text that is the fruit of *theōria*.

56. *De Vita Moysis* II.319–320; Malherbe and Ferguson, trans., *The Life of Moses*, 136–37; SC 1c, 324–26.

57. "The mind apprehends those things which are external to the body, and draws to itself the images [*ta eidōla*] of phenomena, marking in itself the impressions

[*tous charaktēras*] of the things which are seen." *De Hominis Opificio* X.3; NPNF 396; PG 44, 152C.

58. *De Perfectione et qualem oporteat esse Christianum,* in Saint Gregory of Nyssa, *Ascetical Works,* trans. Virginia Woods Callahan (Washington, D.C.: Catholic University of America Press, 1967), 95–96.

59. *De Perfectione et qualem oporteat esse Christianum,* trans. in Callahan, 102.

60. *De Vita Moysis* I.42; SC 1c, 78–80.

61. *De Vita Moysis* I.45; SC 1c, 82.

62. *De Anima et Resurrectione* PG 46, 53C.

63. *De Vita Moysis* I.62; SC 1c, 94s.

64. Since Macrina proceeds to define *thymos* not as a feeling (of fire around the heart), but as the impulse to do harm to those who annoy one, it is possible that Nyssen means that Moses was estranged from the impulse to seek retribution. If this is the definition he has in mind, then the comment that *thymos* is alien to Moses' nature means, not that he never feels anger or irritation, but that he never feels the impulse to inflict injury upon those, such as Aaron and Miriam, who were jealous of him and sought to usurp his authority. See *De Anima et Resurrectione* PG 46, 56A.

65. See Andreas Spira, "Gregor von Nyssa, *De Beatitudinibus,* Oratio II: 'Selig sind die Sanftmütigen; denn sie werden das Erdreich besitzen' (Mt.5,4)," in *Gregory of Nyssa: Homilies on the Beatitudes; An English Version with Commentary and Supporting Studies; Proceedings of the Eighth International Colloquium on Gregory of Nyssa (Paderborn, 14–18 September 1998),* ed. H. Drobner and A. Viciano (Leiden: Brill, 2000), 111–38.

66. *De Beatitudinibus* II, GNO VII, 2 93.

67. *De Beatitudinibus* II, GNO VII, 2 94.

68. *De Beatitudinibus* II, GNO VII, 2 95.

69. According to Cicero (*Academica Posteriora* I.38), although Antiochus criticized Zeno for his denial of any positive role of irrational goods, Antiochus, nonetheless, held that the passions should be extirpated. However, because Antiochus saw no difference between the ethics of the Old Academy and the Stoics (except in the latter's belief in the self-sufficiency of virtue for happiness), John M. Dillon suggests that he must have equated *eupatheia* with the Peripatetic view of moderation. Similarly, Plutarch (*Consolation to Apollinius* 102C–D), having rejected *apatheia* as neither a possible nor helpful moral goal, feared that the pain of excessive grief compromised one's reason. Consequently, he sought a moderation (*metriopatheia*) of grief. See Dillon, "*Metriopatheia* and *Apatheia:* Some Reflections on a Controversy in Later Greek Ethics," 510–11. Robert Gregg suggests that Plutarch's use of *metriopatheia* reflects a greater confidence in the intellect's power to control the emotions, such as grief, preventing them from plunging into excess. See Robert C. Gregg, *Consolation Philosophy: Greek and Christian Paideia in Basil and the Two Gregories* (Philadelphia: Philadelphia Patristic Foundation, 1975), 94.

70. Richard Sorabji recognizes that in *De Anima et Resurrectione* Nyssen use *apatheia* with the sense of *metriopatheia.* Commenting on Nyssen's appeal to Daniel's desire and Phineas's righteous anger, Sorabji says, "This looks like a plea for *metriopatheia,* but Macrina converts it into a case for *apatheia* of a sort." See Richard Sorabji, *Emotion and Peace of Mind: From Stoic Agitation to Christian Temptation* (Oxford: Oxford University Press, 2000), 393.

71. *De Beatitudinibus* II, GNO VII, 2 95.14–16. In this context, *pathos* is being used in a morally neutral sense of an impulse toward a desired object. It differs from Macrina's initial use of *pathos* in a pejorative sense as recounted in chapter 3. Yet Nyssen retains the final view of *pathē* in *De Anima et Resurrectione* that because the emotions derive from the appetitive faculties of the sentient soul they are inherently inclined toward material goods and thus have a downward tendency or sensual orientation that will lead to sin unless they are held in check by reason. It is hard to see, however, how one can reconcile this view of the passionate impulses as inherent in our material existence with Nyssen's earlier insistence in *De Hominis Opificio* 16–18 that the passions came to human nature along with the impulses for sexual procreation rather than with God's plan to create humanity as an embodied creature.

72. "He [i.e., Christ] does not require complete passionlessness of human nature—for that is not the command of a just law which requires what nature cannot do.... On account of this, moderation [*to metrion*] and meekness [*praon*] not the absolute [*pantapasin*] elimination of emotions are blessedness." *De Beatitudinibus* II, GNO VII, 2 95.22–96.1.

73. *De Beatitudinibus* II, 36; GNO VII, 2 96.9–12.

74. This judgment is fully consistent with Macrina's conclusion that without desire the soul could never ascend to God. See *De Anima et Resurrectione* PG 46, 65A.

75. *De Vita Moysis* II.65; SC 1c, 142–44. This interpretation follows Origen's explanation (*De Principiis* 3.1.10) of God's hardening Pharaoh's heart. Grace is like sunshine and rain that can cause erosion of the uncultivated field, ultimately turning it hard, but that also can enable the well tilled field to bear fruit. So too, if the soul is not cultivated in virtue, it is not moved to repentance by God's grace, but is hardened and obdurate. For Origen's treatment of the relation of grace and human freedom, see Rowan A. Greer, *The Captain of Our Salvation: A Study in Patristic Exegesis of Hebrews* (Tübingen: J. C. B. Mohr, 1973), 31–34.

76. *De Vita Moysis* II.66; SC 1c, 144. The expression "evils of the Egyptians" is ambiguous. Is Nyssen intending *Aigyptiōn* to be taken as a subjective genitive, meaning that the Hebrews were unaffected by the evils inflicted on them by their Egyptian masters? Or is it an objective genitive, suggesting that the Hebrews were unaffected by the plagues that befell their Egyptian neighbors? In the context of the plague narrative, the latter interpretation would make sense. Yet in Nyssen's spiritual interpretation, the Hebrews are unaffected—in the sense of uncorrupted—by the unorthodox views of their neighbors. They are also unaffected in the sense of not being harmed by true doctrine since they have the right disposition.

77. *De Vita Moysis* II.301; SC 1c, 310–12.

78. *De Vita Moysis* II.302, Malherbe and Ferguson, trans., *The Life of Moses*, 132; SC 1c, 312. Italics are mine.

79. *De Vita Moysis* II, 303, Malherbe and Ferguson, trans., 132; SC 1c, 312.

80. See my discussion of the meaning of *pathos* in the context of the fifth-century Christological controversy in "Suffering Impassibly: Christ's Passion in Cyril of Alexandria's Soteriology," *Pro Ecclesia* 11, no. 4 (Fall 2002): 469–71.

81. "When he was manifest to us from the bosom of the Father, he was changed to be like us.... What is impassible [*apathes*] by nature did not change into what is passible [*eis pathos*], but what is mutable [*to trepton*] and subject to passions [*empathes*] was transformed into impassibility [*to atrepton*] through its participation

in the immutable [*eis apatheian*]." *De Vita Moysis* II.30, Malherbe and Ferguson, *The Life of Moses,* 61; SC 1c, 122–24. It is significant that in this passage Nyssen equates immutability with impassibility.

82. *De Hominis Opificio* V.1; PG 44, 137B.

83. *De Vita Moysis* II.282; SC 1c, 296–98.

84. *De Vita Moysis* II.153, Malherbe and Ferguson, trans., *The Life of Moses,* 92; SC 1c, 202–4.

85. *De Vita Moysis* II.158; SC 1c, 206.

86. Heine (*Perfection in the Virtuous Life,* 107–8) argues that *De Vita Moysis* does not follow the pattern of purgation, illumination, and unification that characterizes Origen's account of the soul's mystical ascent. Rather, he claims, Nyssen simply follows the meandering account of the story of the exodus, interpreting different episodes as representing various aspects of the virtuous life. Heine is certainly correct that Nyssen is not giving a strictly linear account of the soul's ascent. He is also correct that Moses never achieves freedom from the passions. This is true if he means that Moses is not absolutely free of the impulses of the appetitive faculties. However, *De Vita Moysis* II.153 is clear evidence that Nyssen sees the life of virtue as building up to the mystical moment. And while the Christian must always be on guard against the passions, he insists that the ascetic disciplines, though hard at first, become less disagreeable as the soul is separated more and more from sensual pleasures. Thus however one construes the ascent or growth in virtue, Nyssen's account does have a certain linear movement toward profound intimacy with God that comes only after a long process of purification and progressive revelations.

87. *De Vita Moysis* I.44; SC 1c, 80–82.

88. *De Vita Moysis* I.46; SC 1c, 82–84.

89. *De Vita Moysis* I.47; SC 1c, 84.

90. *De Vita Moysis* I.49; Malherbe and Ferguson, trans., *The Life of Moses,* 44; SC 1c, 86.

91. *De Vita Moysis* I.49; SC 1c, 86.

92. *Poikilia* refers to elaborately embroidered tapestry (cf. Plato, *Republic* 373a), thus gaining the metaphorical sense of that which is ornate, detailed (as the designs of Daedalus, Plato, *Republic* 529d), multifaceted or varied (of musical notes, Plato, *Laws* 812d). Nyssen employs the term in *Contra Eunomium* I; PG 45, 313B).

93. *Commentarius in Canticum Canticorum* XI; Jaeger, 324.

94. *De Vita Moysis* II.285–86; SC 1c, 298–300.

95. *De Vita Moysis* II.315; SC 1c, 320.

96. *De Vita Moysis* II.314; SC 1c, 318.

97. Our nature bears the image of the one who rules creation. Virtue, immortality, and righteousness, like a scepter and diadem, denote the royal character of this nature. Thus man "is shown to be perfectly like to the beauty of its archetype in all that belongs to the dignity of royalty" (*De Hominis Opificio* 4; PG 44, 136D).

98. *De Vita Moysis* II.285–86; SC 1c, 298–300.

99. *De Hominis Opificio* 2.1; PG 44, 132D.

100. *De Hominis Opificio* 4; PG 44, 136B–C.

101. *De Hominis Opificio* 16.11; PG 44, 184B.

102. *De Vita Moysis* II.283; SC 1c, 298.

103. *De Vita Moysis* II. 284; SC 1c, 298.

104. *De Vita Moysis* II.319; SC 1c, 324.

105. *De Vita Moysis* II. 307; Malherbe and Ferguson, trans., *The Life of Moses*, 133; SC 1c, 314. In *In Psalmorum Inscriptiones* (I.8; PG 44, 465C–D), Nyssen likens human souls to the flight patterns of flies and eagles. The flies, which stay close to the earth and so are snagged in the sticky webs of the spider, are comparable to the soul that is so preoccupied with sensual goods that it becomes entangled in worldly delights and is prevented from ascending to God. By contrast the eagle, which strains upward with such force and zeal to lofty peaks that its powerful wings brush aside the spider webs, is like the soul which aims "with the undistracted [*atreptōi*] eye of his soul to the ray of light" from God guiding its contemplative ascent ever higher.

106. Plato dramatically represents the transformation in Socrates' attitude toward the sensually beautiful in the speech of Alcibiades, whose great beauty cannot seduce Socrates. In Alcibiades' account of Socrates' lifestyle while on military campaign, Socrates exhibits the ascetic virtues of one disinterested in the things of the body: he was content with small rations and in the winter he wore only a simple old coat (219d–220b).

107. *De Vita Moysis* II.224; SC 1c, 260–62.

108. "[Since] the nature of the Good attracts to itself those who look to it, the soul rises ever higher and will always make its flight yet higher — by its desire of the heavenly things 'straining ahead for what is still to come,' as the Apostle says." *De Vita Moysis* II. 225, Malherbe and Ferguson, *The Life of Moses*, 113; SC 1c, 262.

109. *De Vita Moysis* II.313, Malherbe and Ferguson, trans., *The Life of Moses*, 134; SC 1c, 316–18.

110. *De Vita Moysis* II.320, Malherbe and Ferguson, trans., 137; SC 1c, 326.

111. *De Vita Moysis*, Preface 6; SC 1c, 48.

112. Aristotle's description of perfection (*to teleion*) in *Categoriae* 4b.22 and *Physics* 207a.8–15 as completeness necessarily entails the notion of limitation. That which is complete lacks nothing and therefore cannot have anything added; for it is fully actualized. The perfect conforms to the boundaries or limits that define the form of a thing. Nyssen's conception of perfection is not an Aristotelian understanding of "completeness," but a Pauline sense of "stretching beyond to what lies ahead [*epekteinomenos*]." See Heine, *Perfection in the Virtuous Life*, 66–67.

113. *De Vita Moysis*, Preface 10; SC 1c, 50.

114. *De Vita Moysis* II. 243; SC 1c, 272–74.

115. *De Anima et Resurrectione*, Callahan, 214; PG 46, 45C.

116. *De Anima et Resurrectione*, Callahan, 244; PG 46, 105B.

117. *De Anima et Resurrectione*, Callahan, 244–25; PG 46, 105B.

118. "Since the source of all goods flows continuously, the nature of the one who has a share in them converts everything that flows into it to its own size because nothing that is taken is superfluous or useless." *De Anima et Resurrectione*, Callahan, 245; PG 46,

119. "Only after we are purged of the sympathy we had with it [i.e., the sensual pleasures of the body] in this life are we able to be joined in purity to that to which we are similar." *De Anima et Resurrectione*, Callahan, 245; PG 46, 105D.

120. *De Anima et Resurrectione*, Callahan, 245; PG 46, 105C.

Chapter Seven: "When God Shall Be All and in All"

1. For a discussion of the variety of Nyssen's treatments of the eschaton see Brian Daley, *The Hope of the Early Church: A Handbook of Patristic Eschatology*

(Cambridge: Cambridge University Press, 1991), and Rowan A. Greer, *Christian Hope and Christian Life: Raids on the Inarticulate* (New York: Crossroad, 2001), 64–111.

2. For excellent discussion of Nyssen's complex and confused accounts of the resurrection body, see T. J. Dennis, "Gregory on the Resurrection of the Body," in *The Easter Sermons of Gregory of Nyssa,* ed. Andreas Spira and Christoph Klock (Philadelphia: Philadelphia Patristic Foundation, 1981), 55–80; Caroline Walker Bynum, *The Resurrection of the Body in Western Christianity, 200–1336* (New York: Columbia University Press, 1995); and Morwenna Ludlow, *Universal Salvation: Eschatology in the Thought of Gregory of Nyssa and Karl Rahner* (Oxford: Oxford University Press, 2000).

3. God allows both godly and sensual impulses to grow together in the soul because man needs the force of the appetitive drives of *epithymia* and *thymos* since "each of them contributes to the virtuous life and...we are led to God through desire, being drawn up to him from below as if by a choir." *De Anima et Resurrectione,* in Saint Gregory of Nyssa, *Ascetical Works,* trans. Virginia Woods Callahan (Washington, D.C.: Catholic University of America Press, 1967), 236–37; PG 46, 88C–89A.

4. *De Anima et Resurrectione,* Callahan, 220; PG 46, 57C.

5. *De Anima et Resurrectione,* PG 46, 49B, 52A, 53C–D.

6. *De Anima et Resurrectione,* Callahan, 232–33; PG 46, 81A.

7. *De Anima et Resurrectione,* Callahan, 237; PG 46, 89B.

8. *De Anima et Resurrectione,* PG 46, 89A.

9. *Contra Eunomium* I.19; GNO I, 94, 1.15–96, 1.12 and *Contra Eunomium* II; GNO I, 245, 1.19–247, 1.4.

10. *De Anima et Resurrectione,* Callahan, 240; PG 46, 96C–97A.

11. "But beautiful is the divine to which the soul will be joined on account of its purity, uniting with what is proper to it." *De Anima et Resurrectione,* 237; PG 46, 89B.

12. *De Anima et Resurrectione,* Callahan, 220; PG 46, 57B–C.

13. *De Anima et Resurrectione,* Callahan, 238; PG 46, 92A.

14. *De Anima et Resurrectione,* Callahan, 238; PG 46, 92C.

15. In contrast with those boys who attach themselves to older men for the sake of money or political prospects, which is scandalous, Pausanias says, "there is left one sort of voluntary enslavement which is not scandalous; this is servile attachment for the sake of virtue. For it is the established custom and conviction for me that if anyone, guided for the end that he might be made better either according to a certain wisdom or some other aspect of virtue, wants to treat a certain one as his superior, this voluntary servitude is neither shameful nor a form of fawning" (*Symposium* 184c).

16. Plato appears to have made Aristophanes, the author of comic plays, tell a tragic tale and Agathon, the great tragedian offer a comic account of love. Robert Lloyd Mitchell, however, contends that Aristophanes' story is true comedy, which expresses "a fundamental sadness, anger, and even pessimism" in reaction to humanity's situation in a meaningless existence. See Robert Lloyd Mitchell, *The Hymn to Eros: A Reading of Plato's Symposium* (Lanham, Md.: University Press of America, 1993), 86.

17. The term *symbolon* refers to a stick divided into two parts, each of which has complementary edges; they are exchanged between two people as tokens of friendship. Plato, *Symposium* 191d, trans. W. R. M. Lamb, Loeb Classical Library 166, (Cambridge, Mass.: Harvard University Press, 1925), 141, n. 1.

18. Plato does not explain how the cultivation of such virtues enables one to attain immortality. Perhaps his idea is that by our participation in the Beautiful which is something, "subsisting of itself and by itself in an eternal oneness" (211b) one gains a share in its immortal nature.

19. Plato, *Symposium*, 195A. Agathon, presumably arguing from the traditional axiom associated with Plato that like is known by and attracted to like, asserts that love's attraction to that which is beautiful implies that love itself is beautiful. "Clear evidence of its fit proportion and pliancy of form is found in his shapely grace, a quality wherein Love is in every quarter allowed to excel . . . for Love will not settle on body or soul or aught else that is flowerless or whose flower has faded away" (196A–B).

20. *Symposium* 202B and 204B.

21. The character of the philosopher as being an intermediate between being ignorant and being all-knowing is a theme at the core of Plato's writings as early as *Apology*. The developmental or intermediate character of philosophy Plato does not apply to love until *Lysis* (217E–218B). In *Symposium,* Plato portrays the philosopher's love of wisdom as a love of the transcendent Form of Beauty itself. W. K. C. Guthrie, *Plato: The Man and His Dialogues Early Period* (Cambridge: Cambridge University Press, 1975), 386. Because the Beautiful in which all beautiful things participate transcends all, including the philosopher who alone has beheld its splendor, it can never be possessed. Thus the lover of the Beautiful is ever desiring what he can never fully possess.

22. *De Anima et Resurrectione*, Callahan, 237; PG 46, 89D–92A. The soul's union with God is nothing less than assimilation into the divine nature through imitation. This assimilation is not absorption into the divine nature in such a way that the distinction between the creature and the creator is lost. Nyssen's choice of words is careful. Through our imitation (*entoi mimeisthai*) of God' virtues, he says, we share a likeness (*homoiōsin*) to God's nature. Writing after the resolution of the dispute between the defenders of the Nicene language of *homoousios* and the Homoeans, who championed the term *homoios*, the distinction between "the same" nature and "a similar" nature was very much in the consciousness of Nyssen and his readers. Thus when Nyssen speaks of our perfected nature as being *homoiosin*, he is clear that, despite our similarities to God's perfection, we are at best only a reflection of God's nature, not a consubstantial constituent member of the Godhead in a way that the Son and Spirit who possess the "same being" as the Father. The Homoeans were an ecclesiastical party formed by Akakius, bishop of Caesarea, at the Synod of Seleucia in 359. The aim of the synod was to advance a compromise formula that would avoided the neo-Sabellian theology suggested by *homoousios* and any language suggestive of essential unity (*ousia*) between the Son and the Father. R. P. C. Hanson, *The Search for the Christian Doctrine of God: The Arian Controversy 318–381 A.D.* (Edinburgh: T & T Clark, 1993), 371–80.

23. *De Anima et Resurrectione*, Callahan, 241; PG 46, 97B.

24. "The rich man, even after death, clung to the carnal aspects of life which he did not put aside although he was no longer living. . . . He was not yet free from fleshly

inclinations from which people must be separated." *De Anima et Resurrectione,* Callahan, 235–36; PG 46, 85C.

25. *De Anima et Resurrectione,* Callahan, 236; PG 46, 88B–C.

26. *De Anima et Resurrectione,* Callahan, 243; PG 46, 101C.

27. *De Anima et Resurrectione,* Callahan, 241; PG 46, 100A.

28. *De Anima et Resurrectione,* Callahan, 243; PG 46, 101C–D.

29. *De Hominis Opificio* 8.1; NPNF 391a; PG 44, 136B.

30. *De Hominis Opificio* 5.1; NPNF 391; PG 44, 137B.

31. *De Hominis Opificio* 16.11; NPNF 405; PG44, 184B.

32. *De Hominis Opificio* 16.10; NPNF 405; PG 44, 184B.

33. *De Anima et Resurrectione,* Callahan, 239; PG 46, 93C.

34. By equating freedom with the pure embodiment of virtue, Nyssen is able to identify perfect participation in God's nature with Paul's eschatological vision that "when all things are subject to him, then the Son himself will be subjected to him who put all things under him, that God may be everything to everyone"(1 Cor. 15:28). *De Anima et Resurrectione,* Callahan, 243; PG 46, 104A.

35. *De Anima et Resurrectione,* Callahan, 243–44; PG 46, 104A–B.

36. *De Hominis Opificio* 18.9; PG 44, 196A–B.

37. Nyssen recognizes that this suggestion is problematic for his conception of the resurrection. For Gregory objects to his sister, "If it is true, as it certainly is, that there is no provision for marriage in the life after the resurrection and that our life then will not depend on eating or drinking, what use will the parts of the body be, since in that life we will no longer expect these activities for whose sake the parts of the body now exist." Callahan, 264; PG 46, 144C.

38. *De Anima et Resurrectione,* Callahan, 237; PG 46, 89C.

39. *De Anima et Resurrectione,* Callahan, 237; PG 46, 92C.

40. *De Anima et Resurrectione,* Callahan, 239; PG 46, 93C.

41. *De Anima et Resurrectione,* Callahan, 238; PG 46, 93A.

42. *De Anima et Resurrectione,* Callahan, 239; PG 46, 96A.

43. *De Anima et Resurrectione,* Callahan, 237; PG 46, 89C.

44. David L. Balás, "Eternity and Time in Gregory of Nyssa's *Contra Eunomium,*" in *Gregor von Nyssa und Die Philosophie,* zweites Internationales Kolloquium über Gregor von Nyssa, ed. H. Dörrie, M. Altenburger, and V. Schramm (Leiden: E. J. Brill, 1976), 144.

45. For a detailed discussion of Nyssen's theory of time, see Brooks Otis, "Gregory of Nyssa and the Cappadocian Conception of Time," *Studia Patristica* 14 (Berlin: Akademie-Verlag, 1976), 327–57.

46. "Time's lapse sweeps away everything that is past, whereas that which is expected subsists by hope." *Contra Eunomium* I.674; GNO I.220, 13–15.

47. Balás ("Eternity and Time," 134–35) explains that, for Nyssen, God who is "self-sufficient, eternal, and contains all beings" is above time and place. Thus there is no temporal distance between past and future for God as there is for creatures. Past and future are "the passions [*ta pathē*] proper to those within creation, whose life is split into hope and memory according to the division of time" whereas God "is always equally present as if it were now, is seen as comprehending by its all-encircling power both past and future." *Contra Eunomium* I.370–72; GNO I, 136, 8–27.

48. "By positing the adiastemic and infinite character of God, Gregory at once overcomes the naive Platonism of Eunomius with his reductionist and creaturely

view of Christ, and at the same time overcame the prevailing views of salvation conceived as a Plotinian-Origenist unity with God. He replaced them with a new view that fully preserved both the temporal, genetic, or diastemic nature of creatures and the eternity, infinity, and fully agenetic nature of God, while at the same time giving a far more dynamic, in fact, a supremely dynamic, character to both salvation and creation. For the first time the church possessed a doctrine that gave meaning to the agenetic-genetic dichotomy of Platonism as well as to the Creator-creature dichotomy of the Bible." Otis, "Cappadocian Conception of Time," 341–42.

49. Hans Urs von Balthasar, *Presence and Thought: An Essay on the Religious Philosophy of Gregory of Nyssa,* trans. Mark Sebanc (San Francisco: Ignatius Press, 1995), 31, n. 46. For Aristotle, time is not to be identified with motion or change but it simply the number or measurement of a particular motion relative to a starting point and an ending point. Thus time is not inherent in the motion but an accident since the measure of movement might have been different. See John F. Callahan, *Four Views of Time in Ancient Philosophy* (Cambridge, Mass.: Harvard University Press, 1948), 49.

50. "For hope motivates a person as long as he is not enjoying what is hoped for.... What is hoped for arrives, the other emotions desist, and what remains is the activity connected with love which finds nothing to succeed it." *De Anima et Resurrectione,* in Saint Gregory of Nyssa, *Ascetical Works,* trans. Virginia Woods Callahan (Washington, D.C.: Catholic University of America Press, 1967), 240; PG 46, 96B.

51. *De Anima et Resurrectione,* Callahan, 238; PG 46, 93A. Nyssen also appeals to Romans 8:24: "Why does one hope for what one already has?"

52. *De Anima et Resurrectione,* Callahan, 239; PG 46, 93A.

53. *De Anima et Resurrectione,* Callahan, 239; PG 46, 93B.

54. This claim is not without its problems for Nyssen. The logic of his argument is that hope is an emotion of the soul that is focused on a future time. But when hope is fulfilled, the soul's emotion is no longer one of hope but of enjoyment — a reveling in the anticipated goodness finally realized. Yet Nyssen must deal with the famous words of Paul from 1 Corinthians 13, that unlike tongues, prophecy, knowledge, etc., which imperfect and so pass away when the perfection of God's Kingdom is fully actualized, "faith, hope, and love abide" into the next age. Hope endures in the sense that what is hoped for, namely, communion with God, endures. The emotion of hope, however, is fully replaced by the activities of love. *De Anima et Resurrectione,* Callahan, 240; PG 46, 96B.

55. *De Anima et Resurrectione,* Callahan, 239; PG 46, 93C.

56. *De Anima et Resurrectione,* Callahan, 234; PG 46, 84C.

57. *De Anima et Resurrectione,* Callahan, 237; PG 46, 89C.

58. While Cahill agrees with Daniélou on the dating, he argues that the homilies were not preached at Constantinople before Olympias. Had Olympias heard the homilies herself, Nyssen would not have needed to attach the explanatory preface. Moreover, Cahill conjectures, it is unlikely that Nyssen would have left his parish for an extended time during the holy season of Lent. See J. B. Cahill, "The Date and Setting of Gregory of Nyssa's *Commentary on the Song of Songs," Journal of Theological Studies,* new series 31 no. 2 (October 1981): 449–50, and Jean Daniélou, "Chronologie des oeuvres de Grégoire de Nysse," *Studia Patristica* 7.

59. His interpretation of the maidens, the concubines, and the queens (Song of Songs 6:8) as referring to a hierarchy of Christians all of whom will be united and transformed by the Holy Spirit suggests that the homilies end with an address to all the different listeners to strive and put on the glory of God that is the Holy Spirit that they all might become the bride of Christ. See *Commentarius in Canticum Canticorum* XV, GNO 6, 460–62 and 67.

60. *Commentarius in Canticum Canticorum* prologus, GNO VI, 4.

61. *Commentarius in Canticum Canticorum* I, GNO VI, 22–23.

62. For a detailed discussion of the Nyssen's defense of allegory, presumably in response to Theodore of Mopsuestia and Diodore of Tarsus, see Ronald E. Heine, "Gregory of Nyssa's Apology for Allegory," *Vigiliae Christianae* 38 (1984): 360–70, and Anthony Meredith, "Allegory in Porphyry and Gregory of Nyssa," *Studia Patristica,* vol. 16, ed. Elizabeth A. Livingstone (Berlin: Akademie-Verlag, 1985), 422–27.

63. R. A. Norris, "The Soul Takes Flight: Gregory of Nyssa and the Song of Songs," *Anglican Theological Review* 80, no. 4 (Fall 1998): 521.

64. *Commentarius in Canticum Canticorum* II, GNO VI, 45.6.

65. Martin Laird says of Nyssen's identification of the Song of Songs with the Holy of Holies, it is "rich with passionate image … [and as] the innermost sanctuary, the Holy of Holies, [is] the apophatic space where God is encountered in the darkness of unknowing, beyond the grasps of images and concepts." See "Under Solomon's Tutelage: The Education of Desire in the *Homilies on the Song of Songs,*" *Modern Theology* 18, no. 4 (October 2002): 514–15.

66. Sarah Coakley, "Re-thinking Gregory of Nyssa: Introduction — Gender, Trinitarian Analogies, and the Pedagogy of the *Song,*" in *Modern Theology* 18, no. 4 (October 2002): 437.

67. Coakley, "Re-thinking Gregory of Nyssa," 439–40.

68. *Commentarius in Canticum Canticorum* I, trans. in Norris, "The Soul Takes Flight: Gregory of Nyssa and the Song of Songs," 525; GNO VI, 23, 9–12.

69. *Commentarius in Canticum Canticorum* I, Norris, 525, GNO VI, 25, 2–9.

70. Norris, "The Soul Takes Flight," 525.

71. Laird, "Under Solomon's Tutelage," 512.

72. Morwenna Ludlow, *Universal Salvation: Eschatology in the Thought of Gregory of Nyssa and Karl Rahner* (Oxford: Oxford University Press, 2000), 57.

73. *Commentarius in Canticum Canticorum* XV, trans. C. McCambley (Brookline, Mass.: Hellenistic College Press, 1987), 265–66; GNO VI, 440.14–441.1.

74. *Commentarius in Canticum Canticorum* XV, 269; GNO VI, 451–52.

75. *In Ecclesiasten,* GNO V, 368.10 and 372.3; *Commentarius in Canticum Canticorum* I, GNO VI, 31.6; X, GNO VI, 306.11; XII, GNO VI, 369.21–370.2; *Epistula* III.4.5; XVIII.3.3–6.

76. Comparing a man who experiences an insatiable greed to an infinite sea that has waters continually fed into it from many rivers, Gregory exhorts the man to be like the sea that does not exceed its natural limits. So too each man must not exceed the natural limits of his capacity for enjoyment. *In Ecclesiasten* I, GNO V, 289.3–289.15.

77. He employs the term to describe the seduction of rulers and the wealthy captivated by vainglorious aspirations. *Commentarius in Canticum Canticorum* XI, McCambley, trans., 199; GNO VI, 316.4.

78. *Commentarius in Canticum Canticorum* IX, McCambley, trans., 180; GNO VI, 283.3–12.

79. *Commentarius in Canticum Canticorum* II, McCambley, trans., 67; GNO VI, 63.2–8.

80. *Commentarius in Canticum Canticorum* III, McCambley, trans., 86; GNO VI, 95.19–96.7. Worth noting is Nyssen's remarks on Song of Songs 1:1–2: "Your breasts are better than wine." He reads this as expressing the contrast between the milk from divine breasts, which corresponds to "the simple nourishment of divine teachings" for those young in the faith (cf. 1 Cor. 3:2 and Heb. 5:12–13) and wine, which is a type for worldly wisdom, science, and learning. Although the wine in this case does not refer to Christ, it is still described as that which by virtue of "its strength and warming capacity, is [the source of] enjoyment for the more perfect." *Commentarius in Canticum Canticorum* I, McCambley, trans., 52; GNO VI, 35.1–13. Even though he goes on to say that the perfect wisdom of the world does not provide the same nourishment to the soul as the "childlike teaching of the divine Word," the suggestion is that the mature Christian can take delight in the wisdom of the world when it is added to foundational wisdom revealed in divine teaching. Thus in both cases "enjoyment" in its true form is reserved for the mature or perfect Christians.

81. *Commentarius in Canticum Canticorum* III, McCambley, trans., 86; GNO VI, 97.2.

82. *Commentarius in Canticum Canticorum* X, McCambley, trans., 192; GNO VI, 306.11.

83. *Commentarius in Canticum Canticorum* X, McCambley, trans., 192; GNO VI, 307.1.

84. A similar line of argument is implied by Nyssen's interpretation of Moses' staff, which sweetens the waters of Marah (Exod. 15:23–25) in *De Vita Moysis* II.131–32.

85. *Commentarius in Canticum Canticorum* I, McCambley, trans., 50; GNO VI, 30.8–19. Gregory's description of the healing of conflict between the passion and the mind in terms of the hegemonic control of the flesh and the spirit by one spirit suggests that Nyssen when he was writing the homilies still identified the passions with the flesh rather than his more sophisticated view of the passions as residing in a borderland between the sensual and rational souls articulated in *De Anima et Resurrectione*. This suggests that the homilies were written before his more developed anthropological theory.

86. *Commentarius in Canticum Canticorum* I, McCambley, trans., 50; GNO VI, 31.2–8.

87. The confusion stems from his sudden shift from a discussion of the life after the resurrection to our present life in the flesh. "Thus the text of Song of Songs exhorts us, even if we now live in the flesh, not to turn to it in our thoughts; rather we should only regard the soul.... For God alone is truly dear." *Commentarius in Canticum Canticorum* I, McCambley, trans., 50; GNO VI, 30.20–31.3.

88. *Commentarius in Canticum Canticorum* XII, McCambley, trans., 218; GNO VI, 353–54.

89. *Commentarius in Canticum Canticorum* I, McCambley, trans., 51; GNO VI, 32. 1–9.

90. *Commentarius in Canticum Canticorum* XII, McCambley, trans., 217; GNO VI, 352.1.

91. *Commentarius in Canticum Canticorum* McCambley, trans., 219; GNO VI, 356–57.

92. *Commentarius in Canticum Canticorum* McCambley, trans., 219; GNO VI, 356.

93. "Indeed, how can anyone list all of Moses' ascents and various theophanies? But as great and exalted as he was with such experiences, Moses still had an insatiable desire for more. He implored God to see him face to face, despite the fact that Scripture already says that he had been allowed to speak with God face to face. But neither did the act of intimately speaking with God as a friend make him cease to desire more." *Commentarius in Canticum Canticorum* XII, McCambley, trans., 219; GNO VI, 355–56.

94. "Even now the soul united to God never has its fill of enjoyment. The more it enjoys his beauty, the more its desire for him increases." *Commentarius in Canticum Canticorum* I, McCambley, trans., 51; GNO VI, 32.8–9.

95. *Commentarius in Canticum Canticorum* XI, McCambley, trans., 208; GNO VI, 336.9.

96. In the very next paragraph, Nyssen remarks, "Human nature is not able to contain the infinite, unbounded divine nature." *Commentarius in Canticum Canticorum* XI, McCambley, trans., 208; GNO VI, 337.1.

97. For an insightful discussion of the Nyssen's description of the soul in masculine and feminine images, see Verna E. F. Harrison, "A Gender Reversal in Gregory of Nyssa's *First Homily on the Song of Songs*," *Studia Patristica* 27, ed. Elizabeth A. Livingstone (Leuven: Peeters Press, 1993), 35–36.

98. *Commentarius in Canticum Canticorum* XII, McCambley, trans., 225; GNO VI, 369.

99. *Commentarius in Canticum Canticorum* McCambley, trans., 225; GNO VI, 369.21–270.2.

100. *Commentarius in Canticum Canticorum* McCambley, trans., 225; GNO VI, 370.2.

101. *Commentarius in Canticum Canticorum* McCambley, trans., 218; GNO VI, 354.

102. *De Vita Moysis* II.225, in Gregory of Nyssa, *The Life of Moses*, trans. Abraham J. Malherbe and Everett Ferguson (New York: Paulist, 1978), 113; SC 1c, 262.

103. *De Vita Moysis* II.227, in Malherbe and Ferguson, trans., 113; SC 1c, 262–63.

104. "This truly is the vision of God: never to be satisfied in the desire to see him. . . . Thus, no limit would interrupt growth in the ascent to God, since no limit to the Good can be found nor is the increase of desire for the Good brought to an end because it is satisfied." *De Vita Moysis* II.239, in Malherbe and Ferguson, trans., 116; SC 1c, 270. Although Nyssen's theory of epectasy predated *De Vita Moysis*, he follows closely Philo's discussion of Exodus 33 (*De Specialibus Legibus* 1.32–50). There Philo contends that God's essence is difficult if not impossible to grasp and our vision of God, like that of Moses, will never be clear; yet we should not cease searching because the quest is beneficial even if God is never seen. See Albert C.

Geljon, *Philonic Exegesis on Gregory of Nyssa's De Vita Moysis* (Providence, R.I.: Brown Judaic Studies, 2002), 144.

105. *De Vita Moysis* II.243, Malherbe and Ferguson, trans., 117; SC 1c, 272. Translation is altered.

106. *De Vita Moysis* II. 243–44, in Malherbe and Ferguson, trans., 117; SC 1c, 274.

107. *De Vita Moysis* II. 248, in Malherbe and Ferguson, trans., 118; SC 1c, 276.

108. *De Vita Moysis* II. 250, in Malherbe and Ferguson, trans., 119; SC 1c, 278.

109. *De Vita Moysis* II. 253, in Malherbe and Ferguson, trans., 120; SC 1c, 280.

110. Paul Plass, "Transcendent Time and Eternity in Gregory of Nyssa," *Vigiliae Christianae* 34 (June 1980): 186.

111. *Commentarius in Canticum Canticorum* XII, McCambley, trans., 218; GNO VI, 354.

112. Ludlow, *Universal Salvation Eschatology,* 62.

113. Although Nyssen ends *Commentarius in Canticum Canticorum* (Homily XV, GNO VI, 469.6) with a reference to 1 Corinthians 15, he explains God's being "all and in all" by saying that all people, regardless of their degree of holiness in this life, will put on the glory of God, i.e., the Holy Spirit, and so be united by a single love of God. He does not explain how this single love affects the character of our desire for God.

114. In Nyssen's Easter homily *In Sanctum Pascha,* he exhorts his congregation to celebrate Easter by living on that day as they shall live in the resurrection. Thus masters must treat their slaves as they shall be treated in the resurrection. He tells them, "Take away the pain of the oppressed souls as the Lord does the deadness from bodies, transform their disgrace into honour, their oppression into joy, their fear of speaking into openness; bring out the prostrate from their corner as if from their graves, let the beauty of the feast blossom like a flower upon everyone. If a royal birthday or victory celebration opens a prison, shall not Christ's rising relieve those in affliction?" *In Sanctum Pascha,* trans. S. G. Hall in *The Easter Sermons of Gregory of Nyssa,* ed. Andreas Spira and Christoph Klock (Cambridge, Mass.: Philadelphia Patristic Foundation, 1981), 9; GNO IX, 251.

115. Mitchell, *The Hymn to Eros,* 76. "All men, we learn from Aristophanes, are sick, diseased to the core. We seek wholeness. The name for this drive towards wholeness which we *are,* entirely, in our present estate — is *love*" (85).

116. Stanley Rosen, *Plato's Symposium,* 2nd ed. (New Haven, Conn.: Yale University Press, 1987), 143.

117. Plass, "Transcendent Time and Eternity," 183.

118. Norris ("The Soul Takes Flight," 531) ends his analysis of *Commentarius in Canticum Canticorum* with this question. He answers, "Gregory would have agreed — had he not died about the time Augustine wrote those words — on the condition that 'rest in thee' be understood to mean the unending leap of faith in which love finds, and loses, and then finds again, its divine lover." My own reading is different. To be fair, Norris's analysis is restricted to the homilies whereas I am offering a synthesis of his earlier and later views of epectasy. Inasmuch as the image of the bride pursuing, finding, but then losing the Bridegroom is a representation of the erotic nature of human love, given ontological separation of the creature from the Creator, then Norris is right that any "resting" occurs in the context of an *erōs* ontology. The soul's growth in the knowledge of God, therefore, will resemble the

bride's pursuit of her Husband. Yet the rest that Augustine describes is psychological, as well as ontological. Nyssen's interpretation of the bride is an ontological, and consequently epistemological, description of the soul in this life and in the life to come. It may even be a psychological account of the soul striving after God in the present life. It is hard to see how this is a psychological description of the soul in the eschaton. Psychologically, the soul's experience of God as the "all in all" entails a resting in God that is qualitatively different than the resting of Christians in this life.

Discussion Questions

Chapter One: The Imago Dei

1. Why must God make man in his image in order for man to have "dominion" over the earth? Given Nyssen's list of virtues that he associates with God's nature, what type of "dominion" over the earth does Nyssen think creatures made in God's image should exercise?

2. Why might it seem odd to speak of God's moral goodness as "beautiful"? How can virtues be thought of as "beautiful"?

3. At the beginning of *On the Making of Man* 18, Nyssen, commenting on the creation of gender for the purpose of the bestial mode of procreation, says, "I think that from this beginning all our passions issue as from a spring, and pour their flood over man's life; and an evidence of my words is the kinship of passions which appears alike in ourselves and in the brutes." How might the division of the human race into male and female be the source of the passions? What, if anything, is problematic about this assertion?

Chapter Two: Nyssen's Eclectic Psychology

1. Does Nyssen's eclecticism with respect to classical models of the soul lead him to a mere "patchwork" description of the soul (in which the models from Plato and Aristotle do not really hold together) or does he integrate them to create a coherent picture of the soul?

2. In the previous chapter, we saw that Nyssen links his theories of creation and eschatology. The end is like the beginning. If the eschaton brings the completion or restoration of humanity to its unalloyed essence, what picture of eschatological humanity might Nyssen's theory of predication lead him to paint?

Chapter Three: The Nature of the Passions

1. In a famous passage in Augustine's *Confessions* (II. 4, 9), Augustine describes how he and his adolescent friends under cover of night stole from a neighbor's pear tree a vast quantity of pears, not principally to eat for themselves, for he had better pears at home, but for the sake of doing what was forbidden. Could Nyssen's view of passion as impulses of the sentient faculties of the soul uncontrolled by reason provide an adequate account of the cause of Augustine's sin? Why or why not?

2. Given Nyssen's description of the dynamic between the rational and nonrational faculties of the soul, sin seems to begin among the movements of the nonrational faculties. Does Nyssen provide an adequate account of how the powers of the intellect might be coopted to serve the aims of the soul's lower impulses?

3. Nyssen makes a distinction between *hormai*, the natural and morally neutral impulses of the sentient soul, and *pathos,* the corrupt form of *hormai* directed toward evil rather than good. Given this distinction, what might he mean when he says that Moses attained *apatheia* (i.e., freedom from passion)? Does he mean that Moses experienced no emotions at all?

4. According to Nyssen, the theological virtues heal the soul of passion by creating correcting judgments about reality. If hope heals grief by replacing despair with confidence in eternal life, of what forms of passion might the virtue of faith heal the soul?

Chapter Four: Satiation and Epectasy

1. Origen's theory of *apokatastasis* claims that the end will be like the beginning. How is the end sufficiently different than the beginning in order to prevent the possibility of a second fall?

2. Nyssen's theory of epectasy argues that the soul can never be satiated with God because God is infinite and therefore can never be known in his entirety. Is it enough, however, to say that God is infinite? What other qualities must God's infinite nature have in order to keep the soul eternally interested and in love with the Divine?

3. Nyssen distinguishes between the soul's present experience of God *indirectly* through his activities and its *immediate* eschatological contemplation of the Divine. Does this view of the eschaton give to the material world any lasting significance or must the soul overcome the material world altogether?

Chapter Five: The Infinitely Wondrous Being of God

1. How does the Christian doctrine of the Trinity alter the way the Cappadocians appropriate the Plotinian concept of divine infinity? What theological concerns drive the Cappadocians to locate God *within* the realm of being rather than *beyond* being (à la Plotinus)?

2. What is the relation between divine simplicity and divine infinity for the Cappadocians? Are they synonymous or do they point to slightly different aspects of God's transcendence? Are they necessary conditions for an account of God's perfection?

3. Does the doctrine of divine infinity fully resolve the problem of satiation for Nyssen? What problems might the doctrine of divine simplicity introduce to his theory of the soul's eternal participation in God?

4. Does Nyssen's account of the body-soul relation provide a more positive view of the body than Origen's theory? How might his view of the soul's dependence upon the body inform his theory of the resurrection?

Chapter Six: Purgation and Illumination

1. According to Origen, the first stage in the soul's ascent to God is that of purgation, the purification of the soul necessary for seeing God. How, according to Nyssen's *theōria* (i.e., speculative commentary) on Exodus, is Moses' flight from Egypt into Midian a moment of purgation that prepares him for illumination? Moses' retreat into Midian is a type or symbol for the soul's training in virtue. In the context of the Christian's ascent to God, what preparatory disciplines might the retreat to Midian symbolically represent?

2. For Nyssen, the moments of purgation and illumination are linked together in an unending dialectical pattern. Purgation gives purity to the soul's constitution so that it can receive the illumination of God's self-revelation. But the illumination of the soul with new insight into God's goodness purifies the soul's desires. Thus illumination is itself purgative. How, then, might the moment of illumination on Mt. Horeb, when the divine Logos speaks from the burning bush, be a purgative moment that prepares Moses/the soul for further growth in virtue and for even higher levels of illumination?

3. Nyssen views *theōria*, or contemplative speculation, as a means for purifying the soul. Given his view of the trichotomous soul

(described in chapters 1 and 2), how does the intellectual process of contemplation purify and sublimate the soul's appetitive drives? What implications might this view of *theōria* have for one's view of icons, religious statues, and other forms of Christian art?

4. How can the apophatic experience of the soul, represented by Moses in the dark cloud, be thought of as a moment of illumination? Why might *apatheia*, understood as detachment from the desire for sensual pleasure, be a necessary condition for the soul's mystical encounter with God?

5. How is Moses' encounter with God in the cloud a moment of illumination and purification? How is his knowledge of God different after passing through the cloud than it was after encountering God in the Burning Bush on Mt. Horeb?

6. How does Moses' apophatic experience in the cloud affect that nature of the kataphatic experience of God in the Heavenly Tabernacle?

Chapter Seven: "When God Shall Be All and in All"

1. According to *On the Soul and Resurrection,* how do the soul's appetitive impulses (desire and spirit) act as the soul's principles of movement? Can there be, according to Macrina, intellectual movement not initiated by desire? Why? Do you agree or disagree with her conclusion?

2. Nyssen views time as both an ontological reality and a subjective reality, i.e., a state of consciousness. How is time consciousness the product of desire? How, according to Nyssen, does the soul's experience of God as the "all in all" bring to an end time consciousness?

3. In *Commentary on the Song of Songs* and *Life of Moses,* Nyssen describes Christian love, eschatological or otherwise, as *erōs,* or desire, which reverses his account of love in *On the Soul and Resurrection.* What aspect of his doctrine of epectasy forced Nyssen to change his view of eschatological love to a form of *erōs?*

4. How does Nyssen distinguish desire and enjoyment in *On the Soul and Resurrection?* How does his account of this relationship change in *Commentary on the Song of Songs?* How might Nyssen's expression "soaring *stasis*" be descriptive of the dialectic between enjoyment and desire in the eschaton?

Bibliography

Primary Sources

Aristotle. *De Anima.*
————. *De Caelo.*
————. *De Motu Animalium.*
————. *Metaphysics.*
————. *Nichomachean Ethics.*
————. *Physics.*
Athanasius. *Life of Saint Antony.*
Basil of Caesarea. *Epistle.*
Cicero. *Academica* I.
Clement of Alexandria. *Stromata.* PG 9.
Diogenes Laertius. *Lives and Opinions of Eminent Philosophers.*
Epictetus. *Enchiridion.*
Galen. *On the Doctrines of Hippocrates and Plato.*
Gospel according to Thomas. *The Gnostic Scriptures.* Trans. Bentley Layton. Garden City, N.Y.: Doubleday, 1987.
Gregory of Nazianzus. *Theological Orations.*
Gregory of Nyssa. *Apologia in Hexaëmeron.* PG 44.
————. *Canonical Epistle.* PG 45.
————. *Commentarius in Canticum Canticorum.* GNO VI.
————. *Contra Eunomium.* GNO I.
————. *De Anima et Resurrectione.* PG 46.
————. *De Beatitudinibus.* 2, PG 44. Trans. Stuart George Hall. In *Gregory of Nyssa: Homilies on the Beatitudes.* Ed. H. Drobner and A. Viciano. Leiden: Brill, 2000.
————. *De Hominis Opificio.* PG 44.
————. *De Infantibus Premature Abreptis.* GNO III/II.
————. *De Virginitate.* PG 46.
————. *De Vita Macrinae.* SC 178.
————. *De Vita Moysis.* SC 1c.
————. *In Ecclesiasten.* GNO 5.
————. *In Inscriptiones Psalmorum.* GNO 5.
————. *In Sanctum Pascha.* Trans. S. G. Hall. In *The Easter Sermons of Gregory of Nyssa.* Ed. Andreas Spira and Christoph Klock. Cambridge, Mass.: Philadelphia Patristic Foundation, 1981. GNO IX.
————. *Oratio Catechetica.* GNO III/IV. Trans. E. R. Hardy and C. C. Richardson. In *Christology of the Later Fathers.* Philadelphia: Westminster Press, 1954.
————. *Panegyric on Gregory Thaumaturgus.* PG 46.
Marcus Aurelius. *Meditations.*
Origen. *De Principiis.* Trans. G. W. Butterworth. Gloucester, Mass.: Peter Smith, 1973. *Traite des Principes.* II. Trans. H. Crouzel and M. Simonetti. SC 253.

281

————. *Homilae in Genesim.* PG 12.

Philo of Alexandria. *De Opificio Mundi.*

————. *Legum Allegoriarum.*

Plato. *Phaedo Plato* I. Trans. Harold North Fowler. Cambridge, Mass.: Harvard University Press, 1914.

————. *Phaedrus.*

————. *Republic.*

————. *Symposium.* Trans. W. R. M. Lamb. Loeb Classical Library 166. Cambridge, Mass.: Harvard University Press, 1925.

————. *Timaeus.*

Plotinus. *Enneads.* Trans. A. H. Armstrong. Cambridge, Mass.: Harvard University Press, 1984.

Plutarch. *Consolation to Apollinius.*

Seneca. *De Ira.*

————. *Epistles.*

Xenophon. "The Art of Horsemanship," IX.5–8. Trans. E. C. Marchant. Loeb Classical Library. Cambridge: Harvard University Press, 1971.

Secondary Sources

Apostolopoulos, Charalambos. *Phaedo Christianus Studien zur Verindung und Abwägung des Verhältnisses zwischen dem platonischen "Phaidon" und dem Dialog Gregors von Nyssa "Über die Seele und die Auferstehung."* Frankfurt: Peter Lang, 1986.

Armstrong, A. H. "Platonic Elements in Gregory of Nyssa's Doctrine of Man." *Dominican Studies* 1 (1948): 113–26.

Ayres, Lewis. "On Not Three People: The Fundamental Themes of Gregory of Nyssa's Trinitarian Theology as Seen in *To Ablabius: On Not Three Gods.*" *Modern Theology* 18 (October 2002).

Balás, David L. "Eternity and Time in Gregory of Nyssa's *Contra Eunomium.*" In *Gregor von Nyssa und Die Philosophie.* Zweites Internationales Kolloquium über Gregor von Nyssa. Ed. H. Dörrie, M. Altenburger, and V. Schramm. Leiden: E. J. Brill, 1976.

————. *METOUSIA THEOU: Man's Participation in God's Perfections according to Saint Gregory of Nyssa.* Rome: I.B.C. Libreria Herder, 1966.

Balthasar, Hans Urs von. *Présence et Pensée: Essai sur la philosophie religieuse de Grégoire de Nysse.* Paris: G. Beauchesne, 1942.

Barnes, Michel. *The Power of God: DYNAMIS in Gregory of Nyssa's Trinitarian Theology.* Washington, D.C.: Catholic University of America Press, 2001.

————. "The Polemical Context and Content of Gregory of Nyssa's Psychology." *Medieval Philosophy and Theology* 4 (1994): 1–24.

Bebis, George S. "Gregory of Nyssa's 'De Vita Moysis': A Philosophical and Theological Analysis." *Greek Orthodox Theological Review* 12, no. 3 (1967).

Behr, John. "The Rational Animal: A Rereading of Gregory of Nyssa's *De hominis opificio.*" *Journal of Early Christian Studies* 7 (1999): 227–46.

Brown, Peter. *The Body and Society: Men, Women, and Sexual Renunciation in Early Christianity.* New York: Columbia University Press, 1988.

Bynum, Caroline Walker. *The Resurrection of the Body in Western Christianity, 200–1336.* New York: Columbia University Press, 1995.

Cahill, J. B. "The Date and Setting of Gregory of Nyssa's *Commentary on the Song of Songs.*" *Journal of Theological Studies* ns 31 no. 2 (October 1981).

Callahan, John F. *Four Views of Time in Ancient Philosophy.* Cambridge, Mass.: Harvard University Press, 1948.

————. "Greek Philosophy and the Cappadocian Cosmology." *Dumbarton Oaks Papers* 12 (1958): 29–57.

Cherniss, Herald. *The Platonism of Gregory of Nyssa.* Berkeley: University of California Publications in Classical Philology, 1930.

Clark, Elizabeth. "Devil's Gateway and Bride of Christ: Women in the Early Christian World." In *Ascetic Piety and Women's Faith.* Ed. E. Clark. Lewiston, N.Y.: E. Mellen Press, 1986.

Clark, Norris. "Infinity in Plotinus: A Reply." *Gregorianum* 60 (1959).

Clarke, W. K. L. *St. Basil the Great: A Study in Monasticism.* Cambridge: Cambridge University Press, 1913.

Coakley, Sarah. "The Eschatological Body: Gender, Transformation, and God." *Modern Theology* 16 (2000): 61–73.

———. "Re-thinking Gregory of Nyssa: Introduction – Gender, Trinitarian Analogies, and the Pedagogy of the Song." *Modern Theology* 18 (October 2002).

Corsini, Eugenio. "Plérôme humain et plérôme cosmique chez Grégoire de Nysse." In *Écriture et culture philosophique dans la pensée de Grégoire de Nysse.* Ed. Marguerite Harl. Leiden: Brill, 1971.

Crouzel, Henri. *Origen: The Life and Thought of the First Great Theologian.* Trans. A. S. Worrall. San Francisco: Harper & Row Publishers, 1989.

Daley, Brian E. "Divine Transcendence and Human Transformation: Gregory of Nyssa's Anti-Apollinarian Christology." *Modern Theology* 18 (October 2002): 497–506.

———. *The Hope of the Early Church: A Handbook of Patristic Eschatology.* Cambridge: Cambridge University Press, 1991.

Daniélou, Jean. "Chronologie des oeuvres de Grégoire de Nysse." *Studia Patristica* VII.

———. *Platonisme et théologie mystique: Essai sur la doctrine spirituelle de Saint Grégoire de Nysse.* Aubier: Éditions Montaigne, 1944.

Dennis, T. J. "Gregory on the Resurrection of the Body." In *The Easter Sermons of Gregory of Nyssa.* Ed. Andreas Spira and Christopher Klock. Philadelphia: Philadelphia Patristic Foundation, 1981.

Dihle, Albrecht. *The Theory of Will in Classical Antiquity.* Berkeley: University of California Press, 1982.

Dillon, John. "*Metriopatheia* and *Apatheia*: Some Reflections on a Controversy in Later Greek Ethic." In *Essays in Ancient Greek Philosophy* II. Ed. J. P. Anton and A. Preus. Albany: State University of New York Press, 1983.

———. *The Middle Platonists, 80 B.C. to A.D. 220.* Ithaca, N.Y.: Cornell University Press, 1996.

Donini, Pierlungi. "The History of the Concept of Eclecticism." In *The Question of "Eclecticism": Studies in Later Greek Philosophy.* Berkeley: University of California Press, 1988.

Ferguson, Everett. "God's Infinity and Man's Mutability: Perpetual Progress according to Gregory of Nyssa." *Greek Orthodox Theological Review* 18 (1973).

Geljon, Albert C. *Philonic Exegesis on Gregory of Nyssa's De Vita Moysis.* Providence, R.I.: Brown Judaic Studies, 2002.

Greer, Rowan A. "Augustine's Transformation of the Free Will Defense." *Faith and Philosophy* 13 (1996): 471–86.

———. *The Captain of Our Salvation: A Study in Patristic Exegesis of Hebrews.* Tübingen: J. C. B. Mohr, 1973.

———. *Christian Hope and Christian Life: Raids on the Inarticulate.* New York: Crossroad Publishing Co., 2001.

———. "The Leaven and the Lamb: Christ and Gregory of Nyssa's Vision of Human Destiny." In *Jesus in History and Myth.* Ed. R. Joseph Hoffmann and Gerald Larue. Buffalo, N.Y.: Prometheus Books, 1986.

Gregg, Robert C. *Consolation Philosophy Greek and Christian: Paideia in Basil and the Two Gregories.* Philadelphia: Philadelphia Patristic Foundation, 1975.

Gribomont, J. "Le Monachisme au sein de l'église en Syrie et en Cappadoce." *Studia Monastica* 7 (1965): 7–24.

Griswold, Jr., Charles L. *Self-Knowledge in Plato's* Phaedrus. University Park: Pennsylvania State University Press, 1996.

Gronau, Karl. *Poseidonios und die jüdisch-christliche Genesisexegese.* Berlin: B. G. Teubner, 1914.

Guthrie, W. K. C. *Aristotle: An Encounter.* Vol. 6 of *A History of Greek Philosophy.* Cambridge: Cambridge University Press, 1981.

———. *Plato: The Man and His Dialogues: Early Period.* Vol. 4 of *A History of Greek Philosophy.* Cambridge: Cambridge University Press, 1975.

———. *The Later Plato and the Academy.* Vol. 5 of *A History of Greek Philosophy.* Cambridge: Cambridge University Press, 1989.

Hankinson, R. J. *The Skeptics.* London: Routledge, 1995.

Hanson, R. P. C. *The Search for the Christian Doctrine of God.* Edinburgh: T. & T. Clark, 1988.

Harl, Marguerite. "Recherches sur l'origenisme d'Origene: La 'satieté' (*koros*) de la contemplation comme motif de la chute des ames." *Studia Patristica* 8, no. 2 (1966).

Harrison, Verna E. F. "A Gender Reversal in Gregory of Nyssa." *Studia Patristica* 27 (1993): 34–38.

———. "Male and Female in Cappadocian Theology." *Journal of Theological Studies* ns 41 (1990): 441–71.

———. "Receptacle Imagery in St. Gregory of Nyssa's Anthropology." *Studia Patristica* 22 (1989): 23–27.

Hart, Mark. "Gregory of Nyssa's Ironic Praise of the Celibate Life." *Heythrop Journal* 33 (January 1992): 1–19.

———. "Reconciliation of Body and Soul: Gregory of Nyssa's Deeper Theology of Marriage." *Theological Studies* 51 (1990): 450–78.

Heine, Ronald E. "Gregory of Nyssa's Apology for Allegory." *Vigiliae Christianae* 38 (1984): 360–70.

———. *Perfection in the Virtuous Life: A Study in the Relationship between Edification and Polemical Theology in Gregory of Nyssa's* De Vita Moysis. Cambridge, Mass.: Philadelphia Patristic Foundation, 1975.

Holman, Susan R. *The Hungry Are Dying: Beggars and Bishops in Roman Cappadocia.* Oxford: Oxford University Press, 2001.

Horowitz, Maryanne Cline. "The Image of God in Man: Is Woman Included?" *Harvard Theological Review* 72 (1979): 175–206.

Hübner, Reinhard M. *Die Einheit des Leibes Christi bei Gregor von Nyssa: Untersuchungen zum Ursprung der "Physischen" Erlösungslehre.* Leiden: E. J. Brill, 1974.

Jaeger, Werner. *Early Christianity and Greek Paideia.* Cambridge: Belknap Press of Harvard University Press, 1961.

———. *Two Rediscovered Works of Ancient Christian Literature: Gregory of Nyssa and Macarius.* Leiden: E. J. Brill, 1954.

Konstan, David. "Stoics and Epicureans on the Nature of Man." *International Studies in Philosophy* 14 (1982): 27–34.

Kopecek, Thomas A. *A History of Neo-Arianism.* Cambridge, Mass.: Philadelphia Patristic Foundation, 1979.

Ladner, Gerhart B. "The Philosophical Anthropology of Saint Gregory of Nyssa." *Dumbarton Oaks Papers* 12 (1958): 61–64.

Laird, Martin. "Under Solomon's Tutelage: The Education of Desire in the *Homilies on the Song of Songs.*" *Modern Theology* 18 (October 2002): 507–25.

Landesman, Charles. *Skepticism: The Central Issue.* Oxford: Blackwell Publishers, 2002.

Leys, Roger. *L'image de Dieu chez Saint Gregoire de Nysse.* Bruxelles: Edition universelle, 1951.

Long, A. A. *Hellenistic Philosophy: Stoics, Epicureans, Skeptics.* Berkeley: University of California Press, 1986.

———. "Soul and Body in Stoicism." *Phronesis* 27 (1982).

Louth, Andrew. "Eros and Mysticism Early Christian Interpretation of the Song of Songs." In *Jung and the Monotheisms: Judaism, Christianity, and Islam.* Ed. Joel Ryce-Menuhin. London: Routledge, 1994.

———. *Origins of the Christian Mystical Tradition: From Plato to Denys.* Oxford: Oxford University Press, 1981.

Ludlow, Morwenna. *Universal Salvation: Eschatology in the Thought of Gregory of Nyssa and Karl Rahner.* Oxford: Oxford University Press, 2000.

Meeks, Wayne. "The Image of the Androgyne: Some Uses of a Symbol in Earliest Christianity." *History of Religions* 13, no. 3 (1974).

Meredith, Anthony. "Allegory in Porphyry and Gregory of Nyssa." *Studia Patristica* 16 (1985): 422–27.

Miles, Margaret R. *Plotinus on Body and Beauty: Society, Philosophy, and Religion in Third-century Rome.* Oxford: Blackwell Publishers, 1999.

Mitchell, Robert Lloyd. *The Hymn to Eros: A Reading of Plato's Symposium.* Lanham, Md.: University Press of America, 1993.

Mongrain, Kevin. *The Systematic Thought of Hans Urs Von Balthasar: An Irenaean Retrieval.* New York: Crossroad Publishing Company, 2002.

Mohammed, Ovey N. "Averroes, Aristotle, and the Qur'an on Immortality and Body and Soul." *International Philosophical Quarterly* 33 (March 1993): 37–55.

Muckle, J. T. "The Doctrine of St. Gregory of Nyssa on Man as the Image of God." *Mediaeval Studies* 7 (1945): 55–84.

Murphy, M. G. *St. Basil and Monasticism.* Washington, D.C.: Catholic University of America Press, 1930.

Negro, Giovanni. "Soul and Corporeal Dimension in the Aristotelian Conception of Immortality." *Gregorianum* 79, no. 4 (1998): 719–42.

Norris, Richard A. "The Soul Takes Flight: Gregory of Nyssa and the Song of Songs." *Anglican Theological Review* 80, no. 4 (Fall 1998).

Nussbaum, Martha. *The Therapy of Desire: Theory and Practice in Hellenistic Ethics.* Princeton: Princeton University Press, 1994.

Nuyens, François. *L'Evolution de la psychologie d'Aristotle.* Louvain: Institut Superieur de Philosophie, 1948.

Nygren, Anders. *Agape and Eros.* Trans. Philip S. Watson. Chicago: University of Chicago Press, 1982.

O'Keefe, John J. "Sin, *Apatheia* and Freedom of the Will in Gregory of Nyssa." *Studia Patristica* 22 (1989): 52–59.

Otis, Brooks. "Gregory of Nyssa and the Cappadocian Conception of Time." *Studia Patristica* 14 (1976): 327–57.

———. "Cappadocian Thought as a Coherent System." *Dumbarton Oaks Papers* 12 (1958): 97–124.

Pelikan, Jaroslav. *Christianity and Classical Culture: The Metamorphosis of Natural Theology in the Christian Encounter with Hellenism.* New Haven, Conn.: Yale University Press, 1993.

Plass, Paul. "Transcendent Time and Eternity in Gregory of Nyssa." *Vigiliae Christianae* 34 (June 1980).

Rist, John M. *Stoic Philosophy.* Cambridge: Cambridge University Press, 1969.

Robinson, T. M. "Aristotle's Psycho-Physiological Account of the Soul-Body Relationship." In *Psyche and Soma: Physicians and Metaphysicians on the Mind-Body Problem from Antiquity to Enlightenment.* Ed. John P. Wright and Paul Potter. New York: Oxford University Press, 2000.

———. *Plato's Psychology.* 2nd ed. Toronto: University of Toronto Press, 1995.

Rosen, Stanley. *Plato's Symposium.* 2nd ed. New Haven, Conn.: Yale University Press, 1987.

Shaw, Teresa M. *The Burden of the Flesh: Fasting and Sexuality in Early Christianity.* Minneapolis: Fortress Press, 1998.

Smith, J. Warren. "A Just and Reasonable Grief: The Death and Function of a Holy Woman in Gregory of Nyssa's *Life of Macrina. Journal of Early Christian Studies* 12, no. 1 (2004): 56–84.

———. "Macrina, Tamer of Horses and Healer of Souls: Grief and the Therapy of Hope in Gregory of Nyssa's *De Anima et Resurrectione." Journal of Theological Studies* ns. 52 (April 2001): 37–60.

———. "Suffering Impassibly: Christ's Passion in Cyril of Alexandria's Soteriology." *Pro Ecclesia* 11, no. 4 (Fall 2002).

Sorabji, Richard. *Emotion and Peace of Mind: From Stoic Agitation to Christian Temptation.* Oxford: Oxford University Press, 2000.

Spira, Andreas. "Gregor von Nyssa, *De Beatitudinibus,* Oratio II: 'Selig sind die Sanftmütigen; denn sie werden das Erdreich besitzen' (Mt.5,4)." In *Gregory of Nyssa: Homilies on the Beatitudes. An English Version with Commentary and Supporting Studies. Proceedings of the Eighth International Colloquium on Gregory of Nyssa (Paderborn, 14–18 September 1998).* Ed. H. Drobner and A. Viciano. Leiden: Brill, 2000.

Stead, Christopher. "The Concept of Mind and the Concept of God in the Christian Fathers." *The Philosophical Frontiers of Christian Theology: Essays Presented to D. M. Mackinnon.* Cambridge: Cambridge University Press, 1982.

Sweeney, Leo. *Divine Infinity in Greek and Medieval Thought.* New York: Peter Lang, 1998.

Turcescu, Lucian. " 'Person' versus 'Individual,' and Other Modern Misreadings of Gregory of Nyssa." *Modern Theology* 18 (October 2002).

Van Dam, Raymond. *Becoming Christian: The Conversion of Roman Cappadocia.* Philadelphia: University of Pennsylvania Press, 2003.

———. *Families and Friends in Late Roman Cappadocia.* Philadelphia: University of Pennsylvania Press, 2003.

———. *Kingdom of Snow: Roman Rule and Greek Culture in Cappadocia.* Philadelphia: University of Pennsylvania Press, 2003.

Verghese, T. Paul. "*DIASTHMA* and *DIASTASIS* in Gregory of Nyssa: Introduction to a Concept and the Posing of a Problem." In *Gregor Von Nyssa und Die Philosophie.* Ed. H. Dörrie, M. Altenburger, U. Schramm. Leiden: E. J. Brill, 1976.

Völker, Walther. *Gregor Von Nyssa Als Mystiker.* Wiesbaden: Franz Steiner Verlag, 1955.

Wheelwright, Philip. *The Pre-Socratics.* Indianapolis: Odyssey Press, 1966.

Williams, Rowan. "Macrina's Deathbed Revisited: Gregory of Nyssa on Mind and Passion." In *Christian Faith and Greek Philosophy in Late Antiquity: Essays in Tribute to George Christopher Stead.* Ed. L. Wickham and C. Bammel. Leiden: E. J. Brill, 1993.

Winslow, Donald F. *The Dynamics of Salvation: A Study in Gregory of Nazianzus.* Cambridge, Mass.: Philadelphia Patristic Foundation, 1979.

Young, Frances M. "Adam and Anthropos: A Study of the Interaction of Science and the Bible in Two Anthropological Treatises of the Fourth Century." *Vigiliae Christianae* 37, no. 2 (1983).

Zachhuber, Johannes. *Human Nature in Gregory of Nyssa: Philosophical Background and Theological Significance.* Leiden: Brill, 2000.

Index

Of Related Interest

Rowan A. Greer
CHRISTIAN HOPE AND CHRISTIAN LIFE
Raids on the Inarticulate

Chosen as "Book of the Year" by the Association of Theological Booksellers, this is already one of the most honored works in early church spirituality in the past thirty years. What is the destiny of the human soul in this life and the next? Dare we hope to "see God face to face," or will our vision of God remain forever filtered "through a glass, darkly"? In this remarkable volume, Rowan A. Greer turns to the New Testament, the church fathers, and later writers to throw light on their own visions of the human soul.

He suggests that Augustine of Hippo and Gregory of Nyssa represent two distinct strands of Christian thinking that find expression later in writers such as John Donne and Jeremy Taylor. Greer, who has trained two generations of historians and theologians in the rich thought of the early church, has succeeded in writing a volume that is both full of original scholarly insight and, by virtue of his elegant writing, accessible to laypeople and nonspecialists.

0-8245-1916-7, $24.95 paperback

Bernard McGinn
THE MYSTICAL THOUGHT OF MEISTER ECKHART
The Man From Whom God Hid Nothing

Centuries after his work as a preacher, philosopher, and spiritual guide, Meister Eckhart remains one of the most widely read mystics of the Western tradition. Yet as he has come to be studied more closely in recent decades, a number of different Eckharts have emerged. Is he the prophet of the God known only in radical negation and darkness, or of the intimate God in Christ born in the human soul? Are his evocative German sermons the truest form of his mystical vision, or do we find the key to his vision in the more scholastic, seemingly drier Latin works? For the first time, Bernard McGinn, the greatest living scholar of Western Christian mysticism, brings together in one volume the fruition of decades of reflection on these questions, offering a view of Eckhart that unites his strands as preacher, philosopher, and theologian.

0-8245-1914-0, $45.00 hardcover

crossroad

Of Related Interest

Edward Howells
JOHN OF THE CROSS AND TERESA OF AVILA
Mystical Knowing and Selfhood

Half a millennium after they lived and wrote, Teresa and John continue to
inspire and confound readers: How can the turn inward to solitude and quiet
also bring a person closer to creation? Howells shows how, for them, the
dynamic life of the Trinitarian God unites the mind within and the world
outside.

0-8245-1943-4, $39.95 paperback

Siegmar Doepp and Wilhelm Geerlings, Editors
DICTIONARY OF EARLY CHRISTIAN LITERATURE

"I would recommend this work highly to specialists and non-specialists alike
who have an interest in the period of early Christianity."

— *Thomas F. Martin, O.S.A., Ph.D.,*
Villanova University

A wealth of information on the literature of early Christianity. Rich in detail
and bibliographical information while remaining accessible to general readers.

0-8245-1805-5, $75.00 hardcover

Please support your local bookstore,
or call 1-800-707-0670 for Customer Service.

For a free catalog, write us at

THE CROSSROAD PUBLISHING COMPANY
16 Penn Plaza, 481 Eighth Avenue
New York, NY 10001

Visit our website at
www.crossroadpublishing.com
All prices subject to change.

crossroad